8/10.
1443

INTERSTATE 69

THE UNFINISHED HISTORY OF THE LAST
GREAT AMERICAN HIGHWAY

Matt Dellinger

SCRIBNER

New York   London   Toronto   Sydney

SCRIBNER
A Division of Simon & Schuster, Inc.
1230 Avenue of the Americas
New York, NY 10020

First Scribner hardcover edition August 2010

SCRIBNER and design are registered trademarks of The Gale Group, Inc.,
used under license by Simon & Schuster, Inc., the publisher of this work.

For information about special discounts for bulk purchases,
please contact Simon & Schuster Special Sales at 1-866-506-1949
or business@simonandschuster.com.

The Simon & Schuster Speakers Bureau can bring authors to your live event.
For more information or to book an event contact the Simon & Schuster Speakers Bureau
at 1-866-248-3049 or visit our website at www.simonspeakers.com.

Manufactured in the United States of America

1   3   5   7   9   10   8   6   4   2

Library of Congress Control Number: 2010008519

ISBN 978-1-4165-4249-0
ISBN 978-1-4391-7573-6 (ebook)

For my grandparents Ordie and Mary Dellinger

They gave up a house in Cleveland for Interstate 71.
He worked thirty years for General Motors.
She never learned to drive.

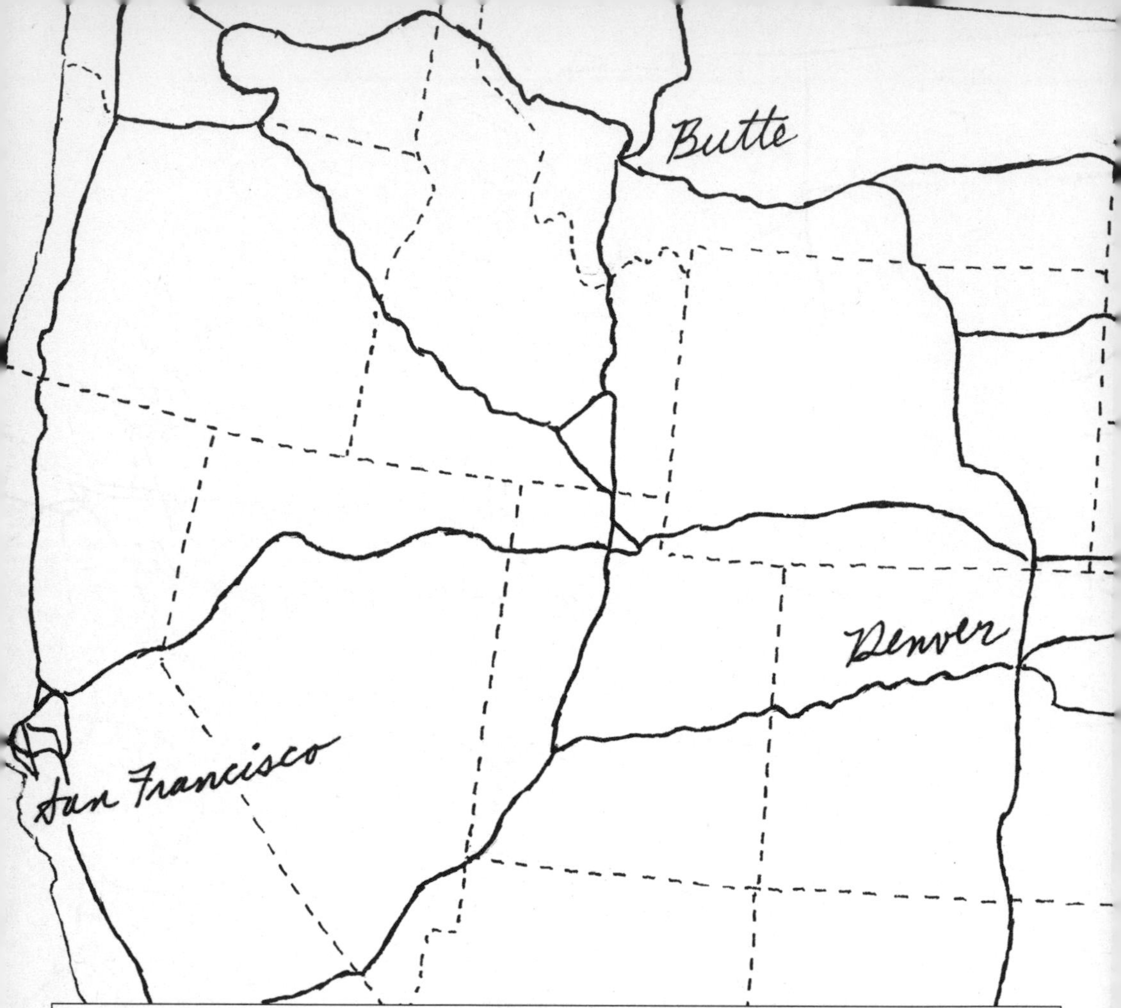
Butte
Denver
San Francisco

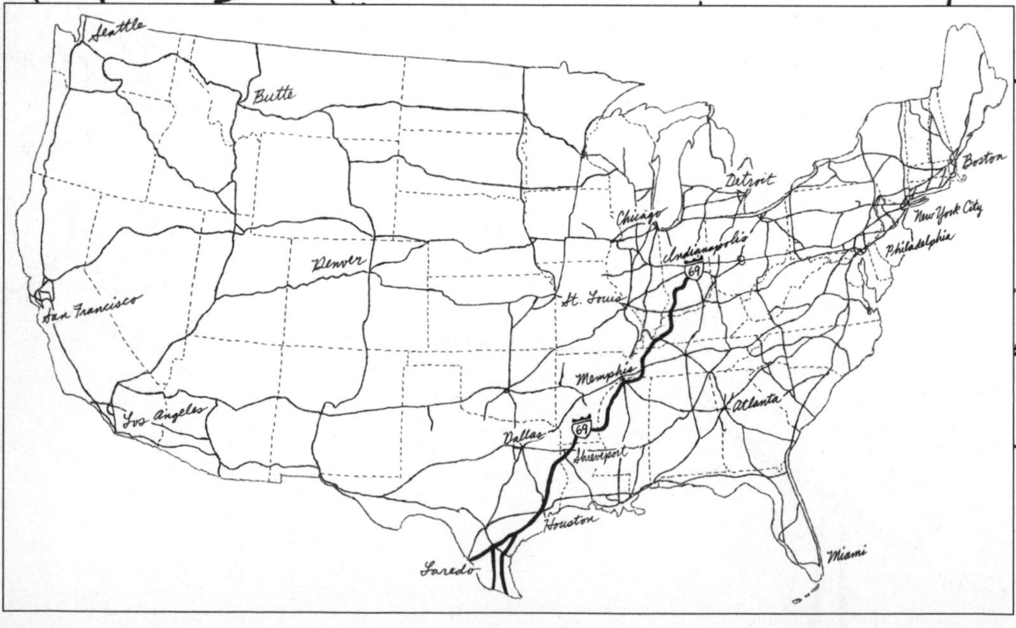
Seattle
Butte
Detroit
Boston
Chicago
New York City
Indianapolis
Philadelphia
Denver
St. Louis
San Francisco
69
Memphis
Atlanta
Los Angeles
Dallas
69
Shreveport
Houston
Miami
Laredo

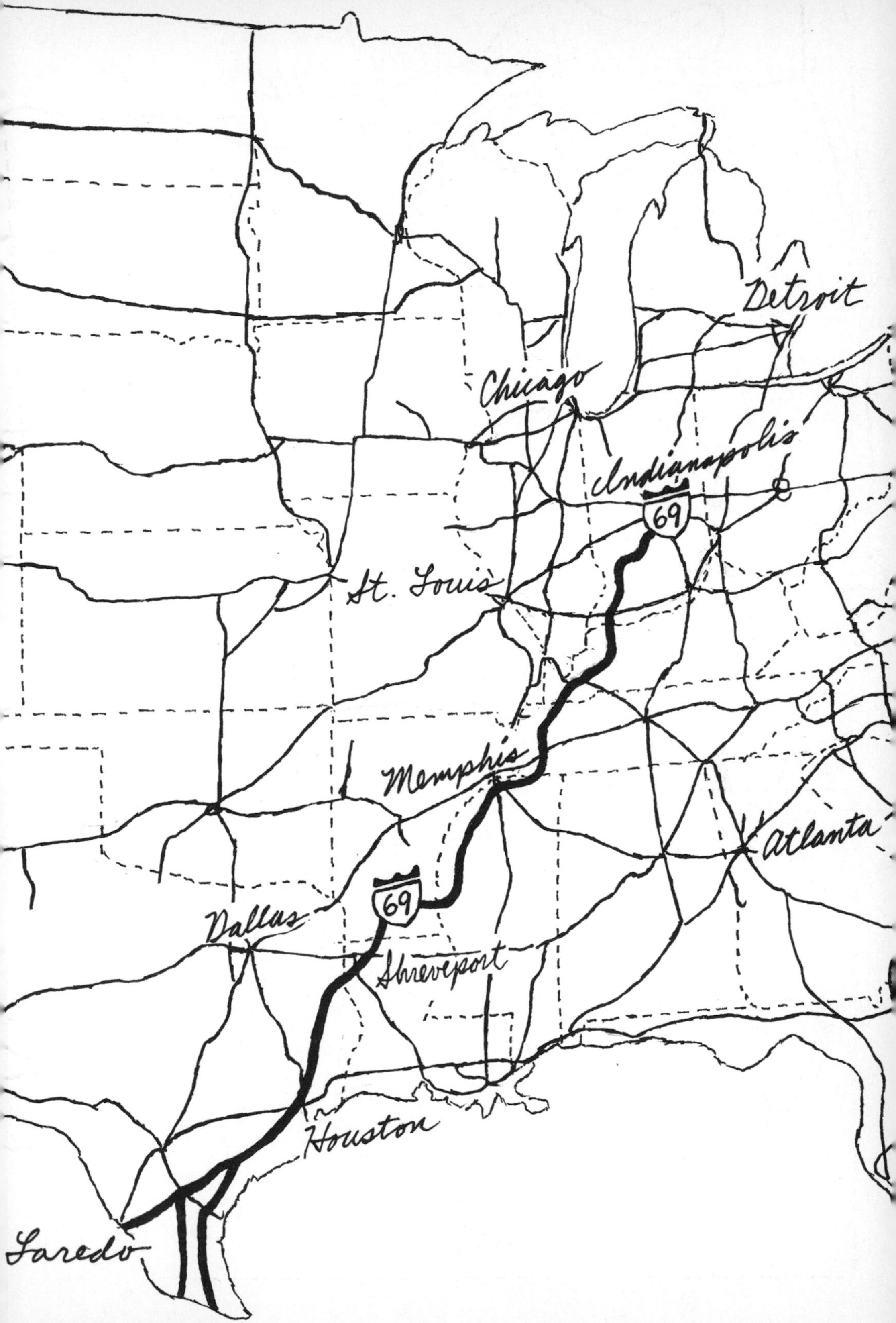
Detroit
Chicago
Indianapolis
69
St. Louis
Memphis
Atlanta
69
Dallas
Shreveport
Houston
Laredo

You road I enter upon and look around, I believe you are not all
that is here,
I believe that much unseen is also here.

Walt Whitman, from "Song of the Open Road"

Contents

- - - - - - - - -

CONTENTS

IV
TEXAS

V
A LINE IN THE DIRT

I

A Line on the Map

Overture

- - - - - - - - -

You have to hand it to Haynesville: The town keeps its chin up. The busted little oil boomtown in the northwest corner of Louisiana has been in decline for thirty years. Its population, which peaked at 20,000, is now around 2,500, and its onetime great wealth is all but gone. Most of Main Street is closed down and boarded up; even the barber gave up and went back to driving a forklift. But Haynesville looks a little different from the desolate American small town you may be imagining. A few years ago Keith Killgore, an art teacher and pharmacist who operates one of the few surviving businesses in town, decided the place could use a little sprucing up. Onto the plywood veneer covering one row of Main Street buildings, Killgore and a handful of his students painted a row of false storefronts: a charming little café with a round French table and chairs, a stylish ladies' boutique offering dresses and shoes and hats for whatever make-believe special occasions might be happening around town, a cartoon flower shop, a pretend toy store.

The renderings aren't intended to fool anyone. They're not lifelike enough to make you reach for a door handle or try to stand under one of the two-dimensional awnings in the rain. They're just a patch, meant to show that the idea of a complete town survives even if the fact of one doesn't. *We know what's supposed to be here,* they say, *and we're saving its place for when it comes back.*

Killgore's imagination is at work elsewhere in the town as well. When the old Planter's Bank building burned down at the corner of Main and First streets several years ago, Killgore got a few people together, cleaned up the lot, and fashioned it into a rudimentary park with a grassy patch of yard bisected by a paved walkway leading to a white-columned "porch" with American flags adorning the corners and rose trellises on either side. This too is a faux facade, a mask worn by the charred brick wall of the adjacent building. You can sit in a wooden rocking chair here, but you can't step inside for a glass of lemonade.

From this prosthetic porch there is an excellent view of the "Welcome to Haynesville" mural on the opposite alley wall, made visible by the collapse of the bank. Killgore painted this montage with slogans and icons that represent points of local pride: GATEWAY TO NORTH LOUISIANA, it says (true, if you're driving in from Arkansas on the two-lane Highway 79), and HOME OF THE BUTTERFLY FESTIVAL (the area is not particularly rich in butterfly specimens, but the town needed something to replace the now-defunct Oil Patch Festival), and HOME OF THE GOLDEN TORNADO (the Haynesville High School football team, fourteen-time state champions). On the left we see a set of railroad tracks and two young men bass fishing (the boy in the front of the boat's got one on the line!). On the right we see an oil pumpjack and, between a truck hauling logs and an eight-point buck leaping past a pair of pheasants, a fat stripe of black paint with yellow dashes and an Interstate 69 highway shield that's moving so fast it has a motion-blur tail.

This mural, mind you, is a good forty-five-minute drive from the nearest interstate—which is Interstate 20, not 69. But a town can dream. While the railroad tracks in this representation of Haynesville are a nod to the past and the present—freight trains still come through town, but they don't stop anymore—the highway totem is a tribute to an anticipated future. I-69 in this mural is like the figure of Jesus in a fresco of the second coming: the long-awaited savior that shall come one day from above to reward all who believe.

"Above" in this case is north. I-69, as it now exists, starts up at the Canadian border in Port Huron, Michigan, makes a wide curve along the outer orbit of Detroit through Flint and Lansing, plunges south into Indiana, through Fort Wayne, Muncie, and some of the wealthiest and fastest-sprawling suburbs of Indianapolis, and then halts abruptly on the north side of the city's squared loop, I-465, where a flashing yellow sign reads FREEWAY ENDS. This relatively short 360-mile piece of interstate is really no big deal. It's a stretch of dotted, divided asphalt that gets a little wider and more congested near the big towns, a little boring in between. Along it, people drive, listen to the radio, sit in traffic, talk on cell phones, get into sometimes fatal accidents. Hotels and restaurants cluster at the interchanges. Trucks stop for gas. Factories close and move overseas. And in the outskirts of the larger urban areas, bunches of houses with green lawns sprout up from the fields.

But I-69 is remarkable—for where it *doesn't* yet go but where it one day might: another fourteen hundred miles south to Mexico, through Evansville, Indiana; Paducah, Kentucky; Memphis, Tennessee; Clarksdale, Mississippi; El Dorado, Arkansas; Shreveport (and, yes, Haynesville), Louisiana; Houston, Texas; and on down to the border towns of Brownsville and Laredo. This corridor, in the vast gaps between the major cities that prop it up like tent poles, is made up of the kind of America that Americans think of least. It's not the familiar Interstate America, nor the wild, beautiful America of adventure magazines. It's not even the quirky roadside America portrayed in kitschy travel shows. If you were to drive this unbeaten path as best one can on the state roads and U.S. highways that I-69 is meant to replace, you would have a chance to appreciate the subtle variety of our nation's seemingly mundane body of grain elevators, water towers, and county courthouse squares. You would go for many hours without seeing a building taller than two stories. You would begin to suspect that some of the smaller towns in this country are nothing more than elaborate speed traps.

You would pass tractors and combines—not just in the fields around you, but on the road in front of you. If your window was down, you would catch the aromas of turkey sheds and sawmills and coal-fired power plants and vast acres of wet crops. The roads you traveled would be "uncontrolled access," as the engineers say, and "at grade": There would be driveways and stoplights, and you would be at the mercy of whatever surrounded you. Over hills, the road would rise and dip and twist. Where the landscape is flat and agricultural, the road would be barren and straight. And to towns of any size you would have to slow down and succumb, if only for a quarter mile.

When I drove this route, I decided that these old main drags look best at dusk. The cracked paint on the aging buildings smooths out in dim light. Power lines recede against the darkened sky, and the crappy old signs look rich and warm—bulbs, at least, don't rust. When the lights come on in modern, newly developed America, fast-food places and retail strips can look cheap and alien, their vast parking lots lit up like airport runways. But along the smaller routes the mix of chain stores and mom-and-pops that remain looks more human and handmade. They nestle right up against the roadway, glowing like a string of Christmas lights. Somewhere on the interstate billboards blare and logos hover high like UFOs. But when the off-interstate motorist starts to think about stopping for supper or sleep, the minor highway village slips into something more comfortable, puts on earrings, and hums a slow, sweet tune.

Yes, living away from interstates has its privileges. It also has its pains. These same charming highways, which were the backbone of automobile transportation just fifty years ago, are now considered secondary routes, obsolete and inefficient. The interstates have guided a half century of industrial, residential, and commercial development in America, and very little of it has touched these towns, the populations of which, on the whole, are dwindling while the average age of their citizens is rising. The rural I-69 corridor is an America where things are manufactured, but not as many things as once were. It's an America where great quantities of food are produced, but that task now employs far fewer people than it once did. Those who remain in small towns don't necessarily do so as an aesthetic choice. They might not describe it quite the way I do. They might feel ready for something bigger.

Sometimes new infrastructure projects are mocked as "bridges to nowhere" or "roads to nowhere." But a truth gets lost in that rhetoric: Once you build a bridge—or a highway, or a transit line—the "nowhere" at the other end becomes a somewhere. This is often the very point. It's the reason people want bridges. It's the reason people wanted canals and railroads, and it's the reason that for the better part of two decades, the Mid-Continent Highway Coalition, a group of politicians, businessmen, and community leaders from seven states, has been lobbying to "finish" I-69.

If built, Interstate 69 would be by far the most significant new highway construction since the original interstate system. The road, as supporters envision it, would connect the busiest trade crossings on the Canadian border to the busiest trade crossings on the Mexican border. The plan was hatched in the early, relatively innocent days of the North American Free Trade Agreement, when the highest hopes about it seemed as plausible as the fears. The coalition, thinking grandly, dubbed the project "the NAFTA highway" and promised the forlorn regions in its path all the perks of international trade and economic development—trucks, tourists, and Toyota plants. Most of the communities along the proposed route are, like Haynesville, eager for its construction. They've waited for federal funding like farmers praying for rain.

While there's no knowing what I-69 will bring, there is plenty of speculating. In Memphis and Houston, it is said it will support booming suburban growth, decrease congestion, and improve air quality. In the notoriously poverty-stricken Mississippi and Arkansas Delta, it is supposed to lure new industrial jobs and droves of tourists. In the piney woods of northwest Louisiana and east Texas, it could bring baby-boomer retirees looking for a pleasant place to settle down. On the Texas Gulf Coast, it is expected to provide more efficient connectivity to the ports. Up and down the proposed corridor, eager towns have fought one another for inclusion. Local papers publish frequent editorials extolling its coming and breathlessly cover each small step toward construction.

But it takes an awful lot of time and money to build a highway these days. Tonight there will be licensed teenagers out driving (doing God knows what) who weren't even born when this last great highway was first imagined. More than $2.5 billion in federal and state money has been devoted to the project, much of it for pre-construction planning, but the full cost is estimated to be $27 billion, a figure that may rise as plans become reality. Federal laws and policies such as the National Environmental Policy Act have, since the 1960s, placed hurdles in the way of new highways: To win funding, states must enumerate the potential benefits, catalog consequences, and consider alternatives. The requisite studies for I-69 have been costly, tedious, and time-consuming, and the intervening years have given people time to think. Local conversations about where to put the road have morphed into larger questions about whether it's worth the expense, whether it's needed or even wanted, and whether it might actually harm the middles of nowhere it's projected to pass through.

In southern Indiana, organized opposition to I-69 is as old as the plans for building it. In the forested hills and small farms around the college town of Bloomington, stopping I-69 has become the cause célèbre, the stuff of bumper stickers and yard signs, heated public meetings, pointed folk songs, and federal lawsuits. The road's proponents have tried to dismiss the growing chorus of rabble-rousers as knee-jerk environmentalists and selfish NIMBYs. But their grievances extend beyond the lines of property and cut across ideologies. Democrats and Republicans, young and old, hippies and hicks alike have come together to insist that the area's lack of interstate is more of a lucky break than a curse. *We like things the way they are*, they say, *so take your progress someplace else.*

In the last decade, the I-69 project has also found itself tangled in a wider debate over how roads should be funded. For more than fifty years, gasoline taxes have paid for the major portion of highway construction. But the federal fuel tax has remained a flat 18.4 cents per gallon since 1993, and revenue can no longer keep up with the price of maintenance and the hunger for new capacity. Many state governments have turned to privatization as a way to fill the gap. Banks and toll-road operators, many of them foreign-owned, have eagerly obliged, paying multibillion-dollar up-front sums for the privilege of operating American roadways—and tolling them for profit. In Indiana, a Spanish and Australian consortium paid $3.8 billion for a seventy-five-year lease of the state's toll road, and Governor Mitch Daniels earmarked a portion of the proceeds for construction of Interstate 69. In Texas, I-69 became a component of the Trans-Texas Corridor plan, an ambitious vision for a new four-thousand-mile web of privately financed toll highways, railroads, and utility lines. The banking crisis and ensuing recession cooled this rush toward privatization, but only temporarily: Stimulus money wasn't enough to clear a backlog of maintenance work, the gas-tax-financed Federal Highway Trust Fund required congressional intervention to avoid insolvency in 2009, and there are reportedly billions of dollars still stockpiled in private funds, ready for investment.

There are those who take for granted that roads should remain under public control, who reject the notion of an international corporation making money on American drivers, and many of these same people believe that the United States has been hurt by globalization. The pairing of these issues has turned I-69's NAFTA branding into a serious liability. Citizens have alleged that the road is part of a corporate and governmental scheme to bring Canada, Mexico, and the United States together into a North American Union, opening our borders and forfeiting our sovereignty while lining the pockets of global profiteers. Rural ranchers in Texas and young vegan anarchists in Indiana share these fears (if not much else), and with the arrival of these disparate demographics, the grassroots resistance to I-69 grew stronger and spread wider. Activists in Indiana occupied trees along the planned right-of-way and chained themselves to trucks at an asphalt yard. At rallies in Austin, farmers drove tractors down Congress Avenue with flags bearing the taunt of Texas independence: COME AND TAKE IT!

On ultraconservative talk-radio programs and liberal independent-media websites, commentators have told their audiences that I-69 is not just a road but an important symbol—even an instrument—of geopolitical oppression. These strong feelings have occasionally spilled onto the national scene. The Republican congressman Ron Paul made thwarting the "NAFTA superhighway" a keystone of his failed presidential bid. The long-dormant John Birch Society found new purpose in these perceived threats to freedom and warned of the coming North American Union and its telltale roadways. And Lou Dobbs took regular umbrage at these highway plans, which he called a secret plot by the "super elite." "It is absolutely a transformational moment," he said ominously, and vaguely, after one report on his CNN show. "People of this country . . . are going to have to decide what is going to happen with this nation."

The people of this country made one big decision in 2008, and the election of Barack Obama took the transportation conversation in new directions. President Obama has championed high-speed rail and mass transit over new highways. "The days where we're just building sprawl forever, those days are over," he told a Florida audience in 2009. With the interstate system now built and its effects clear, a growing alliance of transportation progressives is hungry to chart a new future largely by bringing back the neglected modes of the past. We have plenty of roads, these people argue, and unbuilt "zombie highways" like I-69 should be put out of their misery. They say it's time to reconsider the way we design our communities, to rethink how America moves.

Not that these weighty issues seem very relevant to a hungry town like Haynesville. But over time, the magnitude of the project has made Interstate 69 a fault line for many of the key questions confronting Americans: not just matters of transportation policy, macroeconomics, and land-use planning, but also the tug-of-war between urban and rural, and the blurry distinction between standard of living and quality of life. This is what struck me in piecing together this complex story—how the face of America is shaped in places struggling with preservation and progress, how the character of this country is decided a little more every time a factory closes, a farmer sells his fields, a town opens its first Walmart, a city allows its first casino, or a daughter moves to the big city. In all of this, our transportation system plays a significant role, helping to determine where we work and live, how well, and with whom. Developers and speculators have always known the power of transportation, and people living happily or unhappily in quiet, forgotten places learn it quickly when the surveyors show up.

So who makes these decisions on which so much depends? The future is hammered out every week in boardrooms, state capitals, public hearings, kitchens, and courtrooms, where business leaders, elected officials, and everyday citizens haggle over issues of eminent domain, urban planning, and development. Along an imaginary line down the center of the country, these struggles have a name—I-69.

The highway has spread optimism and dread. It has inspired extravagant plans and incited rebellion. Advocates and opponents alike say they're fighting on behalf of future generations; both sides warn that communities will suffer if the other side gets its way; and everyone accuses everyone else of living in the past. In its absence, this hypothetical highway has become a powerful presence, a conductor of grand hopes and fears: It will come one day to save or destroy the places in its path. It will bring jobs and culture. It will be the end of beauty and peace. It is a bridge to the future. It is a relic of the past. It will keep the young people from leaving. It will carry them away faster. It will save small towns. It will plow them under.

I-69 is the best of highways. It is the worst of highways. It could be the last great interstate built in America. Or it might never be finished at all.

A Big Breakfast

- - - - - - - - - - - - - - -

There is some disagreement about who makes the best omelets in Daviess County, Indiana, but the consensus seems to be that the honor belongs to David Graham. There's a chance that this is only a case of prudent flattery, for David Graham is a wealthy and important man in these parts: His family has been preeminent in this rural pocket of southwestern Indiana for more than a century. Through farming, banking, industry, and real estate, generation after generation has left its mark. Graham's paternal forebears were pillars of their communities, each one an exemplar of his respective era, and each left the town of Washington better off than he found it.

David's great-great-grandfather James Graham came to the wilderness of Daviess County from Paris, Kentucky, in 1826, just ten years after Indiana became a state, and bought 121 acres to farm. His son Thomas became a saddler and merchant and owned a shop in the growing frontier town. Ziba Graham, Thomas's son and David's grandfather, was born in 1853, about the time that a rich vein of bituminous coal was discovered under the region. Ziba would shepherd the family—and the town—into the industrial age.

At thirty-one, when his father died, Ziba became head of the family businesses, including the Graham farm, which by then had grown to over a thousand acres. That same year, the Ohio and Mississippi Railway, which had a stop in Washington, was making plans to build a roundhouse for servicing steam engines somewhere on its line between Cincinnati and East Saint Louis. The competition among neighboring towns was intense. Ziba led a local effort to bring the business to Washington, a successful courtship that involved incentives totaling sixty acres of public land and seventy-five thousand dollars of private money, much of it Graham's. It was worth it: The railroad became part of the venerable B&O line, and the Shops, as the yard came to be known, put Washington on the map, creating several hundred jobs and guaranteeing years of prosperity for the town. Soon after the Shops opened, Ziba, convinced of the power and appeal of transportation, acquired the horse-drawn streetcar operation downtown. The saddler's son also bought the local coal-fired power plant, then dismissed the draft horses and mules and installed a two-and-a-half-mile electrified streetcar line featuring state-of-the-art winter and summer cars complete with headlights and leather seats.

By the turn of the century, Washington, Indiana, was a modern, bustling small town, and Ziba's three sons, Joseph, Robert, and Ray, all came home after college. With a little help from their father, who acted as venture capitalist, the three Graham brothers went into business together, achieving success in the glass-bottle business, and then, more famously, manufacturing automobiles. A factory they ran in Evansville, on the Ohio River sixty miles south of Washington, produced the first trucks for Dodge Brothers, and in the early twenties the brothers established factories in Detroit and California. In 1927 they bought the Paige-Detroit Motor Car Company and started making passenger vehicles. The first line of Graham-Paige cars was an instant triumph, and the Graham Brothers, who remained partners their entire adult lives, saw their fortunes grow. Their cars became known around the world, and they became heroes at home. A new Graham-Paige plant in Evansville, Indiana, made the Grahams the city's largest employer, and to mark its opening, the city declared November 20, 1928, Graham Brothers Day. A parade wound through the streets downtown, a hundred floats long. Kids were let out of school. Stores closed at noon. A local paper estimated that more than a hundred thousand people came out to celebrate these automobile princes of southern Indiana—the largest civic celebration in Evansville's history.

It was into these fine circumstances that David Graham, Robert's youngest son, was born, in February 1927. Graham was a well-traveled child. He spent his early years shuttling—by car—between his father's winter home in Florida, his house in Detroit, a Graham family compound on the northern tip of the lower peninsula of Michigan, and the family farm in Washington. By then, Graham Farms totaled more than five thousand acres. The Depression-era Federal Writers' Project *Guide to Indiana* swooned about its rows of corn a-mile-and-a-half long and the ton-and-a-half of cheese its dairy produced daily. David, like his father and uncles, got his education out of state, first at Georgetown Preparatory School and then at Georgetown University. Then he, too, came home.

Graham's career was every bit as eclectic as the family businesses into which he was born. In his early twenties he worked alongside his father selling real estate near Miami, Florida, but after a few years he came back up to Washington and took charge of the Graham Farms turkey operation. He became chairman of a local bank, and for a time he led the city planning commission. Graham never ran for office, but he became involved in local Republican party politics as a fund-raiser and organizer. His wife, a woman he'd met at Georgetown named Stuart Hill Smith, was a descendant of one of the founding families of Maryland and suffered a bit of culture shock when the couple moved to Indiana from Florida. But she eventually took well to the landlocked flatlands of Daviess County, teaching at the local public high school. She and David had eight children, five girls and three boys, whom they watched grow up and leave Washington, Indiana, one by one, for good.

You can't really blame the Graham kids. The second half of the twentieth century was not as kind to Daviess County as the preceding hundred years had been. By the late 1980s, when David Graham retired at the age of sixty, as all Grahams in the family business are compelled to do, he was contemplating pulling up stakes and leaving town himself. But Stuart enjoyed her job teaching social studies, and they decided to stay. Graham, perhaps wanting to continue the family legacy, endeavored to spend his retirement years helping his community become the kind of place where young people might be less inclined to leave. A number of economic-development schemes were floating around in those days, but one concept in particular was tailor-made for a Graham: an effort by the Southwestern Indiana Regional Highway Coalition, or SWIRHC, to get an interstate highway built between Indianapolis and Evansville.

A hundred years before, with his grandfather Ziba's financial encouragement, the railroad had shone its light on Washington, bringing jobs and immigrants and vitality to the town. Forty years later, the growing demand for trucks and cars had brought his father and two uncles wealth and influence. But the all-important interstate highway system, which defined and directed American mobility after the automotive revolution, had turned a cold shoulder on southwestern Indiana. The government planners who laid out the web of divided highways saw no need to connect Indiana's capital to its third-largest city, so Evansville, already geographically isolated in the dangling southern tip of the state, was left secluded, served by only a single east-west interstate, I-64, that tied it to

Louisville and Saint Louis. The shortest path to Indianapolis remained a folksy two-lane meander, and Washington, the small town the Graham family had helped make great, found itself stuck in a tangle of back roads, forty miles from the nearest on-ramp.

Since then, southwestern Indiana has suffered from a slow deterioration of its agricultural and manufacturing economy, and many have decided that a lack of good highways is to blame. As David's eight children were born, raised, and bid farewell, a string of highway proposals were raised and rejected—a divided freeway north to Terre Haute, a toll expressway to Lafayette through Terre Haute, a freeway northwest to Indianapolis through Bloomington, and a toll road to Indianapolis through Bloomington. None of these, upon examination, was judged worthy of construction. By the time David Graham joined the crusade to remedy Evansville's isolation problem, the highway effort had been creeping along unsuccessfully for four decades.

"Endless meetings" is how Graham remembers the activities of SWIRHC, an offshoot of the Metropolitan Evansville Chamber of Commerce. "It was so discouraging. We had these big meetings down in Evansville. The same old half dozen people would show up, but we never really accomplished anything." In the late eighties, the group was able to convince Congressman Frank McCloskey, a former Democratic mayor of Bloomington whose district also included Washington and Evansville, to earmark half a million dollars for a study of possible new highway routes through southern Indiana. But inconveniently, the consultants that were hired with those funds, Donohue & Associates, came to the conclusion that no highway should be built at all. It wouldn't be worth the money, according to their analysis, which was published in a report in February 1990. Only one of the three routes studied was seen to have a potentially positive cost-benefit ratio, that was only under the most optimistic economic models, and the positive ratio was still below the commonly accepted threshold for green-lighting projects. To move forward, the report said, "would assume that the highway is the highest priority for each of the counties along the route and that each county government is willing to devote significant revenue resources to the project for about thirty years. There is no such precedent of this type in the area." The Federal Highway Administration forwarded the bad news to Congress, calling the proposed road "at best marginal from a cost-effectiveness standpoint." A federal earmark would be all but impossible to obtain, the

FHWA made clear, but Indiana was free to proceed with the Evansville-to-Indianapolis highway if the state wanted to waste its own good money. The Indiana Department of Transportation initiated a preliminary study, but the matter seemed increasingly hopeless.

That spring of 1990, after the Donohue study came out, an economist named David Reed was working as a senior research fellow at the Hudson Institute, the conservative think tank known for future-oriented research on, among other things, economic development. Hudson was headquartered in Indianapolis back then, and at the behest of Democratic congressman Lee Hamilton, the Eli Lilly Foundation funded a study by Hudson on the future of southern rural Indiana, its economic troubles and opportunities for improvement. As the lead researcher, Reed canvassed the countryside, interviewing civic leaders, business owners, farmers, and people who had lost their jobs. Because one symptom of the economic woe that brought him to those parts was a dearth of decent hotels, when he came to Washington, Reed stayed with Graham, who had known the CEO of the Hudson Institute, Mitch Daniels, since 1976, when Daniels managed Richard Lugar's first senatorial campaign and Graham was its chairman for Daviess County.

One morning for breakfast Graham invited two people whom he wanted Reed to meet: his friend David Cox, who ran the Daviess County Growth Council, and a woman named Jo Arthur, who worked for the Southern Indiana Development Corporation. Graham cooked omelets and made mournful conversation with his houseguests about the "brain drain" that had carried his children and so many other well-educated Hoosiers off to bigger cities and healthier job markets. Inevitably, talk around the table turned to the campaign for a new interstate highway through the area. Graham cleared the table, laid out some maps, and showed Reed where an extension of I-69 might go from Indianapolis to Evansville. Reed was cynical—extending the highway to Evansville struck him as fundamentally unsound policy. But he stared a little longer at the map.

"You'll never get to first base unless you can get other people interested in this highway," he said, "other *states* interested. Because nobody gives a damn about Indiana." If you're going to spend a couple billion, Reed asked his breakfast companions, why not be in for a penny, in for a pound? Why not build something that made sense in a broader context, that would have benefits outside southern Indiana? Running his finger over the map, Reed pointed out that the existing I-69 connected to Canada. What if they could extend I-69 all the way south to Mexico? Such a route would tie together the three countries and pass through a trio of manufacturing and distribution centers—Indianapolis, Memphis, Houston—that hadn't been so directly connected before. Reed knew how feasibility studies worked, and he was sure that the inclusion of those major cities would make the numbers jump. And if the road went through multiple states, he reasoned, it would undoubtedly garner broader support in Congress.

Were the plans for the southwest Indiana highway not too big but too small? Graham, Cox, and Arthur immediately recognized Reed's early-morning epiphany as a breakthrough. It rendered obsolete the decades of naysaying studies and elevated their regional highway proposal to one of national importance. With their encouragement, Reed, in his report for the Hudson Institute, "The Future of Southern Rural Indiana: Paradigms and Prospects for Rural Development," made the first public case for a multistate Interstate 69. The facilitation of international trade and the potential for rural economic growth were enough to trump the costs, Reed maintained, regardless of what any consultants may say. "Major public investments are almost always made in the absence of complete and totally reliable analytical information," he wrote. "Often, as with the initial commitment to the interstate highway system in the 1950s, they are made more on the basis of faith."

The report's treatment of I-69 was limited to a four-and-a-half-page addendum that focused almost exclusively on the need for the highway through southern Indiana. In his original draft, Reed told me, the recommendations "were much stronger and focused on the entire route, the NAFTA highway concept." But his language was toned down for print, he says, over his objections, by Mitch Daniels. In 1987 "Hudson began to take on a more predictable conservative orientation with the advent of Daniels as president," Reed explained. "When we came back with the southern Indiana study talking about highways, that landed with a dull thud. It just wasn't sexy."

And what *was* sexy in 1991? The Hudson report's last full chapter, to which the brief annex about I-69 was attached, heralded advanced digital telecommunications infrastructure, specifically a system then under development that "could carry telephone, television, computer, facsimile, and other signals into every home, office, or plant in the nation and do so on a single thread of glass extending into each." Reed implored policy makers to ensure that such a system be brought into smaller towns and rural communities, because this information network had "even greater potential to affect the course of rural economic development and social change than did the current telephone system."

But enough about the information superhighway. There was infrastructure of a more well-established nature that Reed sought to emphasize. "One concept that is being explored involves the completion of the I-69 route, not just in Indiana but as a link between the central Great Lakes region and the central Gulf states," his addendum reported. "If a congressional coalition of the affected states could be assembled, then the task of obtaining federal support for the Indiana segment of the project would not fall solely to the state's delegation."

The Hudson Institute had a fine reputation, but a four-and-a-half-page essay, particularly one neutered by revision and appearing as an afterthought to a hundred-page paper about a forgotten region of a Midwestern state, was unlikely to launch any multibillion-dollar, thousand-plus-mile interstate project. David Reed's study granted the national I-69 concept a certain amount of credibility, but his offhand brainstorm over omelets had already done much more: It had excited the mind of the eager and industrious David Graham. Not everyone would have seen the merit in taking a highway proposal that a federal study had deemed too large and expensive and multiplying its size and cost by a factor of ten. But the dream of an international highway was so well suited to Graham's interests and biography that he internalized it immediately. It was Graham who would take the idea and run with it—or drive with it, as the case turned out to be.

The Long Drive

The house in Washington, Indiana, where David Reed woke up for breakfast that morning in 1990 is a historically registered prairie-style mansion known locally as Mimi's Place. It sits on a leafy, block-and-a-half-size lot in a neighborhood of much more modest homes near the middle of town. The house had belonged to David Graham's parents, Robert and Bertha (friends called her Mimi), and it was still full of his father's personal effects. Maybe a little of his spirit, too. Robert Graham would have been very proud of the highway conceived in his kitchen.

"My father represented the automobile industry in the original Pan-American highway committee," Graham said, explaining his quick embrace of Reed's expanded vision of I-69. "He used to tell me about it when I was a boy, and I got interested in it because he was interested in it." Robert Graham was the director of the National Automobile Chamber of Commerce and had good reasons for wanting to encourage the construction of international roads. "The automobile manufacturers wanted to sell more cars. And you gotta have a place to go," Graham said bluntly. "That was one of the things that the automobile people developed, like air brakes. They had to have good roads." When the first Pan-American Congress for Highways convened in Buenos Aires in 1925, the Graham Brothers truck company sent a delegate to the meeting, where he joined a few dozen other Americans, including representatives from the American Hoist and Derrick Company, the Western Wheeled Scraper Company, Armco Steel, and the Barber Asphalt Company— industry men who wanted to see the great road unite the nations of the hemisphere, and who were no less excited by the prospect of being hired to build it.

As head of the Automobile Chamber of Commerce, Robert Graham wanted people to have more places to drive. As head of sales for Graham Brothers, he understood that international roads also meant new markets for trucks. And because truck advertising then was a lot like truck advertising now, those rugged far-off markets also made for an effective selling point back home. "In Every Business—in Every Part of the World," a full-page magazine advertisement for Graham Brothers bragged in 1925. "Road conditions in foreign lands are generally worse than in America. To operate successfully over there, a truck must have exceptional power and endurance."

This ad, which shows a few smiling men in international dress, hangs framed on the wall of the den in David Graham's current home, which is not a prairie-school mansion surrounded by grand old trees. Mimi's Place was full of wonderful memories, but it was also full of dust and mold that had begun to bother Graham's breathing. Several years ago, with their kids all grown and gone away, David and Stuart made the hard decision to move to a smaller house with a master bedroom on the ground floor so they wouldn't have to climb too many stairs. They sold Robert and Bertha's old home and relocated a few miles east of Washington on Highway 50. A painted sign in the front yard of the new place said QUAIL's ROOST, a name borrowed from an old hunting lodge his father had kept a few miles from there. Graham's new house was surrounded on three sides by cornfields; on the fourth side is a church cemetery. "The neighbors are pretty quiet," Graham joked.

When I first met David Graham, in May 2004, he was seventy-seven years old. His hair, like that of many I-69 boosters I would meet, was white, and he walked carefully but with a practiced poise. His barrel chest and strong jaw gave him—or reflected—an abiding assertiveness, which he could reinforce or mitigate by the expression of his pale blue eyes. Those, he kept locked on the person to whom he was speaking. He was hesitant to talk to a journalist, he told me, having long ago decided that "the less I could have my name in the papers, the more of a success my activities would be. My philosophy is that things never get completely finished if you have to worry about who gets the credit." The fact that I lived in New York City was of particular concern to him. He didn't think that the East Coast press treated the Midwest fairly. But when I explained that I was originally from Indianapolis and that I had attended nearby DePauw University, he softened a little and said, "Well, can I show you around the house?"

We went through a small wet bar and into the den, where the curtains were closed and two plush blue electric recliners sat facing a small television, which was switched on and tuned to the Turner Classic Movies station, flickering in black and white. On the walls hung clippings, photographs, and other mementos pertaining, in oddly equal measure, to Graham's life and that of his father. Just inside the door to the room hung a near-life-scale drawing of a knight in armor wearing a sword and holding a spear and shield. "That was the Spirit of Graham-Paige," he explained. "The three men on the shield are Dad and his two brothers. That was the symbol that they had. You see how strong and tough."

"Now that's a car that my dad and his brothers gave the pope," he said, moving on to a nearby picture of what turned out to be a custom Graham-Paige. "It was open in front and closed in the back. He used that car more than any other." There were old Graham Brothers hubcaps on the wall, and a collection of framed clippings chronicling his father's and uncles' local celebrity. One Evansville newspaper article from Graham Brothers Day in 1928 read, "Like kings going to coronation, the three important figures in the motor world will find an entire city massed to show them its gratitude," and a *Saturday Evening Post* article reported "a public outpouring probably without parallel in the history of American life."

"Down in Florida, my father developed a property called Bal Harbour. It's right there," Graham said, pointing to a large aerial photograph of a sandy peninsula covered with trees and houses. "There was nothing there when he bought it. He pumped it in." When Graham was born, in February 1927, his parents were staying at their winter home in Miami Beach. A major hurricane had hit south Florida the previous September, causing a dip in what had been a skyrocketing real estate market. It must have seemed like a good time to buy. While Graham was still an infant, his father—out of boredom, Graham says—bought 254 acres of swampland just up the coast and formed the Miami Beach Heights Corporation with his fellow automobile industrialists C. T. Fisher and Walter Briggs. Two years later the Great Depression hit, and for the next decade development advanced at a cautious crawl. They filled in the swamp with sand and hired Harland Bartholomew and Associates, the most prestigious American planning firm at the time, to design the new community. Things were still a blank slate in 1941 when the United States entered World War II, so Robert Graham offered the land (at $1 a year) to the U.S. Army Air Corps, which promptly built a prisoner-of-war camp, a training ground, and a rifle range on the sandy Bal Harbour site.

Graham, who was in high school at Georgetown Prep in Washington, D.C., during the war, remembers walking the beach during his summers and seeing black oil sludge in the sand from the freighters that German submarines had sunk off the Florida coast. His senior year, Graham signed up for the U.S. Army Air Corps, but by the time he finished high school the war was coming to a close. After graduation, he said, "I was in Florida, goofing around the bath club down there, and Dad didn't like me spending that much time doing nothing." So Robert Graham called on a friend, an Air Corps general, and David soon had orders to report to South America, where he spent a summer before returning to D.C. for college.

"That's a great picture," Graham said, pointing to a black-and-white photograph of R. E. Olds of Oldsmobile fame; Charles Nash, who ran General Motors; Henry Ford; and Robert Graham. The men were sitting in a circle, wearing suits, leaning forward and grinning at each other. "They're at the Detroit Athletic Club talking about things. And Mr. Ford asked Dad, 'How many kids do you have?' And Dad said, 'I have four. Four boys.' And Ford said, 'What are they gonna do?' And Dad said, 'Well, I hope they'll join me in my activities.' And Ford said—I don't know exactly what he said. But he never would let his son Edsel get ahead."

Robert Graham's sons did join his activities. By the time David graduated from Georgetown University, his brother Bob was the president of the family companies, his brother Ziba was the financial man, and his brother Tom was managing Graham Farms. David went to work running the family's feed mill. "I was home for a couple years. And it's pretty boring for a young kid," he said. (I told him I could relate.) "Well, Dad called up one day from Bal Harbour and said, 'I've got too much business down here and I need one of you boys to come down.'" David was eager to go. From the time his father turned over the first ceremonial shovel of earth in 1946, construction had been constant. There were luxury hotels along the oceanfront, apartment houses along Collins Avenue, and a cluster of exclusive homes. By this time, most of Bal Harbour had been sold—to all the right people—and it was becoming a fashionable place. "Harry Sinclair came down and put in a filling station," Graham remembered. Howard Johnson, a "good friend of Dad's," operated a restaurant at the Beach Club.

Not long after he moved to Florida, Graham passed his brokerage exam and had a job lined up at the prestigious Miami real estate office of Oscar Dooly. "But I thought about it and I decided to come back to Indiana," Graham said. "I would have been a very wealthy person if I'd stayed down there. No matter what you bought, the value exploded." He paused for a moment. He hadn't thought about these things in years, he said. "Stuart never tried to influence me on where we were going, but coming back here was kind of a cultural shock for her."

That's not to say that David and Stuart were destined to live a prosaic life in Indiana. Across one stretch of wall in his den, Graham kept a selection of souvenirs from his turkey days that hints at a life of world travel and, for a poultry farmer, relative fame. "There I am getting a special award from a Czechoslovakian turkey grower," he said, pointing to another black-and-white photograph. "And over here, I gave a speech in London about growing turkey farms. I was president of the National Turkey Federation for about one year. Here's a picture of Stuart and me in *Vogue*." It was taken on the White House lawn during the annual Thanksgiving pardoning ceremony in 1969. "We're presenting President Nixon with a turkey. A turkey to the turkey."

Seeing these photos of a younger David Graham and looking again at the Detroit Athletic Club photo of Robert Graham, I noted how much the two looked alike. It struck me, suddenly, how the arrangement of artifacts in the room seemed to blend the achievements of father and son, as if the one's life was a seamless continuation of the other. Robert had fathered four sons, but it was David who went down to work in the real estate office when his father beckoned from Florida, David who would make his home at Mimi's Place, David who would keep and display so faithfully his father's memorabilia. And it was David who would seize the chance to continue Robert Graham's pursuit of new highways.

After the omelet breakfast with Reed, Graham took the new jumbo-size I-69 idea back to the Southwestern Indiana Regional Highway Coalition. The committee embraced the new plan, with some slight caution. At a meeting in August 1990, Rolland Eckels, a public-affairs man from the Bristol-Myers Squibb Company, warned that the coalition should be prepared to answer challenges regarding the need for such a vast highway. An answer came from Keith Lochmueller, the cofounder of an Evansville transportation planning firm called Bernardin, Lochmueller & Associates, who suggested that their response "should be safety and economics." This turned out to be more than idle chitchat—Bernardin Lochmueller was eventually hired to conduct Indiana's formal I-69 study, which measured potential benefits in terms of safety and economics.

The committee tried to convince Lieutenant Governor Frank O'Bannon, a Democrat, and Senator Richard Lugar, a Republican, that Indiana should host a meeting of key people from the various states along the newly imagined I-69 corridor. Several statewide officeholders voiced nominal support—Fred Glass, the chief of staff to then-governor Evan Bayh, wrote a letter to the group promising that the state would try to have the link designated a corridor "of national significance" in an upcoming federal transportation bill—but no one was ready to accept the responsibility of organizing a multistate campaign for the project.

But perhaps momentum could be created from the bottom up? Or rather, from nearer to the bottom? The movers and shakers in Evansville were not the phone-tree, petition-circulating kind, but they were accomplished networkers. And at least one of them had some time on his hands. The newly retired David Graham kept a home in Cuernavaca, south of Mexico City, to which he and Stuart traveled every summer on Stuart's break from teaching. "I love the trip down. The triple-A book would say things like, 'Don't travel on this highway in Mexico after four o'clock,'" Graham said with a chuckle. "So we wouldn't. They had policemen out there that might stop you. In fact, we got stopped by a policeman in Mexico City. It cost five hundred bucks to pay them off. Maybe it was seven hundred. Seven cops came up and each one of them wanted payment. But, you know, the men don't make enough money—they have to buy their own bullets," he added magnanimously. "You go to a poor country, you tip heavily. Not to be a big shot, but because you know it might put something on the table for their kids, or buy a new coat or dress."

In the summer of 1991, on the way home with Stuart, Graham did a little soliciting himself. Driving his big blue diesel Chevy Suburban, he stopped off in a few cities along what he reckoned would be the route of I-69. He had laid no groundwork before his visits—the trip *was* the groundwork. Rather, like a traveling salesman, Graham called cold on the chambers of commerce or economic-development corporations in Laredo, Corpus Christi, Houston, Shreveport, and Memphis, presenting the I-69 concept to whoever was available to listen while Stuart waited in the car. While he was at it, he also paid visits to Mexico City and Fort Worth to speak with newspaper reporters who he thought might be supportive of the idea of a brand-new free-trade highway. One of them, Dane Schiller, was a writer for *The News*, an English-language daily in

Mexico City. He now covers border issues for the *Houston Chronicle*, and he recalls being somewhat perplexed by Graham's visit. The idea of I-69, Schiller wrote in an e-mail, seemed like "pie in the sky" back then, at best "many years away if, in a wild dream, it could even happen." He thought Graham was "gutsy to come down and roam around Mexico," but "there was no need to believe such a corridor could ever happen." His overall impression? "That dude must be seriously eccentric."

Fortunately for Graham, the economic-development people he met, attuned as they were to the potential benefits of new infrastructure, found his pitch much more convincing. For a few, like John D. Caruthers in Shreveport, agreeing to take a meeting with Graham that summer led to a commitment of a decade or more. In the same way that Graham had adopted David Reed's expanded-highway idea the moment he heard it, these men became disciples on the spot—not of Graham, but of I-69. "It just so happened that it captured everyone's imagination," Graham recalled, "because by accident of geography, it goes through some of the poorest places in the United States. Western Kentucky, western Tennessee, and then on down through Arkansas and Louisiana. All those people needed help. They needed a road."

Graham's traveling medicine show was, among other things, another homage to his father, the sales guru of the three Graham brothers. Robert's pitchman philosophies made a lasting impression on Graham, just as his work on the Pan American highway had. In his book *The Graham Legacy*, Michael Keller, a funeral director and amateur Graham-Paige historian, quotes David as saying that his father believed people "had basic needs which should be made known to them." "Dad's chief stock in trade," Graham told Keller, "was his ability to sell you on an idea, make you think it was yours, and then subtly encourage you to develop it as fast as possible."

A Plane Ride

Some years back, John D. Caruthers sent a warm and rambling reminiscence to the *Shreveport Times* that recalled his childhood in the 1930s and '40s, his early-morning paper route, stickball games in vacant lots, and summer nights before air-conditioning. "In the morning," he wrote, "we sat barefooted on the cool curb and ate ice from the Dairyland horse-drawn milk wagon or from the ice truck that supplied those that had iceboxes rather than new refrigerators." After the young Caruthers graduated from high school, he attended undergrad at Louisiana Tech and then law school at Louisiana State. In the 1950s, he joined the army as a JAG lawyer and was sent to Germany, but four years later he came back home to Shreveport and has never left.

Caruthers started working in the oil and gas business in the early sixties, just after the federal power commission put a cap on natural-gas prices, a move that eventually prompted the major oil companies to abandon the smaller northern Louisiana fields for the oil-rich Gulf of Mexico and to leave Shreveport for Houston and Dallas. "Shreveport lost three thousand white-collar jobs," Caruthers told me. "This was around the same time that the two-car family was producing the mall concept of shopping. And so that double-barrel deal just blew the hell out of downtown." But Caruthers didn't go to Houston or Dallas. He hired a geologist and started an independent company, Caruthers Producing, that specialized in small local leases, and he ran it from an office tower in the cleared-out center of Shreveport.

When David Graham wandered into the Shreveport Chamber of Commerce with a map in his hands, talking about a new highway, they sent him across the street to Caruthers, who was sixty-two, a former chamber president, and known for having a firm grasp of transportation matters, a résumé full of successful economic-development projects, and friends with political power. "They sent him to me to get *rid* of him," is how Caruthers put it, with a chuckle. "I was a lame-duck past president and had nothing to do. And the reason I got involved in 1991—I was concerned, having just seen the demise of fourteen local banks in the savings-and-loan crisis, that this town didn't have a guaranteed future."

When I first went to speak with Caruthers in 2004, he was seventy-five years old and had recently sold Caruthers Producing to his son Witt and his lead engineer, Art Walker (whose own son Todd, Caruthers made a point of telling me, played second base for the Chicago Cubs and the Boston Red Sox). Caruthers seemed younger than seventy-five—he was tall and gregarious with a decent amount of white hair, combed back, and windshield glasses. He had a voice like George Bush the elder, at once soft and sharp, and a generous manner that bespoke a Southern upbringing and perhaps a certain degree of wealth. He had kept his office, a large corner room ten stories above Shreveport, where he still spent many days working on I-69 Mid-Continent Highway Coalition business and other odds and ends. "I come in at ten o'clock usually and leave at about three for racquetball. At my age, I have to do *something* to stay alive," he said. I assumed that he meant racquetball, not highway promoting, but I didn't ask him to clarify. "I'm also writing a novel. I've been working on that for about twelve months."

I asked him what the book was about. "It's about this area, this city," he said. "It's a story of prejudice. It's really an interesting town in that we had a lot of people migrate in here from different areas." He told me about the influx of African Americans who moved from the farms into the industrialized city after World War II. "It was as if you had a hundred plantation slave quarters set up in the Red River bottoms over here. Shotgun houses, eave to eave." Earlier, before the Civil War, a wave of mostly Scotch-Irish settlers, including Caruthers's kin, had come through northern Louisiana in the great western migration of the 1830s and '40s.

It was a partly sunny afternoon in March, and before long Caruthers and I were standing at the northeast-facing windows of his office, looking out at Shreveport. As I was driving in, the city had reminded me of a model-railroad town. There are just enough tall buildings to give Shreveport a skyline, but you can see the entirety of downtown in a glance, even from up close. The office towers, medium-size and architecturally humble, are clustered together several streets up from the waterfront, as if keeping their distance from a string of gaudy casino hotels that popped up along the river in the mid-1990s. In between, I noticed, many of the blocks had been turned into parking lots or had reverted to weedy dirt. Caruthers read the panorama like an old map, pointing to the Texas Street truss bridge that carries U.S. 79 and U.S. 80 over the Red River to Shreveport's smaller sister city of Bossier. "Back in the nineteenth century, the Texas trail started right there at the river. This was where the wagon trains were made up, right where that bridge is, to the right of El Dorado Casino," he said. "All the ironworkers were there on the riverfront, building wagons."

Until the 1830s, a hundred-mile-long logjam clogged the Red River. "You could walk across it," he said. "Every tree in Oklahoma and Texas had floated down here. There was green grass growing on parts of it." This snag was known as the Great Raft, and in 1832 the U.S. secretary of war, Lewis Cass, ordered it cleared so that the Red River, which connected via the Mississippi to the Gulf of Mexico, might be free for navigation. This hefty job was given to Captain Henry Miller Shreve, the U.S. Superintendent of Western River Improvements, a trader and an engineer who had designed a special steam-powered snagboat, the *Heliopolis,* capable of clearing dead wood from the water. By 1834, Shreve had opened up the river to as far north as where the casinos now stood, and the next year the U.S. government, wanting to make the most of the river's new navigability, invested in some local real estate. The white man offered a treaty to the Caddo Indians, who vacated their lands in northwest Louisiana for the sum of eighty thousand dollars.

In negotiating the agreement, the Caddo set aside an unspecified 640-acre piece of land for an interpreter, Larkin Edwards, who was friendly with the tribe and who had married one of the Caddo chief's daughters. Edwards picked out a nice square-mile tract of land along the newly opened river, which was already becoming a major trade route, and then he turned around and sold that 640 acres, in 1837, to a group of developers led by none other than Captain Shreve, who apparently wasn't satisfied with merely professional or altruistic rewards. The Shreve Town Company paid five thousand dollars for what is now downtown Shreveport. "If you look at the way they laid it out," Caruthers said, pointing out the window at the grid below us, "since the Alamo had occurred in 1836, the main street was Texas Street. And Travis is this street here—Colonel Travis headed up the Alamo. Fannin was another Texas colonel, if you remember, and that street there is named for him." There is a Crockett Street, too, for Davy Crockett.

Modern-day developers often reach back into local history—or into a pile of generically pleasing motifs, like trees—to find a theme on which to base the names of subdivisions and their streets. Caruthers, for instance, is an investor in the Highland Ranch community west of town, which consists of subdivisions called Cherry Hill and Summerwood. His son Witt is involved with a development called Provenance, a neighborhood south of town that has streets named Silver Maple Lane and Winterberry Lane. For the Shreve Town Company the branding would have been obvious: The relevant themes were "Shreve" and "Texas." The city was viable, after all, thanks to the Red River being unlocked for trade, and the great mass of people heading west through town were bound for the newly independent Texas. Many of them found Shreveport a worthy place to settle down, and the Shreve Town Company sold lots with ease. Before long, antebellum cotton growers had made Shreveport a major hub.

"When cotton was king—and I'm talking about before the railroads," Caruthers told me, "there was a place over there where the boats picked up bales and took them to New Orleans." The Red, which forms the squiggly northern border of Texas before flowing through Shreveport, continues southeast through Alexandria, and when cotton was king, it entered the Mississippi River right at the place where the foot of Louisiana's geographical boot kicks under the southwestern butt of Mississippi and relieves that state of its eponymous river. The Atchafalaya River, the watery main street of Cajun country, originated *out* of the Mississippi near that very same spot. This was all too much for the various riverbanks to handle, and in the 1940s—around the time when Caruthers was working his paper route—the Atchafalaya captured the Red's discharge.

If left alone, the Mississippi's prime flow eventually would have become the Atchafalaya's, and the great river would have changed channels, a phenomenon not out of line geologically speaking, but one that nevertheless would have been deeply troubling to any person or place that had a stake in the lower Miss remaining mighty. This included, most notably, the cities of New Orleans and Baton Rouge, whose existence historically relied on the Mississippi River the way Shreveport's relied on the Red. Thanks to the Army Corps of Engineers, however, America didn't have to stand there and take such insubordination. As John McPhee writes in "The Control of Nature," his authoritative account of this natural event and the heroic unnatural efforts that followed, in 1950 "the United States Congress, in its deliberations, decided that 'the distribution of flow and sediment in the Mississippi and Atchafalaya Rivers is now in desirable proportions and should be so maintained.' The Corps was thereby ordered to preserve 1950."

By then, the Red River was tangled up in a different kind of trouble farther upstream. It, too, had been usurped—not by the Atchafalaya or any other river, but by the railroads, which after the Civil War had become the primary mode of transporting goods and people through the country. The Red, which Shreve had gone to such pains to clear, had fallen into a state of neglect: It would periodically flood farms and towns, whose residents liked to dump garbage into it. The wild Red may have been fine for the keelboats and rafts of old, but it was inhospitable to the kind of barge traffic that had become the mainstay of modern inland agricultural and petrochemical shipping. By the time John D. Caruthers became involved with the Shreveport Chamber of Commerce in the late 1960s, restoring and modernizing Red River navigation had become one of the local business community's top priorities.

"I was vice president of economic development in 1971 when we printed a bunch of bumper stickers that said BIG RED BY '80," Caruthers told me. "Everyone thought the stickers meant Big Red Oklahoma, the football team." In fact, the River and Harbor Act of 1968 had authorized a Red River improvement project, again by the Army Corps of Engineers, that would eventually include the installation of five locks and dams and a series of shortcuts along a 236-mile stretch of river from Shreveport to the Mississippi. The Corps would dredge the river's channel to a minimum of nine feet deep and two hundred feet wide, and reinforce its banks—in essence taming the Red River into a barge-worthy water highway. "Bank stabilization was a big thing," Caruthers said, "because it kept going back and forth, it was such a young river." The Red River Navigation Project took decades. Despite the chamber's sticker campaign, 1980 came and went without a new Red River, in part because of strong opposition to the two-billion-dollar project. "We had a newspaper here that was opposed to navigation on the Red River," Caruthers said. "They called it a boondoggle."

They weren't the only ones. Over the years, most administrations and members of Congress not from the state of Louisiana received the undertaking lukewarmly. In addition to the costs involved, there was also a broader philosophical concern: that the business-oriented push for navigation projects was at odds, financially and physically, with the prerogatives of flood control, which many believed should have been the Corps' main mission. But the river had a formidable champion in the Democratic Louisiana senator J. Bennett Johnston Jr., a Shreveport native whose older sister, incidentally, went to high school with John D. Caruthers. Johnston and Caruthers are old friends and they maintain a great mutual respect. "He actually built the damn thing," Caruthers said of Johnston and the river project. "Bennett funded it, over the objections of Bush, Carter, and Reagan."

The money came mostly in dribs, but sometimes in buckets—in August 1990, Johnston, who chaired the relevant subcommittee of Senate Appropriations, added an earmark to a far-reaching energy and water funding bill. It gave the Red River Waterway $92.6 million, "to remain available until expended." It was the largest single expenditure in the bill, and its passage sped the project toward completion. The locks and dams were finally opened a few short years later, in 1994, and on April 19, 2000, after he had retired from the Senate, Johnston spoke at a renaming ceremony for the Red River Waterway. "This river route connects us to every part of the world," he told a crowd of several hundred. "It gives us the ability to attract industries from everywhere." On that day, the Red River Waterway became the J. Bennett Johnston Waterway. What Shreve had done for the Red with steam power, Johnston had done again with political power. And Caruthers had watched it all unfold.

"When this guy from Indiana told me the concept of I-69," Caruthers said, "a light came on." His meeting with Graham, which took place there in the offices of Caruthers Producing, didn't last long, he recalled. Possibly as little as twenty minutes. But Graham's presentation grabbed him. "I said, 'Let's see where this thing would go if we just made it straight as an arrow and picked up Memphis and Houston.'" The two men took a map that Graham had brought along and they drew a line, freehand, connecting the dots from Detroit to Indianapolis to Evansville to Memphis to Shreveport to Houston to Laredo.

I remember a time, not so long ago, when I saw the map of the United States as something more or less finished. I assumed that the rivers and the roads were where they were supposed to be, that the cities had evolved by logic or luck. Previous generations had toiled, I knew, to build towns and to connect them. But wasn't that work finished? Wasn't construction these days just a matter of fleshing out those bones? Well, you can't spend much time looking out a window at Shreveport with John D. Caruthers without realizing that there are men (they seem to most often be men) who still view the map as a work in progress. Caruthers knew that the America I took for granted had been the arbitrary work of individuals and small groups. And it could be remade by more individuals and small groups. In short, there were still Shreves among us, and I was talking to one. "So you two drew that line in this office?" I asked Caruthers. "It all happened right here?"

"It all happened on an airplane. I took the map that David Graham and I drew and showed it to Bennett Johnston," he said. "I happened to be flying back from Louisiana Tech with Bennett. It was a private plane. And I said, 'Senator, here is something we've just drawn. Look what it can mean to Shreveport. Is this a doable deal? I don't want to get involved in something that's not doable.' And he said, 'It's doable—let's do it!'" Caruthers chuckled. "And I figured we'd do it next week! That's how he made it sound. Of course he didn't tell me he was going to resign from the Senate."

Never mind that the Red River had taken twenty-six years to complete—fourteen years longer than the chamber's stickers had hoped. On that plane ride in 1991, Caruthers heard all the encouragement he needed from a senator friend who had just conjured ninety million dollars for a project few others wanted. Caruthers was convinced, and by February 1992 Senator Johnston was talking up I-69 to the *Shreveport Times*. "Can you imagine Shreveport having north-south and east-and-west interstates and Red River navigation and a diagonal highway?" he said, referring to the existing I-20, the ongoing construction of I-49 from New Orleans through Shreveport to Kansas City, and, of course, I-69. "It would make the city one of the major distribution centers in the country.

"We need to organize all the states in the route," Johnston told the paper. "It will [require] a lot of work from everyone, but it will work." By this time the task of organizing the Mid-Continent Highway Coalition was in full swing. That month, David Graham made a second pass through Houston, Memphis, and Shreveport to shore up support among the people he'd met on his first trip. Caruthers took to the road, too, sometimes traveling with Lindy Broderick from the Shreveport Chamber. He traveled to Nacogdoches, Texas; Magnolia and El Dorado, Arkansas; Cleveland, Greenville, and Clarksdale, Mississippi; and Memphis and Dyersburg, Tennessee. Caruthers's tactics were somewhat more methodical than Graham's improvisational barnstorming: He often targeted people he knew and relied on their advice about whom else to call. He set up his appointments in advance, gave public talks to chambers of commerce, and spoke to a string of small-town mayors. "My first trip was to Lufkin, Texas," he recalled. "I rode down in Lindy's Volkswagen bug with my knees on the dashboard. I remember it vividly."

In Memphis, Caruthers visited the office of Mayor W. W. Herenton, whom he describes as "a distinguished black man, tall, slender. He looks like an African prince, actually." Herenton found the idea of I-69 thrilling—Memphis was already the kind of major distribution center Shreveport hoped one day to become, and the more highways the merrier. The mayor offered to host the coalition's first meeting, and a date was set for November 1992. At that meeting Caruthers would become president of the Mid-Continent Highway Coalition and I-69 would become the focus of his working life.

It so happens that a highway dominates his domestic life, too, as he explained while we were standing at his office window. We had stepped over to the northwest-facing view, away from the city. In the middle distance, past the downtown grid, we could see Cross Lake—which provides Shreveport with both tap water and leisure—and Interstate 220 cutting across the eastern quarter of it. "I live on that lake and I hear every eighteen-wheeler that goes up that grade," he said. Caruthers had helped campaign for the I-220 bypass years ago, and he has a certain affection for the long stretch over the lake. "Just to the left of that section of the bridge there's a bunch of pine trees. I live in those pine trees over there, facing the bridge," Caruthers told me. "If you go under the bridge you look for two straight miles at nothing but arches. Like a church. So whenever I take my friends out there in a boat, I always put it in neutral under the bridge." He smiled. "Then I start singing 'Ave Maria.'"

The Hotel Lobby

Mayor Herenton made good on his offer to host the first meeting of the Mid-Continent Highway Coalition, and he hosted it in style. Memphis is a major cargo hub and always has been. The coalition might have found a boardroom at the FedEx headquarters east of town, or at the massive Port of Memphis on the Mississippi River. But if you're going to make big plans in Memphis, you might as well do it at the Peabody Hotel, an establishment that has played host to celebrity visitors, society weddings, grand balls, and deal-making lunches since 1869. The hotel moved to its current location, a majestic Italian renaissance–style building on Union Avenue, in the 1920s and quickly became a home base for blues talent scouts. It was in a room at the Peabody in 1929 that the great Furry Lewis recorded his version of "John Henry," a folk song about a superhumanly efficient railroad builder. The Peabody is a cathedral of Southern culture but also a local symbol of renewal—the assassination of Martin Luther King Jr. at the Lorraine Motel in 1968 is widely cited as the event that began urban Memphis's steep decline, and the reopening of the Peabody after extensive renovations, in 1981, is generally considered the beginning of the downtown's renaissance. Today it is perhaps most celebrated for its resident ducks, which take an elevator to the ground floor from their rooftop dormitory every morning and march through an adoring crowd. They spend the day in the lobby fountain, then march back to the elevator at cocktail time.

"The Mississippi Delta begins in the lobby of the Peabody Hotel," David Cohn, from Greenville, Mississippi, wrote in 1935. "If you stand near its fountain in the middle of the lobby, where ducks waddle and turtles drowse, ultimately you will see everybody who is anybody in the Delta." If there were people watchers there on November 10, 1992, they were likely underwhelmed when the members of the Mid-Continent Highway Coalition made their way through to their appointed confer-

33

ence room. Those assembled were pillars of their local communities but not well known outside of their respective home counties. There was David Graham and his breakfast companion David Cox. There was John D. Caruthers. There were the mayors of Evansville, Indiana; El Dorado, Arkansas; Lufkin, Texas; and Dyersburg, Tennessee. Heads probably did not turn at the sight of the man from the Pine Bluff, Arkansas, Port Authority or the woman from the Pike County, Indiana, Economic Development Corporation, but the consequences of their anonymous work that day, they hoped, would be far from obscure.

All told, between forty and fifty like-minded highway lovers traveled to Memphis from the seven I-69 states that morning. Mayor Herenton welcomed the group and then gave the floor over to Caruthers, who made introductions and presented an overview of the project. The group tackled organizational business, namely hashing out a structure for the nonprofit corporation they would form. It was decided that each state delegation would elect a vice president and four directors to represent it on the coalition's board, and each state vice president would be responsible for raising twenty thousand dollars per year to cover operating expenses. Caruthers was elected president and chairman of the corporation. David Graham would be the vice president for Indiana, and the coalition's executive director would be James Newland, a longtime friend of Graham's who also grew up in Daviess County.

Newland, who was already seventy-three years old in 1992, was steeped in the world of transportation. He had worked for decades as a publicist and lobbyist—first for a railroad consortium on the East Coast and then for an association of highway contractors in the Midwest. He served as a transportation aide to Governor Evan Bayh before semiretiring to a volunteer position as the secretary of the Southwestern Indiana Regional Highway Coalition. Newland went from being the lone staffer at the SWIRHC office to being the lone staffer (paid, this time) at the Mid-Continent Highway Coalition headquarters. The transition for Newland was easy: The office stayed the same—it was a suite on Monument Circle, in the very center of Indianapolis—and, for a while, so did the stationery.

The new I-69 coalition members were eager and, perhaps to their advantage, a little naïve. Advancing the construction of a new national highway would be a huge and unwieldy mission under any circumstances. But the Mid-Continent Highway Coalition happened to form at the very time when national transportation policy was being revamped for a post-interstate future. Many of those who had gathered in Memphis, including Graham and Newland and Caruthers, were of a generation whose adult lives had coincided with the interstate age: The planning for the system we know today took off in 1941, with President Franklin D. Roosevelt's appointment of a National Interregional Highway Committee. That group—seven men—was smaller than the one assembled at the Peabody, but their recommendations, which Roosevelt sent to Congress in January 1944, would change the face of the country. Their report, *Interregional Highways*, offered maps of ideal routes, traffic and population analysis, design principles, and, most important, a compelling vision of a highly connected and more mobile America. Congress obliged by promptly authorizing a national system of interstate highways "to connect by routes, direct as practical, the principal metropolitan areas, cities, and industrial centers, to serve the National Defense, and to connect at suitable points, routes of continental importance in the Dominion of Canada and the Republic of Mexico." But they balked on paying for it. Their mandate went more or less unfunded until twelve years later, when President Dwight D. Eisenhower signed the Federal-Aid Highway Act of 1956.

Eisenhower had established his own committee, led by General Lucius Clay, a friend and colleague from his West Point days. The Clay Committee proposed financing the interstate construction through bonds, an idea supported by Connecticut senator Prescott Bush, a Wall Street banker and father and grandfather to future presidents. But the bonding solution would have cost taxpayers some eleven billion dollars in interest over thirty years—an unnecessary handout to the financial industry, many complained. In the end, Congress negotiated the creation of a tax-based, pay-as-you-go funding system, and Albert Gore Sr., the junior senator from Tennessee and father of the future vice president, sponsored his chamber's legislation. The relevant House bills, later combined with Gore's, were by Representative George Fallon of Maryland, who introduced the construction-oriented language, and Louisiana's Hale Boggs, who contributed the funding solution. Boggs's language created a new highway trust fund, a dedicated stream of money that would pool federal gas-tax dollars and related fees and redistribute them as the federal government's share of interstate construction costs.

By 1991, the interstate system, as planned, was nearly complete, but because of the way the program had been structured, it would never be finished. The Eisenhower bill guaranteed that the federal government, through the highway trust fund, would pay 90 percent of the "cost to complete" the interstates. But this meant that every time a new design standard or innovation was introduced—better guardrails, say—the Interstate Construction Program was obliged to update all of the highways that had already been built to the old standards. "Completion" was a moving target, so the federal funding liability, in theory, was infinite. This seemed like a bad way of doing things, and many in Washington understood that the Interstate Construction Program needed to end.

What's more, national priorities had grown more complex in the intervening decades, and an increased emphasis on historic and environmental preservation, energy conservation, and responsible urban planning had made major-highway building a thornier, less appealing endeavor. With sprawl, congestion, and urban decay, the shortcomings of a roads-only strategy had become widely appreciated, and state highway departments had morphed (at least in name) into state *transportation* departments. New economic, political, and environmental hurdles had been placed between big projects and their funding. While David Graham was making his all-important drive from Cuernavaca back to Indiana, President George H. W. Bush was haggling with lawmakers from both parties and negotiating with nongovernmental stakeholders over a new transportation authorization bill that would signal an end to the Interstate Construction Program and a paradigm shift away from the decades-long focus on the Eisenhower interstate system.

In June 1991, around the time that Graham and Caruthers drew I-69 onto the map in Shreveport, California congressman Norman Mineta, the chairman of the House Surface Transportation Subcommittee, stood before a conference of the American Road and Transportation Builders Association and told them, "America needs more of a transportation vision for the future than endless ribbons of asphalt, overpasses, and off-ramps." The new transportation bill, as drafted, gave greater flexibility to state governments and municipal-planning organizations, allowing them to spend federal "highway" dollars on trains, trolleys, trails, or whatever nonroad projects they decided met their more holistic needs.

The final bill, signed a week before Christmas, was called the Intermodal Surface Transportation Efficiency Act, or ISTEA. It opened with a declaration of policy outlining the new federal mission, which would include "significant improvements in public transportation necessary to achieve national goals for improved air quality, energy conservation, international competitiveness, and mobility for elderly persons, persons with disabilities, and economically disadvantaged persons in urban and rural areas of the country," it said. "Social benefits must be considered with particular attention to the external benefits of reduced air pollution, reduced traffic congestion, and other aspects of the quality of life in the United States." It was a kinder, gentler transportation bill made possible by the closing of a long chapter: ISTEA's appropriations for the Interstate Construction Program, Congress declared, would be the last.

It was less than a year later, in the early morning light of this new era, that the Mid-Continent Highway Coalition arose to ask for one more interstate, as if for old times' sake. I-69, if it was to exist, would have to be an exception to the rule, and that exception would have to be made official by Congress. Luckily for the coalition, that was already under way. Thanks to the machinations of a few legislators, I-69 had stuck a foot in the closing door that was ISTEA. The bill may have ordered an end to the old interstate program per se, but it preserved a federal commitment to roadways by calling for the designation of a national highway system that the U.S. government would remain largely responsible for maintaining and improving. The system would consist almost entirely of existing roads—the interstate system plus a certain number of secondary highways—but its specific makeup was to be decided at a later date in consultation with state and local officials, subject to the approval of the secretary of transportation.

Just to get the ball rolling, ISTEA went ahead and identified a small group of "High Priority Corridors" and directed the secretary of transportation to include these in the new system. "The construction of the Interstate Highway System connected the major population centers of the Nation," the law explained, but "many regions of the Nation are not now adequately served by the Interstate System or comparable highways and require further highway development in order to serve the travel and economic development needs of the region." There were sixteen corridors listed in the initial House version of the bill, introduced in July 1991, all of them regional pet projects in various stages of development—the I-49 extension from Shreveport to Kansas City; an expressway from Denver to Rapid City; a couple of Appalachian highways; and an "Economic Lifeline Corridor" along I-50 and I-40 in California, Arizona, and Nevada.

A week later, when the bill was referred to the Committee on Ways and Means, the list of High Priority Corridors had grown by two. There was a Corridor 17, along existing roads between Greensboro and the District of Columbia, and a Corridor 18, "from Indianapolis, Indiana, to Memphis, Tennessee, via Evansville, Indiana." Congressman Frank McCloskey, who had previously stood up for SWIRHC's interests by earmarking funding for Indiana's Donohue study, was responsible for this bit of legislative rainmaking, and his efforts were simultaneous with David Graham's traveling campaign. By the time ISTEA was signed into law, there were twenty-one High Priority Corridors, including another piece of what would become the Interstate 69 route: Corridor 20 along U.S. 59 "from Laredo, Texas, through Houston, Texas, to the vicinity of Texarkana, Texas."

Maneuvering continued the next summer. In 1992, while John D. Caruthers was filling out the roster of the Mid-Continent Highway Coalition in Arkansas, Louisiana, and Texas, his friend Bennett Johnston was working to insert language into the yearly transportation appropriations bill that would amend the definition of Corridor 18, extending it through Shreveport and all the way to Houston, where it would effectively meet with Corridor 20. With this amendment, which became law that October, the federal description of the two High Priority Corridors coincided fully with the rudimentary map of I-69 that Caruthers had shown Johnston in that airplane above Louisiana. Despite the federal policy headwind against new highways and the fact that the governors and highway departments from the seven states hadn't yet been fully briefed on the I-69 concept, by the time the coalition members first sat down around their conference table at the Peabody that November, the rough lines of I-69 had been staked out in the federal books.

In the loose definition of Corridor 18 there was significant wiggle room, especially in the segment between Memphis and Shreveport, where there was no obvious path. The degree of leeway must have been clear to the new coalition members from Arkansas and Mississippi, who came to Memphis from towns not all of which could possibly be joined by a single highway of any reasonable shape. To pass near Pine Bluff, Arkansas; Cleveland and Greenville, Mississippi; and El Dorado, Arkansas, I-69 would need to carve a large S through the two states, crossing the Mississippi River three times. The folks at the Peabody, in the spirit of cooperation, agreed they would all support whatever route made the best sense for the region. In the first coalition newsletter, Newland wrote a short profile of Caruthers in which the new president promised that the group would "'stay focused on the construction of the highway,' thus steering clear of many of the political issues and traps that often haunt a project of this nature."

For the next several years the invisible highway would shift around, like the young Red River had, until engineers and politicians put it in its place. The final routing of the interstate would be a complex decision—part logic, part luck, and part influence. But to suggest it could avoid politics was out of touch with history. Carl Fisher, the man who organized the effort to build the Lincoln Highway, the country's first coast-to-coast roadway, observed in 1912, with disgust, that "the highways of America are built chiefly of politics, whereas the proper material is crushed rock, or concrete." In the Mid-Continent Highway Coalition's two main objectives—solidifying a route for I-69 and getting the government to pay for its construction—political influence would play a major role as both a tool and a monkey wrench.

The Washington Lobby

The first newsletter of the I-69 Mid-Continent Highway Coalition was mailed out from the group's downtown Indianapolis headquarters in 1993. It was a four-page black-and-white bit of desktop publishing, as modest in appearance as its subject was grand. On page one, below the banner AN INVESTMENT IN AMERICA'S FUTURE, was an essay titled "The Reason Why," by David Reed, whom the newsletter did not identify as the conceptual father of the coalition.

"Interstate highways are significant to most Americans only as the shortest routes for their daily commute to work, or the fastest way to get to the spot they've chosen for their annual vacation," Reed wrote. "For those who think of the Interstate system in this way, it must seem to make little sense to build yet another stretch of road, distinguishable from others only by the names of the towns on the exit signs." But, he continued, the interstates were also the primary arteries of the national economy and a magnet for jobs, and the proposed route of I-69 "traverses areas that are, in large part, among the slowest growing, poorest, least developed and most isolated in their respective states. Many of these regions are desperate for something to spark growth, and the road has the potential to do so."

The North American Free Trade Agreement, which had been hammered out by the George H. W. Bush administration, was on track to be ratified by Congress and signed by President Bill Clinton just weeks after the newsletter reached mailboxes on Capitol Hill and elsewhere. "A completely unique element will also influence the outcome of this project," Reed wrote. "By accident of geography, history, and timing, the Mid-Continent Highway could become the main surface transportation link between Canada, the United States, and Mexico at a time when economic ties between these countries are being strengthened and barriers to trade are dropping."

In February of that year, just three months after the Peabody meeting, the coalition took the first of what would become annual trips to Washington, D.C., to sell Congress on the dual arguments Reed put forth for I-69. Senator Bennett Johnston hosted a breakfast at the L'Enfant Plaza Hotel and invited the members of Congress from the seven states. It was a bipartisan affair: The coalition included devoted members of both political parties, as did the gang of lawmakers that would make up the I-69 congressional caucus. At breakfast, after the lofty I-69 vision was introduced, boosters from each state offered three-minute presentations highlighting the unique benefits a highway would bring to their fellow constituents. The big-picture selling points—NAFTA, economic development, rural empowerment—would be key in justifying the road on a national level. But the appeal to caucus members was more personal, more parochial. A highway was bacon to be brought home. Whatever was ailing their state or district, I-69 could surely help fix it.

The most urgent and tangible request that the coalition made during that first meeting in Washington was for a lump of federal funds to pay for the obligatory feasibility study that would establish the highway's purpose and need and identify possible routes and impacts. The caucus saw to this wish: Later that year, Congress appropriated eight hundred thousand dollars for a study of Corridor 18 from Indianapolis to Houston. The sum was enough to hire two of the largest transportation firms in America, Wilbur Smith Associates and HNTB Corporation, which maintained contact with the Mid-Continent Highway Coalition during the course of their work. Both corporations are also in the business of building major infrastructure projects, a common overlap that troubles purists and cynics. A company that could (and would, in this case) benefit from future contracts on a project should not be trusted with the objective preliminary assessment of it, some argue. But there's no rule against it, it happens quite often, and it happened with I-69.

In 1995, the firms released their report, which concluded that the project did indeed make sense and that, "on balance, the Nation and the corridor would be better off" with I-69. The highway would facilitate the increased truck traffic projected to come out of the implementation of NAFTA and would bring economic benefits to depressed regions, the report determined, echoing Reed. It would connect a number of river ports, airports, and military facilities. It would save time and lives. Yes, there were environmental challenges to overcome, the report noted, but nothing insurmountable.

The main issue to tackle was how exactly to pay for such a thing. "For every dollar spent on it," the report calculated, "Corridor 18 will produce $1.39 in user benefits." The bad news was that the dollars spent on it would total an estimated five and a half billion. (That price tag, after state-by-state studies and construction-cost inflation, is now more like twenty-seven billion.) Cognizant of the end to the Interstate Construction Program, the consultants offered a few interesting funding schemes in their report, ranging from tolls to possible advertising opportunities to even the off chance that private individuals and interested companies would want to chip in money and land. Most likely, the study warned, the public funding needs would be substantial. "If these requirements are to be met by existing revenue sources, then Corridor 18 will have to compete with other funding needs of the corridor states, including preservation of existing infrastructure."

But if ever there was a moment for I-69 to gain traction in Washington, it was in 1995. Feelings about NAFTA were high and the political stars were aligned on both sides of the aisle and both ends of Pennsylvania Avenue. David Reed had suggested that by extending the route of I-69 beyond Indiana, the project could gain the vital support of additional members of Congress. But what he could not have foreseen was that just one week after the first Peabody meeting in Memphis, in 1992, Governor William Jefferson Clinton, of Arkansas, and Senator Albert Gore Jr., of Tennessee, would be elected president and vice president of the United States. Both hailed from I-69 states (two joined at Memphis, no less), and there was pretty good reason to believe that they both would be friendly to the road's development. Gore's father, after all, had been a key player in the passage of the Federal-Aid Highway Act of 1956. And Clinton, as governor, had been chairman of the Lower Mississippi Delta Development Commission, which endorsed new highway construction as an economic-development tool. The Midsouth regional bias spread down the transportation policy chain, too: In March 1993, Clinton appointed Rodney Slater, a former chairman of the Arkansas Highway Commission, as federal highway administrator (and later, as secretary of transportation).

The project also got a considerable boost from the 1994 midterm elections, in which the Republicans won control of both the House and the Senate. Although bad news for the president's agenda, the changes in congressional leadership enhanced I-69's clout. Trent Lott, of Mississippi, became the Senate majority whip; Dick Armey, a congressman from north of Dallas, became House majority leader; and Tom DeLay, who represented an irregularly shaped district of south Houston exurbs, became the House majority whip. The relationship between these men and the White House would be famously antagonistic, but moving I-69 forward was one of the few goals they could all agree on.

The ascent of DeLay in particular punctuated an increased level of interest and participation in the coalition's efforts on the part of Texas, and specifically Houston. The year before, there had been clear evidence of intrastate strife: Louis Bronaugh, the mayor of Lufkin and the leader of the Texas contingent to the Mid-Continent Highway Coalition, complained to the *Houston Chronicle* that the city had yet to produce a representative. A spokesman from the Houston office of the Texas Department of Transportation told the paper that the I-69 idea "doesn't seem to offer new solutions. It seems to be tied to a technology which is not attractive to federal funds. It doesn't seem to be the way we're going." The *Chronicle* was left to wonder what the real chances for I-69 were, given that the new Clinton administration's infrastructure initiatives would likely be focused on the "'electronic information highways' rather than ones made of concrete." Houston already had decent highway access, and the city's chamber, the Greater Houston Partnership, was happy for the moment to let the smaller, hungrier towns in east Texas lead the charge for I-69.

But that would change. After NAFTA took effect on January 1, 1994, there was a new north-south stream of truck commerce to be captured, and the extant Interstate 35—which springs forth from the border at Laredo and heads north through San Antonio, Austin, Dallas–Fort Worth, and Kansas City on its way to Minneapolis, Duluth, and (via I-29) Winnipeg—was becoming the continent's de facto Main Street. They knew it, too: The string of cities along I-35 quickly formed a coalition to seek federal money to improve and expand the road they were branding the North American SuperCorridor, or NASCO. The president of the Greater Houston Partnership at the time—Kenneth Lay, chairman of Enron—saw NASCO's activities as a direct threat to Houston's own potential for NAFTA-related growth, and he decided that pushing Interstate 69 should be one of the partnership's top priorities. Lay was prepared to pitch in staff and extra money—$350,000 over two years—if the Mid-Continent Highway Coalition was willing to take things up a notch. It was. In September, a group that included the mayor of Houston, Harris County judge John Lindsay, Caruthers, and local business leaders held a symbolic ribbon-cutting ceremony at the Four Seasons hotel in Houston to publicly announce an escalated campaign to promote I-69.

The coalition's executive committee held its next meeting, in January 1995, at the downtown headquarters of the Greater Houston Partnership, and the discussion focused on ways in which the group might escalate its lobbying efforts beyond the do-it-yourself strategy it had started with. Up to that point, the coalition had been relying on James Newland, who sent out the newsletters, and a government-affairs consultant in Indiana named Garry Petersen, who helped coordinate the group's trips to Washington. It was time to hire real Washington representation, the Houston hosts insisted. They presented the committee with two options: The coalition could retain a public-relations firm to market the project to the public, or it could hire a lobbying firm that would "work the 'back rooms.'" A woman from the Evansville Chamber broke the silence that followed and suggested that it might make more sense for public-relations work to be carried out at the state level. What the coalition really needed was a lobbyist.

The Greater Houston Partnership led a search over the next few months, and soon they had found their backroom worker: Carolina Mederos from Patton Boggs, the largest lobbying firm in Washington. It was founded, coincidentally, by the son of Hale Boggs, creator of the highway trust fund. Mederos seemed like a perfect fit. She had worked at the U.S. Department of Transportation from 1976 until 1990, including stints as an assistant deputy secretary and as director of programs and evaluation—a position that had made her responsible for developing the department's appropriations bills and defending them before Congress. As a career USDOT executive and then as a lobbyist, Mederos had played a role in every major federal transportation law over the last twenty years. She was short but spunky and extremely well versed. She knew the law, the legislative process, and the transportation bureaucracy intimately.

"Having been at DOT in the office of the secretary, writing all this stuff, I probably knew better than anybody how to change it," Mederos told me. "I wrote it. I can *rewrite* it." She also had "genetic memory" on her side, she told me with a smile. "My parents were born in Cuba. And my great-grandfather was Basque and he went to Cuba to develop the highway system there. Isn't that funny?" Mederos began her career working on health and labor issues. But she liked transportation better, she told me, "because you can see the results of your work. And I felt like in some of these other areas you never really knew if you were winning or losing."

The coalition's entire annual budget had started out at $140,000, but it would have to increase—the initial contract with Mederos was for $200,000. She went to work helping shape I-69-friendly language in the National Highway System Designation Act, a law that would solidify the evolution in priorities foreshadowed by ISTEA. Among other things, the bill was a chance to refine the definition of High Priority Corridor 18, which until then specified only the inclusion of Indianapolis, Evansville, Memphis, Shreveport, and Houston. The coalition members and their congressional representatives were particularly keen on nailing down the route between Memphis and Shreveport, where vast areas of Arkansas and Mississippi stood to lose or gain mileage. A more or less straight route would go through Arkansas exclusively, and the initial House version of the bill added that state alone to the Corridor 18 definition. But Trent Lott of Mississippi, then the Senate majority whip, made it clear that his state would not be left out. Ken Murphree, who was the county administrator in Tunica, Mississippi, remembers when an elderly and influential aide to Lott visited a coalition meeting at the University Club in Washington. "He said, 'Let me tell y'all something,'" Murphree recalled. "'I just got back from Trent Lott's office. And Trent said to tell y'all if that road doesn't go through Mississippi, there isn't going to *be* an I-69.'"

In the end, the bill did not address where exactly the highway would cross the river—that battle was postponed—but it did officially determine that I-69 would run through both Mississippi *and* Arkansas. The NHS Designation Act, which passed in September 1995, also extended Corridor 18 farther south, beyond Houston and down along the Gulf of Mexico into the Lower Rio Grande Valley, a region of over a million people at the very tip of Texas that was not yet served by an interstate highway. Republican senator Kay Bailey Hutchison of Texas was responsible for adding this second leg south. Corridors 18 and 20, while not yet officially named I-69, were "designated as future parts of the Interstate System" by the law so that any segment could officially become an interstate as soon as it met interstate design standards and connected to any other existing interstate. The states, which would be individually responsible for building their respective sections of highway, would not need to wait for the entire length of I-69 to be finished before reaping whatever benefits came from the interstate shield.

Mederos, it seemed, was making things happen. But some thought a second lobbyist might be beneficial. When the executive committee met again in Memphis on the morning of January 29, 1996, just before a meeting of the full coalition, Caruthers began by reading aloud a memo from the Greater Houston Partnership. The Texans were asking him to sign one more lobbying contract, for $126,000 a year, with Randy DeLay. DeLay represented a number of clients in Texas whose interests did not conflict with their organization, Caruthers explained. He also delicately noted that Randy was the brother of Congressman Tom DeLay. The minutes of this meeting describe the lively discussion that followed:

> Caruthers asked if the group thought there might be a conflict of inter-est there. Roger Hord, Greater Houston Partnership, stated that they had addressed that issue with Randy and do not believe there is a con-flict . . . "to the contrary" Hord thought that it may be a BENEFIT to us. David Graham stated that "it's just a perception."
>
> Louis Bronaugh asked whether Randy's affiliation with his congress-man brother or Randy's accounts presented the appearance of conflict . . . Caruthers stated that as long as it's OK for members of Congress to be lobbied by their brothers, then it's legal.

In fact, there was no rule against relatives lobbying members of Con-gress, and the House Ethics Committee would make that clear in 1997 when it dismissed a complaint filed against Tom DeLay alleging that he allowed Randy to influence his congressional actions. "You have demon-strated," the committee told Congressman DeLay in clearing him, "that in each issue involving your brother, your involvement either predated his hiring or made sense in terms of your representation of your dis-trict." DeLay's town of Sugar Land was along the path of I-69. But for whatever reason, the Greater Houston Partnership considered Randy's involvement "critical," according to the coalition meeting minutes, and offered to pay an additional hundred thousand dollars toward his hiring.

The arrangement proposed by the Greater Houston Partnership was that Randy's contract would be considered a "continuation" of the coali-tion's association with Patton Boggs, and Mederos's firm gave its blessing.

By then, Tom DeLay, with the conservative strategist Grover Norquist, had already initiated the now-infamous K Street Project. Following the Republican takeover of Congress, aides to Republican congressmen had compiled lists of hundreds of lobbyists and their party affiliations and had distributed the lists to Republican lawmakers. This was not about black-balling Democrats, they insisted, but rather it was meant to encourage the hiring of more Republicans into what had been for years a Democrat-dominated industry. "K Street's future," according to a July 1995 article in the *National Journal,* was embodied in a new, thirty-six-year-old Republican lobbyist named Jack Abramoff. "What the Republicans need is fifty Jack Abramoffs," the article quoted Norquist as saying. "Then this becomes a different town."

If the guard was changing in Washington, perhaps it was best for the coalition to cover its bets, and there would seem to be no better hedge than hiring the brother of the House majority whip. Many members of the coalition held private misgivings about bringing Randy DeLay aboard, but the Partnership's suggestion felt to everyone like a mandate.

That morning in 1996, the coalition executive committee voted unanimously to approve the contract with Randy DeLay, who was conveniently waiting in the wings at the Peabody. At a meeting of the larger group a few hours later, Caruthers introduced the new member of the team. "Let's talk politics!" DeLay said to the group before delivering a pep talk about the bipartisan support for I-69 on Capitol Hill.

The coalition was going to need all the support it could get—another big reauthorization bill was coming up, a renewal of ISTEA, and this would be a crucial moment for I-69. When Mederos first went to work for the Peabody group, she told me, "they didn't even realize there was no interstate program to fund I-69, but *I* knew there wasn't." Mederos and Randy DeLay would have to find funding, and they'd have to do better than conjuring small earmarks. They decided the best strategy was to contrive a whole new federal program. Mederos began collecting traffic-flow and demographic data to make the case for a new category of infrastructure. The argument would be that the original interstate system had been laid out primarily east to west in the 1950s, and that today's north-south trade patterns—and the southwestern migration of manufacturing and population—justified new highways, and one in particular. To Congress and the Clinton administration, she presented their findings and proposed two new initiatives: a "National Corridor Planning and Development Program" and a "Coordinated Border Infrastructure Program."

"We got the programs into the administration bill. And then we got it in the House and the Senate versions," she said. Next, they went after votes. "I had folks do all this research to figure out what other corridors might be in the same boat. Then I had to go around to all those other legislators. I remember talking to people up and down the West Coast, along I-5, and saying, 'You know, I'd rather have all this money for ourselves, but we're never going to get a national program unless we have a big enough group of folks who are for it.'"

In 1998, Congress passed the Transportation Equity Act for the 21st Century, or TEA-21. The law did wonders for I-69—for one, it gave it that name. Corridors 18 and 20 were officially designated Interstate 69, and the route was expanded in definition—again—to include the existing portion of I-69 through Michigan and northern Indiana. This placed the corridor's end points at the borders with Canada and Mexico. And just for good measure, the existing Interstate 94 between Port Huron, Detroit, and Chicago was thrown in as part of the package, so that the greater "I-69 Corridor" could pick up the Ambassador Bridge and the Detroit-Windsor tunnel crossings, bolstering the trade statistics and strengthening the rationale for the project. On the southern end, the route from Houston to Mexico split again, from two routes to three. It would now include US-59 to Laredo (the old Corridor 20 route, now "I-69 West") as well as U.S. 77 to Brownsville ("I-69 East"), and U.S. 281 to McAllen ("I-69 Central"). These crossing points together—three in the north and three in the south—accounted for half of the truck traffic across each border.

In this new configuration, Interstate 69 would have strong claim on funding from both of Mederos's new creations. The stated purpose of her corridor program was to fund planning, design, and construction of "corridors of national significance, economic growth, and international or interregional trade." The border program was meant to improve existing crossings but also pay for the construction of new highways "that will facilitate vehicle and cargo movements related to international trade." TEA-21 put an annual $140 million into these two initiatives for the first five years. The only problem was that Mederos's efforts to recruit other roadways to her programs had been a bit too successful. What started out as a grant program allocated by the DOT soon became a haven for earmarks. "The thing mushroomed later," she said. "I mean, some of the corridors are two blocks long!" But all told, over the seven-year life of the bill, I-69 would end up getting a respectable $70 million. Serendipitously, the bill was signed by President Clinton on June 9: 6/9.

One last touch: TEA-21 allowed any state with jurisdiction over any segment of Corridor 18 or 20 to erect signs identifying those segments as the future route of I-69. The law specifically ordered Texas to erect such markers along U.S. 59 and on the two roadways to the valley. (Randy DeLay takes credit for this bit of branding.) "Future I-69 Corridor" signs did go up, in south Texas and Tennessee, to remind people, like the mural in Haynesville does, what greatness was in store. The day when I-69 would stretch from border to border was still years away, if it was to come at all. But there it was—an interstate-in-waiting, a real thing, sort of. Eight years after David Reed was struck by his inadvertent breakfast epiphany, seven years after David Graham got into his car to spread the gospel, five years after the Mid-Continent Highway Coalition first stormed Washington, Interstate 69 was written into federal law and was moving forward.

The big idea of I-69 had matured into an official plan, but it still had a long way to go before it was a reality. Federal money would help things along, but the hard details would be left to the states. The route would be broken up into thirty-two "sections of independent utility," each one its own design and routing puzzle, engineering problem, and funding challenge. The members of the coalition would continue to meet every year in Memphis and in Washington, but more important, they were tasked with rallying the anxious citizens and local and state politicians back home. They would have to market I-69, defend it, and translate its importance to their respective regions. The road would take on a life of its own—*lives* of its own—in Indiana, Texas, and the Midsouth between.

Although I-69 became the work of Congress, it began as nothing more than an ad hoc, homegrown enterprise that got very, very lucky in its formative years. Interstate 69 was baptized in Washington, D.C., but it was born in the town of Washington, Indiana, as a happy accident hatched over eggs. As the I-69 effort spread into the small corners of middle America, however, the highway's early history would be lost. Even the folks who sat at the conference table at the Peabody didn't know—or would forget—about David Graham's long drive that had led them all there. They understood vaguely that the cradle of I-69 was Indiana, the state where the stub of an old interstate yearned to break free and head south through their towns. But maybe the genesis didn't really matter anymore. The coalition members were working now for reasons unique to their own communities and their own lives. As much as the effort might seem, from a distance, to belong to a world of decisive action in smoke-filled rooms, the truth was that the unfolding of this highway was destined to be many different stories, not one.

II

Indiana

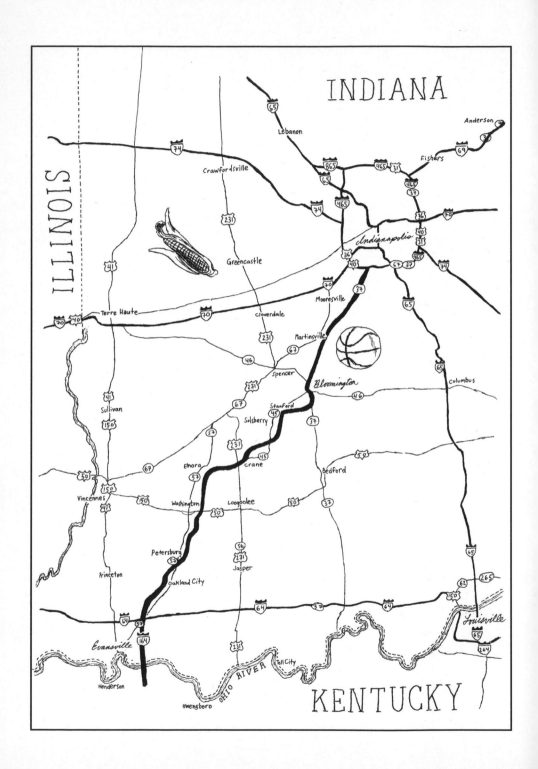

The Crossroads of America

People tend to think of Indiana, if they think of it at all, as a place to drive *through*. "It was an ordinary bus trip," Jack Kerouac writes in *On the Road*, "till we got on the plain of Ohio and really rolled, up by Ashtabula and straight across Indiana in the night." John Steinbeck, crossing the country in *Travels with Charley*, wrote, "I became impatient, stuck to the huge toll road that strings the northern border of Indiana." Even the state's motto, "The Crossroads of America," boasts its historic transportation prowess above all else. Other states choose to associate themselves with less tangible symbols—Hope, Liberty, Freedom, Friendship, God—but Hoosiers are meant to swell with pride thinking about the railroads and highways that once made their state the main intersection of a passionately mobile country. These days, though, it can feel like the slogan refers to the millions of people crossing Indiana on their way to someplace else, and to the thousands of young people who use that awesome web of highways to get the hell out.

When you grow up in Indiana, as I did, you learn a whole litany of natives who made good upon leaving—Don Mattingly, Cole Porter, Kurt Vonnegut, Jane Pauley, Hoagy Carmichael, Colonel Sanders, Florence Henderson, Michael Jackson, Axl Rose, David Lee Roth, Tavis Smiley, Twyla Tharp. After his heart surgery in 2000, David Letterman publicly offered his hometown of Indianapolis ten million dollars to rename its interstate loop, I-465, the David Letterman Bypass. It was partly a joke but a fitting idea nevertheless—Indiana defines itself by the famous people who've left it, and by the roads they drove away on.

James Dean, the actor, amateur race driver, and car-crash victim, grew up an hour northeast of Indianapolis in Grant County, where they still celebrate him as a favorite son and economic engine. For sixteen years, a collector named David Loehr kept a small museum of memorabilia—Dean's high school artwork, the jeans he wore in the movie *Giant*, a replica of the

Porsche he died in, the speeding ticket he got earlier that same fateful day—in a quaint little house on Main Street in Fairmount, the rebel's hometown and final resting place. In 2004, Loehr moved the James Dean Gallery eight miles east to the town of Gas City, into a new building right next to the existing stretch of I-69. He had hoped that the new location would provide greater visibility and access to interstate-bound tourists. But the highway let him down. Besieged by debt, he closed the building after only two years and moved the exhibit back to Fairmount, tucked away again.

There was a time not long ago when "tucked away" was considered an Indiana forte. The state nowadays offers a variety of license-plate flavors—"In God We Trust," "Support Our Troops," "Lincoln's Boyhood Home"—but in the mid-1980s, when I was a boy and cars were boxy and gasoline was cheap, everyone's passenger plate was emblazoned with three wide stripes of red, green, and yellow and the simple words "Wander Indiana." The slogan was mocked by purposeful adults who didn't care for the characterization of Indianans as an aimless tribe. But I liked it. Wandering sounded good to me. The smoky end of every car enticed me with the idea that my state was full of hidden jewels—small towns and back roads that should not be overlooked and need not be programmed. Never mind big-ticket attractions, whatever those might be. In Indiana, every place was worth seeing. The state was rich in obscure nooks and wide-open stretches where the driving soul could explore and graze. New York, around this same time, put the Statue of Liberty on its plates. They just didn't get it.

Wandering *away* from Indiana is a well-celebrated phenomenon, too. A pair of Tin Pan Alley composers wrote the expatriate anthem "Back Home Again in Indiana" in New York City in 1916, the same year that the journalist Theodore Dreiser published *A Hoosier Holiday,* an account of his first trip home in twenty-six years. Dreiser had left the sycamores, the new-mown hay, and the moonlight on the Wabash for the big city, and one evening at a party at his apartment on the Upper West Side of Manhattan he struck up a conversation with his friend and fellow Hoosier Franklin Booth, a well-known illustrator. Booth had dual citizenship—a home in New York and another in Carmel, Indiana. He also had a Pathfinder touring car ("very presentable and shiny") and a mechanic they called Speed. Booth lured Dreiser back to the Midwest with him, and the two agreed to record their adventure in a book with Dreiser's words and Booth's illustrations. *A Hoosier Holiday* became one of the first great American road books.

Like the road writers who followed, Dreiser put a premium on authenticity, insisting they take "the scenic route" west rather than the popular Hudson-Albany-State road, which he was worried would be crowded and dusty with traffic. "Give me the poor, undernourished routes which the dull, imitative rabble shun," he wrote, "and where, because of this very fact, you have some peace and quiet." Dreiser, as pleased as he was to come home, grew cynical, wistful, and annoyed by the signs of growth and attempts at progress he saw in Indiana, especially in Bloomington, where he had spent his unfinished college days at Indiana University. "Now [the town] seemed more or less tame," he observed. "It had grown so in size and architectural pretentiousness as to have obliterated most of that rural inadequacy and backwoods charm which had been its most delightful characteristic to me in 1889."

If Dreiser thought that Bloomington was overdeveloped in 1914, then he's probably rolling in his grave today. Booth might be, too; his beloved Carmel has been fully absorbed by the sprawling north side of Indianapolis, where the final suburban stretch of I-69 gets choked with commuter traffic each weekday. Dreiser and Booth would no doubt be impressed by the speed and mobility and reliable amenities that highways offer today. But they might be surprised to discover how little peace and quiet driving affords—unless one ventures out from the metropolitan blob, finds an undernourished exit, ignores the fast-food restaurants and gas stations clustered there, and wanders into that rural inadequacy one would normally just speed past.

In any case, sentimental attachment to the way things used to be didn't end with Dreiser. The anti-I-69 struggle that pervades Bloomington today is focused on saving what's left of that backwoods charm from further obliteration. And, generally, keeping Indiana the same has been something of a state obsession. Until just a few years ago, for instance, most of the state shunned the voodoo practice of daylight savings time. Tradition-minded farmers, who set their schedules by the sun, didn't want to be out of sync with their clock-watching neighbors and local businesses, and movie theaters and drive-ins feared losing customers if darkness fell an hour later. When I was growing up, we never had to change our clocks. In the winter we were with the eastern time zone and in the summer we were with the central time zone. We moved by standing still. But times have changed, literally. Daylight savings turned out not to be a passing fad, and in 2005, a governor who was hell-bent on shaking things up came along and broke the spell. His reasons had to do with the needs of modern business in the new global economy.

On one of my own recent trips back home I paid a visit to the Indiana State Museum, a place uniquely suited to indulge in both nostalgia and worldly sophistication. In one exhibit, "Global Indiana," a placard explains that economics, entertainment, and information know no borders. "Today Hoosiers greet this new world with their customary mix of optimism and caution," it says. "Their challenge is to embrace both their heritage and their future, retaining Indiana's distinctive viewpoint and values in a global age." A nearby display—for city folk, I guess—lets visitors sniff the odors of manure, corn bread, and mown hay through small openings in the Plexiglas. In an exhibit on the early twentieth century, the museum's display text, phrased in the present tense to transport visitors into the past, tiptoes through the state's difficult racial history: "Hoosiers welcome increasing prosperity, but they do not always welcome the new neighbors that come with prosperity. Jobs attract both immigrants and migrant workers, bringing social changes that ignite tensions and friction," it explains. "Wary of moving too fast, Hoosiers reject radical transformations of any sort."

But they always managed to get around pretty well. The museum's Hall of Transportation takes visitors through successive eras of American infrastructure, explaining how each one played out in the Crossroads of America. The earliest corridor of any sort through the state was forged over the course of centuries by the now-extinct Eastern American bison. These animals, though known for their roaming, reached consensus when it came to hauling ass between the grasslands of Illinois and the salt licks of Kentucky. They beat such a deep path through Indiana that parts of the route are still visible today. This "buffalo trace" later became a convenient route for Native Americans, and then for early settlers and traders.

The first human roads of any note in Indiana were built in the 1830s. The museum itself sits on U.S. 40 (in Indianapolis it's called Washington Street), which follows the route of the National Road, the first federally funded highway in America. Started during the Thomas Jefferson administration, the all-weather, wagon-ready road originated in Cumberland, Maryland, at the terminus of the privately funded Baltimore Pike, and ran some six hundred miles west toward Saint Louis. It would have reached Saint Louis were it not for the fact that funding ran out, as funding sometimes does. The Michigan Road, which was financed by the state of Indiana, was a precursor to Interstate 65. It connected Lake Michigan, near Chicago, via Indianapolis to the Ohio River between Cincinnati and Louisville. The Michigan road "disrupts Native American communities, severing Potawatomi lands while stimulating white settlement," the exhibit explains. "Though these routes are muddy, rutted, and stump-filled, [they] bring trade, settlement, and changes in the mid-nineteenth century."

For smooth, stumpless travel, nothing beat a canal. Boating was still the easy way to travel in the early nineteenth century, and just as we build bridges today to get our cars over rivers, canals were built to get boats across inconvenient bodies of land. In 1825, the Erie Canal joined together the Hudson River and the Great Lakes, a breakthrough that, along with the National Road, would open the western interior to greater settlement and trade. The Erie also set off something of a canal craze that (naturally) swept the young state of Indiana. In 1827, Congress provided a land grant to encourage Indiana to build a canal connecting Lake Erie down to the Wabash and Ohio rivers. The Wabash & Erie Canal, as it was called, became the longest canal system in America. It cut a southwesterly trench through Toledo, Fort Wayne, Lafayette, and Terre Haute before bending east toward Bloomington and then southwest again, past Washington to Evansville—along the approximate route of what may one day be I-69.

Communities near canals reaped big-time economic rewards, and nearby farms flourished because of the access to markets. The Wabash & Erie was no exception, but its construction suffered frequent delays. The canal wasn't fully completed until 1853, just in time for its obsolescence, a fate brought about by the railroads. With passengers and shippers switching to the iron horse, business on the canal dried up. The water roads became a crippling financial burden for the state. Portions of the southern end of the Wabash and Erie were closed down less than a decade after they were completed, and in 1876, the entire canal was sold at auction. There were more Indiana canals proposed and under way, but these were abandoned, including the Central Canal, which was supposed to connect Indianapolis to the Wabash and Erie near Bloomington— again along the proposed route of I-69.

The canal crash apparently hardened some hearts. In 1851, when Indiana approved its state constitution, the document restricted public debt, and the state played only a minor role in financing transportation improvements in the years before and after the Civil War. Private investors stepped in to fill the gap, building railroads and turnpikes—so called because travelers had to pay tollhouse attendants to turn pikes that blocked free passage. "Savvy and often ruthless in business, many prosper by exploiting political connections and inside information," the museum narrative explains. "Railroads often decide which towns thrive and which decline, making railroad building and planning not just a source of wealth but also a source of power."

This was all true, of course—just ask Ziba Graham. It was in 1884 that the town of Washington, Indiana, with the help of Ziba's cash and the city's land, scored the B&O maintenance site that secured the town's economy for decades and affected the map forever. There was a time when the routes of commerce and migration were predetermined by nature—the rivers, the oceans, the shortest, flattest pieces of ground. But each new mode of transportation made place-making more and more a matter of human engineering. Sometimes those humans worked for business, sometimes for government, but rarely were the masses consulted. If there is truly such a thing as democratic transportation planning, then the Eastern American bison were probably the first—and last—practitioners.

At the turn of the century, streetcar operations like Ziba's in Washington were branching out into a system of regional electric rail lines between towns. These "interurbans," as they came to be known, were privately operated and were often constructed in tandem with the expansion of electrical power services. Rides on the interurban passenger cars, which traveled individually like trolleys, were cheaper and more frequent than on the steam railroads, and the service proved very popular. Indiana's network was the longest in the country. A route up to South Bend connected to the Chicago area system, and a line over to Dayton tied into Ohio's. At their peak, Indiana's interurbans totaled some eighteen hundred route miles radiating from Indianapolis, where Traction Terminal on Market Street handled some four hundred cars a day.

By the 1910s, when Ziba Graham's three children were manufacturing trucks in Evansville and Dreiser was wandering back home in a touring car, the popularity of the internal-combustion engine was gaining fast, and the network of paved roads was growing. By the 1920s, the interurbans faced serious competition from upstart motor-coach outfits. Several of the electric rail companies simply bought rival bus operations—or started their own—rather than fight them head-on, and the relationship between the two modes of transportation proved, for a time, symbiotic. With fleets of trains *and* buses, companies could offer expanded service and coordinated schedules. But eventually even the combined ridership began to decline. Americans had struck up their now-famous love affair with the automobile, and no advertising about the cost of gasoline or the dangers of winter roads could reverse the trend. After a decade of corporate consolidation and an admirable effort to win customers with "high-speed" travel (sixty to seventy miles per hour), the Indiana interurban railcars made their last runs on January 18, 1941. The next morning, their routes were handled by motor coaches. And for still another decade, passengers rode from town to town in buses painted with the old name "Indiana Railroad" on their sides.

Modern-day Hoosiers find it difficult to fathom how easily their predecessors got around the state by rail. That's what museums are for, I suppose. In the Hall of Transportation, there is a spot where you can stand and hear the sounds of an old interurban station: the clanging of bells, the calling out of stops, the squeal of metal wheel on metal rail. There is still a romance to the train, still men of a certain age (they are most often men) who speak of trains with great yearning. We are as far away in time now from the end of the interurban as the end of the interurban was from the end of the canal. Were there old-timers who would bore train-happy youngsters in the 1930s with stories of the bygone canal days, and stare off into the distance with sad eyes at the very mention of the Wabash & Erie? Probably. And are there aspects of our transportation life today that will seem crude, dull, or absurd to young people another sixty-five years from now?

The museum offers a chance to reflect on this as well. The building itself sits at a rich historical cross section of the Crossroads of America. Washington Street—the old National Road—runs out front, a right-of-way once shared by the interurban train to Terre Haute. The downtown stretch of the old Michigan Road, now named Martin Luther King Jr. Boulevard, passes a few blocks away. And a section of the abandoned Central Canal comes through the museum property, separating the main building from a west wing. When visitors cross a footbridge over the canal, they come to "Tomorrow's Indiana," an interactive environment that occupies a large, dark room full of video monitors. (There will be no charm in the future, evidently.) On one wall, a large screen shows short episodes of a trigenerational family talking through some of the real-life issues of the future. Should we grow genetically modified crops like the big corporation wants us to, or work the land the old-fashioned way, like

Grandpa did? Should Mom partake of elective in utero gene therapy to enhance her unborn son's sports abilities, or leave things to nature, as she had to with her older son? Museumgoers hear all sides and weigh in using keypads. The results (which reflected a collective conservatism the day I visited) are shown on the big screen.

At a series of smaller monitors, a racially ambiguous girl named Ismee asks visitors to take part in an exercise. "Your mission, if you choose to accept it, is to tackle some tough decisions facing Indiana's future," she says. "Depending on your choices, the state may be a very different place in twenty-five years." A multiple-choice touch screen allows you to address pointed problems about education, immigration, energy, economic strategy, and transportation. After a series of judgments, you're informed of their consequences. Maybe Indiana develops into a high-tech network of small semiagrarian villages where everyone is linked by computer (but where, Ismee warns, your constituency might go stir-crazy). Or maybe the state goes übergreen, with electric cars, clean air and water, and energy-efficient homes. (But without a thriving economy, Ismee quips, "how long can *that* last?")

From the museum's very first dramatically lit gallery, where a big swirling electronic globe shows that the history of Indiana began, in fact, millions of years ago with continental drift—the state was once under a great sea!—on through to this last room, full of pixels and dilemmas, you can feel the curators doing their best to expand young (or closed) minds. The museum seems to want to promote the rather revolutionary notion that Indiana will not hold still in this crazy world of ours, that it will inevitably become something else, and furthermore that this something else will be determined by a series of subjective decisions, made by people. Like you.

As you leave the Indiana State Museum (after perhaps stopping in the gift shop to buy some Indiana-themed apparel manufactured in Nicaragua or China), change is everywhere to be seen. Over the last thirty years the city of Indianapolis has experienced a suburban population explosion into the surrounding rural counties. Where interurban trains once traveled, congested highways now roll. But over the last twenty years or so, the city's downtown has undergone a healthy renewal as well, and in the White River Park area, on the near west side, a new minor-league ballpark, the national headquarters for the NCAA, and the state museum have replaced blight and brownfields.

Among those responsible for setting Indianapolis's inner rebirth in motion is William H. Hudnut III, a former Presbyterian minister who served for sixteen years as mayor, from 1976 to 1992. Now a senior fellow at the Urban Land Institute in Washington, D.C., Hudnut preaches the gospel of smart growth, a development philosophy that aims to fight economic stagnation without encouraging sprawl. He hasn't lived in Indiana for years—he left office just before I-69 went from a southern Indiana pipe dream to a national Big Deal—but I called him anyway a while back. He was the mayor of my hometown for my entire childhood, and I figured he would have a thing or two to say about highways in Indiana and evolving communities.

The controversy surrounding I-69 needed no introduction. We talked a bit about the forests and farms of southern Indiana, and I asked him how one chooses wisely if the very thing that is supposed to bring jobs might also harm the quality of life. He was quick to answer. "I don't know exactly what a farmer's going to benefit from a bunch of interstate trucks and cars zipping through on their way down to Mexico," he said, echoing a sentiment common among the farmers themselves. "There probably would be some development. But one of the principles of smart growth, in addition to conservation of the environment, is compact development, as opposed to sprawling development—and development that is of good quality, where there's a sense of place."

Another cornerstone of smart growth is promoting mass transit and encouraging denser, more walkable neighborhoods around stations. I asked him—from one Indiana expatriate to another—if he believed that this kind of planning could ever take hold in a place like Indianapolis. He sighed. "It's just an automobile-oriented town, there's no question about that, in an automobile-oriented state," Hudnut said. He told me that in his sixteen years as mayor he had three big dreams that went unfulfilled. The first was a triangle of high-speed rail between IU, Purdue, and Indianapolis. The second was a high-speed line from the Indianapolis airport up to the Chicago loop. "And my third dream was a restoration of some of the interurban commuter lines.

"One of the problems in Indiana is a lack of what you might call an aspiration to excellence, particularly in the rural parts," the reverend mayor said next. "We just go along. I sort of get the impression a lot of them are happy just to have a pickup truck and a regular old job.

"Well, the good book says, 'For lack of vision, the people perish.'"

Small Towns, Big Dreams

For lack of jobs, the towns perish. That's what it would say in the Chamber of Commerce Bible, if there were such a book. Any mayor or economic-development official in any struggling or growing town will tell you: Jobs (regular old or otherwise) are the bottom line for civic survival. The places that keep them prosper, and the places that lose them fade away.

The dichotomy tends to be self-perpetuating, too. A growing town with ample jobs attracts smart, mobile young workers who can afford to support local culture and small businesses. This creates the kind of atmosphere that attracts new employers looking for talent. Companies put down roots, people put down roots, and the place grows. But when a town lacks good jobs, the well-educated kids tend to pursue their careers elsewhere. This "brain drain," in addition to whatever familial heartache it causes, decreases the quality of the workforce, which dissuades potential new businesses, in turn driving more kids to leave. Roots are severed and the place contracts.

This downward cycle is the very thing that worried the community pillars who gathered at David Graham's breakfast table to meet with David Reed that morning in 1990. And it was still worrying them almost twenty years later when Graham brought them back together to meet with me. Jo Arthur, who had recently retired after thirty years at the Southern Indiana Development Commission, came to Graham's house on U.S. 50 with her husband, Tom, a judge. David Cox, who had retired several years before as head of the Daviess County Growth Council, brought his wife, Marjorie. It was late afternoon, so scotch whisky was served in lieu of omelets. Cox, Arthur, and Graham rehashed the big moment when, over maps, Reed suggested that I-69 go international. The detail that seemed to have remained most clear in their minds was the reason that Reed believed that an Indianapolis-to-Evansville highway would never be built: because "no one gives a damn about southern Indiana."

Reed's harsh statement still rang true for the three, who feel as though they live in a forgotten world. They remember a time when small-town jobs were more plentiful, when agriculture and manufacturing and mining were enough to keep most local sons and daughters happy and productive. Now a family farm can barely support two people. "The husband works in the post office while the wife teaches school or something, and that's what keeps the farm going," Graham said. The grown children of Cox and Arthur and Graham, without exception, had left. The city of Washington had become stagnant. "Every time a baby was born," Cox joked, "somebody would leave town."

Washington did get a Walmart, Judge Arthur pointed out. But Jo Arthur, like many, saw that as a mixed blessing. "It's difficult in today's economy for small businesses to make it in small towns. They just can't compete with the Walmart," she said. "But we haven't boarded up and given up on the downtown." As part of her development work, she had been encouraging service professionals like doctors, lawyers, and insurance agents to occupy the emptying storefronts. The movie theater and a local hamburger joint, the White Steamer, have survived. And a quilting store called the Stitching Post was able to stay in business, Arthur said, by connecting with new customers online. "A vast majority of what they sell goes out in the mail every night to places all over the world," she bragged.

Modest gains and incremental improvements are the bread and butter of small-town economic work. Arthur spent much of her time competing for relatively meager federal community-development grants to pay for infrastructure improvements such as water and sewer-system work. David Cox bent over backward to woo new businesses, including a drawer factory, a grain-processing plant, and a Perdue turkey operation, which took over and expanded the turkey farms that David Graham had so famously run. The hard, unglamorous, and often unnoticed work that Cox and Arthur performed over several decades had been, by any reasonable reckoning, successful. But that didn't stop them from envying nearby counties that scored even bigger victories—Princeton, a town about an hour's drive away, got a Toyota assembly plant in 1996—and fretting over the prospects that had slipped through their fingers.

Cox doesn't mind talking about the ones that got away. He told me a story about a helicopter that flew over the county one afternoon some years back. The helicopter, he says, carried representatives from a major company that was hunting for a site on which to build a new plant. Which is to say: The chopper contained *jobs*. "Well, the helicopter flew right over. It didn't even land," Cox told me. "They saw how far we were from an interstate highway, and they went home."

Cox doesn't know what kind of jobs, or how many, were hovering above Washington that day. Even if the chopper had landed and he had met with the passengers, he says, there's a good chance he may not have known what company they represented. The business of site selection is an oddly cloak-and-dagger affair. Oftentimes, especially when the stakes are high, the interested party won't identify itself. An economic-development official like Cox might receive an e-mail from the governor's office or a fax from an independent site-selection consulting firm. The notice will refer to the potential project by a code name—sometimes a fierce mammal, sometimes a letter of the Greek alphabet—and offer only basic information such as how much land and what kind of water and sewer and electrical capacity would be required. Cox replies to these inquiries with demographic data, a few selling points (the median center of population for the United States, he likes to boast, is in Daviess County), and a menu of potential sites. If things match up the company will arrange an in-person visit. Sometimes the meeting is a week or two later. Sometimes it's that same day. Men in suits appear, talking obliquely and using aliases. "You give them your business card," Cox told me. "But they don't give you theirs." The mysterious persons case the town and might meet discreetly with community leaders or local bank presidents.

These obscure mating rituals protect the prospective employer and its reputation. If the company's identity is known, key landowners could extort a premium. "Until it's time for nut cracking," Cox says, "speculation runs rampant." Word travels fast in small towns, as do hungry expectations. A flirtatious company could hold the very fate of the town—or the whole county, or several counties—in its hands, and no corporation wants to openly disappoint such an expanse of potential customers.

The moral of Cox's helicopter parable was clear: Big employers have needs, and if a town wants to have a shot at attracting a game-changing auto-assembly plant or major distribution center, then it needs to be near a divided four-lane highway, preferably an interstate. But, as Cox explained in well-thought-out detail, I-69 would likely help many of the existing industries in the county, too. It would increase the trucking radius for Perdue, he said, since loading a truck full of live turkeys bruises them, and the company has only eight to ten hours to transport and slaughter the birds before the bruises show up on the meat and prevent it from being classified as Grade A. The local Amish community would benefit as well, since their crews of carpenters, who make daily round-trips in trucks driven by Mennonites, would be able to cover a wider service area. "The women don't like them working too far from home," Cox said. "If the men have to stay in hotels, they might be exposed to TVs and strange women."

The interstate would also help the town's corn-processing plant, GPC, operate more efficiently. Graham had invited Ken Jones, the vice president and plant manager of GPC, to join Cox and Arthur and me that afternoon for drinks. Jones came with his wife, Paula, and the two sat together on an antique sofa between pillows decorated with the likenesses of old Graham automobiles. He rattled off some impressive numbers: The plant operates around the clock, seven days a week, and each day it processes about ninety thousand bushels of corn, which comes in on 125 trucks and represents about five hundred acres of crop. Their electrical bill is about six hundred thousand dollars a month, and their natural-gas bill is a little over two million. The facility, which opened in 1996, the same year as Toyota in Princeton, represents an investment of half a billion dollars and employs about 150 people, making it the second largest in the county behind Perdue (which employs over 800).

I asked Jones how the prospect of I-69 affected the decision to locate the plant in Washington. It didn't really. "When we first came to town, why, I-69 was just a dream or talk or whatever," Jones said. "There's always talk, talk, talk. 'We gotta build I-69!' But most people said we wouldn't see it in our lifetimes." What convinced them to come here, if it wasn't the promise of I-69? "David Cox is the reason GPC came here," Jones said. "He had a drive, an aggressiveness. To give you an example, we had a company jet. And it was questionable whether the airport here could land it, because of the width. So David Cox widened the runway."

Cox, who had reddened a shade, told the story of the runway. "The FAA said if we widened it, our runway lights had to be moved," he said. "Well, that's a deal breaker because we didn't have the money. So we asked, 'Can we do shoulder work?' They said sure. So we did eight-foot shoulders on each side. And then the FAA came in a little bit later and said, 'Now that you've got a wider runway, we'll move the lights for you.'"

"There was just a lot of little things like that," Jones said. Cox also saw to the building of a rail spur the company needed, and Jo Arthur got grant money to pay for it.

"The city rolled out the red carpet," Paula remembered. "All you had to do was go into the grocery store and they'd say, 'Oh, you're from Iowa, with the GPC project.' Everybody knew about it and they'd say, 'Oh, we're so glad you're here.' And I think that was Dave Cox politicking, telling the community how much they'd like this company."

The company's location decision, Ken Jones said, came down to two options: Washington and Paducah, Kentucky, a river-port town with direct access to an interstate highway. "Paducah thought they had us," Jones recalled. "And then we did a survey for corn. And Washington, Indiana, is right in the heart of corn land." Transportation infrastructure matters a lot to a business like GPC. But in the end it didn't mean as much as other factors: the human qualities that David Cox was able to exude and the proximity of raw materials. All those cornfields might look like nothingness to certain corporate types in rented helicopters, but to the right executive they can look bountiful, even better than a barge dock or an on-ramp.

When This Was All Field

I remember I used to ride in cars through the Midwest and see old farm-houses a stone's throw from the interstate and wonder why on earth anyone would build their house that close to the highway. They didn't, of course—the road came to them. It can be difficult to imagine a land-scape as it was before its dominant man-made feature was built. It's even harder, perhaps, to come before that man-made feature and imagine the scene to follow.

I suffered this cognitive dissonance whenever I visited Thomas and Sandra Tokarski, the mother and father of Indiana's anti-I-69 movement, at their home in Stanford, Indiana, twenty minutes southwest of Bloom-ington. The Tokarskis have lived on a wooded thirty-five-acre lot there since 1975, and every time I stopped by they were up to something folksy. They had just baked bread or lemon pie, or they were trying to figure out what to do with all of the fresh blueberries or sugar snap peas from their garden, or Thomas was midway through weaving a blanket on the loom in the living room, or Sandra was getting ready to fire up the kiln and finish some pots she had thrown with clay from the creek bed out back.

Their house is a good distance off the road. Their driveway, sloped and rutted enough for a Jeep commercial, winds through a few acres of maple and oak and tulip trees before coming to a high clearing on which the house, the garden, and a chicken coop are situated. If you walk a little farther beyond the house, past a small meadow and a raised observation deck that the Tokarskis built for stargazing, you come to a wooded ravine with the creek running through the bottom. Just across that, on a ridge along the back line of their property, is where the great NAFTA high-way is supposed to run.

The interstate's construction, if it happens, will leave the Tokarskis' house where it is but will strip them of their rural seclusion and a nice chunk of their land. Fighting such a fate has already consumed a significant portion of their lives. For twenty years now, half of their life together, while raising two children and working jobs, the Tokarskis have led a statewide crusade against Interstate 69. Their dissent began even before they knew the road might affect them directly, but knowing that it will has added a certain heat to their conviction. The paper detritus from their public battles occupies an entire room of their home, where clippings and binders fill file boxes, shelves, a desk, and much of the floor. This in a house that cannot easily afford to lose rooms to paper. "Thomas would say it's a crummy house," Sandra told me. It's comfortable, and they can't imagine ever leaving, she said, but every time you turn around, something needs to be fixed. "You know how they talk about the old farmhouses that are so well built? Well, this wasn't one of them."

The Tokarskis seem at first like an unlikely pair of rabble-rousers. They are in their sixties, with hair that's turning white (his) or salt-and-pepper gray (hers). Thomas retired recently after thirty years as a lab researcher at the Indiana University School of Optometry, where he coauthored such papers as "Regional Morphological Variations within the Crayfish Eye" and "Retinal Development in the Lobster *Homarus americanus*." He is scrupulous and thoughtful, wears glasses and a mustache, and has a slight lateral lisp that turns his *s*'s a bit slushy, more so when he's agitated, which is often when he's talking about I-69. Sandra works at an art-supply store in downtown Bloomington and is short and maternal, with hair cut above her shoulders and wire-rimmed glasses over cheeks that often appear red from sun. The Tokarskis share a healthy sense of humor, and they take a serene pleasure and pride in caring for their small section of earth. But never far away is an anxiety and frustration about the highway plan that they view as scandalous government malpractice. When discussing the interstate, they take turns finishing each other's points, but each has a unique strength—Sandra is a particularly soulful communicator and a tireless organizer, and Thomas picks apart government reports and composes arguments with the attention to detail of a prosecuting attorney.

They have been do-gooders for as long as they've known each other. They met in 1969 while teaching at different schools in inner-city Louisville. Thomas had grown up in Port Huron, Michigan, where the existing I-69 now connects to Canada via the Blue Water Bridge. There was no interstate when Thomas was a boy; his father worked on the Grand Trunk Western Railroad, part of a major system that connected the auto industry in Detroit to the industrial centers of Chicago and Toronto.

During the Vietnam War, Thomas asked the draft board for conscientious-objector status but was denied. So he joined the Peace Corps and spent two years assisting with malaria control in Thailand, where he often had to travel by longboat, he says, since there were so few good roads. He got his master's in biological sciences at Indiana University, and before moving to Louisville he taught for a time at an all-white school in a small town outside Peoria. He brought the controversial black comedian Dick Gregory to speak to students, and soon after, the school allowed his contract to expire.

Not long after the couple moved to Indiana, Thomas got involved with a group that was fighting to stop construction of a nuclear power plant down on the Ohio River. In 1978, he joined three dozen other marchers who climbed a fence around the perimeter of the construction site, got arrested, and spent a night in jail. The power company, after more protests and the infamous accident at the Three Mile Island nuclear plant in Pennsylvania, abandoned its plans. A few years later Thomas and Sandra got behind another local cause: stopping a planned waste incinerator in Monroe County that was meant to dispose of the toxic PCBs that a Westinghouse capacitor plant had left in the soil and water around Bloomington. Concerned citizens like the Tokarskis raised serious questions about the environmental effects of burning PCBs, and ultimately those plans, too, were scrapped.

It was with these two victories in mind that Thomas, in the late eighties, took an interest in the Evansville-to-Indianapolis highway. He went to several of the public meetings that were part of the federally funded Donohue study. Like a lot of people in Bloomington, he and Sandra had been reading about various proposed highways to Evansville for years, and they were of the opinion that a new freeway was a terrible idea—an environmental disaster and a waste of tax dollars and good farmland. When the Donohue consultants recommended *against* construction of the road in February 1990, the Tokarskis were relieved. They perused the damning report and figured that the matter had been put to rest.

But that summer (soon after David Graham and David Reed had their breakthrough omelet breakfast), the Tokarskis went to a community-planning session at the county fairgrounds and were surprised to hear Department of Transportation people still talking about a new highway through Bloomington. Hadn't the DOT read the Donohue study? Did they plan to ignore it? The couple drove home from the fairgrounds that night bewildered and upset. Thomas, feeling a need to vent, penned a pointed opinion piece for the Bloomington *Herald-Times*, and a few days later, on August 20, the Tokarskis sat down to compose a handwritten letter to Senator Richard Lugar, for whom they had high regard.

"As you know, all of the unbiased economic feasibility studies on the highway have been negative," they wrote to Lugar. "But because some people who will gain a great deal have persisted, it now seems the highway might be built." The Tokarskis had only a vague notion of who "some people" were. They knew that a Southwest Indiana Regional Highway Coalition had formed out of the Evansville Chamber of Commerce, but they didn't have any idea who David Graham was, or David Reed. And they certainly weren't aware that the Evansville-to-Indianapolis highway had morphed, at least in the minds of a few, into a Canada-to-Mexico highway. "I can assure you we are not alone in our opposition. This is not a threat, it is a statement of fact," the Tokarskis warned Lugar. "You will hear increased opposition not only from environmentalists and owners of homes and family farms in the road path, but also from citizens concerned about the priorities of government spending."

The Tokarskis were comfortable predicting this, as they put themselves in the latter category. They weren't NIMBYs. They were watchdogs. And their letter, typical of them, was constructive in tone, political rather than personal, and tough without being harsh. "We strongly urge you to reconsider your position on this project," they told Lugar. "Indiana needs a lot of things, but it does not need this highway. Surely there are less destructive, more creative ways to help our communities." The letter was signed by Thomas, Sandra, and their daughter, Lara, who was eighteen. Their son, Ben, was only ten—too young for attribution.

One autumn Saturday evening, October 13, the Tokarskis came home to find, among their mail, a notice from the Indiana Department of Transportation requesting access to their property for surveying. They couldn't believe what they were reading. Not only was the Indianapolis-to-Evansville highway concept alive and well, but the state was already mapping routes, including one that came right through their property. The Tokarskis were mortified. They wondered at first if Thomas's piece in the newspaper had provoked retribution by the highway planners. *They're out to get us!* Sandra thought. They didn't really take this suspicion seriously—it would drive them crazy if they did, Sandra said—and the intervening years have made them more or less numb to that initial sense of shock and loss. But Sandra says she feels the pang again whenever she watches a landowner learn for the first time that his home might be taken: "I've been there, and you have this incredible, just, boulder in your stomach. You feel like you've been kicked in the gut. A lot of people who live in rural areas, they move to rural areas because that's where they *want* to live." Sandra is one of those. As a kid she was shuffled around from town to town because her father was in the air force. "All I ever wanted," she told me once, "was to stay in one place."

After they got the survey notice, the Tokarskis called a Department of Transportation phone number listed on the mailing and asked for maps of whatever routes the state was considering and more information about who had authorized the study and what the state thought the road would cost. They received none of it. A series of frustrated letters followed, including a handwritten note to Governor Evan Bayh, and over the next several weeks the Tokarskis telephoned their local elected officials and the *Herald-Times*. No one they spoke with, apart from the neighbors who had received similar notices, seemed to know anything about the highway study. As it happens, in April *The Evansville Courier* had published an item announcing the contract for preliminary engineering studies, but these were pre-Yahoo! days and the news hadn't traveled far. That is, until the Tokarskis got started.

As with the initial idea about extending the road to Mexico, the first organized opposition to the highway came together around a kitchen table. One night in late October 1990, the Tokarskis and their friends Scott and Jackie Wilson met at the home of their neighbors Brian and Nancy Garvey. The six sat around after dinner drinking wine, drafting a petition, and throwing around ideas about what to name themselves. HOWL was one thought—Hoosiers Opposed to Wasting Land—but land was just one of many reasons to oppose a new highway, and maybe their name should be positive? "We didn't want to be *against highways*, for God's sake," Sandra said. "We wanted to be *for* something." By the end of the night they had a petition ("This highway would place an unacceptable tax burden on small communities and would be extremely damaging to the environment . . .") seeded with their six signatures. They also had a name: the Citizens for Appropriate Rural Roads, or CARR. "Fix the roads we have" became their slogan.

The next order of business was to hold a public information meeting of their own. Congressman Frank McCloskey's office had provided them with a copy of the Donohue study, which Thomas went through line by line, extracting all of the consultants' damning assessments about the great costs and limited benefits of the road. In December, they booked the Center Township fire station in neighboring Greene County and started putting out the word. This first event was a test both for CARR and their fellow Hoosiers. "We didn't know what we were doing," Sandra said. "We had not a clue. But we talked to neighbors and sent out hand flyers and put a notice in the paper." Brian Garvey, an artist, drew up a poster with a Paul Revere theme: *The highway is coming! The highway is coming!* They decided that if thirty people showed up to the tiny rural fire station, that would indicate that there was sufficient interest to keep going. One hundred people came. Requests for more meetings, in more towns, came pouring in. Over the next few weeks, at gatherings in towns such as Scotland, Newberry, and Bloomfield, people turned up by the dozens, got upset by what they heard, and signed the CARR petition. Soon local environmental groups—the Audubon Society, the Hoosier Environmental Council, and others—started their own anti-I-69 advocacy campaigns, piggybacking on the information the Tokarskis were able to distill from the Donohue study.

While proselytizing to the masses, the Tokarskis were also busy sending appeals up what they perceived to be the chain of authority. Late at night and on weekends with the other members of CARR, they laid out their case in letters to Representative McCloskey, Senators Lugar and Coats, Governor Bayh, Indiana Department of Transportation executives, and the U.S. secretary of transportation, Samuel Skinner. Their correspondence didn't appear to change any minds, but they did get a few answers, some more helpful than others. In response to a presumably rhetorical question about whether the purchase of land by eminent domain included any payment for the tranquillity that would also be lost, an INDOT official responded, "Loss of serenity is a non-compensable item."

Eugene W. Cleckley, environmental-operations chief at the Federal Highway Administration, wrote back to the Tokarskis on behalf of Secretary Skinner. "We do not select projects, or tell the states which projects to fund," he informed them. Yes, the USDOT was aware of the Donohue study. And yes, the department had reported the study's findings to Congress. But the Indiana Department of Transportation, under the direction of the governor, "has the sole authority to select projects," he wrote.

"Our role . . . is to review the states' work to make sure it meets federal requirements." There were laws, regulations, and policies that the Indiana DOT would have to follow, Cleckley told the Tokarskis, including the National Environmental Policy Act of 1969, or NEPA, which requires preparation of an environmental impact statement and prescribes an open public-involvement process. Cleckley suggested the Tokarskis participate in that process.

Participate they did. In a time before the Internet made information ubiquitous, the Tokarskis scoured every report and article and pertinent law they could get their hands on. The piles of paper that clog that room of their house hint at just how meticulously the Tokarskis have worked to tackle I-69, and how sophisticated they became in doing so. No detail was too small. No damning contradiction escaped their notice. Judging from the state's own facts and figures, there were fiscal, environmental, and social reasons to forgo the road, they argued: It would cause severe damage to the environment, paving over wetlands, fragmenting forests, disrupting delicate limestone karst features such as caves, springs, and sinkholes. It would upset protected species, consume good farmland, and destroy the integrity of rural areas.

Proponents claimed that these were small prices to pay for the economic benefits the road would bring, but the state's own Donohue study, the Tokarskis pointed out, predicted that the vast majority of these benefits would fall to Bloomington and Evansville, and the growth on either end of the road was likely to come at the expense of the places between. The idea that the highway might save dying places like Odon and Petersburg was a wish not supported by the state's own study, they insisted. It was just as likely, if not more so, that some of the communities could become ghost towns after the highway reshuffled jobs and businesses. And these questionable results, the Tokarskis maintained, would come at a cost of over a billion dollars that could be spent on needed repairs and maintenance to the appropriate rural roads that gave CARR its name. I-69, they said, was the economic-development equivalent of an overpriced lottery ticket. The state could do more good driving around the sleepy backwoods highways throwing hundred-dollar bills out the window.

The case that the Tokarskis made against the Indianapolis-to-Evansville highway amounted to an indictment of the nation's interstate culture in general. The arguments they made were colored by hindsight—the interstates were largely completed, their effects were clear, and not everyone was a fan. Their criticism rang true in the environmentalist culture of Bloomington and among many land-loving residents of rural communities to the south who preferred to think of their region as "undisturbed" rather than "undeveloped." Everyone wanted more jobs and better economic opportunity. But they weren't all eager to make the deal that the rest of Interstate America had been given. They didn't want prosperity to come in the form of traffic and pollution and chain stores and truck stops.

So what did they want instead? The Tokarskis offered their alternative in an essay sent to supporters shortly after the ISTEA legislation passed in late 1991. "Like all other states, Indiana must begin to plan and build a transportation system that will meet our needs in the future," the Tokarskis wrote. "The new six-year transportation act strongly supports mass transit, bicycles, and increased use of railroads to help solve our transportation needs. These, along with repairing and upgrading our existing roads, will help . . . all of Indiana." People who oppose the highway, they wrote, "are frequently accused of being afraid of change. That is not true. We want change—real, significant change in the transportation system of this state, and of this country. It is the highway boosters and the elected officials who support this project who are afraid of change . . . They want the rest of us to continue to pay for their outdated, destructive, fiscally irresponsible projects."

The Tokarskis' vision was at odds with the norms of contemporary development and the popularity of suburbs that attracted people and jobs from the smaller towns and center cities. But it wasn't out of line with Indiana's past or its self-image. Governor Bayh had recently unveiled a new state license plate at the Farm Bureau convention, the Tokarskis pointed out in their essay. The tags depicted a sunset-colored farming scene with the slogan "Amber Waves of Grain." "Did you intend to honor and help rural Indiana," they asked the governor, "or were you eulogizing rural Indiana? Indiana's license plate may proclaim 'Amber Waves of Grain' now, but if we continue to exploit what's left of our beautiful, productive rural lands, future plates may read, 'Indiana—Easy to Get Through, No Reason to Stay.'"

The effectiveness of the arguments put forth by CARR and other advocacy groups caught local proponents flat-footed. In March 1991, James Newland spoke to a dinner meeting of the Odon, Indiana, Business and Professional Association in a small town in Daviess County twenty miles northeast of David Graham's home. An article in the local paper the next day quoted Newland talking about the growing cacophony of objections: "We must recognize the fact that the infrastructure of this country is in trouble," Newland told the group. "It's old, inadequate, and worn-out. It may be difficult to make a case for new highway construction." Members of Congress who backed the road were increasingly hearing negative comments, he said, so anyone who supported the new highway had better organize and present its positive aspects to lawmakers. "I'm afraid those who favor this project are not exerting the kind of influence necessary to get the job done," he said.

But as Newland surely knew, influence was being exerted—in ways quieter and more potent than CARR or the Odon Business and Professional Association were able to match. In just a few months, the Hudson Institute would issue David Reed's paper calling for the development of a multistate I-69 corridor; in July Congressman Frank McCloskey would insert High Priority Corridor 18 into ISTEA; and by mid-August, David Graham would be in Shreveport drawing his line on the map with John D. Caruthers while Stuart waited in the car.

The Tokarskis caught wind of Reed's paper in time to refute its suggestions in written testimony to the Senate Appropriations Subcommittee on Transportation that spring. Thomas prepared a long and thorough briefing—ten pages of detailed argument with thirteen attachments—in the hopes of discouraging any federal funding for the Indianapolis-to-Evansville highway. He mentioned the NAFTA highway notion just long enough to dismiss it as bunk. Proponents claimed the Southwest Indiana Highway might be part of a Canada-to-Mexico route, he wrote, but "we believe this is a poorly disguised ploy to justify a local highway project that has been shown . . . to have little economic justification." Several good highway routes from Canada to Mexico already existed, Thomas pointed out. "To argue that another north-south highway, one that of course has to go through Evansville, will somehow have national significance, is clearly self-serving and not credible."

These arguments did not sufficiently impress Congress. The Tokarskis soon learned that the final ISTEA bill contained an earmark for a new highway from Indianapolis, and that in fact the road had grown southward. "Memphis? Nobody had heard of this!" Sandra recalled. "I got on the telephone and called the DOT in Tennessee, and I said, 'We're just curious about this. This came as a complete surprise to us. Do you know anything about this? Have you done any studies?' They said, 'Nope. This is the first we've heard about it.' They just heard about it in the news!" Then came Senator Bennett Johnston's legislative tweak in the fall of 1992. "Lo and behold," Sandra said, "technical correction time! All of a sudden the highway's going to Houston? And then all the talk is about NAFTA. All of a sudden it's Canada to Mexico!"

The Tokarskis had built a formidable local opposition, but their kitchen campaign was hardly equipped to fight a national I-69 effort. In late 1993, the couple mailed out a letter to twenty or so Sierra Club members in the other affected states in the hopes of drumming up a national coalition against the highway. "The myth of the interstate, the notion that prosperity is inseparably tied to major highways, is again threatening to cause real problems in the American Heartland," they wrote. "Promoters speak as if their highway would be the mythical rainbow. Spanning the countryside, it would spin off glittering paths to fill pots of gold in every town and hamlet. They're only doing us a big favor, they insist." The Tokarskis warned that the highway would ruin the very places it was claiming to save: "What slops over the edges of the cities into the rural areas is all glitz and despoilment," they wrote. "The rainbow is nothing more than a concrete slab laid over our forests and wetlands, across our streams and rivers and farms."

Extending the road to Mexico had given the highway boosters a justification to lay before Congress, but in their letter the Tokarskis turned this NAFTA rhetoric on its head. "Now [interstates] are being justified as taxpayer subsidized infrastructure improvements for fugitive companies that move their factories and jobs to Mexico," they told their potential compatriots. "There they hope to exploit cheap labor and the lack of enforcement of environmental regulations.

"We need to awaken people all along the route to the disaster that is building. This is a politically driven project so politicians must be confronted," Thomas and Sandra pleaded. "If we act quickly, forcefully, and together, we can bring reason to the debate on the future of transportation in the U.S."

The Tokarskis sent their letter and they waited. Eventually, a few responses trickled in from sympathetic environmentalists, many of whom were learned in these matters and jaded by their experiences. A man in Arkansas warned the Tokarskis that they should be prepared to hire private investigators and lawyers. A man in Tennessee informed the

Tokarskis that "little old ladies in tennis shoes" had stopped a highway from going through Overton Park in Memphis in the early 1970s—good news—but the legal battle had taken twenty-five years and had gone all the way to the Supreme Court. The Tokarskis found the correspondence encouraging, but they were surprised to find that no one seemed eager to act. It would be a decade before another married couple would stand up against massive new highway plans in Texas as forcefully as the Tokarskis had in Indiana. For now, Thomas and Sandra and their local allies were the only real thorn in the side of I-69.

That thorn was growing sharper, though. They didn't hire a private detective, but in early 1995, a young lawyer named Alexander "Sandy" Ewing joined the Environmental Law and Policy Center, an advocacy group in Chicago that took an interest in the battle over I-69 in Indiana. Ewing had grown up on a cattle farm in Dutchess County, New York, and after he met the Tokarskis he developed strong feelings about their struggle. "The Tokarskis are some of the greatest people I've ever met in my life," he told me recently at his apartment in New York City, where he now lives. "They're smart and totally sincere and without pretension." His heart had gone out to clients before, of course, but the case against new-terrain I-69 was "much more black-and-white" than any other he'd handled, he said. "This was just *wrong*."

Ewing worked on a variety of issues for the ELPC, but he found himself putting thousands of miles on his car shuttling between Chicago and southern Indiana, and he wound up dedicating many more hours to the cause than the ELPC had funding to cover. Ewing and Andy Knott, a policy director at the Hoosier Environmental Council, proved indispensable in bolstering CARR's homemade crusade. The two nonprofits had staff and resources and experience, and Ewing and Knott shared the Tokarskis' command of the issues and their appetite for government documents that could turn weaker minds to mush. As a plaintiff's attorney, Ewing also had the legal expertise to pull apart the environmental-impact studies that were being conducted. The collective critique was now much stronger: The road was still a bad idea for all the reasons the Tokarskis had laid out, they argued, but the state's justifications also failed to live up to the requirements of federal law.

Specifically, NEPA required the state to "rigorously explore and objectively evaluate all reasonable alternatives" to the project, including the option of building nothing at all. But the state had considered only new-terrain routes that went through Bloomington and Washington. There was another course of action, the critics pointed out, that would improve the connection between Indianapolis and Evansville and fulfill Indiana's obligation to build its piece of the now federally designated I-69 route: The state could use the existing leg of Interstate 70 from Indianapolis west to Terre Haute, then upgrade U.S. Highway 41 between Terre Haute and Evansville. Using these existing highways would reduce construction costs by roughly half and spare thousands of acres of farmland, forest, and wetlands. What's more, they said, this alternative would continue to feed the towns that already depended on U.S. 41, rather than siphoning traffic elsewhere at those same towns' peril. The 41/70 route would be slightly longer, of course, but the difference in driving time, one state document suggested, might be only eight minutes.

They called it the "common sense" alternative and took up the more nuanced slogan "No New Terrain." Putting this forth did wonders for the cause. The debate was no longer simply about whether to build I-69 or not. It was about how to do so responsibly. The state could have its cake and eat it, too, it seemed—an interstate connection from Indianapolis to Evansville and an undisturbed Bloomington; a piece of the NAFTA highway, and peace.

A moment of truth came in 1996 when Indiana released a Draft Environmental Impact Statement, or DEIS, for the Southwest Indiana Highway. Not surprisingly, it identified a preferred route connecting Evansville to Bloomington and Washington through the Tokarskis' backyard. By this time, the Mid-Continent Highway Coalition had hired Carolina Mederos and Randy DeLay as lobbyists; HNTB and Wilbur Smith had released their positive feasibility study of Corridor 18, which now reached all the way down to the Lower Rio Grande Valley thanks to the National Highway System Designation Act of 1995. On the whole, I-69 was chugging along, and the completion of the DEIS should have put Indiana far ahead of any other state in the slow crawl toward construction.

But the Environmental Protection Agency, which reviews all impact statements as part of the NEPA process, dropped a bombshell. In a letter from Valdas V. Adamkus, a regional administrator for the EPA, the agency lambasted Indiana's study. "Based on a thorough review," Adamkus wrote, "EPA has determined that the DEIS is insufficient." The reasons for the project were questionable, he said, the environmental consequences had not been fully explored, and the state had not given proper consideration to all viable options. "In view of the wide range of our objections to this project, I am urgently requesting that a supplemental DEIS be developed," Adamkus wrote. "I simply do not believe that either the decision makers or the interested public can be adequately apprised of the full range of issues related to this project without a supplemental DEIS." In short, the study was no good. The Tokarskis, Ewing, and Knott were right.

Sort of. INDOT had been slapped on the wrist and sent back to the drawing board. But they had not been told no. The emphasis on "appraisal" in the EPA's letter was telling: As Cleckley had pointed out in his letter to the Tokarskis five years earlier, the NEPA process is only that—a process. As Ewing explained to me, the National Environmental Policy Act "does not say you have to do the best thing for the environment or minimize harm to the environment." Rather, it compels the government to "examine all of the alternatives and set forth what the impacts are. And the idea—the nice idea—is that once that's all studied, the public and the policy makers will make an informed decision."

This last, subjective step in an otherwise technical process tends to limit the power of environmentalist activists. "Everyone always thinks the silver bullet is a lawsuit," Ewing told me. "Really all that a lawsuit or maneuvering over NEPA can win you is time." Time is a valuable thing, though—budgets often tighten, governors change, priorities change. "We weren't trying to win a legal battle. We were trying to win a *public-opinion* battle. All the legal stuff is just a weapon to win time to win the public-opinion battle."

The EPA's letter promised to buy the Indiana opponents months if not years, and indeed the governor had already changed. Shortly after the release of the DEIS, Evan Bayh ended his second term with a successful bid for the Senate, and his lieutenant governor, Frank O'Bannon, was elected as his successor. This wasn't necessarily good news for CARR, though. As the Tokarskis had frequently pointed out, O'Bannon (along with Bayh, McCloskey, and other state politicians) was listed on the letterhead of the Southwest Indiana Regional Highway Coalition as a member. But he was an elected politician, after all, and theoretically he could be swayed by the strong feelings of his constituents. There was hope, and the public-opinion battle seemed to be shifting in their favor.

While the state worked to overcome the EPA's objections, Ewing and

Knott visited the editorial boards of the largest newspapers in the state to make the case for the cheaper "common sense" route. If INDOT wastes money on I-69, Ewing and Knott reasoned, that means fewer highway dollars for projects important to other cities. This tax-dollar angle gained wider traction than the environmental arguments ever did. By the time Ewing left the trenches, in 2000, to move with his wife back to New York, dozens of papers from across Indiana had editorialized against the new-terrain route. *The Indianapolis Star, The Indianapolis News,* the Terre Haute *Tribune-Star,* the *South Bend Tribune,* the Gary *Post-Tribune,* the Fort Wayne *News-Sentinel,* and the Louisville *Courier-Journal* came out in favor of upgrading 41/70. The national group Taxpayers for Common Sense attacked Indiana's plans, *NBC Nightly News* with Tom Brokaw featured I-69 as part of a series called "The Fleecing of America," and ABC's *World News Tonight* with Peter Jennings followed suit with a segment in their antiwaste series "It's Your Money."

Sandra attributes much of this groundswell to Ewing and Knott, whom she considers godsends. "They would wear us out because they were so good at working the media," she said. One night, she remembers, after a marathon meeting of the Bloomington City Council at which the opponents convinced the council to pass a formal declaration against new-terrain I-69, the two men came back to the Tokarskis' house. "These meetings would go until one o'clock in the morning, and they would come and spend the night here," she told me at her kitchen table. "And they would be like, 'Gotta get this done!' I remember sitting in that room there, and they were going nuts writing this press release and faxing it off and I'm like—" Sandra slumped in her chair, miming sleep.

The camaraderie was strong, and occasionally their work morphed into fun. "We've done this so long, and basically this stuff's all pretty boring," Sandra said. "So we do things like we have a little jar, usually a canning jar, with these little teeny plastic pigs. And it's guess-how-many-pigs-in-the-I-69-pork-barrel. We do a lot of pig-motif things. There's a place up in Indianapolis that has a great pig costume that you can rent . . ." In January 1999, Sandra drove up to the Indiana Statehouse with "Arnold the Pig" to present a ham to the governor. She informed O'Bannon's press secretary, who accepted the ham, that Arnold represented Hogs Opposed to Government Waste and Silly Highways—HOGWASH.

Soon after, the Tokarskis were named Environmentalists of the Year, an award presented, somewhat paradoxically, by the state's largest power company. Ewing shared with me a copy of a letter he had sent in support of their nomination. "The highway battle is of David-and-Goliath proportions, and has been fought against enormous odds," he wrote. "An impressive array of business and real estate interests, many of whom stand to gain financially from the highway, have spent literally millions of dollars lobbying for it in Indianapolis and Washington, D.C. Practically no one questioned that the highway was needed, and practically no one doubted that it would get built." But the Tokarskis, he said, despite having day jobs and no paid staff, had identified flaws in the proposal and publicized its environmental and economic impacts. "No one knows how it will be resolved. But win or lose, the Tokarskis' years of hard work on this project will pay big dividends . . . They have demonstrated that 'ordinary' citizens . . . can take on the powers that be and transform an ill-conceived project from a 'done deal' to a question mark."

Once, sitting with the Tokarskis in their house, I asked them if they could remember a time when they felt as if they were ahead in the I-69 struggle.

"When the EPA slammed the state's study," Thomas replied quickly, nodding. "That was good."

"Sandy and Andy came with champagne," Sandra said, smiling at Thomas. Did they think they had won, I asked? "No. We *knew* we hadn't won."

"I don't think there's ever been a point where we thought we'd won," Thomas said.

"Sometimes I've dreamed that it was over," Sandra said.

"Yeah. I've dreamed about it once in a while," Thomas muttered.

"It's always this great feeling of relief," Sandra said.

"Incredible relief," Thomas went on. "Every once in a while you say, 'I'm just going to imagine it's over, it's done with. What would I do?' And it's like, everything just opens up, this tremendous feeling of relief, and you're free to do all the stuff you always wanted to do but didn't have enough time for. Finally we can go on with our lives."

How Things Have Changed

The Tokarskis are not alone in wanting the I-69 ordeal to end. When I met James Newland at the headquarters of the Mid-Continent Highway Coalition in October 2002, he had been serving as its director for one month shy of a decade and had been agitating for the Indianapolis-to-Evansville highway for four years longer than that. He was eighty-three years old and he spoke in the measured, over-enunciated way of an older man who has led countless meetings and had been forced to repeat himself to myriad reporters.

"There are two ways really to look at whether—or why—I-69 simply must be finished," he said. "The first is from a sense of fact, economically and otherwise. And the other is looking at it in terms of what is called a no-growth syndrome, a perpetuation of the status quo. They don't wanna change. 'Don't change!' This leads to the irrational, really." We discussed a poll that had just come out in the Bloomington *Herald-Times* that found that 65 percent of respondents wanted I-69 to be built, but only 49 percent thought it should be built over new terrain. Newland interpreted those figures as evidence of overall support for the highway. "I know there's some folks that don't want this road built," he said. "And I admire them for saying what they want. And they're not a dang-gone bit timid about this." But he learned "a hell of a long time ago," he said, that the shortest distance between two points is a straight line. "Some people say, well, you know, it's going to cost too much money. Whatever that means. My answer to them is this: It isn't necessarily the investment. It's the *return* on investment which is going to be immense.

"The North American Free Trade Agreement changed everything, really," Newland told me. Truck traffic on the interstates had doubled since NAFTA, he explained, while the interstates themselves had increased just 2 percent. "President Eisenhower—I served under him during the war, in England, France, Germany, and other places—he saw what a modern transportation system means," Newland said. "And we must move with the times. We are living now in a *globalized* society. We couldn't withdraw from the world economy if we wanted to. And I don't think we want to."

Newland's points about the modern economy and the need for modern infrastructure were colored somewhat by a detail that had struck me when I first walked into his office: He had no computer. The headquarters of the I-69 Mid-Continent Highway Coalition turned out to be a single sparsely appointed room on the third floor of a suburban office building on the north side of Indianapolis. Newland was its sole occupant. He had a desk, a telephone, a few filing cabinets, and, on a table against one wall, a large manual typewriter. "I have carried that around with me literally all over the world," Newland told me when I asked about it. The steel, German-made Olympia weighed about fifteen pounds, and it had traveled with Newland decades ago when he worked in public relations for the Eastern Railroad Presidents' Conference, which represented thirty companies including the New York Central, the Pennsylvania, and the Baltimore railroads. Newland bought the typewriter in 1956, the same year, coincidentally, that Eisenhower signed the law that created the interstate system. It was now an antique. "I wouldn't give it up for anything," he said.

Newland is also nostalgic for the manner in which interstates were planned years ago. He sympathized with those being asked to sacrifice their land, he wanted me to know, but the project had been studied to death. "I wish I were smart enough to build a road that's not gonna impact or affect somebody. But that cannot be done," he said. "My family was personally impacted when they built I-70 years ago. But we didn't have this problem in those days. They *built* the interstate!"

I related Newland's comments to Sandra Tokarski, and she surprised me with her response. "James Newland, bless his heart," she said. "He's totally wrong, understand. But I have some compassion for these old people whose world has changed. They just don't know it yet." She felt pity, too, she said, for Governor O'Bannon, who had supported the highway his entire public life. "But what he doesn't understand is that times have changed. And it's not 1950 anymore. You know? It's 2002, and rural people are just not gonna roll over and play dead anymore."

The fact that road building wasn't like it used to be had an awful lot to do with the National Environmental Policy Act of 1969. NEPA, which was signed into law by President Richard Nixon, was a groundbreaking piece of legislation intended, according to its preamble, to "encourage productive and enjoyable harmony between man and his environment; to promote efforts which will prevent or eliminate damage to the environment and biosphere and stimulate the health and welfare of man." In more practical terms, NEPA mandated the preparation of an environmental impact statement for any major federal actions "significantly affecting the quality of the human environment." This included things like dam and levee construction, oil and gas development, and of course transportation projects, which have accounted for most of the EISes completed under the law.

It happens that one of the principal authors of NEPA worked in Bloomington. Lynton Caldwell was a professor of government at Indiana University, and in the early sixties he began to work out ways in which the U.S. government might institutionalize the concern for the earth that was by then pervading the country. Caldwell wanted federal policy to have its heart in the right place, and he wanted it to have teeth as well. So he invented the environmental impact statement, which forced agencies to catalog the foreseeable social, economic, and environmental effects of a proposed action and any possible alternatives. If we take a good hard look at the consequences of our actions, the thinking went, we will make informed decisions that are in the best interest of the biosphere and the health and welfare of man.

But things didn't quite work out that way. Within a decade after the passage of NEPA, it became rather clear to Caldwell that the EIS was not performing its ideal function. "Virtually nobody seems to read and make use of environmental impact statements," he wrote in an essay in 1978, including "the decision-makers who must act on the projects." He worried that governments merely saw the EIS as an obstacle around which to steer their foregone conclusions, rather than as an opportunity to inform a more responsible judgment. And he worried that court battles over EISes were drawing attention away from the more important values underpinning the procedural rules. "The NEPA process has overshadowed the NEPA purpose," he wrote in 1993. And in 1998: "There is a NEPA process larger than impact statement procedure. It is a process of policy leadership, social learning, scientific advancement, and psychological and behavioral change reflected in the ends and operations of society, government, and the economy."

A tall order for a bill that ran just a few pages. But Caldwell never gave up hope that the spirit of his law would be realized. Near the end of his life—he died in 2006—Caldwell watched a battle over these very issues consume Bloomington, his home of more than fifty years. He spoke out publicly only once, in a letter to the *Herald-Times* in 1996. The state's I-69 study was flawed, he wrote, and inconsistent with the intent of NEPA. The EIS did not adequately evaluate "the non-quantifiable values impaired by the proposed route," and "the objectivity of the EIS is suspect, having been prepared by a private consulting firm in Evansville. The practice of farming out impact analysis to consulting firms is contrary to the purpose of the law," he informed.

After Caldwell's scolding and the Environmental Protection Agency's critique of that first-draft EIS for I-69, the state spent a few years looking for some way to address the study's shortcomings without starting from scratch. But the opposition held the state's feet to the fire, and ultimately INDOT announced in 1999 that it would complete a new, expanded study that would properly measure all of the various alternatives. This new study would be conducted in two phases—first the state would decide whether a highway should be built, and, if so, what general route it should take; then, with the most contentious issues out of the way, a second layer of studies would determine the exact alignment of the road. For this new study, the "purpose and need" statement was also revised. The stated goals for I-69 in Indiana were now threefold: to provide a new link that "strengthens the transportation network in Southwest Indiana, supports economic development in Southwest Indiana, and completes the portion of the National I-69 project between Evansville and Indianapolis."

Right away, the opposition detected a slant to these objectives. Thomas Tokarski, Ewing, and Knott wrote a letter to the Federal Highway Administration pleading that "the first and presumably most important criterion creates a strong bias toward the new-terrain route and against U.S. 41/I-70." It was clear, the three men complained, that the state would not feel bound by any obligation to minimize environmental impacts. "A biased purpose and need statement," they wrote, "turns the NEPA process into an empty charade . . . INDOT will simply go through the motions."

For further evidence of a slanted study, CARR et al. pointed to the firm that would conduct it. The state, without putting the work out for bid, had awarded a $7.7 million consulting contract to Bernardin, Lochmueller & Associates, the same Evansville firm that had worked on the earlier, discredited study. What's more, critics discovered, employees of Bernardin Lochmueller had given more than $120,000 in political contributions to Governor O'Bannon and the Indiana Democratic Party since 1996, including $18,000 that poured into the governor's reelection campaign within seven weeks of the contract's being awarded. Ewing, Knott, and the Tokarskis mused in press releases and news interviews about whether the public could really trust the advice of such well-repaid political donors. "It appears that Bernardin Lochmueller is being rewarded for playing politics, rather than doing credible work," Thomas wrote in one.

To be fair, Bernardin Lochmueller employees gave generously to both parties, often to competing candidates. BLA's largesse was moot, an INDOT spokesperson answered at the time. It was simply the best-qualified firm for the job and its familiarity with the project would prove valuable to the taxpayers. That familiarity went considerably deeper than the 1996 study, however. David Graham had known Vince Bernardin, a cofounder of the firm, since the two were young. The Bernardins were from Evansville and had a house next to the Grahams up in Michigan. On at least one occasion in the early days of the first I-69 study, Graham recalled, representatives from BLA met at his house for dinner and cocktails to practice their I-69 presentations. Keith Lochmueller, the company's other principal, attended some of the very first strategy sessions about the highway at the Evansville Chamber of Commerce. At a meeting in 1990, even before David Graham's long car trip, Lochmueller suggested that the highway boosters, who favored a route through Bloomington, should respond to any potential challenges regarding the need for an interstate by emphasizing "safety and economics." Ten years later, Lochmueller's consultancy was being asked to conduct an objective analysis of the road's impacts, and how various alternatives measured up as far as safety and economics.

As David Reed astutely observed in his Hudson Institute paper, quantifying the costs and benefits of major infrastructure projects is tricky business. Skeptics go a step further and say that such work is susceptible to actual trickery: If the analysis is inherently subjective and the company evaluating a project is also in the business of planning or building infrastructure of the same type—as is often the case—doesn't this encourage the company to find virtue in any project the government wants to build? The I-69 opposition believed it was up against a consulting firm that was inherently friendly to highways, friendly to the new-terrain route in particular, friendly with the governor, and tasked with project goals that almost immediately discounted the use of existing highways.

By the time the showdown over the first-tier study reached its climax, in 2002, the opposition was stronger than ever. The Tokarskis, with Knott and Ewing, had succeeded in making I-69 the hot political issue in Indiana. As one person put it to me, "You can't get three people together in a room around here and not have a heated discussion about the highway." The sides taken were not always predictable. The vocal chorus in favor of upgrading existing highways—the "common sense" alternative, as the Tokarskis had branded it—contained a mix of local politicians worried about jobs, editorial boards worried about the state budget, and the chambers of commerce of towns that stood to lose if the highway cut through new terrain. The debate had also made friends of longtime foes: those involved in agriculture and those interested in counterculture. "Ours was an amazing coalition," Ewing told me. "Farmers *never* liked environmentalists, the idea of long-haired hippies telling them they couldn't grow genetically modified corn or plant in wetlands. And we got chambers of commerce. Talk about people who don't like environmentalists! But we worked it and worked it and worked it. That coalition should have been the death blow."

This strange synergy was on dramatic display that August at three public hearings following the release of the revamped-draft EIS. The study stopped short of identifying a route. Instead, of the twelve corridor variations studied, five were identified as "preferred alternatives," and the final choice was left to Governor O'Bannon. Bernardin Lochmueller had made his decision significantly easier, however: The opposition's 41/70 alternative did not make the preferred list. Using existing highways "would have relatively low impacts on the natural environment," the study admitted, but that scenario "performs much more poorly than any other alternative in terms of satisfying the goals of the project." The high-performing alternatives were those that featured shorter mileage and service to Bloomington.

It was still theoretically possible that the governor would surprise everyone and choose the cheaper, "common sense" option. But with the study pointing to new-terrain, the job of convincing O'Bannon otherwise would be left to the public, who turned out in droves to fill auditoriums in Evansville, Terre Haute, and Bloomington. At each of the public hearings, the crowds sat and scowled through opening presentations by INDOT and Bernardin Lochmueller, after which they were allowed to speak. One by one they came to a podium facing their peers. The format allowed two minutes for each commenter to speak, and in an absurd bit of stage managing, their time was kept by a traffic light, which shone green until thirty seconds remained, then yellow, and finally red when their time had expired.

In Bloomington, only a handful of speakers voiced support for the highway; they were met with heckling and boos. Those ardent in opposition (the majority) were applauded and cheered. Sandy Ewing had left the Midwest and moved to New York City in 2000, so a colleague spoke on behalf of the Environmental Law and Policy Center. "You know, I like nostalgia," she said. "I like to relive the 1950s by watching *I Love Lucy* reruns. The DOT, on the other hand, seems to like to relive the fifties by taking us back to the time when government was a political machine that brought home pork without a second thought about public opinion or collaborative planning, and before the law required the consideration of environmental impacts."

A young man in a green T-shirt stood before the people and declared I-69 "a hoax." It would provide only lowly gas-station jobs, he said, while more decent-paying jobs would be shipped to Mexico. "I think if we pave this highway with the teeth of workers and farmers from Indiana, and then hired immigrant Mexicans to brush them every morning, then we would create jobs," he said. "That would be about equivalent to what this highway is really doing."

"Many of us agree that God works in mysterious ways," a woman said. "God gives us messages. To Governor O'Bannon, to those of you at INDOT, and to those of you at Bernardin, Lochmueller & Associates: You need to wake up and you need to listen. God is speaking to you very loudly and very clearly through the voices of twelve thousand Hoosiers. *Use I-70 and U.S. 41.* It will save six hundred million of our hard-earned taxpayer dollars. It will save seven thousand acres of God's creation. And it very well may save your soul come Judgment Day."

Sandra Tokarski got a standing ovation as she walked to the podium. "You all are great," she told them. Then she turned to the men on the dais. "Listen to the people in this room. Sometimes we aren't always perfectly correct and polite, but it comes from our hearts. We do *not* want a new-terrain highway." Then she over-enunciated. "We are here. We are *not* going to allow any new-terrain highway built in southwest Indiana." She made a plug for the "common sense" route, and then told the crowd—her crowd—"blessings on all of you for taking time out of your lives to come and express your concerns."

The woman who followed struck a more militant tone. She stood tall in a purple dress. "Like most environmentalists, I believe in nonviolence. I believe in civility and politeness. I respect the person and property of others. But you know, we might need to be *present* soon. I intend to have to sit down in front of an earthmover," she said, then, raising her voice above the swelling applause, "and I invite all of you to join me, especially the elderly. Bring your wheelchairs! And when we come together, let's all bring *books*."

A short while later, Sean Connelly, a local writer who would soon self-publish *I-69 Does Not Stop,* a novel about corruption and anarchist rebellion, came to the microphone. He pointed out the various ways citizens could submit comments—by mail, by telephone hotline, over the Internet, at the meeting that night. "How is it, with all this technology and all these ways to listen," he asked, pounding the podium, "they haven't heard. One. Damn. Thing!" Everyone in the room, he said, knew someone who had lost a job due to a factory's moving overseas. "Who here thinks the NAFTA corridor is going to be our savior? . . . Let's see it stopped, or let's see Governor O'Bannon stopped."

Kay Connelly, Sean's wife, reminded the auditorium that the 1990 Donohue study had judged a new highway unwise. "Today, INDOT is presenting us with a *new* study and trying to make it look objective by using terms like 'computer model,'" she said. But Kay was on the faculty of IU's computer-science department, and "I can tell you that basing such a major decision on computer modeling is *wrong.* As any computer programmer will tell you, it's impossible to write a computer model without flaws. Any computer model is only as objective as the programmer."

A Bloomington resident in a tan suit and beard addressed a Federal Highway Administration official who was present. "We are a unique place," he said. "We want to *stay* a unique place. We don't want to become a common place along the road."

Brian Garvey, the illustrator who was one of the six founding members of CARR, had lived in southwestern Monroe County for twenty-seven years. "The big reason why I'm still there is the devotion people have to my neighborhood—and those *are* neighborhoods, even though there's more acreage and more fields," he said. "To say that economic development will 'improve our lives,' I do not see that. I see massive disruption to sense of place. Not a little line on the map, but big waves. And that makes me *ill* to think that. What renews my spirit is to look out and see this fight."

An exasperated woman asked the men from INDOT, "Where are your brains? We live in southern Indiana because it is southern Indiana. Call us hicks, call us what you want, but we're not stupid. We will save this land."

Thomas Tokarski received wild cheers when he spoke, saying, "We are *not* going away. If the government chooses any of the routes that are destructive to our environment, our community, and our economy, we will continue to fight it—in the meetings, in the courts if necessary, and in the streets. We are going to do whatever it takes to defend our homes, our farms, our forests, and our communities. And that is a fact!"

A woman who was a retired marine officer rose a short while later to say that she was ashamed of her government but proud that night to be a Hoosier. "I've not heard us express ourselves with such enthusiasm. We're quiet folk," she said. "My family has been here for six generations. Their bones are in some of these counties. But they're dead. Those yet to come deserve our best efforts. And we're not giving them that."

An older man's voice was full of disappointment. "This is about growth? *Cancer* is a growth," he said. "We produce and consume enough for each person fifty times over. More wealth will not benefit society if it only puts more economic power in the hands of a few." He talked about empty apartments and storefronts he knew about, and asked why people weren't filling those instead of mass-producing houses out into the countryside. "We're using up natural resources faster than they can regenerate."

Another woman spoke of Bedford, down south, a small town that was bypassed by an upgraded state road. "Bedford was a booming town," she said. "Now Thirty-seven runs beside it, and all the development you've got is big box stores. You've got Wendy's. You've got two Kmarts. But you don't have real development. The downtown is shuttered. They don't have a downtown movie theater. They don't have much of a downtown. They have a *highway* town."

A little while later, John Smith, a Bloomington bike-shop owner, read from an essay he wrote comparing I-69 to a natural disaster. "I've tried to think of an act of nature that would destroy so permanently so many homes, families, and lives," he said. "It's like the biggest tornado ever that knocks down flat every house in a wide swath from Evansville to Bloomington, with a lasting roar that may never stop." But unlike the highway, nature doesn't take land, he said. "It's there to rebuild on, with lifelong ties to one's neighbors and family. Nature is not as cruel as the moneyed persons and the brainwashed who would request this unnatural disaster to sweep across our state."

After each of these passionate speeches, a stoic INDOT public-hearing manager, who stood the entire time at his own, higher podium on the audi-

torium stage, deadpanned the same response: "Thank you for those comments." After four hours—ninety comments—he brought the hearing to
a close, apologizing to the thirty speakers who remained. He encouraged
them to deliver their comments in writing, and informed them that the
public-comment period would end on November 7, 2002.

The three months between the public hearings and the end of the
comment period were busy ones for John Smith. The man who compared
I-69 to a tornado became something of a tempest himself. With the
state's route maps in hand, Smith drove all over southern Indiana knock-
ing on the doors of homes along the various paths being considered.
Some of the residents were aware of their situation, but others weren't—
the two-tiered study meant that the state wouldn't survey property until
a corridor had been chosen. For many, Smith was the bearer of very bad
news. He would show them the map, commiserate with them about the
possibility of losing their home, and then invite them to submit formal
objections to the state. He also offered each household a yard sign, to be
placed along the road at the spot where I-69 would cross.

I rode with him one Saturday as he traveled through Greene County,
southwest of Bloomington and northeast of Washington. We met a
woman who stood in her doorway in bare feet and explained that she
had seen the study map at a local apple festival. "So much for living in the
country, right?" she said, sounding resigned. "I guess we'll have to move
to Kentucky."

Down the road we found another man in his horse pen, cleaning the
foot of a mare with a wire brush. "I've really tried to look at it as—it could
be a positive for me. I can't say that it will be, but I can't guarantee it won't.
Depends on the size of the check that's written how this thing pans out,"
the man told Smith. "If it's gonna hit me, I want it to take *all* of me." He had
heard some guidance from a city engineer in town, he said: "'Turn down the
first offer, and take the second one. Don't fight it.' That's what he advised."

Smith felt somewhat differently. His antihighway activism began after
he discovered that his house was on one of the routes—3B, which cut
near Bloomington but gave the town a wider berth than 3C, the route
that crossed the Tokarskis' property. Smith's ten acres were off to the west
in Solsberry, where he says you can stand for fifteen minutes or more and
not hear a single human sound. "We looked for three years to find our
place. We'd look in the daytime and my wife would say, 'We have to come
back at night.' We didn't want to live near any streetlights."

Smith is fifty-two, athletic, and wears a graying ponytail and wire-rimmed spectacles. He is not an environmentalist, he told me. "I recycle, but I don't lose sleep over it." One night some years ago, Smith found himself screaming at the evening news and decided he would run for Congress. He ran as a Democrat and lost convincingly in the primary. "When I ran," he told me, "I said I was antigrowth. No politician says they're antigrowth. But with people on the other side fighting so hard towards growth, if we're going to come to a compromise, someone has to take the other point of view."

Smith runs a popular bike shop on the county courthouse square in Bloomington and makes a good living. Bikes are a fetish there, and Smith caters to students training seriously for Little 500, an annual race patterned after the Indianapolis 500 and made famous by the movie *Breaking Away*, which, like other Indiana sports movies—*Hoosiers, Rudy*—tells the story of a young hardworking local underdog who stays true to his purpose and eventually triumphs through sheer force of will. "When you're on the right side of an issue, it seems to just win," Smith told me as we drove around identifying endangered homesteads. "I guess I'm kind of an optimist. But what I said to a lot of people is, 'I sell bicycles for a living. If it were as easy to sell bicycles as it is to convince people that this highway is a bad idea, I would be a rich man.'"

On the last Saturday of October, days before the end of the public-comment period, Smith led a mass demonstration drive through the countryside that the new-terrain routes would bisect. The car tour kicked off just south of Washington, at the farm of Jim and Jane Gillooly. Just past noon, a hay field full of cars started up and the tour moseyed north, rambling and zigzagging along the back roads, many of which were gravel or dirt. It was a rough ride, an exercise that highway proponents might have used to show the gross inefficiency of the agrarian infrastructure. But Smith's point was more about the beauty of it all, the way the fall foliage looks from across a field of soybeans, the way you can reach the top of a hill and see the next hill and nothing but valley in between. He wanted to show that there are people who find peace in inefficiency, who don't care to go anywhere they can't get to already.

Smith led the caravan in his pickup truck and sliced with his hand in a rigid wave out his window every time the road crossed the imaginary footprint of I-69. Outside Elnora, Indiana, in the heart of Daviess County's Amish community, he pulled off to the side of the road. The riders all got out of their cars and solemnly gathered in a circle for one of the quieter, sweeter moments in the decade-long controversy. "We stop and pause for a group of people who have very little voice, a group of people who some find annoying because they're slow, a group of people that can't use this interstate, a group of people that will be cut in half," Smith told the group, who stood holding their keys and squinting in the sun. He was speaking of the Amish, but those listening felt included. "We wish we could have stopped next to a buggy. They don't like that very well, so we stopped here. We silence our cars and our gasoline engines and we have a moment of healing for this very spiritually wealthy community."

The tour ended just shy of Indianapolis at a suburban park, where tables were set up with protest literature and a collage of landscape photographs taken by affected landowners along the route. The several hundred participants congregated on the grass around a portable public-address system for a series of pep talks, but first a Bloomington resident named Mitch Rice, who served as master of ceremonies, brought out a guitar and sang a song he wrote in 1994 called "Highway 69 Revisited":

> *Well, the big boys up in Indy, they like to spend our dough,*
> *And when they drive to Evansville, they feel it is too slow,*
> *So they want a billion dollars just to save eight minutes' time*
> *While they tear up southern Indian', a land still in its prime!*

> *CHORUS:*
> *And we've been down this road before, one too many times,*
> *Paving over Mother Earth, it really is a crime!*
> *We don't need more semis roaring through our land,*
> *Back down home in Paradise, southern Indian'*

> *They say we need this highway to trade with Mexico,*
> *Just trade off jobs and industry, and southward they will go,*
> *In the land of revolutions and cheap labor they will hide,*
> *And so the average Hoosier is just taken for a ride!*

> *Highway 69, they say, will bring us all great wealth,*
> *But breathing all those diesel fumes, it ain't good for your health!*
> *While working at the truck stop is the best job you can find,*
> *You know the nation's better jobs and days are now behind . . .*

John Smith thanked the crowd for coming. He especially thanked Thomas and Sandra Tokarski. "Let's keep up the fight," he said. "The Tokarskis should be able to live their life in peace."

Thomas spoke next. "We were down in Washington today and we drove up here," he said, "and we did not see any grinding poverty that this highway is supposed to solve. So why are we talking about still building this highway?"

And then Sandra. "We started our organization in 1990 with six people around a kitchen table," she told the crowd. "And all of you have come and are standing up and speaking out to protect our farms, our rural communities, our homes. It's—I can't thank you enough for your steadfast dedication for so many years," she said. "We are going to fight this boondoggle highway every step of the way."

As the autumn light faded there were more testimonials and more songs. The mood was celebratory and bellicose, but also a little valedictory. The environmental study, with its public meetings and its alarming route maps, had brought scores of new opponents on board for the fight. There was no telling how many would remain a few months later, after the study was done and a route was chosen.

When the comment period ended, it was revealed that some 90 percent of citizen input had been in opposition to a new-terrain highway. But on January 9, 2003, Governor O'Bannon announced the state's official decision: I-69 would follow route 3C, which came through Washington, Bloomington, and the Tokarskis' backwoods. "I know all of you waited for years for this decision. I know many will be pleased by this decision, and I know some certainly will be upset," O'Bannon said at a news conference full of both heckling and applause. "Indiana has always been the Crossroads of America, and with the completion of this project, Indiana will move beyond that billing to become the economic-opportunity state of the twenty-first century."

The governor did his best to make the announcement sound final. But with more years' worth of bureaucratic hurdles to jump before construction could begin, and with federal funding uncertain, and with dissenters vowing to continue their fight—in the courts, in the nation's capital, and, if need be, in front of bulldozers—O'Bannon's decision amounted only to the end of a battle in a much longer war.

New Developments, Old Dreams

At the hearings and public demonstrations that surrounded the environmental studies for I-69 in Indiana, it was common to see a distraught farmer stand up to object that one of the routes under consideration would split his family's farm in two. Maybe the bisection would leave a piece of his land isolated and far from any overpass, and how, the farmer wanted to know, was he supposed to get across that highway with a tractor? Some complained that the highway would sever their land diagonally, and has anyone from the Indiana Department of Transportation ever tried to farm a triangle?

It was routine for these farmers to mention, when it was the case, that the endangered land had been in the family for several generations. Jim and Jane Gillooly, who hosted the kickoff of John Smith's car tour, were two such farmers. They raised cattle in Daviess County on a piece of property that their son, Kyle, was the fifth generation to work. Jane's great-grandfather bought the original acreage in 1884, as she told me when the three of them drove me around, in 2002, to show me their operation. Kyle, who had just graduated from Purdue with a degree in animal science, had been quiet the whole drive, so I asked him what he thought about the proponents' argument that the region needed the highway to keep young people around. "In high school, everybody talks about moving away—they gotta get out of this small town. But you talk to them four or five years after high school, and it's amazing the number that have stuck around and found a decent job. That may not be the job they wanted in high school, but it's something that they're happy with," he said. "But if the highway comes, I won't be able to do what I wanna do, and that's be here and raise cattle and raise a family and enjoy the life that I've lived the last twenty-three years. To stay here, try to work cattle around a four-lane highway, that's not quite doing it."

Unfortunately for the Gilloolys, the route that Governor O'Bannon chose in 2003 will indeed have a major impact on their farm. It will also cut across another multigenerational farm nearby, through land belonging to a family that had been in the county even longer: the Grahams. David Graham shared this fact with me when we first spoke as a way of demonstrating that some landowners, unlike the noisemakers up near Bloomington, were sacrificing gracefully. He wanted me to know that he and his family were taking one for the team. "It just so happens that the road goes through one of our farms," Graham told me. "And I'm not happy about that, and neither are my brothers. But we decided we're gonna put up with it."

One thing that sometimes helps landowners put up with the loss of hard-worked acreage, I knew, was the expectation, even in the face of any misgivings, that proximity to the new highway might mean a windfall. I asked Graham whether his family might be able to bring themselves to develop any of their farmland. He didn't have to think about it. "Yes," he answered. "But I don't know what that would be. We've been hoping for Washington, Indiana, to get some of the ancillary plants from Toyota"— an assembly factory had opened fifty miles away, in Princeton, in 1996— "but so far we haven't had any."

It made sense that Graham would believe personally the buoyant predictions that he and his fellow interstate proponents had been floating publicly. But his answer sounded a little overly optimistic to me. Even if I-69 were to be completed and growth did follow, few parcels along the highway would benefit from anything like an auto-parts plant. Most affected families would have to wait years before they saw anything better than billboards spring up along their frontage. True development would likely come first to the lucky property owners with sizable chunks near new interchanges.

But it turns out that Graham wasn't being naïve. One afternoon a while later, while we were touring the area in my rented car, he showed me the piece of his family's land that I-69 would touch. Heading west from his house toward Washington, we took the four-lane U.S. 50 bypass as it swung south, splitting off from the old two-lane highway through town. Graham motioned out the window toward a vast expanse to our left. "We have a farm stretch right there. And the interstate," he said, motioning with his hand perpendicularly to the bypass, "goes right through it. It's going to come up from Petersburg. And this will be an interchange." The cornfield he had shown me on our left continued for some distance more. Is this still yours? I asked, pointing to the piece on the other side of I-69's path. "Yes. And on this side, too," he said, motioning to the right, on the north side of the bypass. The Grahams owned close to a thousand acres here, on three corners of a planned interchange. If Interstate 69 were to be built, this would become a very valuable piece of property.

U.S. 50 was certainly worthy of an exit off a new I-69. And this eastern edge of town seemed a natural enough place to put an interstate if you were going to build one, because there's a river on the western edge of town. But I could guess what the Tokarskis and other opponents would make of Graham's good fortune, if they knew: They would call it a most blatant bit of cronyism. And that perception would not have been discouraged by an anecdote Graham told me later that same day. As I drove him back to his house, we were talking about the U.S. 50 bypass, which had been built almost twenty years earlier but along which commercial and industrial development was still scarce. I asked Graham if he had pushed for this road, too. "Oh, yes," he said. He and David Cox were at the forefront of that effort, which for a while moved very slowly, like I-69. "Then all of a sudden the governor had the money, and they were able to put it in." Robert Orr, the governor of Indiana from 1981 until 1989, had grown up in Evansville. "He was a personal friend," Graham said. "He named the bridge over the White River after Dad."

At the western end of Washington's humble bypass, near the much-celebrated grain-processing plant, a double span of Highway 50 crossed over into Knox County. It was christened the Robert C. Graham Memorial Bridge when it opened in 1988, an event commemorated by one of the mementos in Graham's den, where I stood once again when we returned to his house. The room put the revelations of that afternoon into a certain context. There, on the walls, were the advertisement for Graham Automobiles that bragged about their prowess across the globe; the photo of Robert Graham, the Pan-American Highway promoter, sitting with R. E. Olds and Henry Ford; and the aerial shot of Robert Graham's housing development in southern Florida. A man who had lived his early life in the times and places commemorated here would not necessarily be squeamish about an overlap between the people who advocated for highways and the people who stood to profit from them.

That type of synergy, though often frowned upon, has a long and glorious history in America. Yes, the twentieth-century highways we know today were planned and financed by government, and the politicians and public servants who decide the fate of projects are expected to do so with personal disinterest. But a hundred years ago and before, the operation of our national transportation network was a largely private affair, and many corridors of commerce were developed jointly with the land along them. Captain Henry Miller Shreve, of course, started his namesake town along the river he had cleared on behalf of the American people. The great railroad companies often established new towns along their for-profit routes as well, particularly in the sparsely populated West, on land granted them by the federal government. And in the early days of the nation, a private transportation-and-land-development scheme was undertaken by a man whose name is synonymous with America itself.

George Washington, the first president and the man after whom David Graham's town was named, was into real estate. After the Revolutionary War, the general returned to his farm at Mount Vernon and, cheered on by Thomas Jefferson, started campaigning for a water highway that would connect the eastern states to the western frontier. Washington was a surveyor before he was a soldier, and so, like Graham after him, he embarked on his own route-finding expedition. He soon took the reins of the Patowmack Company, which endeavored to build a passage west to the Ohio River by way of the Potomac, along which Washington happened to own considerable land. "Nature then has declared in favor of the Potomac," Jefferson wrote to Washington in 1784, "and through that channel offers to pour into our lap the whole commerce of the Western world." Washington relinquished control of the Patowmack Company after he was elected president in 1788, and the company later fell into bankruptcy after Washington's death in 1799. As Peter Bernstein describes thoroughly in his book *Wedding of the Waters,* the Patowmack Company's private efforts were ultimately eclipsed by the state-sponsored Erie Canal. But the marriage of patriotic dreams and personal enrichment would live on.

At the turn of the last century, a man named Carl Graham Fisher (no relation to Graham or Bal Harbour partner C. T. Fisher) harnessed the self-interest of auto companies to create America's first cross-country highway. During the early days of automobiling, leaving town in a "horseless carriage" was a muddy ordeal. In 1903, three decades after the completion of the transcontinental railroad allowed coast-to-coast travel in roughly four days, it took Horatio Nelson Jackson a whopping sixty-three and a half days to make the first successful cross-country automobile trip, from San Francisco to New York. Jackson's ride was the equivalent of flying a hot-air balloon around the world or climbing Mount Everest. At the time, there were only 150 miles of paved roads, all of them city streets. Excursion driving, most believed then, was a luxury diversion for the rich and a daredevil hobby for those who liked to tinker with machines or otherwise couldn't sit still.

Carl Fisher fell into all of those categories, but he had a more catholic vision for motoring. A clever entrepreneur, a gifted pitchman, and a travel-hungry Hoosier, Fisher made his initial fortune manufacturing early headlights for automobiles and turned his bike shop in downtown Indianapolis into one of the nation's first car dealerships. Jerry M. Fisher, a cousin of Carl's, wrote a biography, *The Pacesetter*, that explains how, with an inner circle of business partners, Fisher built the Indianapolis Motor Speedway—he also drove the pace car at the first Indianapolis 500—and paid to improve a mile-and-a-half-long section of road that led to his racetrack. Fisher understood sooner than most the powerful pull of the automobile and what it could mean to the nation, and he knew that good roads were the key to it all.

In 1912, when Fisher started talking up his dream for what would become the Lincoln Highway, it was not yet conventional wisdom that road building was the task of government. There was no federal road program. But Fisher saw no reason to wait for one; he knew exactly who could pay for the first coast-to-coast highway. "The automobile industry should be willing to finance a road across the country," Fisher told his friend James Allison. "Think what it would do for the American automobile!" Around the fireplace at his home in Indianapolis and in correspondence with his friends in the industry, Fisher made his case. "Our idea is to collect one third of one percent each year for three years . . . from the gross receipts of all automobile manufacturers and dealers of automobiles and automobile sundries and accessories," Fisher wrote to Henry Ford that September, "and with these receipts, which if all manufacturers enter into this game—as it now appears they will—we will have a fund considerably in excess of $10,000,000." In addition, he wrote, the Lincoln Highway Association planned to ask all automobile owners to join as members, paying dues of five dollars or one hundred (the premium members would receive a Lincoln Highway button).

"I am of the opinion that the automobile people can build and present . . . this road without any outside assistance, and [it] can be handled by the large automobile men in the same way they handle their business affairs, and the road will be finished and pushed thru without delay," he wrote to Ford. "If we attempt to mix up with government appropriations or if politics is allowed in any way to creep into the proposition, there will be numerous delays and wrangles and possibly graft." The privately funded Lincoln Highway Association would be able to "make very splendid terms with a great many states," Fisher predicted, because there would be such intense competition to be on the route.

His logic was unabashed: The auto industry had the means to make the road a reality, and they stood to gain the most from enabling people to drive. Just four days after his letter to Ford, Fisher hosted a kickoff dinner in Indianapolis and he implored those present, "Let's build it, before we're too old to enjoy it." The group pledged a total of three hundred thousand dollars that night. Frank Seiberling, president of the Goodyear Tire and Rubber Company, soon contributed another three hundred thousand. Within a month, a million dollars was pledged. Henry Bourne Joy, of Packard, gave money and became president of the association. And they indeed made splendid terms with a great many states. Utah and Wyoming promised to pay for road work if the highway went through their territory. The Colorado legislature took out a $1.5 million bond to help pay for their section after businessmen in Salt Lake City promised to raise the same amount. Telegrams and dignitaries from western states flooded the association's office, begging for inclusion, and a few towns even built miles of improved road out into the countryside in the hopes that their speculative roads might provide an obvious path for the Lincoln Highway.

But Ford held out. James Couzens, secretary-treasurer of the Ford Motor Company, wrote Fisher a letter notifying him that the company's board of directors had voted unanimously to decline his invitation. There were several reasons, Couzens wrote, "principal among them being that we do not believe in building roads by private subscription, and secondly we believe that it is better to spend our money in making the price of the cars low, as this will have the beneficial effect of putting more cars into use, and the more cars there are in use, the greater demand there will be for the government building Good Roads."

Ford's contributions to the democratization of driving are now legendary, and the philosophical line in the sand that the company's board drew in answering Fisher would soon become a high wall: The auto industry would not stay in the road-building business long, and the federal government soon would enter it. In 1916, Congress would pass the first Federal-Aid Highway Act, and the Lincoln Highway's completion, like I-69's, would depend on whatever money trickled down to the states through that bill and its successors.

As the momentum shifted toward government sponsorship of roads, Fisher started promoting a second grand project, the Dixie Highway. In 1914, he convinced Indiana governor Samuel Ralston to convene a meeting of governors from Illinois, Kentucky, Ohio, Tennessee, Georgia, and Florida. Fisher's dream this time? To construct a great highway that would unite the north and the south. Not coincidentally, it would also provide convenient travel from the industrial centers of Detroit, Indianapolis, and Chicago to the southern tip of Florida, where Fisher was busy developing Miami Beach.

Fisher first visited Miami by railroad in the winter of 1910 with his wife, Jane, and he became enchanted with the place. He bought a house and soon acquired two hundred acres of beachfront property from John Collins, a septuagenarian farmer who had started building a wooden bridge across Biscayne Bay but couldn't afford to finish it. Fisher could. In 1912, he financed the completion of Collins's bridge in exchange for a piece of the overgrown strip of sand and swamp on the other side. Today this would be lampooned as a "bridge to nowhere," and back then Jane thought her husband was crazy. In her biography of him, *Fabulous Hoosier*, she tells of a day when the two stood on the muddy, mosquito-covered beach while Fisher sketched out his plans in the sand. "Look, honey, I'm going to build a city here," he told her, "a city like magic, like romantic places you read and dream about, but never see."

Fisher's word was good. He bought more land, dredged sand to fill in the lowlands, cut down mangrove jungles, and erected grand hotels. His Miami Beach properties were sold and resold in an accelerating boom, and for Fisher's northern industrialist friends and many others the city became a winter playground, a place of polo ponies and boat races. The Collins Bridge brought people to his resort from the train station in Miami, and the Dixie Highway carried drivers from the north. Fisher would lose most of his fortune in the late twenties after a devastating hurricane in 1926, the stock crash of 1929, and an expensive attempt to develop a resort in Montauk, New York, but by then the things he had built no longer depended on his frenetic participation. In Miami Beach today a strange little monument with a bust of Fisher stands at the corner of Fiftieth Street and Alton Road. CARL GRAHAM FISHER, an inscription reads. HE CARVED A GREAT CITY OUT OF A JUNGLE.

Robert and David Graham made themselves heirs to Carl Fisher's bold lifework. Whether knowingly or not, their respective efforts to promote the Pan-American Highway and I-69 followed in the footsteps of Fisher's Dixie Highway Association: In all three cases groups of states or nations worked idiosyncratically toward their stated altruistic purpose, reporting to each other at annual meetings and through periodic newsletters. After the Great Miami Hurricane of 1926 punched back the Florida real estate bubble, Robert Graham and his partners bought their own chunk of land at the northern end of the same sandy strip that Fisher had made viable. Although the Bal Harbour development languished until after World War II, Robert Graham spent his winters there, and his young son David grew up in the afterglow of Fisher's grand imagination.

Standing with David Graham in his den, I asked him if he had ever met Carl Fisher, who died in 1938, when Graham was eleven. "No," he said. "But my father knew him. In fact, my father bought one of the houses that Carl Fisher had built himself down there. That's where I was born. I was baptized in Carl Fisher's old polo-pony stables, which they had turned into a little Catholic church." I expressed some surprised delight at this coincidence, and Graham walked me through a side room with a wet bar to show me a small framed picture hanging in a hallway. It was an old photograph, faded, of a group of children dressed in light-colored clothes, riding in a basket atop an elephant. "That's Rosie. In those days they didn't have many bulldozers. So they had to use elephants." Rosie, he explained, belonged to Fisher. She was a mascot for Miami Beach and a regular prop in publicity pictures, including one in which she posed as a golf caddy for President Warren G. Harding. "Carl Fisher sent his elephant to my birthday party! That's me right there." He beamed.

I had seen elephants everywhere in Graham's home: stuffed elephants on the floor outside a bedroom. Ceramic elephants placed delicately on a shelf. Tiny stone elephants on an old wooden desk by the door. I had assumed these were Republican Party mascots, but no. They were a childhood totem. They reminded Graham of his Depression-era childhood spent in Carl Fisher's ocean-side dreamworld.

What an amazing place to grow up, I said.

"In grammar school down there, we had a club that would cut off the end of a conch shell and blow it like a bugle," he told me, as if he was remembering it fresh. "It was a spooky noise. That was the sign for our club. We used to go plant coconuts. I helped plant the first coconut trees out there. About half of them sprouted. Sometimes you wouldn't have to bury them. Sometimes we'd dig a little hole and put them in." He paused. "That's just one of those things that people don't realize was done."

A lot of people don't know about all the things Carl Fisher did, I said—the Indianapolis Motor Speedway, the Lincoln and Dixie highways, Miami Beach.

Graham raised his eyebrows. "Those are the kind of people that build America," he answered sharply. "And if we don't have a lot more of those people, we're going to be passed up, by China or somebody."

The kind of people that build America. Carl Fisher had dreamed up the earliest national highways and carved a great city out of a jungle. Robert Graham had advanced the cause of the Pan-American Highway and built a beautiful town on a sandbar. It remained to be seen what would come of the road David Graham had worked to build, or what new developments might rise up from the cornfields of Indiana at his family's interchange. But that ground that Graham wanted so badly to break was the same terrain that the Tokarskis and other opponents were struggling to save. This wasn't the twenties anymore. Or the fifties. No one could say for sure whether I-69 would be built at all. Or whether David Graham would live long enough to see it.

III

Down South

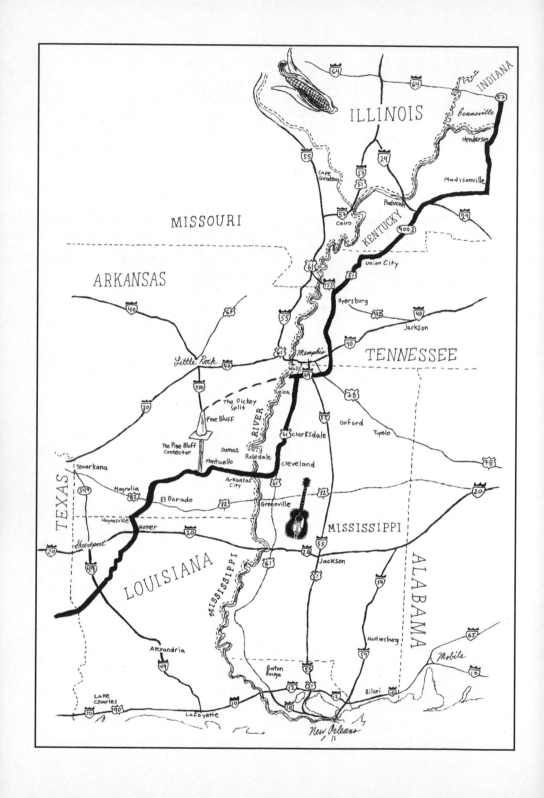

The Scenic Route

When David Graham and James Newland would journey south for their Mid-Continent Highway Coalition meetings at the Peabody Hotel, they got a taste of a simpler world. Simpler for highway proponents, anyway. On the other side of the Ohio River, they didn't see any yard signs demanding that I-69 be stopped. No one compared the highway to a man-made natural disaster. No one wrote protest songs. In short, there were no Tokarskis or John Smiths stirring up doubts. Sure, there were farmers unhappy about losing their land, but in the South the main disagreements were between counties and states that *wanted* I-69 and were jockeying for a spot along it.

At the Peabody powwows in Memphis, Graham and Newland would report on the troubles back home and do their best to assure their counterparts from other states that the Hoosier hostility would be overcome. From Kentucky on south, the highway plans brought no such resistance, and the other coalition members were perplexed by the news that so many in Indiana opposed I-69. They shared Graham's reverence for do-it-yourself America building and saw themselves as carrying on that great tradition. Geraldine "Gerry" Montgomery, who was mayor of Paducah at the time of the first meeting in 1992, first heard about I-69 from John Caruthers, who called to invite her to Memphis. "I thought it was great that citizens had stepped up to the plate," she said. "I believe that's how our country started to begin with. And we ought to be out there, looking for ways we can make our area, our country, better."

Montgomery had me to her home, just outside of town near the Paducah Country Club, where she lives with her husband, Wally, a retired surgeon and bank director. Except for philanthropy and various board positions they are retired, but she met me at the front door looking as if she might have just come from an office, or church—she wore a blue pantsuit and jewelry, and her short feathered blond hair was done to perfection. We sat down in a well-appointed room off the foyer and we talked about simpler times: Montgomery, who is seventy-two, remembers when you couldn't drive from the river-port town of Paducah to the middle part of the state without the assistance of a boat. "We had the Tennessee and Ohio rivers right here. We had a lot of barge traffic," she said. "But when the car came into the picture, the only way to cross the Tennessee River was in a ferry."

The southwestern nub of the state, between the Mississippi and Tennessee rivers, was not, like the rest of Kentucky, part of the Louisiana Purchase. It was acquired later, under President Andrew Jackson, and the "Jackson Purchase" region around Paducah still suffers from a bit of a stepchild complex. "As mayor, I used to kid and say the message hadn't gotten to Frankfort that we're part of the state," Montgomery said. Connectivity was one of her major issues. By the time Caruthers informed her of the NAFTA highway plans, she had already been pushing for another new highway near Paducah: a proposed stretch of Interstate 66 that was designated as High Priority Corridor 3 by ISTEA, the same federal legislation that included I-69's Corridors 18 and 20. "I was very interested in roads. In today's world, that is the way we're doing things," she said. "Paducah was a big railroad town, but the railroads are not what they were. These days, you gotta have roads."

Montgomery eventually became the I-69 coalition's vice president for Kentucky, and she was always puzzled to hear of the growing dissent in Indiana. "Nobody feels that way here," she said, "or at least it was never more than a very small segment of the population." There was comparatively little to quarrel over in Kentucky, though. In 1999, Governor Paul Patton approved a plan to fashion I-69 by upgrading existing highways. Interstate 69 will cross the Ohio River on a new bridge from Evansville to Henderson, Kentucky, take over the Pennyrile Parkway for forty-five miles south, then make a hard right turn onto the Western Kentucky Parkway, which it will supplant for thirty-five miles until it feeds into Interstate 24. It will share I-24 for a fifteen-mile stretch, then curve left and piggyback on the Purchase Parkway for fifty miles down to the Tennessee border. This isn't a very straight line, but by not cutting any new swaths, the Bluegrass State has saved hundreds of millions of dollars and avoided any potential strife over environmental destruction or eminent domain.

To many in Indiana, Kentucky's approach seemed deliciously wise and conservative—using the existing right-of-way was exactly the kind of "common-sense" approach that the Tokarskis and other new-terrain opponents had been advocating up north. But this path of least resistance was available to the people of Kentucky only because they had done the hard work of building their own state parkways back in the late fifties and sixties, when ambitious construction was more in vogue and there was no National Environmental Policy Act to contend with.

The map of what became the interstate highway system was first drawn in 1944 by the National Interregional Highway Committee. Its objective was to connect the nation's major cities, not necessarily its rural regions, many of which felt snubbed. In Kentucky, as in southern Indiana, no interstates were initially planned west of I-65. (I-24 through Paducah was added later to better connect Nashville to Saint Louis.) But while Indiana hemmed and hawed and repeatedly balked on building its own highway to Evansville, the state of Kentucky implemented an aggressive program of statewide toll roads almost immediately. In 1956, after Eisenhower signed the bill initiating the interstate program, voters in Kentucky approved a state bond measure to fund new roads of their own—on the promise that the tolls would be removed once the debt was paid off. The state went to work constructing 650 miles of modern connections that the federal government hadn't seen fit to provide.

If Kentucky was going to build these roads itself, why not make them special? With marketing in mind, the state's highway department eschewed the word *turnpike* in favor of the more poetic *parkway*. They laid out the highways to connect state-owned outdoor attractions such as Kentucky Lake, a body of water formed by the dammed Kentucky River. In conjunction with the parkway effort, the Tennessee Valley Authority also built a dam on the Cumberland River, just to the east, and used eminent domain to clear the residents from the "Land Between the Lakes," now a national recreation area.

Local residents were bitter about the condemnation of private property, and there were critics throughout the state who predicted that the new toll roads would never pay for themselves. But not long after the first two parkways opened, in 1963, their traffic counts exceeded expectations. Governor Edward T. Breathitt, who oversaw these statewide construction efforts (and after whom the Pennyrile Parkway was renamed in 2000), spoke triumphantly to a conference of highway builders in March 1964, near the end of his term. "Kentucky has at last become respectable in the matters of highways offered to the driving public and no longer suffers under the onus of being a detour state," he told the attendees. Kentucky's bold efforts had been vindicated, he asserted, and must continue. "If we had waited then until we got the money through taxes, we would still be driving on highways that were not adequate ten or even twenty years ago." The state's citizens and tourists bought their mobility with a slow avalanche of their hard-earned change. Kentucky paid off its construction-bond debt by the early nineties and removed the parkways' tolls as promised.

But impressive as they are, Kentucky's parkways are not *interstates.* Sure, they are four-lane, divided, limited-access highways. But the state's landscape architects specifically designed the parkways to be quainter, to conform more closely to the state's natural terrain. They feel different from interstates. They tread lighter across the ground, and billboards are refreshingly rare. Exits tend to be more discreet, tucked away in patches of trees and uncluttered by chain stores and gas stations. Touring the parkways, I could imagine a slightly different America, where major highways were more modest—just as fast but not so monstrously utilitarian. It was kind of nice. It felt more as if I was driving *through* places rather than past them. But to an engineer, and perhaps to a trucker, the Kentucky parkways are junior varsity. By interstate standards, the medians are too narrow, some hills are too steep, overpass clearances are too low, and the exits are too sudden and their curves too tight—they were engineered for cars pulling slowly through tollbooths. All these shortcomings will have to be remedied, at considerable expense, before the old parkways can be consecrated as I-69.

As far as Gerry Montgomery is concerned, those upgrades can't come soon enough. The parkways "did a good job of connecting point A to point B," she told me, but they came up short economically. Their bucolic character was a strength but also a weakness. "The parkways went mostly to rural areas. That's the way they were built," she said. "So there's not as much development along them." Kentucky parkways have often appeared on maps in a hue different from that of interstates, colored as toll roads (when they were tolled) or as state or scenic routes. To many companies looking for a place to plop down and hire, these subtleties matter.

And so there was great fanfare in 2006 when President George W. Bush signed a bill that included language officially designating the parkway route through Kentucky as the "Future I-69 Corridor." Governor

Ernie Fletcher unveiled reflective road signs to that effect, green and white with the highway shield glorious, and declared that these would be erected along the appropriate parkway routes. Exactly when that "future" would come, no one could say. It will cost Kentucky between one and two billion dollars to upgrade the parkways and pay for its share of the new bridge over the Ohio River. The state transportation secretary at the time, Bill Nighbert, told the Henderson *Gleaner* that the work might need to be spread out over twenty years, and Montgomery predicts that tolls may once again be needed in the end. But the long-suffering local economic-development directors were already heralding the end of parkway mediocrity. The mere presence of the FUTURE I-69 CORRIDOR signs, they told journalists, would improve their chances of attracting industry and jobs to the region.

Of course, Interstate 69 could have a few negative repercussions as well, as Gerry Montgomery knows. Much of her energy as a public official was spent advocating for new highways, but an equal or greater portion was spent dealing with the unintended consequences of earlier ones. When Interstate 24 opened through western Kentucky, in the late 1970s, it had a profound effect on her small city. "I-24 killed downtown Paducah," she told me flatly. "All the businesses went out to the mall, and by the early eighties there wasn't anyone living downtown. It was a ghost town. A war zone." When the concrete river of Interstate 24 came along, Paducah turned its back on the waterways that birthed it. Historic buildings were abandoned. Drugs and crime grew rampant, and the older neighborhoods along the banks of the Ohio were left to disintegrate. "But that doesn't mean you can't bring it back," Montgomery was quick to add. "You just gotta work hard to make it happen."

Before she became mayor, Montgomery was a city commissioner, and in 1986 she led Paducah through a "visioning process" in which citizens were asked to ponder how their town should evolve over the next twenty years. "People at that point thought there was no hope to get a job here," Montgomery said, and so the survey questions were phrased pragmatically. "Maybe they had moved away and were coming back to retire, and what would they like to see here? One thing we heard was we should bring downtown back, make people aware of the river."

When Montgomery became mayor in 1988, she made a habit of taking monthly trips to Frankfort to remind state officials about the needs of Paducah. She went after state and federal community-development money and got it. She hired consultants and courted tourism and business. She encouraged a private effort to build a new quilting museum, which opened in 1991 and has remained an anchor of the revitalized downtown. The faraway year that Montgomery had invited citizens to envision, 2006, has passed, as have Montgomery's two terms as mayor. Paducah seems a better place now; it has embraced its past and its river. A new waterfront promenade stretches along the flood wall, which is painted for several blocks with murals celebrating the city's history—the first Chickasaw Indian settlements, the first white settlements, the steamboat-and-barge heyday, the Illinois Central railroad depot, and the "Atomic City" boom that came with the construction of a U.S. Department of Energy uranium-enrichment facility in 1951. A new performing-arts center has opened nearby, and on the main street of Broadway many of the old three-story buildings have been renovated. Upstairs condos and lofts and street-level restaurants and shops now mingle with still-empty storefronts and threadbare antiques stores.

Lowertown, Paducah's oldest neighborhood, is a few blocks away. It devolved into a slum by the early 1980s—three quarters of the housing was rental, the buildings were dilapidated, and drugs were rampant. But the once-distressed historic district is now teeming with sculptors, painters, photographers, and metalworkers who were recruited to colonize the neighborhood as part of the inventive Artist Relocation Program. In 2000, the city started buying abandoned and underutilized properties, and a local bank agreed to give preferential loans to artists who were willing to fix them up, live in them, work in them, and devote ground-floor space to a public gallery. Today more than seventy artists have set up shop in the LowerTown Arts District, and the neighborhood, while still in transition, has clearly crossed the line from frightening to funky.

The Artist Relocation Program is the work of the current mayor, Bill Paxton, who worked in commercial lending at a local bank for thirty years before running for city commissioner and then mayor. Paxton left banking for government because "the business was not as fun. Large banks were coming in and buying the smaller ones." With consolidations came changes. The big guys at headquarters were calling the shots about who got loans, Paxton said, and he could no longer make decisions based on personal relationships and his own judgment. "My passion is economic development," he told me a couple of years ago in his City Hall office, the decor of which suggests that his other passions include basketball and golf. "And I've found local politics is very rewarding. You can make a lot of things happen. It's really where the rubber meets the road."

Paxton serves as Montgomery's successor on the I-69 Midwest Highway Coalition's executive committee. Interstate 69 is an important project, he told me, and the state did the right thing in choosing a relatively inexpensive plan. He would be happy to see I-69 built as a toll road through Kentucky, but he doubted there was adequate political will to make anything happen quickly. "We're probably a long way off, quite honestly," he said. "And because we're in western Kentucky, there's not the urgency there should be." While he waits, he plans to continue Montgomery's other work, closer to home.

"Without a strong downtown, you don't have a strong heart and consequently don't have a strong community," he said. "I'm interested in revitalizing even more inner-city neighborhoods." There are only so many artists a city can lure, of course, but the mayor has another demographic in mind. "I think a big part of our growth over the next twenty years will be from the baby-boomer generation retiring," Paxton, a baby boomer himself, told me. This was in interesting contrast with Indiana, where people like Paxton seem most obsessed with winning back young people. "A lot of them are gonna want to come where there's a good quality of life, good health care, and affordable housing. And that's why we're working on these inner-city neighborhoods now. To get them ready for the baby boomers."

A Company Town

Bill Revell knows a thing or two about local politics. He was the mayor of Dyersburg, Tennessee, for twenty-six years—a state record for political longevity, he will tell you. That quarter century was a hard one for most agricultural and manufacturing towns like Dyersburg, but Revell had uncommon success. He shepherded in a dozen new industries and transformed a budget deficit into a surplus. And while places like Evansville and Paducah were battling population decline, Revell presided over two decades of steady growth. In 2008, *Southern Business and Development* magazine named Dyersburg number four in its list of "Ten Small Towns in the South That Deserve a Second Look" (number five was Paducah). The writers cited its geographically central location, its plethora of factories, and the fact that it's so accessible—by a major freight rail line, air facilities, the Mississippi River, Amtrak, and interstate highways.

You could say that Dyersburg has always had the best of two worlds when it came to transportation. Though not directly on the Mississippi River, the town rose up as a steamboat hub on the Forked Deer River tributary. Similarly, its place on the interstate system today comes thanks to Interstate 155, a highway spur that reaches into Tennessee from Missouri like a giant arm across the Mississippi (creating the only river crossing south of Cairo, Illinois, and north of Memphis). Twenty-five miles west of Dyersburg, this spur connects to I-55, but a particularly rural stretch of it, and to the northwest, I-155 peters out before it gets to the border of Kentucky. Dyersburg, then, sits on a byway of the interstate system. Its seventeen-thousand-some residents live an hour's drive from Jackson, Tennessee, and two hours from Memphis, but for now at least both connections are by four-lane U.S. highways (U.S. 51 and U.S. 412). As a result, it doesn't feel as though Dyersburg is in the orbit of either city. It's a big small town, connected but independent, solitary but not stranded. It might eventually benefit from I-69, but it doesn't seem to be suffering from its absence.

When I first visited Dyersburg, in the spring of 2007, Revell had just recently lost his bid for a tenth term. "My time was up," he told me. "I shouldn't have run this last time. Everyone was saying my wife has Alzheimer's and I needed to be with her. And they talked about my age. Those were the two things that hurt me." Revell was a spry seventy-seven years old. He was cheerful, stocky but fit (he runs a few miles each morning), with dark gray hair that was perfectly in place and parted severely. His reign as mayor had been over for months, but he wore a suit and tie as though he might not be comfortable in public wearing anything less. His enduring popularity was evident. We met for lunch at a restaurant on the Dyer County courthouse square, and our comfort-food meal was interrupted every few minutes by well-wishing townspeople who offered Revell small pieces of personal gossip and encouragement. To each of them Revell introduced me and explained my purpose there. He was being courteous, but his verbal emphases made it clear that he welcomed any chance to remind people about Interstate 69.

Revell has been pushing for the highway for eighteen years, since that first meeting at the Peabody, and he serves now as the Tennessee chairman for the I-69 Mid-Continent Highway Coalition, a position for which he has no rival. Having been stripped of his mayoral responsibilities, he told me, he planned to devote most of his time to advancing the highway. To support him in that mission, the Dyer County school board had given him an e-mail address and an office in its downtown headquarters, and that is where Revell and I drove after lunch. A metal I-69 highway sign hung on the beige-painted concrete-block wall behind his desk, detailed route maps covered another, and a tall file cabinet full of records sat in one corner. In many ways, Revell's work for the coalition resembles political campaigning. He sends letters to the local newspaper and makes his case in any public meetings that arise. At a meeting down in Millington, Tennessee, Revell had to fend off two large men who were unhappy about the highway plans. "One fella was six foot four and drunk and screaming and hollering. And they had to get the police to get him off me," Revell said. "I thought he was gonna hit me."

But such incidents are rare. Most of Revell's time is spent among supporters, fund-raising. He visits the mayors and county commissioners and civic clubs up and down the western edge of Tennessee, briefs them on the slow-motion march toward construction, and reminds them of the great benefits he predicts will come from construction. Then he asks them to take out their checkbooks so he can keep the whole thing going for another year. "I raise more money than any of the other states," he said. "Because I work at it. I send letters. I'm gonna be talking to thirty groups this month. That's my goal."

Revell let on that some of the other states didn't always pull their weight when it came to funding the coalition. He took a few stapled spreadsheets from one of his file cabinet's drawers—budgets for the Mid-Continent Highway Coalition—to show me how vital his work was to the survival of its collective effort. In 2004, one document showed, the coalition raised $344,600. Of that, the Tennessee contingent kicked in $152,000, thanks to a $100,000-contribution from the state government that bailed the coalition out of debt and allowed it to pay an overdue bill from its lobbyist, Patton Boggs. Tennessee once again outcontributed the other states in 2006. According to that year's budget, Revell collected $65,000, of which $37,000 came from the publicly funded Memphis Regional Chamber. Most of the rest came from other city and county governments and chambers, but Revell had also collected almost $8,000 that year from local businesses. The pages listed receipts from companies like Security Bancorp, First Citizens National Bank, the local Ford Construction (which does paving and bridge building), Komatsu (hydraulic excavators and dump trucks), Millington Telephone Company, and Marvin Windows & Doors. The only state that rivaled Tennessee in private contributions to the I-69 coalition that year was Indiana, where $4,569 came in from businesses that are, or once were, run by the Graham family.

Like other members of the Mid-Continent Highway Coalition, Revell was working for free. Most of his income, he told me, came from cotton; Revell owns a decent-size piece of land west of town that he rents out to farmers. The parcel has been in his family since before the Civil War. His great-grandfather, who fought for the Confederate army, is buried in a small cemetery just off Revell Road, which cuts through a handful of lots on subdivided acreage close to town. I asked whether I-69 would affect any of his land. "Oh, no," he said. "Over the years people have offered to sell me land near the interchange, but I wouldn't touch that with a ten-foot pole! I've got a good name, and I don't want to spoil it."

Revell boasts about Dyersburg's farming heritage—"We're the number one row-crop county in the state of Tennessee," he told me—but actually, working the land lost its allure for the Revells a few generations ago. By the time Revell was born, in 1930, his father had moved up to Michigan to work for General Motors. "He couldn't get a job here," Revell explained. "I grew up my first seven years in Flint. Then Dad was transferred to Buffalo to open up a new plant over there." The family moved back to Dyersburg in 1946, but when Revell graduated from high school, he returned to his childhood homes up north. "I went to General Motors Institute in Flint, and did my co-op work in Buffalo during school," he said. "They taught me how to operate a dealership." Before his quarter century as mayor, Revell spent twenty years operating a string of new and used GM car lots in northwestern Tennessee. His timing couldn't have been better: He opened his first dealership, for GMC trucks, in 1956, the same year that President Dwight Eisenhower signed the bill authorizing the interstate highway system.

Revell understands that his early career path is not one that would be attractive, or even possible, today. For one, the General Motors Institute is now Kettering University, detached from its corporate past. But more important, General Motors itself is still emerging from a devastating meltdown. As it headed into bankruptcy in 2009, the company announced that it would be cutting back to 38,000 union workers, less than a tenth of the 395,000 it employed at its peak in 1970. The number of GM factories would be cut to 34, down from a high of 150 in 1970, and nearly half of its dealerships would be closed. This reorganization and the decades of troubles and off-shoring that preceded it have left dozens of small towns reeling—many of them along the existing I-69 corridor in Michigan and northern Indiana, including the birthplace of GM. "Flint is the most depressed city in the United States," Revell reckoned. "I haven't been there in years, and I don't care about going. It's gone."

Later, I visited Flint, which is indeed a shell of its former self. I saw the vast Buick City, once an American manufacturing marvel with its own neighborhoods of worker housing, now the largest brownfield site in the country. There were empty houses everywhere, houses the city was selling for a dollar each, empty buildings downtown where an iron archway over the main drag of Saginaw Street still says VEHICLE CITY. Flint had a head start on building carriages thanks to the preponderance of pine in Michigan. The timber was harvested, cut, and fashioned into horse-drawn buggies in the nineteenth century. When gasoline engines replaced horses, the factories in Flint adapted gracefully and began producing automobiles. Today, one hundred years after the founding of General Motors, it's time to repurpose that manufacturing power yet again. In October 2009,

GM announced it would spend $230 million overhauling its four factories in Flint to produce the electric Chevy Volt and the crossover Chevy Cruze.

I toured the Flint assembly plant in August 2007, when they were still making enormous trucks and SUVs, the kinds of cars that let you kiss the clean new hood without bending over. Flint Assembly has made big, tough vehicles for years, including the blue diesel Chevy Suburban that David Graham drove on his I-69 barnstorming tour. In the plant visitors' lot I saw signs that said GM PRODUCT PARKING ONLY, which I took to be corny humor along the lines of DETROIT TIGERS FAN PARKING ONLY. But when I checked in at the front desk for the tour, the guard there asked what kind of car I was driving. Luckily, it was a Chevy, or I would have had to move it to another lot. They had gotten sick of seeing vendors park Toyotas and Hondas right outside their front door, the tour guide explained. So they decided to fix things not by making better cars but by punishing visitors who had chosen other makes. Flint Assembly was my second auto-plant tour. I had also been to the much-discussed Toyota plant in Princeton, Indiana, where I was asked to wear a helmet, shop glasses, and steel-toed boots. At Flint Assembly, we wore clip-on badges. Toyota was newer, cleaner, more automated. At Flint Assembly, the men and women on the line listened to classic rock, the blue-collar soundtrack of better times.

Dyersburg has fared much better, but it does share one unfortunate trait with Flint—its most significant job loss came at the hands of the very company that put the town on the map. After our talk in his I-69 office, Revell gave me a driving tour of the town. He wanted to show me, among other things, Dyersburg Fabrics, an old abandoned textile mill that was built in 1929, the year before Revell was born in Flint. R. H. Wheeler took over the mill in 1932 and kept it alive during the Great Depression. Wheeler's commitment to the town was strong. "This is still called Milltown," Revell said as we drove slowly down Wheeler Street past a neighborhood adjacent to the factory. "Mr. Wheeler built all of these houses for his workers to live in. These little houses. And they go for block after block after block."

Wheeler sold the company to a New York private-equity firm in 1987 and died a few years later. Through the nineties, Dyersburg Fabrics struggled to compete with lower-wage factories overseas, and six or seven years ago the mill closed. Revell stopped the car on the empty street in front of a mammoth brick building. A few months later, in July 2007, the empty factory would burn down in an extraordinary three-alarm blaze that was visible for miles. But out Revell's windshield, the old mill still stood, surrounded by a chicken-wire fence, its windows boarded up. "They made material for a lot of things," Revell said wistfully. "They had about twelve hundred employees. But they couldn't compete with China and Mexico." Since the closing of the factory, he said, Milltown "has been run down pretty bad." The area now saw a lot of crime and drugs. "We lost something when we lost Dyersburg Fabrics."

A factory closing is the kind of thing that can keep a mayor up at night. But, luckily, Revell had a lot more to show me. We drove over to the city's newer industrial area, where Revell's refrain was "All of that's been built since I became mayor." He showed me the Heckethorn factory, where they make welded exhaust system parts, Colonial Diversified Polymer Products, which makes custom plastics and compounds for Goodyear, and ERMCO, which makes electrical transformers. "We kept expanding our industrial park," Revell said. He pointed out a speculative building that the town built in order to entice a company to occupy it. "You take a chance on getting industry. And it works! We already landed a new industry in it. NSK. It's a Japanese company, the world's largest steering-column manufacturer.

"And we have Caterpillar, of course," Revell said, referring to the manufacturer of earthmoving and road-building equipment. One of Revell's favorite parables, which he told me as we drove past the plant, involves a bittersweet announcement that Caterpillar made a few years ago. "They called us out there, and I thought they were going to tell us they were gonna close the plant. But they said, 'We've got good news for you, but bad news for a lot of the country. We're moving a lot of our plants offshore, but we're going to keep the Dyersburg plant open,'" Revell said. "And they had two big reasons. The first was workforce—people here have a good work ethic—and the other one was I-69."

Revell tells another good story about a company that some years back decided to make Dyersburg its home after a representative came to town incognito. "It was World Color Press and they had the main office in Effingham, Illinois," he said. "And when the guy came here, he didn't come to the mayor. He didn't come to the chamber of commerce. He went to a hotel, put on a pair of overalls, and called a cab to come and get him." Revell giggled. "And he went around town in a pair of overalls and talked to individuals and found out what they thought about the town. And that's the way he decided to come."

I asked what other reasons companies gave Revell for locating in Dyersburg. "Well," he said, hesitating, "a lot of them, to get away from— I got to be careful how I say this. You gotta be *real* careful." I sensed where he was going. Is Tennessee a union state? I asked. "No," he said, "it's a right-to-work state. And we don't have a single union in Dyersburg, not one. That's the reason a lot of them have moved here."

The commercial climate in Dyersburg is such that even Revell is tempted to try his hand again at entrepreneurship. "Even though I'm seventy-seven years old, I still wanna go back in business," he told me. "I was looking at that Smoothie King. You ever had any Smoothie King? They have more than five hundred stores in the United States. They mix the formula for whatever need a person might have. If they have a joint problem, you can buy a smoothie for that. You wanna lose weight? Gain weight? Whatever you want. But I would have to find somebody to run it, because I don't want to do that."

Revell spoke so enthusiastically about opening a franchise that I asked him why he ever left his GM dealerships for politics. I wasn't expecting the answer he gave. He turned to me with his eyebrows raised. "The Lord called me," he said.

It was in 1978. Revell and his wife, who are Methodists, were at a retreat at Oral Roberts University in Tulsa, Oklahoma. He felt happy there and didn't want to leave. "But the Lord spoke to me when I was in the restroom," Revell told me. "In that still, small voice, he said eleven words: 'Go back home. I'm gonna use you where you are.'" The Lord had never spoken to Revell before. He took the command quite seriously. "And one night, after I decided to run, the Lord gave me a vision of what would happen in Dyersburg. I stayed up and I wrote. He gave me—I looked at Dyersburg from the north, the south, the east, and the west. And the Lord said, You'll see a new road coming from Dyersburg to Jackson." U.S. 412 was upgraded after Revell took office. "And you'll see industry in the northern part of the city—he showed me that industrial park!"

That's incredible, I said. Has the Lord ever mentioned Interstate 69?

"No," he said.

But Revell's faith in the interstate and its eventual construction is unwavering, even after the long purgatory he and his fellow advocates have endured. "I thought it would take ten years. I was badly mistaken," he told me. "We started, really, from scratch. And I'm just not the kind of fellow that wants to throw in the towel. I've been at it so long that I— I wanna keep going. I may live to see it built if I live as long as my mother did. She lived to be a hundred."

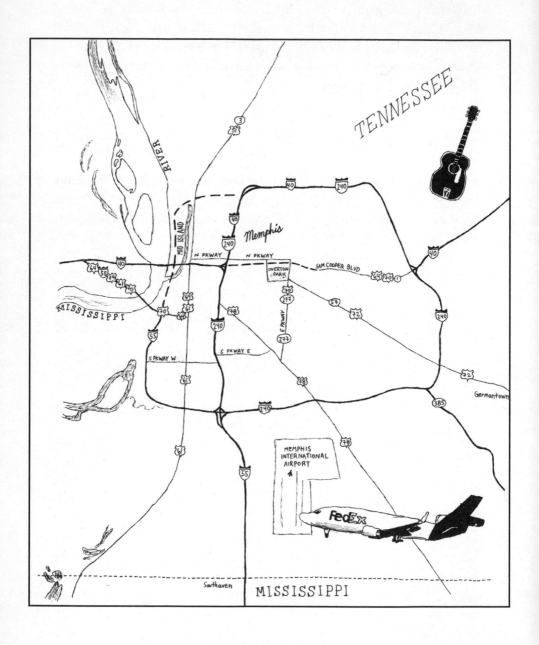

Best-Laid Plans

From the sculpture garden of the National Ornamental Metal Museum, on a high bluff just south of downtown Memphis, you can stand in the early evening and watch the hustle and bustle of America: A steady stream of FedEx planes descends from the sky, barges steer through a wide bend of the Mississippi River, and freight trains and interstate traffic hum across steel bridges to and from Arkansas. The city has been a center of trade since its birth. Memphis was founded in 1819 as a real estate speculation by three men: John Overton, who bought the five thousand acres on which it sat; Andrew Jackson, who had just negotiated a treaty with the Chickasaw Indians that gave Western Tennessee to the United States; and James Winchester, who had served with Jackson in the War of 1812's Battle of New Orleans. The town's big selling points were its web of Indian trails and its high ground along the great water highway, and in its first half century Memphis served as a hub for the cotton trade, the slave trade, the underground railroad, and the occupying Union army. Today, in addition to its port, Memphis boasts interstates and railroads stretching out in all four cardinal directions, plus the FedEx mothership, which has made Memphis International Airport one of the busiest cargo hubs in the world.

And yet somehow, despite all this movement, Memphis holds steady. Through both careful preservation and neglect (artful or otherwise), the town has developed a patina that is quintessentially Southern and distinctly Memphian. It is hot and humid; the pace is languid. You can still smoke in the bars—many do—and the city's jukeboxes tend to play vintage tunes that match the ubiquitous old furniture. Greasy food is celebrated; old cars are plentiful. One encounters everywhere tacky rooms and sunny afternoons that resemble classic William Eggleston photographs. To say that the city wears its history on its sleeve doesn't quite do it. Memphis wears its past like long underwear—a thin film that covers and underlies almost everything. Much Americana was born here—the self-service grocery store, Beale Street blues, early rock'n'roll at Sun Studios, Holiday Inn—and iconic men died here: Martin Luther King Jr. at the Lorraine Motel, Elvis Presley at Graceland. Every few years another book is written about the fertile stretch of space-time that was Memphis in the twentieth century, and every few minutes another tourist arrives to take it all in—the glory, the pain, the saucy pork barbecue.

Although the metropolitan area, which includes parts of Mississippi and Arkansas, weighs in with a population around 1.3 million, with 700,000 living inside the city limits, Memphis feels a lot like a small town. Residents tend to be of the sort who enjoy conversing at length with strangers, and a visitor who stumbles across the right people might get the impression that the normal six degrees of separation have been whittled, in Memphis, to two. You feel this acutely at the Little Tea Shop, on Monroe Avenue downtown, where lawyers, lawmakers, architects, journalists, and other Memphians of minor or major influence eat lunch. Suhair Lauck took over the business with her husband, Jimmy, in 1982, when downtown was near its low point, and the Laucks' loyalty to the neighborhood has been rewarded. Their devoted regulars include both the city and the county mayors (Memphis has a convoluted government structure, to put it mildly). But only one patron has his own table reserved: an attorney named Charles Newman, who has been eating at the tea shop almost every day for forty-seven years. When he sits down, the waitstaff, without any further cue, bring him his plate of fruit, cottage cheese, and corn bread and two glasses of iced tea.

Newman wasn't there the day I first wandered into the Little Tea Shop several years ago, but we were soon introduced. After a very satisfying lunch, I struck up a polite conversation at the cash register with Suhair, who asked what brought me to Memphis. I told her I was writing about Interstate 69.

"What about it? They're building it?" she asked. Yes, in theory, I said. But there didn't seem to be enough money to build it just yet. "So then what are you writing about?"

I told her I was interested in the various people working to build it, the character of the places it would change, and, in some cases, groups of people who were trying to stop it. Her eyes widened under the bill of her baseball cap. "You need to talk to Charlie Newman," she said. She grabbed a cordless phone, dialed, and was put straight through to Newman. She called him baby. She asked if he was busy and told him she was sending over a writer. Then she hustled into the kitchen, came back with a Big-Gulp-size iced tea for me to take to him, and gave me walking directions to his office. Charlie Newman, Suhair explained, was the lawyer who helped stop Interstate 40 back in the seventies.

There has been some debate in Memphis about the proper route for Interstate 69—whether it should come through downtown or go around the city in a circumferential loop—but the temperature of that conversation has never approached the fever of the landmark battle that was fought here—across decades, to the Supreme Court and back—over where to put Interstate 40. In 1969, Charlie Newman signed on as the local attorney for the Citizens to Preserve Overton Park, the "little old ladies in tennis shoes" that a sympathetic Memphian once told the Tokarskis about. Newman then was just five years out of Yale Law School, but his young career had already been eventful: He was one of several lawyers from Burch, Porter & Johnson who represented Martin Luther King Jr. in his efforts to hold a sanitation workers' march in April 1968. The team met with King at the Lorraine Motel the day before his assassination.

Newman is now seventy-three years old. He is cut from the Atticus Finch cloth—tall, thin, handsome, with oval-rimmed glasses over a kind but serious face. I handed him his tea and sat down in his office, a large room in the turret of an old stone building on Court Square. The floors creaked, the ceiling was high, and there were huge bay windows looking out on the square's small park. Sitting at his desk, Newman faced away from these windows and toward two interior walls that were covered with framed editorial cartoons and news clippings from the Overton Park controversy. "It was naturally an extremely interesting and satisfying thing," Newman told me, looking over the caricatures of frustrated bulldozers and triumphant trees. "It was something I could never have predicted that I would have gotten involved in, nor that it would have come out as well as it did."

In the highway boom of the late 1950s and early '60s, it was common for cities and states to route their new expressways through parks—the land was already publicly owned and therefore easy pickings. Memphis was preparing plans for three new highways based on the federal diagrams of what would become the interstate system: a loop around the city (later numbered I-240), a north-south route (which would become I-55), and an east-west expressway (the eventual Interstate 40) that would connect the city's eastern suburbs with downtown on its way between Little Rock and Nashville. The planners and highway department engineers charted this east-west route straight through the middle of Overton Park, a three-hundred-acre preserve that had been set aside in 1901 and that featured a zoo, woodlands, and a band shell where Elvis had recently performed one of his first public concerts. In 1956, the federal Bureau of Public Roads approved this plan, and state highway officials were predicting that construction might begin within a year. But at a public meeting in April 1957, citizens expressed outrage. Overton Park was a city treasure, they argued, and an important fixture of the diverse Midtown neighborhood—surely there must be a better place to put the expressway. The highway engineers stood their ground, cheerfully describing how beautiful the landscaping along the expressway would be, but the park defenders didn't buy it. The next public discussion, at a city commission meeting that September, turned raucous, with angry residents shouting down the city's private planning consultant, William Pollard.

Ironically, the firm that Pollard worked for, Harland Bartholomew and Associates, had made its reputation in the twenties and thirties doing city street plans that emphasized smaller-scale, context-sensitive roads that were in many ways the antithesis of the east-west expressway. Harland Bartholomew himself was an influential figure—he was the first full-time planner employed by an American city (Saint Louis)—and he had strong feelings about the design of urban transportation and its effect on cities. His longtime colleague Eldridge Lovelace, in a biography of his friend and former boss, described Bartholomew's core principle of "society-first" road design, which envisioned highways "serving the greater good of society as a whole. In cities, they would be designed as an integral part of the urban pattern, creating viable neighborhoods," Lovelace wrote. "Highways would respect the traditions and amenities and not preempt parks or require demolition of historic structures."

In 1924, Memphis had hired Bartholomew to do a comprehensive city plan, and the volume that he produced was full of society-first prescriptions. Bartholomew sang the praises of Overton Park, the downtown Riverside Park, and an eleven-mile parkway that connected them. The value of these three properties, designed by George Kessler at the turn of the century, was "beyond computation," he wrote. Kessler had laid out the north, south, and east parkways as a pleasure drive around what had been the outskirts of town, but in 1924, Bartholomew complained, this "splendid drive . . . is carrying an increased number of vehicles that should be diverted to other routes." Parkways, he argued, were no place for trucks and other utilitarian traffic. He suggested that parallel routes be constructed along the parkways for the "wagons" that needed to move about the city, and he proposed an even more extensive system of parks and parkways in Memphis's outer reaches.

Bartholomew's "society-first" highway vision, in which major thoroughfares could move automobiles and transit while also supporting worthwhile frontage and harmony with the existing townscape, had its opposite in the "traffic-first" approach championed in those days by state highway engineers. Lovelace described this competing idea: "If traffic wanted to go from point A to point B, the road should be as direct as possible and as cheap as possible . . . If the result was messed-up cities or spoiled countrysides, that was regrettable but necessary, because the over-riding consideration was to do the best for the traffic." As Jeffrey Brown at the UCLA Institute of Transportation Studies pointed out in a 2002 paper, "A Tale of Two Visions," the "traffic-first" philosophy was probably most fully embodied by Robert Moses, New York's master builder, whose political tactics and city-reshaping work are detailed in Robert Caro's book *The Power Broker*. Moses laid out a number of pleasure-drive parkways in the outer reaches of the New York metropolitan area, but when it came to moving traffic through the city, he was far more heavy-handed. He built immense bridges and carved through the middles of old neighborhoods to make way for new elevated expressways. To Moses, nothing was too sacred to knock down.

These "traffic-first" and "society-first" philosophies were both represented by the members of the National Interregional Highway Committee that President Franklin Roosevelt appointed in 1941. Bartholomew was one of the seven luminaries chosen for the committee, the recommendations of which laid the groundwork for the interstate system. Lovelace assisted Bartholomew, and together they injected "society-first" ideas into the committee's report. A chapter titled "Locating the Interregional Routes in Urban Areas" extolled the virtues of comprehensive citywide planning and explained the importance of integrating new major roads such that they "bear a proper relation in location and character to the other parts of the street system." The two men noted how existing main highways had encouraged the unwanted decentralization of population—sprawl, in today's parlance—and proposed limiting the number of exits on the outskirts of towns to "discourage the creeping of settlement." Bartholomew hoped, as many urban champions did, that new highways would revitalize central business districts and help concentrate development.

In hindsight, it may have been naïve of Bartholomew and Lovelace to believe that new highways could actually counteract the outward spread of cities. (The opposite has occurred.) It was certainly optimistic to think that thoughtful planning could win the day over ruthless traffic engineering and city-state politics. As Lovelace laments in his biography of Bartholomew, national road-building practices in the years after the Interregional Highway report lurched toward "traffic-first" habits despite the two men's best efforts. "The fact remained that state highway departments were in charge . . . They would 'consult' and, later, would make environmental impact studies, but these seldom affected the choice of the cheapest alignment that would carry the most traffic." The results, he wrote, were often the "division of neighborhoods, and destruction of the fabric of historic districts," and, yes, "the preemption of park land."

By the time Memphis hired Harland Bartholomew and Associates to lay out its expressways, Bartholomew himself had stepped away from his namesake organization and was serving as the Eisenhower-appointed chairman of the National Capital Planning Commission in Washington, D.C. There, he remained true to his ideals: He advanced plans for what would become the Capital Beltway road, but he squashed proposals for a new web of radial highways *into* the city that would have required extensive demolition. Instead, Bartholomew made the case for an underground metro rail system (now in place) that could handle the same trips to and from the suburbs but leave the historic city unmolested.

With Bartholomew in Washington, the firm was left in the hands of its five other partners, including Lovelace and Pollard, the man who stood before the angry crowds in Memphis trying to defend the defacement of Overton Park. "The clients for a transportation consultant were a very different group than they had been before," Jeffrey Brown writes. "No longer were they likely to be business associations concerned with maintaining the economic viability of the central business district. Now the clients were state highway departments concerned with moving automobiles safely and inexpensively." If it had been Bartholomew at that City Commission meeting in 1957, would he have been so resolute in sticking to a plan that so jarringly contradicted his earlier convictions, or would he have been sympathetic and responsive to the dissent?

He certainly wouldn't have been surprised, for the little old ladies in tennis shoes were not alone. In New York, Moses's plans were drawing fire from the likes of Jane Jacobs, the activist and author of *The Death and Life of Great American Cities.* She (and her book) argued that cities were delicate and vibrant things that worked well in ways scarcely appreciated. They were not to be hacked at with the meat cleaver of "urban renewal." In 1958, Jacobs organized a successful campaign to stop a roadway through Washington Square Park, and in 1968, the week after King's assassination in Memphis, she was arrested for disorderly conduct at a public hearing on the controversial Lower Manhattan Expressway, which was ultimately defeated.

Jacobs's crusade against freeways in New York and the long fight to protect Overton Park in Memphis were part of a broader rash of "expressway revolts" that rocked New Orleans, San Francisco, Cleveland, Philadelphia, Los Angeles, and a handful of other cities. These preservation-minded uprisings coincided with the ascent of the environmental movement—Rachel Carson's book *Silent Spring,* a seminal polemic, was published in 1962—and the collective political pressure led to acute discomfort in Washington. Even before Nixon's 1969 signature of Lynton Caldwell's National Environmental Policy Act creating the EIS requirement for major projects, Congress moved to put limits on highway construction. The Department of Transportation Act of 1966, which established the agency, included a provision, section 4(f), that prohibited routes through public parks, wildlife refuges, or historical sites unless there was "no feasible and prudent alternative to the use of land" and "all possible planning to minimize harm" had been done. These key terms were subjective, however, and it would be up to the courts to interpret their meaning.

The clash over Interstate 40 in Memphis would become a crucial test case and an important legal precedent for all of the highway trials to follow (including, eventually, a lawsuit over Interstate 69 in Indiana). In the late sixties, after the new laws were in effect, the secretary of transportation, John A. Volpe, gave his approval for the I-40 route through Overton Park, and the state began demolishing houses in the right-of-way. The Citizens to Preserve Overton Park decided to sue, arguing that the route was in violation of section 4(f). The group, led by Anona Stoner, an activist and neighborhood resident, and Arlo Smith, a biology professor at what is now Rhodes College, hired a Washington lawyer named Jack

Vardaman to represent them. Vardaman needed a collaborator in Memphis, and a mutual friend recommended Newman, who joined the team in November 1969. "Having been away at school, I hadn't really been following the controversy. But I was sympathetic to their cause," Newman told me. "Jane Jacobs's book was an important one for me when I was that age."

The first ruling, by the district court of western Tennessee, was a letdown for the Overton Park group. "The parkland statute was broad and rather vague and no one knew what it meant," Newman said. "And the district judge here, not surprisingly, held that the secretary of transportation had pretty broad discretion and dismissed the case." The court of appeals in Cincinnati later affirmed the district court's dismissal, but one judge, Frank Celebrezze, offered a strongly worded dissenting opinion. Volpe had testified that the approved route was the sole feasible and prudent option, but he hadn't backed up his assertions with any documents, Celebrezze complained. "How a reviewing court can determine whether the secretary's findings were supported by sufficient evidence, when the secretary has published no findings, is a source of great puzzlement for me," he wrote.

Encouraged by Judge Celebrezze's dissent, the Citizens to Preserve Overton Park petitioned the Supreme Court and were granted a hearing. The case was argued by Vardaman, with support from Newman, who sat at council table. The Court's decision, handed down on March 2, 1971, was unanimous, and it overturned the lower courts' rulings. While a clear win for the Overton Park group, it was by no means the death knell for I-40. The justices did not expressly forbid construction through the park, and they stopped short of demanding new hearings or studies. Rather, they sent the case back to the district court and ordered a complete review of the highway department's records. To approve the construction through Overton Park under the new laws, Justice Thurgood Marshall wrote, the reviewing court must be certain that "the actual choice made was not arbitrary, capricious, an abuse of discretion, or otherwise not in accordance with law."

After another year of depositions, discovery, and hearings in the district court, Newman said, "the judge held that he could not conclude that Volpe had applied the standards that the Supreme Court required." The district court ordered Volpe to deliberate again with the new strictures in mind. For the Overton Park construction to proceed, the secretary would have to prove that his decision to approve it was not arbitrary or capricious. In math-class terms, he had to *show his work*. Volpe by now had NEPA to deal with, so he ordered the preparation of a full environmental-impact statement. And after all of that was done, in January 1973, Volpe refused to approve the Overton Park route, citing the new federal parklands statutes and the very Supreme Court case he had lost. More litigation followed. The Tennessee state highway department tried to force Volpe to approve the Overton Park route or suggest a different one; they won. The Citizens to Preserve Overton Park then appealed that decision; they won. On and on it went, but no one with the authority to do so would hold the hot potato and approve the highway through the park.

Newman, after years of reflection, believes the Citizens to Preserve Overton Park were lucky to have won. His clients deserved credit for their unwillingness to compromise and their faith in the courts, he told me. But he worried at the time that their faith might have been excessive. Had Newman been on the other side, he said, he would have insisted that the state simply study one of the alternatives in a straightforward and honest way. "They might well have been able to satisfy the courts and the secretaries of transportation. And they might have been allowed to build it straight through the park." Fortunately, Newman said, the decision makers were just as stubborn as his clients, and "they got locked into a position that made it easy for us to get a dramatic victory."

The rhetoric against the victory was equally dramatic. In May 1973, the industry newspaper *Transportation Topics* ran a full-page article with the headline ENVIRONMENTALISTS SPILLING BLOOD. The author, Jesse H. Merrell, opened the piece with a quote from the Gospel of Matthew and then wrote: "Just as the rabble-rousing street mob clamored for the head of Jesus in Jerusalem nearly 2,000 years ago, so have the environmentalists who—through lengthy litigation—blocked construction of Interstate 40 spilled the blood of innocent victims." Merrell quoted figures provided by Pollard that suggested highways were far safer than local roads before lamenting "those unfortunate individuals killed on overcrowded Memphis streets—who would still be alive if the expressway had been built through Overton Park." Beneath a photograph of the cleared but unused right-of-way, a caption suggested the hallowed ground be called "'Potter's Field,' or 'The Field of Blood.'"

Instead, it's Sam Cooper Boulevard. Once the city and state finally came to terms with the fact that there would be no highway through

Overton Park, they decided to reroute Interstate 40 along the northern curve of the city's freeway loop, I-240. But east of the park, the obstinate highway department had already built an expressway, complete with exits. By the time the Supreme Court had ordered construction halted, this soon-to-be stub was two miles shy of the park's entrance. The land between the last exit and the park was bulldozed, and no one was sure what to do with it. Until Henry Turley piped up.

Turley, a Memphis native, is the preeminent developer of downtown Memphis, a distinction he earned in part thanks to a lack of competition. Turley made his first foray into urban revitalization in the late seventies with the purchase of the fourteen-story Al Chymia Shrine building across the street from the Little Tea Shop (where he often comes for the collard greens and corn sticks). He converted the building to apartments in 1981, just as the renovated Peabody Hotel reemerged. Turley turned forty that year, and he took a young man's long view of downtown. "I once walked from City Hall to Beale Street and did not see a human being," he told me. "Not a homeless person, *nobody*. And this was in the early evening, like seven thirty. Now try to imagine that condition in perpetuity." He poked his chest. "I read history books, for chrissake!" As any fan of Elvis knew, nothing good stays dead for long.

Turley's office is on the twelfth floor of the old Cotton Exchange building, which he bought in 1983 (by then the commodity was no longer traded face-to-face). He is sixty-nine years old, buoyant, rascally, and droll with a drawl he sometimes exaggerates for effect. His round nose, wide mouth, expressive eyes, and jowls bring to mind Lyndon Johnson, but his frameless glasses and combed-over gray hair suggest Harry Reid. Turley is rather proud of the role he played in the I-40 epilogue. "I decided it should be a boulevard. So I convened a very few people," he said. "The state senator who represented the area, now-congressman Steve Cohen; the city councilman who represented that area, Johnny Vergos; and an engineer whose office is near there and would probably get the work, Frank Gianotti. I got them together at Bayou Bar and Grill," a few blocks south of Overton Park, "and I said, 'Let's work this out.'" Turley told the men what he was imagining, using the city's parkways as an example. "They're about trees and beauty," he told them, "rather than the expressing of automobiles and trucks." But a boulevard would still move traffic. "If on the expressway you can average fifty miles per hour, on the parkway you can surely average forty. It's not gonna change your life."

Turley wasn't part of any planning committee, and he owned no property in the area. He was just a student of urban history, a fan of Harland Bartholomew, and otherwise "just an average white boy. But in Memphis, you can pretty well do what you wanna do." The Bayou Bar and Grill session proved fruitful, and in 2003, the Turley-inspired Sam Cooper Boulevard opened on the last two miles of the I-40 right-of-way. "Now, I didn't get everything I wanted, because 'parkway' was no longer in the Tennessee Department of Transportation's vocabulary," Turley said. "They had an 'expressway,' a 'collector street,' whatever the terms were. But there wasn't a parkway. It was considered no longer relevant. But if you look at it today, it's better." The boulevard was built at grade (except for a guardrailed overpass across railroad tracks), and, close to the park, there are several contiguous blocks with sidewalks, young trees, and a raised median. Along these the city sold housing lots under the condition that homes be built in traditional style in keeping with the neighborhood.

While he was at it, Turley decided to see if he could fend off another expressway. Originally, the I-240 loop was supposed to come all the way to the Mississippi River and slice down the waterfront. Construction had not begun, but the plans remained on the books. "I said, wait a minute. That waterfront land down there is precious. We cannot allow it to be used for the transportation of cars," Turley remembered. He knew exactly to whom he should gripe. He went to see Bob Snowden, a commercial real estate developer who was a member of the influential downtown business group Future Memphis and was, more important, an Overton heir. When Overton died in 1833, he bequeathed much of the riverfront land to the city for use as a public promenade. Over the years the local courts had permitted the city to interpret this requirement for public use rather broadly, and the strip became home to a library, a fire station, and several parking lots. It wasn't much of a promenade anymore, but Turley argued that an expressway would be the worst possible thing. "I went to Bobby and said, 'Bobby, I'm right about this, aren't I?' And he said, 'Yeah, you are.' I said, 'Let's fight it.'" Turley set out to raise a thousand dollars, one hundred each from ten associates. "And one didn't pay, so I only got nine hundred bucks. And we put together a stop-that-expressway not unlike the one they had for Overton Park."

The city ultimately built the western leg of its loop two miles inland, which brought it closer to Memphis International Airport. This no doubt satisfied Snowden, who was the developer of the Airport Industrial Park and a major evangelist for Memphis's potential as a center of distribution and warehousing. Snowden's commercial real estate projects, along with the growth of FedEx, laid the groundwork for the city's logistics industry. Not surprisingly, Snowden later became an early driving force in the promotion of Interstate 69. Alongside Dexter Muller from the Greater Memphis Chamber, Snowden met with James Newland before the first Peabody meeting. Like Turley and Charlie Newman, Snowden was a fixture at the Little Tea Shop. Since before Suhair's time, he was a member of the "cotton table," a bygone daily gathering of the city's elite, and in his later years he continued to eat there every Friday until he became ill with cancer and died in 2006. "Bobby was a great guy," Turley said. "He was always interested in things he thought were good for the city, and I went to him whenever I would embark on something."

Halting the riverfront elevated expressway also spared Mud Island, a large sandbar that was connected to downtown by a small bridge. Mud Island was sufficiently substantial and underutilized that highway planners initially chose it for the site of the western interchange between I-40 and the I-240 loop. With those highways relocated, Mud Island was ripe for development. Its main disadvantage—being downtown—didn't bother Turley. Together with Jack Belz, the real estate man who had bought and restored the Peabody, Turley bought land on Mud Island in the mid-eighties and started planning a development called Harbor Town, which he wanted to be special. "I realized that I only knew two forms of housing," he told me. "I knew an urban form and a suburban form. And one day, in something of a little tiny and inconsequential epiphany, the kind you have if you're an average white boy, I said, you know, what if I quit thinking that way and started thinking in terms of what my likely customer most wants."

Turley imagined a small-town setting, complete with a village center with grocery store and school, and small streets with sidewalks and traditionally designed houses close together. "I wanna be able to *walk* places, and I want *places* to walk," he told me. "I don't wanna walk around like an athlete. I wanna walk to the store, or walk to school. Or walk to the park, or walk to my neighbor's house. Simple stuff like that." He figured that anyone moving to Mud Island would want to have an intimate relationship with the river, and so he made sure the houses had porches. It was hot and muggy by the river, so he made sure the porches had ceiling fans. He hired a traditional-minded architect from Baltimore and had the streets laid out in a grid with small parks and a main boulevard down the length of the island.

Turley's dream for Harbor Town was against the grain of everything being built in the suburbs, along the interstates. Like the boulevard he proposed in the unused footprint of I-40, his neighborhood idea was something that American professionals had left in the dustbin of history. In early 1988, Turley called the chief appraiser in Memphis and warned him that something strange was coming his way. "'The lots are gonna be smaller, but they're gonna sell for the same thing,'" Turley told him. "'There'll be a diversity of incomes. In fact, there'll be mixed uses, a school right next to a house.'" The development broke almost every rule, Turley said. "And the appraiser sat here and listened and listened— thoughtful guy—and kinda digested it and left," Turley remembered. "He calls me back about three weeks later. He says, 'Henry, you know all that madness you were declaiming in your office the other day?' He says, 'Do you read the *Atlantic Monthly*? Go get you a copy. There's an article in there that's verbatim what you just told me.'"

Turley went outside to a newsstand, bought the magazine, and started reading. The article, "A Good Place to Live," by Philip Langdon, began: "In a small but rapidly growing number of American towns designers and developers are rejecting the dominant modern methods of creating new residential areas. They are coming to view the community-development practices of the past few decades as a terrible blunder and returning to the town-planning traditions of the early twentieth century and before." Though the term was not then in use, Langdon was writing about New Urbanism, a neotraditional school of planning that has since emerged as an influential antidote to suburban sprawl. Langdon's article, which later grew into a book by the same name, focused specifically on Seaside, a porch-festooned coastal resort town that the developer Robert Davis and the planners Andrés Duany and his wife, Elizabeth Plater-Zyberk, created on the Florida panhandle.

"I walked across the street reading this thing," Turley told me. "And I remember feeling violated in a way, that other people had done my idea. But it's so *good* that they did, because it was real lonely doing this." By the late eighties, mainstream developing had little to do with town planning. Houses were built increasingly on quarter-acre lots on cul-de-sacs in suburban subdivisions, and zoning—the separation of residential buildings from industrial buildings from commercial buildings—had become so highly restrictive that traditional neighborhoods, where shops and offices are intertwined with houses and apartments, were illegal. I asked Turley if zoning had been an obstacle for him in building Harbor Town. "Hell no!" he answered. "Everybody'd given up on downtown. Think about it. Wasn't anybody here. They said, 'Look, if you build something downtown, you can build it *upside down*. We don't give a shit *what* you do.'"

Unhindered by zoning regulations, Turley was free to innovate. Instead of building typical housing developments, he accomplished something that hadn't been done since the days of John Overton—laid out a new town on the Memphis riverfront. Here, too, he was walking in the footsteps of Harland Bartholomew, who, in addition to the municipal work he did as a consultant, designed seven "new towns" for private developers. One of these, as it happens, was Robert C. Graham's Bal Harbour, Florida.

When Robert Graham's son came through Memphis to promote his highway, the hubbub over Harland Bartholomew's firm's I-40 plans had only recently quieted. I-69 would create another controversy. Once Trent Lott made it clear that the highway would not be crossing the river at Memphis, city officials had to decide how to get it into Mississippi. Some thought that I-69 should come straight through the city along the downtown edge of I-240 and continue down I-55 into Mississippi. But others saw an opportunity to build a new outer loop around what had become the new edges of Memphis, a solution that would serve the growing suburbs and avoid downtown congestion by giving trucks a bypass route. Critics of the loop worried that a new ring highway would only promote more sprawl at the very moment when, thanks in large part to Turley, downtown revitalization seemed plausible. But the metropolitan planning organization, with Solomon-like wisdom, decided it would build both—an I-69 through the city and a new I-269 around it—although it was less than bullish on when it might be able to pay for either.

Mike Ritz, a Shelby County commissioner, is among those concerned about the new loop's effect on land use and the city's tax base. "With the inner loop, 240, all the development was still in Shelby County," he told me in 2009. "Memphis was able to annex land as people spread out. But the 269 loop will go outside our county entirely. Memphis is not going to be the beneficiary of the development that's following that road. It encourages money and wealth to leave." Ritz speaks with unique authority on these matters. Years ago, in the late seventies, he served as the director of the Memphis and Shelby County Office of Planning and Development, where he helped bring the I-40 debacle to a close by suggesting the interstate follow I-240. In those days, Ritz explained, Congress offered cities that decided not to build an interstate money from the general fund in an amount equal to what that interstate would have cost. "It was a bribe," he said, "a congressional bribe to get you to resolve these expressway revolts." Governor Ronald Reagan, in his 1980 run for the White House, swore to put an end to this governmental largesse, but Ritz maneuvered quickly and submitted his paperwork to the Federal Highway Administration the day before Reagan's inauguration. Memphis walked away with $230 million, which it used to pay for several local roads and a new downtown trolley line up and down Main Street.

After stints in private real estate, banking, and consulting—he was national marketing director at Harland Bartholomew and Associates for a time—Ritz is now retired except for his part-time work on the County Commission, where he is overseeing an effort to revamp the planning and zoning codes in Shelby County. With any luck, Ritz says, the new rules will encourage New Urbanism along the lines of Henry Turley's neighborhoods. "We want the code to allow mixed use to happen, and we want to encourage development inside the I-240 loop and discourage development outside," he said. But the city keeps on sprawling, and reform is always slow. "The whole community is ready to get it done. The only people fighting it are the schools, the transportation department, and the public utilities." He chuckled. "It kinda reminds me—I've been reading about Robert Moses. He was a big utility dude there in New York, and a highway guy, and a parks guy. He had everything. When you can do all that, you really can control what the community looks like."

Highway 61 Remade

As every planning professional from Harland Bartholomew to Mike Ritz has learned the hard way, urban development, with all of its overlapping constituencies, can be overwhelmingly complex. Planners almost never wield the kind of power Robert Moses had, and it's rare to find generous tracts of open land near the geographic center of cities, as Memphis had with Mud Island. Therein lies the catch of New Urbanism: The true believers champion downtowns, but they usually work elsewhere. Most of the movement's defining communities have been built on greenfield—agricultural land on the outskirts of sprawling cities—because developers hoping to create perfect new villages are drawn to the same kind of site that attracts developers looking to build more typical housing subdivisions: several-hundred-acre tracts in the suburbs, in the exurbs, off the next exit on the freeway, or along new highways where a planner has but one client, that client owns all of the land, and that land is a blank slate.

The new I-269 loop, when it draws its circle around Memphis, will fertilize a good many fields with development dust. And the ring road swings so wide—its radius from Turley's office downtown will average about twenty miles—that the southern portion will leave the state of Tennessee entirely and form an east-west corridor through DeSoto County, Mississippi. The county has been booming for decades already, and farmers there are hip to growth. Gene Thach, a DeSoto County supervisor and a member of the Mid-Continent Highway Coalition since its first meeting, told of a time not long ago when landowners in northern Mississippi would actually donate property for roads. "When I went into office fifteen years ago, we didn't pay for right-of-way," he said. "Just to get the road through, they'd *give* it to you. Church Road? Quite a bit of that was given to us. The Bridgeports had thousands of acres down there. Now they have subdivisions going in everywhere. They get to build on both sides."

Church Road, which skirts the southern edge of the older exurban towns of Horn Lake, Southaven, and Olive Branch, is four miles down from the state line, and for years it was considered the outer reaches of the Memphis metropolitan area. But the prospect of Interstate 269, five miles farther south, has DeSoto County landowners and planning officials thinking on a far grander scale. Leland Speed, a real estate executive who served from 2004 to 2006 as the head of the Mississippi Development Authority, calls I-69 "a golden opportunity." "An argument can be made that if you want to have one distribution point in the world, you ought to put it in Memphis, Mississippi," he said to me near the end of his tenure. It was very telling, I said, that he had adopted Memphis into the state of Mississippi. "And we didn't even have to pay for the damn airport!" he answered. "Every one of the big box players is developing land banks in DeSoto County." Williams-Sonoma, for example, owns more than 3.5 million feet of warehouse space in the region, he told me.

But Speed wants DeSoto County to be much more than a logistics mecca. He is also devoted to New Urbanism. When Speed took over the Development Authority, he went around passing out copies of Seaside planners Duany and Plater-Zyberk's book *Suburban Nation,* the popular bible of the movement, to the mayors and state legislators in DeSoto County. His admiration came into play in the days after Hurricane Katrina: Speed introduced Duany to Mississippi governor Haley Barbour, who called in a small army of New Urbanists to help plan the rebuilding of the state's Gulf Coast. In October 2005, Speed joined more than a hundred designers, architects, and planners for a week at the half-wrecked Isle of Capri casino hotel in Biloxi, where they drew up traditional-neighborhood proposals for the eleven communities wiped out by the hurricane.

John Smith, the bike shop owner in Indiana, likes to compare the construction of I-69 to a natural disaster, and it seems that Leland Speed sees the same parallel. His hopes for the aftermath of I-69 are quite similar to his vision for the post-Katrina Gulf Coast. "I-69 is going to be the main street of north Mississippi," he told me, "and my aspiration for our dear state here is not to catch up with anybody. I wanna *leap ahead*. And the way we can do it, while nobody's looking, is through New Urbanism." Advances in telecommunications and transportation had made it easier for a growing number of professionals to live wherever they choose. "You can't show me a town that has high quality of life that's not doing well. If you can have an attractive place with a good school system and reasonable amenities, you're gonna grow."

The massive residential projects popping up along the planned route of I-269 will share a well-regarded county school system, so the developers are playing a game of one-upmanship with amenities. The plans for Hernando West, a four-thousand-home venture that will occupy more than eleven hundred acres of the old Banks Plantation, feature not just a town center (designed by a firm that developed shops and condos at Turley's Harbor Town) but an "active adult" community aimed at customers fifty-five and older. And then there is Riverbend Crossing, a multibillion-dollar, forty-three-hundred-acre plan for the western edge of DeSoto County, where the new loop highway will head south into the Mississippi Delta. Bill Phillips, a veteran developer on whose résumé Disneyland Paris looms large, has decked out his Riverbend proposal with four golf courses, hotels, and an MGM amusement park. The economic promise of this new place was so significant that in 2006 Governor Barbour called a special session of the state legislature to formalize an incentive package for Riverbend: $23 million for roads and water and sewer lines, plus $150 million in tourism tax rebates. Phillips's company has not yet closed on the land—the real estate crash put a slight damper on enthusiasm—but if things go according to plan over the next twenty years, ninety-five hundred new houses will sit among fairways and roller coasters alongside Interstate 69.

Hanging in the balance is the future of Walls, Mississippi, an old farming community that stands ready to annex the Riverbend acreage. Walls today has just eleven hundred residents, but if all of the developments now on paper are built as planned, the tiny town's population will explode to more than thirty thousand. The idea of this kind of exponential growth weighs heavily on the mind of Mayor Gene Alday, whom I visited at the Walls town hall, a low-slung, gray prefabricated building across the street from an abandoned cotton gin a stone's throw from Highway 61. Alday, a solidly built former police officer with blond feathered hair parted in the middle, helped fix up the building himself after an embarrassing incident at the old town hall in 2006. "I'd only been in office for about six months when Bill Phillips and the Riverbend executives came here to meet with us," he said. "We were in the other building then, and it was raining. You couldn't get close to the walls because water was running down them. We didn't have but one computer. I mean, we've changed a lot already."

When not handling odd plumbing and carpentry tasks, the mayor sometimes climbs onto a tractor and mows the tall grass along Highway 161, a piece of the old U.S. 61 that cuts through the middle of town. That two-lane stretch, now bypassed by a four-lane upgrade, was once a heavily trafficked road. Not anymore. Trains used to stop in Walls, too, but now the Amtrak cars just rattle by on their way between Memphis and New Orleans. Automobiles speed past, too. Alday was Walls's chief of police twenty years ago when neighboring Tunica County passed an ordinance permitting gambling. When the first casino opened, in 1992, Walls became the midway point between the riverboat and Memphis. "The traffic was so thick we put a light north of town to slow it down. On Friday and Saturday, the cars would be backed up four or five miles," he recalled. "We had a fatal crash every Sunday morning. People drove down kinda fast, but they came *back* a whole lot faster."

A decade ago, to accommodate this traffic and help spur further growth, the state went to work on an upgrade of Highway 61. It was part of a larger roads program called AHEAD (Advocating Highways for Economic Advancement and Development) that was designed to put every Mississippian within thirty miles (or thirty minutes) of a four-lane highway. The historic "blues highway" was replaced by a wider, faster U.S. 61, much of which was built with an interstate-size right-of-way in anticipation of I-69. Near Walls, the new freeway is littered with billboards advertising loose slots, B-list celebrity appearances, and low-price casino buffets on the way down—and strip clubs and pawnshops on the way back. The Delta towns along the original two-lane road, which is now called Old Highway 61, have been spared the headache of gridlock. "But the bypass killed the town," Alday said. "It totally destroyed what the town was. Everything closed." I asked him if the residents of Walls had fought the bypass plans. "No," he said. "We wanted the traffic out of here. We didn't know. We thought life was gonna stay like it was."

Alday is not so naïve about the coming transformation. Much of his time is spent meeting with developers, and the flat files in his office are filled with their drawings and maps of the town's post-I-69 future. "Sprawl's something we're gonna have," he told me. "When you got major roads you're gonna have stuff moving around, but we're trying to keep it more dense, with town centers and stuff like that," he said, referring to the trend toward smart growth. Alday has had time to get used to the idea of growth, and he shows a sense of humor about his hometown being turned upside down. "When the governor was up here I said, 'We used to raise cotton and soybeans. Looks like we're gonna be raisin' homes now.'" Those new houses, some of which Alday said will be priced in the half-million-dollar range, will have to be filled with people from other places, people with more money (or at least credit) and better education than the current residents have. There will be retirees looking for golf and gambling, young families with jobs in Memphis and DeSoto County looking for more space and better schools, northerners looking for warmer weather, people making a fresh start. Were it not for the recent decades of decline in Walls, this coming revolution might depress Alday, who describes the town in its prime as a kind of Garden of Eden.

"Walls used to be a pretty ideal little place," he said. "We had six stores, we had a picture show, we had a little airport strip down here. And even colored folk, they had their own cafés and restaurants and stuff." When Alday was a boy, his grandfather ran the movie theater and a small garage that serviced farm equipment. "But now remember, they used to farm with little-bitty tractors. Now they've got one tractor that'll do what ten used to do, so that kinda did away with the need for people. All of a sudden, the hands started leaving and moving to Chicago."

The widespread mechanization of farming that replaced sharecropping in the Delta in the middle of the twentieth century spurred the Great Migration of black laborers from the agricultural South to the industrial cities in the North. This demographic shift had its impact on American music, as talented Southerners honed their talents in faraway cities. But it also left a lot of people behind. The African Americans who didn't partake in the exodus faced a dearth of jobs and a fading lifestyle. On Old Highway 61 fifteen miles south of Walls, I met Melvin Johnson, who was spreading pellet fertilizer by hand on a patch of his lawn under a forty-foot tree. Two grandchildren were playing in the yard. Just behind Johnson's property were rice and soybean fields. Four miles away sat the casinos on the Mississippi River. And about a thousand feet beyond the rural two-lane out his front door, on the other side of a narrow strip of cotton, was the new four-lane U.S. 61. There once were more houses along this stretch between Robinsonville and Tunica, Johnson told me, but many were torn down as people moved away. "I used to go to Robinsonville on the weekend and there'd be seven or eight juke joints," he said. "You'd drink two beers, play pool. Some people now ask me, 'Where's Robinsonville?' Well, you just passed it! It don't *look* like Robinsonville. People ain't there. Everything's changed."

Since the four-laning of 61, Johnson has watched apartment complexes pop up along the new road. Fifteen years ago, he says, trucks here were few and far between, but now "it's almost a gateway. And it's gonna *be* a gateway when they get I-69." He stepped around a cluster of flowering cactus toward the road and motioned across to the bypass. "Twenty years ago, couldn't nobody told me that you would have casinos and four-lane highways here. Shit. If they get 69 going through here, this whole country here is gonna change. You drive around and look, there's more houses coming up than you'd ever seen." Johnson, like Alday's grandfather, is a tractor mechanic. He expects to see less work as the fields are replaced with development. "Everybody I know, they're glad I-69 is coming," he said. "Thirty years ago, wasn't a whole lot of money jumping around. But in a way, I think people had a little bit *more,* 'cause everything wasn't so high. The way it is now, it seems like a good thing, but to me everything's stayed the same because if prices go up, wages gotta go up."

Johnson was understating things. Thirty years ago, Tunica was the poorest county in the nation. The 1980 Census found that 53 percent of residents here were living below the poverty level. Jesse Jackson, on a visit in 1985, called Tunica County "America's Ethiopia." The coming of casinos ("the Tunica Miracle," it has been called) had a transformative effect: The windfall of tax revenues financed new schools, civic centers, and a county museum. Country clubs and residential communities have risen out of the cotton fields. The county's boom also attracted several shoot-the-moon plans, never realized, for a Nascar track and the world's first indoor eighteen-hole golf course. But the changes that did materialize haven't benefited everyone—as of 2007, one third of Tunica County residents still lived in poverty—and the recent recession hit the gaming industry particularly hard. The unemployment rate in the county, after reaching a low of 7 percent in 2007, spiked to a startling 19 percent in 2009, a sobering reminder that betting a town's prosperity on gambling can be a risky deal.

"The past is never dead. It's not even past," William Faulkner, a Mississippi local, once wrote. Ken Murphree, a former DeSoto County administrator who was hired away by Tunica in 1994 just as the casino boom went into full gear, believes that no matter how much prosperity comes to Tunica, there will always be a segment of the population that fails to take advantage of it. "Everyone who's capable of working and wants to work can get a job in Tunica, but the unemployment rate is still high," he told me when we met at the clubhouse of the new Tunica National championship golf course in 2007, before the recession. "There are people here who are unemployable, and there can be a lot of reasons for that. It's a cultural, social thing they've been involved with. It's just historic. And all of that's improving, but it's not something that changes in a year or two or a decade or two." The situation will improve, he believes, if I-69 allows the county to diversify its economy. "Essentially, we've taken people who were agricultural workers, displaced, on welfare, and we got them into hospitality jobs. And that's a good industry for our skill level. They've been in that industry now for ten years or better and they're developing skills, and now the thing to do is try to get them into manufacturing, warehousing. Take them to the next level."

Lyn Arnold, the president of the Tunica County Chamber of Commerce, has been trying hard to do just that, starting literally from the ground up. "When I came here in 2000 we had fifteen acres of industrial area," she said. "And we've now rezoned about fifteen *thousand* acres. I'll never fill it up in my lifetime. But we're trying." Arnold's office is in a row of old buildings on Main Street, where a downtown revitalization project has attracted a few small restaurants, shops, and a fresh-market grocery. But the real action is happening out along the new four-lane 61, where I-69 will run. The county has created what's known in the economic-development world as a megasite—a large, flat, open tract clear of wetlands and already stuffed with gas, electric, water, sewer, and fiber-optic lines. The twenty-two hundred acres, which sit near Robinsonville a couple of miles from Melvin Johnson's house, are privately owned but optioned by the county. It is in Arnold's office that I first heard the term *shovel ready*. "All my utilities are in place, all of the pre-engineering work is done, I have all of the environmental stuff done, archeological work is done, wetlands work is done, all of that's done. It's shovel ready. You could literally buy the property today and start building tomorrow."

Megasites are like hope chests, a dowry that a hungry community puts together to attract a mate. A recent evolution in the art of business luring, they go beyond land gifts like those that Ziba Graham gave for the B&O shops in Washington, Indiana, and the speculative buildings like the ones with which Bill Revell seeded the Dyersburg industrial park. Like the eager towns out west that built roads out into the vast empty countryside in the hopes that the Lincoln Highway promoters would see fit to adopt the mileage into their route, the counties that put together megasites are signaling the seriousness of their intentions. They're hunting for big game. And like David Cox in Indiana, Arnold doesn't always know who's scoping out her community. "I know that our site has been looked at on several occasions in a helicopter by people that had not contacted me about being in town. But I have someone in that area who is constantly watching out, and every time there's a helicopter anywhere in the area, they'll call me," she said. Trying to figure out whom she's dealing with is "one of the greater joys in the life of an economic developer," she told me. "And just to tell you how savvy some of these people have gotten, we had a group in here a couple weeks ago and we rented a big bus-type thing to take them around, and those drivers signed confidentiality agreements. They cannot say anything about who was on the bus or anything that they heard."

It's not just corporate types who case Arnold's megasite. She's pretty sure the other megasite purveyors have, too, just as she has checked out theirs. A few months before I visited Arnold, Toyota announced its intention to put a new assembly plant on a megasite near Tupelo, Mississippi. State officials had shown the Tunica location to the auto manufacturer as well, but, according to Dennis Cuneo, a site-selection consultant for Toyota, the deciding factor was the quality of the workforce. "Tupelo is a center of furniture manufacturing, which is now going offshore. Unemployment rate is going up. So we knew we'd have a readily available workforce," he said. "If you've ever been in a furniture plant, that work ethic is pretty strong, and it's handed down." As a vice president at Toyota and then as a private attorney, Cuneo has done scouting work for Toyota for over a decade, during a time when the company's American presence has grown exponentially. He picked out some twenty factory locations that together represented about nine billion dollars of investment. And he is the person perhaps most responsible for the megasite concept.

"It struck me that all the requirements for auto-assembly plants are significant, and there are not that many sites that can meet them," he said. "You have to move fast on these decisions, and sometimes you like a site but there's so many inefficiencies you wipe it off your list." A few years ago, in conversations with executives from the Tennessee Valley Authority, Cuneo mentioned the possibility of preparing sites ahead of time and actually marketing them to companies looking for a new home. "Two facilities engineers from Toyota worked with TVA on criteria, not only for us but for anybody looking for this kind of site," Cuneo said. "For Toyota, site selection is almost like selecting land for a church. We want to make sure it's a good place for us to be for forty, fifty, sixty years." I asked Cuneo if it ever gave him pause that his decisions could make or break a town. "Absolutely," he said. "And we take that very seriously. I must say that the hardest thing to do in my job—and I'm the one who has to do it—is to go to the local officials and the governor of the states that didn't get the plant. And I know exactly what that means. I go in person, and we try to tell them before the information is public."

A rejection from a big company like Toyota can be a soul-searching moment for a town. There are some important site-selection factors that can't be fixed by engineers. The "business climate" comes into play, Cuneo told me, a term that is usually code for low taxes and the absence of unions. "That's why the South is often so attractive." Even after Cuneo identifies a suitable location, a team from the company does a "deep dive" investigation into the local school system, training programs, and population. "The education system in Tupelo is very good. The K-12 is just excellent. Tupelo is a little gem that's kinda hidden. Someone explained to me that Tupelo is actually part of foothills Appalachia, and people a hundred years ago had to work very hard just to eke out a living, and that work ethic continued." Cuneo did not address whether the work ethic in the Delta was comparable, but he did say that the presence of casinos was a concern. "I wouldn't say it's insurmountable, but for some it could be an issue. You're competing for workforce, and you might figure if you have casinos nearby and you're gonna have a substantial part of your workforce spending time in those casinos, they get into debt, and that could affect your business. Garnishments and disrupting families and everything else. It could lead to an unhappy workforce. I'm not saying it's a do-or-die thing, but it's a factor. If you had I-69 going through there, and a nice site and everything else, there could be a lot of pluses that still make that site work."

Lyn Arnold was well aware of Tunica's shortcomings. "I very likely lost a project or two because the casinos were here," she said. "My bigger challenge, I think, is that I have not had housing for people to live in, and that's real difficult for somebody to envision." Sixty percent of Tunica's workers commute daily from Shelby and DeSoto counties, Arnold says, but there are several new residential developments in the works locally, several of the New Urbanist variety. Her biggest problem might be education. "The schools are not as good as they need to be. Physically they're good, they're well funded, but academically, they are not where they need to be," she admitted. "Attracting teachers is hard; we pay high teacher supplements here and we've used Teach for America teachers. But it comes back to leadership, and a lot of it comes back to racial divisiveness back in the sixties. When African Americans got into these positions at some of these school boards, they see that as a sense of power and they hold on to some old traditions, whether they're appropriate today or not." The school boards are elected, she complained, and there are no prerequisite qualifications for service. "I mean, you might have school-board members that don't even have a high school education." In part because of this perception that the public schools are poorly run, de facto segregation is the norm in the Delta. In Tunica, the public Rosa Fort High School is 98 percent black, while the private Tunica Institute of Learning is 97 percent white. In Coahoma County, Clarksdale High School is 92 percent black, while the Lee Academy is 92 percent white.

While the problems of curbed rights and overt hatred have subsided in the Delta, a vestigial racial divide persists. With the exception of DeSoto, the four Mississippi counties through which I-69 will travel have populations that are mostly black, but the officials championing the highway, like those generally in positions of leadership at the chambers of commerce, are nearly all white. These same public and business community leaders, who exalt the interstate and the changes it might bring, speak openly and somberly about the state of the black community, the unusually large number of people on welfare, and the social divisions that undercut their efforts at progress. When pressed, they acknowledge that I-69 won't be a cure-all. But many, like Arnold, believe that it will provide the kind of economic opportunity that could bring everyone together. "Already we have gradually built much more of a black middle class," she said. "When casinos came in, you had the opportunity to have a decent job with benefits. So they've got a good income and they can build a future. And they want more of a future for their children, so therefore they're demanding more from the education system.

"The four-laning of Highway 61 helped tremendously. And I-69 will help even more. Tunica could not play in the manufacturing and distribution world if not for 61 and I-69," she said. Someday soon she hopes that "if a couple comes in here, you might find maybe the man works in a manufacturing facility or a distribution facility, and the woman would work maybe in a casino. Used to be, if you had a good skill, if you could be a good farm manager, if you were a good mechanic, if you were a good plumber or electrician, you could earn a good living just with a high school education and a little bit of training. Or in a lot of cases, without even a high school education. The world just doesn't turn like that anymore."

If the new world that Arnold and Alday and others hope to see finally comes with the completion of I-69, there will certainly be space for it. While the Delta waits for Interstate 69, for jobs and working-class prosperity, for the flood of casino-loving golf-happy retirees, a vast agricultural ocean holds their place. Highway 61 leaves Memphis as Third Street, but the urban thoroughfare quickly becomes rural. By the time you reach Walls, hills have disappeared. There are new trees and tourist-friendly landscaping along the road through Tunica, but once you've passed where gamblers go, driving feels almost like riding in an airplane. The shriveling towns along the old 61 appear off in the distance, if at all. The screen of a GPS shows towns that are invisible to the naked eye—old rumors of hamlets like Clayton, Maud, Dundee, Lula, and Moon. There is a thirty-mile stretch of the new 61 between Tunica and Clarksdale that is said to be the longest segment of highway in the world without horizontal or vertical curves. It certainly feels true. It's as though the highway engineers laid out this road with a rifle shot. For half an hour, the flat landscape and endless sky are broken only by barns and silos, gently arching irrigation booms, low-flying yellow crop dusters, and power lines. When this was a two-lane road there were frequent head-on collisions; the straight shot mesmerized drivers into sleep. Even now, at night with few other cars on the road, your headlights show pavement, the odd reflective sign, and nothing else. Your windshield hits bugs. Big ones.

The fact that it's lonely getting to Clarksdale is, for many, part of the town's charm. It seems like an unlikely place for tourism to bloom, which is part of what has made tourism bloom. Near the intersection of old Highway 61 and Highway 49, a signpost topped by three large blue guitars commemorates the rural crossroads where, according to legend, a mediocre Robert Johnson sold his soul to the devil for the musical talent that would bring him fame, fortune, and immortality. This location is approximate, of course, and since the bulk of through traffic has been rerouted onto the new Highway 61 bypass east of town (the future I-69 corridor), it seems only a matter of time before someone erects a more elaborate crossroads landmark there. A Crossroads Truck Stop and Gift Shop, perhaps.

Clarksdale has sold its soul, too—or at least it's trying: The town has fashioned itself into the epicenter of a Mississippi blues-tourism industry. The few juke joints that remain in the Delta are no longer the local refuges Melvin Johnson remembers. They are precious tourist resources, celebrated and protected by the chambers of commerce and frequented by an increasingly older and more mainstream group of pleasure-seeking whites. Born of necessity and exile, these juke joints now anchor the marketable regional brand and are adored as chapels of authenticity—even when they're deliberately engineered to convey it. When the actor Morgan Freeman and a local lawyer named Bill Luckett opened the Ground Zero Blues Club in May 2001, they made sure that the walls were quickly covered in graffiti, that the furniture and decor looked appropriately threadbare and mismatched. I came through Clarksdale for the first time a month before the club opened, and the bottlecap checker pieces were still sitting in unopened plastic bags. "Morgan wanted the place to be as tacky as possible," Joe Williams, a musician and one of the club's managers, told me back then. They also had loftier goals. "We want this to be a place where whites and blacks can come and be together. We're trying to re-create that happening time, when you come and relax on the weekend and you don't worry about anything."

Happening times are being re-created all over Clarksdale. Just south of town, less than a mile from what will one day be an exit off Interstate 69, the Shack Up Inn offers rustic lodging for blues tourists on the old Hopson plantation. The proprietors have renovated a small row of old sharecropper shacks into vacation bungalows with working bathrooms, kitchenettes, and televisions. The cabins were featured in *Time* magazine's "50 Authentic American Experiences" package in 2009, and shortly thereafter the inn was honored by the Mississippi legislature with the Keeping Blues Alive award. The Clarksdale community has embraced the celebration of its complicated past with no apparent shame. Blues music has always been something of an inspired paradox—party music about hardship and all—but the irony has thickened here. There is still plenty of struggle visible around Clarksdale, but the community that most resembles the one from which the blues sprang has little apparent use for acoustic guitars and harmonicas. Still, commerce is commerce. Just as the four-laned Highway 61 has made it safer and more convenient for insider outsiders to travel where once only a broken-down two-lane road would take them, places like the Delta Blues Museum and events like the annual Juke Joint Festival have provided cover for tourists from across the nation and the globe.

Ron Hudson, the longtime executive director of the Clarksdale Chamber of Commerce, credits the late Sid Graves for lighting the town's blues beacon. Graves is the man who founded the Delta Blues Museum in the town's old freight-rail depot in 1999 after nurturing a small collection of artifacts at the Carnegie Library. "People would bring him this stuff for safekeeping," Hudson said. "He really didn't know what to do with it. Basically it was just lying around in the library. Some of it wasn't even in glass." The museum collection includes guitars that belonged to B. B. King, John Lee Hooker, and Big Joe Williams, as well as original signs from old juke joints. "Sid began to study the blues, and he thought, 'You know, this is a real treasure.'"

As glad as he is that the town's history brings in dollars, Hudson is under no illusion that the area can thrive solely on tourism. "It's part of the mix. The economy here is built on agriculture. It always will be. The major asset—our oil in the ground—is the soil and our crops," he said. "And we got some smart farmers. The dumb guys are long since out of it." Hudson, a lanky white-haired man who is cheerful but seems to have a lot on his mind, was born in 1945 and grew up in the country east of town. His father ran the commissary on the Omega plantation. He remembers being a young boy when the tractors appeared. "It was a huge transition. That's when the migration was occurring. And I guess we were in it, but we didn't really realize what we were in," he said. "There was a huge barn across from our store that must have had fifty mules. The farmers didn't use them anymore except for little jobs. But at Omega they didn't turn them into dog food or anything. They fed them the rest of their lives, till they died. And mules live a long time. They knew these mules. They could tell you, 'This is old Abe, and Abe was born in such and such a year and this is his mother.' I mean they *knew* those mules.

"I grew up here, and it was a glorious life. I wanna tell ya, it was just *heaven*. It really was. I mean, there was money here, there was people here. It was just fun growing up." Hudson left Clarksdale after high school and went to Mississippi State University and then to Ole Miss for his master's in urban planning. He went to work in Greenville and started his family there before moving back to Clarksdale to head up economic-development efforts. He had been gone for twenty-seven years. "And it was really almost sickening to come back here. It was sad to come back here and see it. It was like after the sixties, the riots at Ole Miss, everything went to hell in a handbasket. You had this huge out-migration.

And I'm not sure everybody really understood what was going on, what was happening to us. It was something so much bigger than the individuals. You'd come home and see all these stores that had closed, and the town looked dirty. It just wasn't the same town that we grew up in." Hudson's three children, he told me, have left the Delta, gone to Dallas and Birmingham and North Carolina.

Clarksdale suffers from the same troubles as Tunica—a lack of quality education and housing—and the town's blues tourism doesn't bring in the same kind of service-industry money that the casinos to the north provide. Hudson, like Arnold, has hopes that Interstate 69 will bring in some industrial jobs, but even with the highway, he says, they'll have transportation problems. "The challenge we would have is we don't have a class-one railroad, and to get a car plant, you have to. This used to be on Illinois Central's main line, but now their main lines go through Marks." The Illinois Central tracks, along which Amtrak's City of New Orleans service runs, is fifteen miles away, which precludes a Tunica-caliber megasite along I-69. Clarksdale is also too far from Memphis and DeSoto County to draw commuters, and the local workforce leaves something to be desired. "People who are moving factories, they're not looking for unemployed people," Hudson worried. "They're looking to come in and hire your best people from factories that are already there. But I think we have tremendous potential for smaller suppliers. If Lyn Arnold were to locate a plant up in Tunica County, it would be extremely good for us. And hopefully someday a bigger and better mix of retail, generated out on I-69. And if we can get a thriving downtown going, we'll have kind of a good groove, I think, going here."

Hudson can see the town's future, he says. "It's gonna come back. I hope we've hit the bottom and are on our way back up." He cited Clarksdale's history, beyond the blues heyday, as proof of how many lives a place can live. "Originally Clarksdale was founded by a logger. That's what John Clark was, a logger. We had big trees, big virgin forests of mostly hardwood cypress oaks. The Sunflower River was navigable then, and they actually loaded logs onto barges right here in downtown Clarksdale. At the end of the day it's about money. It's about making a living. You read some of the history, some of the letters in the library, about the malaria and yellow fever they endured. This was a terrible place. And the people who moved in here were true pioneers. They were some tough folks." His eyes squinted wisely and he grew a grin. "I guess we came along for the easy part."

The Great River Bridge

It's never been good luck to be the seat of justice of Desha County, Arkansas. Behold today's Arkansas City—beat-up, broken-down, devoid of the trappings every county seat deserves. No four-lane road. No Chinese restaurant. No muffler shop. No Walmart. The main attractions are a recently renovated county courthouse (if county courthouses are your thing) and, for the well-guided visitor with a generous imagination, the shabby remnants of great things long gone.

"People pulled their steamboats up there and you could walk right off the river into town," Mark McElroy, the Desha County judge, said as we drove along a gravel road atop the town's levee one recent spring afternoon. "They had gambling houses and hotels. This was sin city, man!" Fishing poles and tackle boxes bounced around the back of McElroy's SUV. The judge, a part-time actor and river enthusiast, wore a trimmed beard and jeans. He pointed out the old opera house, barn-shaped, abandoned, and in need of a fresh coat of paint; the trackless railbed scars of the Little Rock, Mississippi River & Texas Railway; and the old drunk tank, which doesn't have a ceiling and never did. "That old jail there," McElroy said, "Miss Dorothy said on Sunday when you went to church you could hear the drunks: *Uuuurgh.* They'd fill it up, too."

"That would be Dorothy Moore," said Charlotte Schexnayder, who was riding shotgun. "She's ninety-four and really one of the anchors of this county." Schexnayder, eighty years old and a pillar of the community herself, had a globe of white hair and a mind for historical details. "Dorothy received her high school diploma from a rowboat, if you can believe it. They rowed her up to the second floor of the school, and the superintendent handed her diploma through the window." McElroy drew our attention to a monument the size of a small gravestone halfway down the levee that marked its former height. A historical sign explained the rowboat commencement: "The flood of 1927 was the greatest disaster ever suffered by the county . . . four to thirty feet of water in April, parts remaining until summer . . . A drought and the depression of the 1930s followed the flood. Years were required for the county to recover."

Recover is a term used loosely here. As John Barry describes in his definitive history, *Rising Tide,* the Great Flood of 1927, which inundated large portions of Mississippi, Arkansas, and Louisiana, devastated the local agricultural economy, sped the Great Migration of black workers to the north, and altered permanently the politics and culture of the South. In the decades after the Depression, more subtle events—the consolidation and mechanization of farming, the decline of railroads, the gradual urbanization of America—have also taken their toll. Desha County may have recovered from the flood per se, but its population today is three quarters what it was in 1926, the year before the flood.

The harder truth, not mentioned on the sign but evidenced by the boarded-up windows and trailer homes and junked cars nearby, is that Arkansas City, the county seat, never recovered at all. When the levee broke upstream, the deluge cut a channel that changed the course of the river, and by the time the waters finally receded, the Mississippi lay two miles to the east. The once rollicking river town found itself landlocked. On the other side of its levee today sit the cypress trees and swampy wetlands of an oxbow lake named Kate Adams, in honor of a popular paddleboat from Memphis that used to dock there, back when "there" was the river. In its heyday, Arkansas City teemed with some 15,000 people. Today there are 517.

When the citizens of Desha County voted to make Arkansas City their county seat in 1879, it was an up-and-coming railroad town with a terminus at the river. The previous seat, a whistle-stop called Watson's Station, had been selected five years before, but it flooded too frequently and the railroad pulled out. The original county seat, Napoleon, was fifteen miles north, where the Arkansas River meets the Mississippi. Mark Twain visited Napoleon on several occasions, and in his autobiographical book *Life on the Mississippi* he recalls coming through on a steamboat in 1875. Napoleon had drowned: "It was an astonishing thing to see the Mississippi rolling between unpeopled shores and straight over the spot where I used to see a good big self-complacent town twenty years ago. Town that was county-seat of a great and important county . . . town of innumerable fights—an inquest every day; town where I had used to know the prettiest girl . . . a town no more—swallowed up, vanished, gone to feed the fishes."

"Napoleon just fell, block by block, into the meandering river," Schexnayder said wistfully as we drove out of town along the levee. Locals assert, perhaps spitefully, that the trenches dug by Yankee occupiers during the Civil War had hastened the erosion of Napoleon's banks. But the reality of life before modern engineering and river channelization was simply more biblical: The river giveth, and the river taketh away. "Literally, the townspeople stood and watched it just decay into the river."

A little farther along, next to a small white ranch house in a meadow full of cows, McElroy came to a stop. "Now, this is the right-of-way line right here," he said, motioning out the windshield, "where Interstate 69 is supposed to come through. The Great River Bridge will start right here, at this levee, and go up and all the way across to the levee on the Mississippi side."

Here, finally, was what McElroy and Schexnayder wanted to show me. According to state and federal plans, this pasture, thirty miles from the nearest bridge and ten miles from the nearest four-lane road, will someday play host to I-69. Near the submerged site of Napoleon, the new NAFTA highway will cross the country's original north-south thoroughfare, the Mississippi River. And because everything the river and the railroad once brought to a town—trade, work, wealth, bustle—comes today on concrete, community leaders like Schexnayder believe this highway is the rope the Delta needs to pull itself up. McElroy drove us to the riverbank. There had been rain earlier in the day, and it was still gray out—the river and the sky—but the trees along the Mississippi were turning green. Schexnayder apologized; there wasn't much to look at. But we parked anyway and got out. Schexnayder took my picture. I took Schexnayder's picture. We took pictures of a barge motoring up the river. She pointed to the patch of horizon that she had spent twenty years trying to fill, and I tried to imagine what she could already see—a huge, modern, four-lane highway bridge bustling with tourists and trucks and commerce. A new river reaching across the old one. A concrete river. A river that never moves away.

The Great River Bridge, which the state legislatures of Mississippi and Arkansas have resolved shall be named the Charles W. Dean Memorial Bridge, will be just over four and a quarter miles long. Bank to bank, the river is a little less than one mile wide at the crossing, but it is prudent for a bridge to soar levee to levee as if everything between were rolling water. Because someday it will be.

Charles W. Dean, the civil engineer who first conceived of the bridge, died rather suddenly of lung cancer in 1998 at the age of seventy. His whole life had been intimately tied to the river. Dean spent the flood of 1927 in the womb, and as the waters rose dangerously high that spring, his grandfather, a county sheriff in Shaw, Mississippi, organized patrols to guard the levee against sabotage. It seemed inevitable that the river would break through somewhere, and it was the job of nervous armed men on both banks to make sure that it was God, or fate, or flimsy engineering—not an armful of dynamite—that decided where.

By the time Dean was born, in December of that year, the waters were gone, and so were his chances for an aristocratic life. The Dean family owned the Buckshot plantation near Shaw, but the flood and the Depression would wipe them out. Fortunately, Dean liked hard work and knew how to make friends. At the University of Mississippi, where he studied engineering, Dean was elected student-body president, president of the Kappa Sigma fraternity, president of his graduating class, president of the National Leadership Honor Society chapter, president of the Ole Miss Hall of Fame, and captain of the varsity football team. Schexnayder, who calls Dean the consummate Southern gentleman, loves the oft-told story of a big game when Dean, a tight end, got injured. "In the first half, Charles got knocked out, and they had to take him to the hospital to work on him," she told me in gleeful disbelief. "And his brother appeared at halftime and said, 'Boy, get up! We've got to have you this second half!' And Charles got up off the emergency-room table and went and played the second half!"

Dean was a father of three, a Boy Scout troop leader, and a faithful churchgoer. And, like any Southern gentleman, he liked to have a good time. He is said to have always had a bottle of whiskey in the trunk of his car, for emergencies, and there are countless stories of him living it up at White House receptions, lunching decadently at Windows on the World in New York City, or chaperoning American beauty queens on a trip to Tokyo. Throughout his lifetime, Dean's congeniality and go-getting won him a network of influential friends, and his expertise in the area of river transportation and economic development made him a coveted expert abroad. He consulted in Japan, Korea, England, Belgium, Germany, and Mexico, and in 1983 the U.S. State Department sent Dean to the People's Republic of China, only recently opened to westerners at the time, to advise them on managing and developing their river systems.

At home, a large part of Dean's work involved domesticating the Mississippi, either by controlling its consequences or by reaping its benefits. During the 1970s and '80s, Dean devised a new drainage system for the town of Cleveland, Mississippi, that solved a decades-old flooding problem, and he led the construction—and, more important, the politics—of an inland shipping port in nearby Rosedale, a facility that has arguably saved that community from extinction.

Ancil Cox also grew up in Shaw and played peewee football with Dean. The two were roommates in college and sidekicks thereafter. Cox, too, moved to Cleveland after Ole Miss. He opened a law practice and loyally performed pro bono legal work for Charles's civic projects. "It was just one of those things you do," he told me. "Charles didn't say, 'Come do this for nothing.' He just said, 'Let's do it.' And we did it." Cox's wood-paneled office in downtown Cleveland is crammed with topographical maps and printed studies for I-69 and the Great River Bridge. On the wall just above his chair is an artist's rendition of the port of Rosedale, drawn thirty years ago when Charles Dean was the only one who could imagine it. "Most of the time Charles came through with what he said he would do," Cox said. "He was conscientious, and not just full of bull."

In 1984, after the port was completed, Dean proposed an even grander scheme. There was no bridge for almost fifty miles north or south of Cleveland. If a two-lane highway and railroad bridge could be built across the Mississippi, he thought, it would stimulate badly needed economic opportunity for the entire Delta—on both sides of the river. This was eight years before NAFTA—and well before the combined Southern clout of Bill Clinton, Al Gore, Tom DeLay, and Trent Lott would advance the idea of I-69. Charles Dean wasn't thinking in terms of an international trade corridor. He wanted, put simply, to get to the other side.

"I don't know how well you know the Mississippi River, but it's a big river," Cox said. "You don't go out there in your little boat and go across to visit Aunt Nellie—it's too big for that. So Arkansas and Mississippi have always been split off from each other by the river. My grandmother grew up in Rosedale back in the late 1880s, and I never heard her ever mention visiting people in Arkansas. She'd ride the *Kate Adams* to Memphis or down south, but they never went across." Cox remembers his own childhood trips to Memphis, a five-hour drive up the two-lane Highway 61. "I can remember sitting there eating in the Peabody Hotel and being astounded when I saw a lady light a cigarette at another table," Cox said.

"It's funny how you remember little things. My mother smoked, but not out in public like that. I guess that's what blew my mind. Like the first time I was sitting in a restaurant with my dad and I saw a lady have a highball at noon." Memphis had it all: rails, rivers, roads, ladies smoking and boozing in lush hotels. But the very same river that brought Memphis prosperity and sophistication kept Cleveland detached from the west. Not every place needs to be Memphis, but if you're no place with no port and no bridge, then that mighty, majestic Mississippi might as well be the Great Wall of China.

Though Charles Dean was an engineer, he did not design his eponymous bridge. Large-scale public projects like this one are no longer the work of visionary independent builders but of huge construction conglomerates that like to trace their histories back to visionary independent builders. In this case it is the HNTB Corporation, a Kansas City firm with historic ties to the 1890s bridge pioneer Dr. John Alexander Low Waddell, whose major design contribution was the large-scale, high-clearance, vertical-lift bridge. Although HNTB branched out to develop airports, sports stadiums, and military facilities, it still studies and builds roadways and has designed hundreds of bridges around the world, including nearly forty over the Mississippi River. HNTB was also one of the two firms hired to study the feasibility of Corridor 18. It is fortunate that the company reached a positive conclusion, or it could never have been hired to design the bridge.

The Charles W. Dean Memorial Bridge will cost around $1 billion, or about $45,700 a foot. The main navigation channel below will be 1,520 feet wide, with additional 685-foot spans on either side. The bridge will be cable-stayed, with tall towers like a suspension bridge, except that the cables supporting its deck will fan down diagonally from its tall piers rather than hang vertically from draped support cables. A cable-stayed bridge has a sharp, angular, and vaguely futuristic look, much less lyrical than the swooping arcs of a suspension bridge. But the beauty of the cable-stayed bridge is its simplicity and efficiency, virtues that made the design popular in Europe after World War II when countries had to rebuild their infrastructure quickly and cheaply.

"The concept of a cable-stayed bridge is four or five centuries old, but they didn't have the technology then to build them," Steve Hague, the project manager and lead designer for the bridge, told me. "They're very highly indeterminate structures, and anything you do in one part of the structure affects everything else." More like a spiderweb than a clothes-line, a cable-stayed structure relies on hundreds of simultaneous mathe-matical equations—essentially, computer modeling. "A suspension bridge is a very determinant structure, and fairly simple to calculate. That's why in the 1800s, people like John Roebling could design and build them."

John Augustus Roebling's bridges conquered several American riv-ers, starting with the Monongahela, in Pittsburgh, in 1846, and ending with the East River, in New York, in 1883, when Roebling's masterpiece, the Brooklyn Bridge, opened for pedestrian, livestock, and carriage traf-fic. Roebling was not there to cross it. He died in 1869, before construc-tion began, from a tetanus infection after a ferry crushed his foot on the Brooklyn waterfront. Roebling's son, Washington, also an engineer, con-tinued his father's work and saw the bridge to completion.

Charles Dean never got to see his bridge either. And as lovely as it would have been for his son, Charles "Chuck" Dean Jr., to pick up the Great River Bridge project where his father left off, life—and the river—pulled Chuck in other directions. He learned surveying from his father as a teenager but ultimately chose to work the river as a barge pilot. "I grew up in the sixties. I was kind of a rebel-type person that resented a lot of different things," he told me, unrepentantly. "And I kinda rebelled. And that's life. But my father always told me, 'Son, whatever you do, I will be one hundred percent behind you.'" At his father's request, Chuck tried a year of junior college. "But I told him, 'Pop, this just isn't for me.'"

The barge pilot and the engineer are the yin and yang of river tamers, conflicting in complete harmony. Both must possess intimate, detailed knowledge of the river. But where the engineer works the river's hard edges to neutralize it, the pilot travels its turbulent middle and exploits its power. "It's a wild, untamed world," Chuck told me. "The Mississippi River is like a woman. She's steady-moving, always changing, never the same." When the first railroad bridge was built across the Mississippi River, in 1857, and the first steamboat hit that first bridge, the boat went up in flames and a legal battle ensued. The steamboat operator, supported by river interests, sued the Rock Island Bridge Company, supported by the railroad interests, claiming that the bridge was a dangerous impedi-ment to the rightful navigation of the river. A brilliant attorney from Illi-nois, Abraham Lincoln—a former river pilot himself—argued the case for the railroad and the bridge. Not only was the accident the boat pilot's fault, Lincoln maintained, but the court must recognize that the railroad had as much right to be there as the boats. Lincoln's case for economic development and westward expansion won, and not long after, as president, he would call for the construction of the transcontinental railroad.

A lot of people—engineers, politicians, environmentalists, consultants—have had a say in where exactly the Great River Bridge should go, and the decision changed a half dozen times. Chuck, for his part, wanted his father to put it in a straightaway. "You don't put it where you've just come out of a bend," he said. They did that with the Greenville bridge, and barges hit it all the time. To get his first-class pilot's license, Chuck took a test in which he had to "draw the river." "They give you the edge of the river," he said, "and you fill in everything else—the sailing lines, the banks, the buoys, the lights." Chuck has drawn the river from Vicksburg up to Memphis, the route of the old *Kate Adams*. He's piloted all the way up to Saint Paul and all the way down to New Orleans. It never gets boring, or easy. "Even the best of the best get stumped. I've seen pilots that I've been with for twenty-seven years all of a sudden hit a bridge. And it's because they just take their eyes off. They lose concentration or lose focus." In the old days, the seventies, before cell phones, Chuck would go out for thirty days at a time. It was like being out at sea. "The river gets in your blood," he said. "You think every trip will be your last, but you always keep going back."

After following jobs to Kentucky and Florida, Chuck quit the river a few years ago to stay closer to his wife and seven children. When his father died, Chuck moved with his family back to Cleveland to help take care of his mother, Martha, with his two sisters, Tommicile and Debbie. The ghost of his father is never far away. "Everybody I ever talked to always says that he was like Moses," he said. "That's what they referred to him as around here. That was his legacy." As father figure for a whole community, Charles Dean was always deeply concerned by the constant exodus of bright young people from Cleveland, Chuck said, and was always trying to build reasons for them to stay.

"The older I've gotten, the more I see what my dad's dream was," Chuck told me. "Being back, I look around Cleveland and I see a lot of things that my father did just to make this a better place to live. I look at the walking park in the middle of town," he said, referring to the renovation of an abandoned railroad line in Cleveland's old downtown, which has helped keep the small Main Street businesses alive. "Back then I would have told you that's not something anyone cares about. But he could visualize things that other people just couldn't imagine. Now I look at it and I say, this is something everyone can use—the blacks, the whites. There's nothing separating us. It's for everybody."

The sole black member of the Great River Bridge Committee and one of the few black members of the Mid-Continent Highway Coalition, the Reverend Dr. Juniper Yates Trice has lived in Rosedale, Mississippi, for thirty-five years. He grew up clear across the state in Verona, a small town you've never heard of that sits just a few miles away from Tupelo, a town you probably have (and not just because of its Toyota plant). Tupelo is where a truck driver named Vernon Presley had a son named Elvis in 1935, when J. Y. Trice was fifteen. "Now, Verona is a little older than Tupelo," he explained. "The Ohio Railroad Company went through Tupelo and Verona. Had a stop in both towns. But just a little later, the San Francisco Railroad came, out of Kansas City to Atlanta, through Birmingham. Tupelo was where the two railroad lines crossed. The Bank of Verona moved to Tupelo, became the Bank of Tupelo. And after that everything started fluxing on Tupelo."

At the end of the Second World War, after some years as a small-town preacher, Trice went for his master's in education. He was the principal of the black school in Itawamba County, Mississippi, on the border with Alabama, when the Supreme Court ordered an end to segregation a decade later. The state closed his school and redistributed his students into the three white schools. Trice became assistant county superintendent and helped manage the transition. He earned a reputation as a great integrator, and in 1968 he was recruited to Rosedale, a poorer Delta community where the mandated changes were causing, as Trice delicately put it, "some confusion." In fact, the confusion was so great that Bolivar County had closed down its schools, and the community was divided in a heated struggle.

In the turbulent late sixties, while Chuck Dean turned down college to work the river, Trice arrived in Rosedale to find many young blacks malnourished, some living with huge families in small shacks without plumbing. Some lived outside. Trice applied for emergency federal funding and got some ten million dollars for a new water pump, basic plumbing services, and a start on public housing. By the time he retired from education in 1985 at the age of sixty-five, he was credited with turning the school system, and indeed the community of Rosedale, around. The townspeople promptly elected Trice their mayor. He served four terms and "retired" again in 2001. When I met him in 2005, he was eighty-four and served as the executive director of the Bolivar County Council on Aging, a group that provides services, one of the most important of which is everyday transportation, for the disadvantaged of Trice's generation. Through the council, Trice bought a fleet of vans and found younger volunteers to drive older people to the store, to church, to the bank.

I gave Trice a ride home from work one afternoon so he could show me some of his accomplishments. We drove to the port of Rosedale, which he worked on with Dean and Cox, and Trice counted all the things that might not have been there were it not for their efforts: grain elevators, truck scales, a small industrial park, barge shop, steel business, lubrication plant, fertilizer company, and a flock of birds eating spilled seed off the dusty road. We drove through the Great River Road State Park, which Trice named and which Charles Dean helped him get for Rosedale. He showed me the campgrounds with water and sewer hookups for recreational vehicles, which are better than tents, he said, because mosquitoes, not to mention the occasional wild boar or brown bear, are a problem by the river. We drove past a federal housing project he built as mayor, a semi-gated cul-de-sac with a dozen small brick dwellings. He asked me to read aloud the sign at the entrance: THE J. Y. TRICE APARTMENTS. A slice of immortality for the Reverend Doctor Mayor and a decent place to live, it seemed. No one had done much to spruce up, but still. Trice was in the process of buying the apartments from the government, he told me, at which point he would become the landlord and the name wouldn't just be honorary.

As we neared his house, Trice began rattling off for me the races of the people in the homes we passed, emphasizing, I think, that one can't always tell from the outside: "Those apartment buildings you see over there, we just put them in three years ago. Black folk live in those houses. That's the last thing I built. We call these self-help projects. Turn here. This is where most of the whites lived. Now a Chinaman lives in that house. And a black boy lives in this house. That house sits back yonder, set back, that's what the farmers were living in. White folk were living in all these houses here. Black living in them now. White folk live in these houses. White lived in these houses but black live in these houses now. Black live in this house. The other two here, white live in. Now, this is my house. Pull in here. At one time this was a doctor's house. A white doctor's house."

The population of Rosedale, which is 82 percent black, has come a long way, Trice told me, but there are still traces of what he calls plantation syndrome. "The black people here don't have enough involvement to be as enthusiastic as they should about the bridge and I-69," he explained. "What's making the white people so enthusiastic about the project is they've either got land that's gonna be bought by the project, or they see the possibility of putting a business by the project. So economics is the whole crux of the situation. That's what this highway is, an *economic* highway. The people in the Delta are getting excited about I-69 because they see it's a new way to make new money," Trice said as we drove. "That's the bottom line. The black people haven't learned to appreciate that. It's gonna be some easy money in this for the whites who are really excited about it." Trice himself is really excited about I-69, and as a board member of the First National Bank of Rosedale, which stands to gain new customers from any development in the region, he can identify with the desire for greater cash flow. But at eighty-four years old, Trice, like Charles Dean and Ancil Cox and Charlotte Schexnayder, seems motivated by a hunger for progress, a desire to leave a legacy.

On the other side of the river, Michael Jones, the president of the Merchants & Farmers Bank of Dumas, drove me around his small town, which at forty-six hundred residents is twice the size of Rosedale. Dumas, he boasted, has more of a moderate attitude on race than one might find elsewhere in the state and even the country. But even still, he said, as the schools "got darker," whites pulled their kids out. Even Jones moved his daughters to a boarding school, he confessed. "I went to some of my black friends and said, 'This is the hardest decision I've ever made.' I wanted them to know that it was not a white-flight thing," he said. "It was not a race thing but a peer-group thing. I'm talking about sex, drugs, and rock 'n' roll, but to the nasty extreme. Just low-down. I know there's nothing to do around here—there wasn't when I was young either, but you created your own fun. It's been harder for me to convey that to my girls than it was for my parents to convey it to me."

Jones is only fifty-six years old, but he looks the part of a town father. He is thin and bald with round spectacles, notably poised, and he speaks with great sincerity. The Delta has changed since he was a boy, and he talked like a man who yearned for something that was gone. He can vaguely recall the passenger trains that used to stop in Dumas until the late fifties. He remembers his Irish grandfather's old one-stand cotton gin, how it smelled almost like peanut butter inside and the noise was so loud you couldn't hear yourself shout. "All up and down this Delta, this is what people did. Came with little or nothing except brains and a willingness to work," he said. "Fast-forward, and now that opportunity isn't here, because the trend in agriculture is to grow. When I was young, a thousand acres made you a large gentleman farmer. Now it's eight thousand. And those guys leverage millions of dollars just to skim a little profit." Jones was only thirty-five when he became president of the bank. It was 1989, and Dumas had started to contract from its 1980 peak population. "It happened to be one of those horrible years for farming, and right off the bat men my dad's age were coming in and sitting down. 'How are you doing, Michael? Congratulations.' And then they'd burst into tears. Their world was ending. They were losing everything they owned."

There are other, less noble ways to lose it all. Jones bemoaned the close presence of the casinos in Greenville, which came along after Tunica's and lack the sheen of their counterparts to the north. I had visited one, I told him, and thought I'd seen the most even mix of blacks and whites anywhere in the Delta. I also saw penny slot machines, I reported, which I gathered were not for tourists. "It's worse than that," Jones said, lowering his voice. "People cash their paychecks there. And they have machines where you can insert your *credit card* and gamble until it maxes out." Jones has seen his fellow townspeople at their most desperate, but he insists that there is cause for optimism, too, remnants of entrepreneurial glory. He drove me past one of the biggest cotton gins in the South, all scientific and air-conditioned, and a plant that makes high-end pet food and feed for zoo animals. We admired the old general store, which had been started in the late 1800s by a Polish Jewish immigrant who came to town by himself at the age of fifteen. There was something plucky about Dumas, even now.

Charlotte Schexnayder spent her career explaining—and encouraging—the little things that set her town apart. Back in 1954, the year Jones was born, Schexnayder and her husband, Melvin, bought the local newspaper, the *Dumas Clarion,* and for more than forty years they used their paper as a pulpit of activism and optimism. "Dumas had a vision that we were gonna go beyond the other small towns. We were gonna have a nice little industrial district," she told me in her unwavering alto. We sat in her living room, the walls of which were covered with certificates and honors and photos. Just above the couch, Schexnayder had hung a framed needlepoint sampler that read, DO NOT FOLLOW WHERE THE PATH MAY LEAD. GO WHERE THERE IS NO PATH, AND LEAVE A TRAIL! "When the town needed $140,000 to buy an industrial park in the early 1960s, people went door-to-door. And if you didn't have the money to pledge, you borrowed the money and pledged it. It took Melvin and me three years to pay back three thousand dollars. And we can laugh about it now. But that's the kind of thing. We had a barber here who had four hundred dollars in his checking account, and he gave two hundred. The *people* are the reason places grow. The people, and their determination."

In 1984, Schexnayder had just been elected state representative in the spring primary (she was a Democrat and would be unopposed in the general election) when she received a letter from the Dumas County Chamber of Commerce asking if she would be interested in meeting with an engineer from across the river regarding a possible bridge connecting his impoverished county to hers. She was, in fact, tremendously interested, and in a matter of days Charles Dean and Ancil Cox and J. Y. Trice showed up in nearby McGehee, Arkansas, to meet Schexnayder and Jones and a few Arkansas colleagues. Dean brought big maps, and all parties could see from those maps exactly how close they all lived to one another—and yet how far they'd had to travel to meet. Afterward, they drove out and looked at the river together and agreed that they had a big wall between them, and that a bridge would be a very big deal indeed.

From the trophy case in her living room, Schexnayder pulled out a frame with a big, shiny blue fountain pen mounted inside—the very instrument that Arkansas governor Bill Clinton used in 1985 to sign the interstate compact legislation that officially initiated the cooperation with Mississippi on the Great River Bridge project. In the black-and-white photograph framed above the pen, Schexnayder stands confidently beside the fresh-faced Clinton, who is seated at his desk, smiling at the camera and signing the papers that Schexnayder needs signed.

The bridge group started making annual trips to Washington, at everyone's own expense, to lobby their congressmen for support and funding. Money for studies trickled in here and there, but nothing significant. Then, in 1992, Charlotte was summoned to yet another meeting, this one called by Arkansas senator David Pryor. The senator told the bridge group about the plans for I-69, which, grasping for adequate superlatives, he said was the most significant project he'd been associated with in his thirty-year political career. "And it was like the blinds opened up.

The door opened," Schexnayder recalled. "Suddenly we had an immense opportunity where we'd had a small opportunity before. I-69 was a godsend for us to get this bridge."

In the early days of the Mid-Continent Highway Coalition, the placement of the river crossing was the subject of great speculation. Until 1995, it wasn't clear that the highway would go through both Arkansas and Mississippi. Bill Revell and others hoped that it might cross at Dyersburg, a possibility that attracted delegates from as far north as Cape Girardeau, Missouri. Or maybe it would cross at Memphis. Or maybe at the bridge at Helena, Arkansas. Or maybe at Greenville, Mississippi. But Trent Lott's insistence that the highway go through the Mississippi Delta narrowed the choices, and in the end, the consultants hired to study the whole corridor, Wilbur Smith and HNTB, settled on Charles Dean's bridge. There were environmental concerns elsewhere, and the Great River Bridge, after all, was already partway through its own study process. Jerome Hafter, a lawyer in Greenville who has been active in the coalition since the start, spoke admiringly of Dean's salesmanship in getting his crossing on the books years ago. "It couldn't have been justified by car traffic counts," he explained. "So his argument for a spare bridge was rail. Then Dean got the defense department to say it was needed to fight the Russians. If an earthquake on the New Madrid fault took out the bridges at Memphis, it would be harder to move equipment to the coast by train. Spell all that out, and the cost-benefit ratio overcomes the economic weaknesses." Dean, he said, "basically cobbled together just enough justifications to drag that idea across the finish line." But approval hadn't meant urgent construction. "Until I-69 came along, the Great River Bridge was faltering—there was no real impetus."

In an early interview about the bridge, in November 1984, Charles Dean warned a reporter from the *Arkansas Democrat-Gazette* that it might be quite some time before actual construction of the bridge would begin, possibly even as long as eight to ten years, "depending on funding." Had even his pessimistic estimate come true, Charles Dean would have lived to see his vision completed. "You get into a project like this, and of course you're not gonna live long enough to see it," Schexnayder said to me. "But it's like the story of the old man planting trees. And somebody asks him why. 'You're not gonna be around to see it grow.' And he says, 'It's for those who come after me. I'm the only one who can give them the fruit, and the shade.'" She winked at me. "That's philosophy."

One afternoon in June 2004, almost twenty years after putting that shiny blue pen to use on Schexnayder's bill, former president Bill Clinton was in Manhattan autographing copies of his presidential memoir while Schexnayder was back in Arkansas with her fellow bridge boosters signing the record of decision for the Great River Bridge. The Federal Highway Administration Record of Decision officially approved the site for the project and deemed it the Mississippi River crossing for the future Interstate 69. The document is normally considered a procedural formality, and its release nearly came without fanfare. "They were just gonna sign it and mail it to us," Schexnayder said. "And we said, 'No! We worked twenty years on this, and we're gonna have a ceremony!'"

The milestone came without any federal funding, so the record of decision was just a promise on a piece of paper, not a bridge at all. But 130 people came out to the courthouse in Arkansas City to celebrate anyway. The town was soggy from twenty-two days of rain. Judge McElroy was there, with Schexnayder, Cox, and Trice. Martha Dean came with her three children and ten of her thirteen grandchildren. It was her first time in Arkansas City, the first time she'd seen what would be the other side of her husband's bridge. Chuck had started piloting again on weekends in Tunica, driving dinner tours on a family-owned paddleboat pleasure cruiser called the *Tunica Queen*. He said he did it partly for fun—he loves the river—but really, he said, he did it to keep his license current, "because I want to be the first person to go under my father's bridge."

Everyone took turns signing the record of decision document that afternoon at the courthouse. Speeches were made. Ancil Cox presented red roses to Schexnayder and Martha Dean. Just as people were about to board vans to visit the site on the river, the Reverend J. Y. Trice cleared his throat. He had a few words, he said. He praised Charles Dean highly, said a prayer for everyone, and said a prayer for the bridge. It seemed a good moment, between thanking God and thanking Charles Dean, to reflect on pitiful old Arkansas City, a town made by the river and the railroads and then forgotten by both, now desperate for a highway bridge. A good time to reflect on how interchangeable, in these affairs, the acts of God and man can be: A river runs through here, they build a railroad there, the highway crosses here, a flood hits, a bridge gets built—and the whole place changes forever.

The Long Wait

"You ever been to Washington searching for money or anything?" Ancil Cox asked me.

"You just can't believe the people that are there every day walking the streets around the Capitol. And, of course, they got the Senate office building on one side and the House office building on the other side. And you have to take appointments when they give them to you. And sometimes you can have an appointment with a senator over here and an hour later you've got one with a representative over there. And it's a pretty good walk all the way around the Capitol. You nearly walk your legs off. And the crowds of people are there from all over the United States. Every week. The sidewalks are full of people, bustling from one side to the other, all doing the same thing. You go in one or the other Senate or House buildings, it doesn't matter which one, and there'll be people walking the halls. And you need to make appointments ahead of time. And sometimes you end up with just one of their representatives, young people that work for them. But they'll usually have a conference room arranged across the hall or something where everyone can go in and sit down, and you can sit there and tell them how far you've gotten on the project and how much you need for the next stage, and you tell them, 'We've talked to Senator So-and-so and his folks are working on it.' They don't have sole control, and they know it. And we know it. I don't see how those people ever get anything done with the people that are there worrying them every day."

Those members of Congress—when it comes to funding the construction of Interstate 69—haven't gotten much done. Every year since 1993 a delegation from the Mid-Continent Highway Coalition has visited Washington, and every year a handful of money has dribbled out to help pay for environmental and engineering studies in the various states. But as those formalities have been settled, it has become clear to those pushing for the road that a quantum leap in appropriations is needed, and that securing such appropriations will require a quantum leap in political will. If Charles Dean was the Moses of the Delta, his people have indeed wandered far—and it may end up being forty years before their luck is known. Even the younger proponents have grown tired of waiting. "I wish they'd just build the thing," Michael Jones, the banker from Dumas, told me once, "or else tell us they're never going to, so we can move on."

But as Cox knows too well, the coalition members are far from alone in their quest for dollars. Especially now, with the federal government overextended and still juggling two expensive wars, the thought of spending $27 billion to build I-69 is a hard sell in Washington. From the vantage point of those struggling in the Delta, the highway seems like the greatest idea anyone has had in decades, something of a last best chance for renewed prosperity. But for members of Congress whose constituents live on the coasts, for instance, or in the Great Plains or Rocky Mountains, rescuing fading towns in Middle America is not necessarily a high priority. And there's a sinking feeling among some in the Delta that even for champions of I-69, the plight of the agricultural South is not a primary concern.

Jerome Hafter, the Greenville attorney, continues to collect coalition lobbying dues (now eight thousand dollars a year) from the participating counties in Mississippi, but he's under no illusion that Washington is pining to save his stretch of rural America. "The truth is if rural Kentucky, rural Tennessee, rural Mississippi, Arkansas, and east Texas didn't exist, it would be more pleasing to the highway department," he said. "People say, 'Gosh, there are four factories in Clarksdale that could really use the highway. It's really important to tell people in Congress how important this is.' But that issue falls very deaf on those ears. It's a nice incidental thing. It's something Trent Lott will tell you he's all in favor of because it'll help this area—and it will—but really this is part of a transportation network to serve major industrial areas, major population and distribution centers."

There was a time during the Clinton administration, Hafter recalled, when the idea of rescuing the rust belt and the Delta was more in vogue. An Arkansan was president, after all, a Tennessean was vice president, and a Mississippian was Senate majority leader. "There was a spirit of a sort of new Tennessee Valley Authority for this part of the country. And I-69 fit with that—accidentally." But that particular fever has subsided in the nation's capital over the last fifteen years, Hafter lamented, and Congress's notion of Interstate 69 (inasmuch as it's thought about) has gravitated back toward the original stated purpose of the interstate system. The language of the Federal-Aid Highway Act of 1944, he reminded me, called for the connection of the country's principal cities and industrial hubs by routes as "direct as practical." Any trickle-down growth in the areas between was gravy.

The rural backers of I-69 don't see themselves as afterthoughts, though, and they've made that clear on their trips to Washington. They've walked office to office. They've taken meetings with notepad-carrying staffers, unloaded barrages of facts and figures about how many bales of cotton or truckloads of fertilizer pass through their towns and how many jobs have gone away. With aides in conference rooms they have fantasized aloud about how the highway could change their lives. They've gone to receptions, had their pictures taken with smiling senators, and sometimes they've left behind donations. During that heady Clinton era, the coalition members were cognizant of their Southern connections but never made much use of them. Charlotte and Melvin Schexnayder spent a night as guests in the Lincoln Bedroom, but they never got to meet with the Clintons. The Mississippi delegation put forth Hafter as their leader because he had gone to Yale Law School with Bill and Hillary, but he never had a serious talk with either one of them about I-69. The small towners who made up the I-69 group, it seemed, were not the type to play hardball. They were persistent, patient, and polite. They flew east every year, took their turns among the great flock of Capitol Hill petitioners, and then came back home to wait for some drizzle of highway funds.

Now and then, Washington came to them. In the mid-nineties, when Representative Bud Shuster of Pennsylvania was chairman of the House Transportation and Infrastructure Committee, he made two fact-finding trips down to Arkansas. Representative Don Young of Alaska continued the tradition after he became chairman in 2001, visiting Arkansas a half dozen times. Shuster and Young got lectures on I-69 on these trips. They also raised money—tens of thousands of dollars each—from local donors who wanted to make very clear their enthusiasm for transportation and infrastructure.

The trips were facilitated by Jay Dickey, who until 2001 was the Republican congressman for the fourth district of Arkansas, an area covering much of the southern half of the state and encompassing the entire proposed path of Interstate 69. Dickey lost his reelection bid in 2000, then again in 2002, but he still had a lot of friends in Washington. So he became a lobbyist. His biggest client—from which he received $729,000 over five years—was the Pine Bluff Sand and Gravel Company, a construction-industry concern in his hometown. Lobbying on the company's behalf meant that Dickey was paid well to do something he had always done as a public servant: fight for federal transportation dollars for south Arkansas. And it allowed him to maintain an involvement with I-69, a project that he had battled over in Washington.

It was Dickey who wrestled with Mississippi's Trent Lott in the late nineties over the alignment of I-69 between Memphis and Shreveport. Lott, of course, wanted as much mileage as possible through Mississippi, while Dickey wanted it to come through the heart of Arkansas and his city of Pine Bluff. The Mid-Continent Highway Coalition included members from both areas, in part because no description of the highway's path between Memphis and Shreveport was made official until the National Highway System Designation Act of 1995. The House version of the bill, introduced by Shuster around the time of his first educational (and lucrative) visit to Dickey's district, inserted Arkansas—and only Arkansas—into the definition of Corridor 18. But Lott, then Senate majority whip, saw to it that the final bill included Mississippi, too.

Still, the precise route was left to the imagination until 1997, when both the HNTB and Wilbur Smith recommended the Great River Bridge as the Mississippi River crossing for I-69. The dormant bridge site near Rosedale, preferred for reasons of environmental sensitivity, economic development, and procedural expediency, afforded healthy stretches of highway of more or less equal mileage to the two states. But Dickey still wanted better for Arkansas and for Pine Bluff. The next year, when Congress took up the federal transportation reauthorization bill TEA-21, Dickey made a bold move. He drafted language adding a second trunk that would split off to the west, cross the river up near Tunica, head straight southwest to Pine Bluff, and then rejoin the eastern route down near Monticello, Arkansas. Once again, Shuster put Dickey's language into the House version of the bill. But Lott, who had ascended by then to Senate majority leader, didn't like this so-called Dickey Split one bit. It would compete with the route through Mississippi—for federal dollars and eventually for traffic.

As Dickey tells it, the matter came down to a phone call from the

Oval Office. "I had gone and made a pitch to Clinton, and he said if I could keep it in the bill he would see that it was done," Dickey explained. "Well, he didn't say *that*. He just said, 'You're talking to the choir.' He never did say yes. He avoided that, as Clinton is able to do." That June, the night before the final bill closed, Shuster told Dickey that for his split to remain, the president needed to call Trent Lott and convince him to leave it in. The White House didn't answer calls from Dickey's office, so the congressman went to Newt Gingrich, the Speaker of the House, who supported Dickey's position, and tried calling from Gingrich's phone. Erskine Bowles, Clinton's chief of staff, picked up the call. "Erskine said that he would talk to the president and get him to call Trent Lott if he could. Okay. So I waited and I waited and I waited and I waited, and finally Erskine called and said, 'The president did call Trent. He was asleep, and the president decided he was not going to wake him up.' And I said, 'Well, is he gonna call in the morning?' He said no. And I said, 'Is that all I get?' And he said yeah." The next day, the bill moved forward with no Dickey Split. "And that's when the people of the delta of Arkansas got shafted," Dickey added. "For Arkansas it would have been a bonanza. It would have been the crown jewel that Clinton could have given us, in my opinion."

It wasn't a total loss for Dickey, though. TEA-21 added an extra little piece to I-69, an interstate-quality spur from the main route up to Pine Bluff, where it would join with I-530, an existing forty-mile spur from Little Rock. The I-69 Pine Bluff Connector—or the I-530 extension, as it's often called by those in Pine Bluff—constituted a full third of the original "split" that Dickey had championed, and it would put Pine Bluff in a very nice spot, on an interstate connecting two bigger interstates. But Dickey wasn't done. In October, four months after the TEA-21 reauthorization bill was signed into law, Dickey, who sat on the House Appropriations Committee, inserted an earmark for the Pine Bluff Connector into an omnibus spending bill being rushed through Congress. The amount he secured that October—one hundred million dollars—was astounding, considering that I-69 had won no earmarks in the recent reauthorization bill. (The coalition's lobbyist, Carolina Mederos, had succeeded in creating new national-corridor and border-infrastructure programs in TEA-21, but I-69 would have to compete for an eventual $70 million of the $700 million allotted to those new programs.)

Dickey's earmark was well hidden, too. It didn't say "Pine Bluff" or

"I-69" or "I-530" or even "Arkansas." The money was set aside for "highway projects in the corridor designated by section 1105(c)(18)(C)(ii)" of the transportation authorization. The avalanche of money took even the Arkansas State Highway and Transportation Department by surprise. "That was nowhere on our radar screen, or anyone's radar screen," an AHTD spokesman told a local paper. The one hundred million dollars was good "until expended," and it came out of the general fund, which meant that the state would not have to cover 20 percent of the project cost, as it normally must do with transportation earmarks. But state highway departments have become accustomed to setting their own priorities. A huge appropriation for a project they'd only known about for two months was a bit off-putting. The AHTD asked if they could redirect the funds to other important projects, but the answer was no. So they did the only thing they could do—they got to work on what might as well be called the "Dickey Connector."

Dickey was nearly as effective a lobbyist as he was a congressman. Working for Pine Bluff Sand and Gravel, he continued to advocate for the connector, and in 2005, when the federal transportation bill was reauthorized, he won another windfall. His friend Don Young, who had by then made several educational (and, again, lucrative) visits to Dickey's former district, went to bat for the connector as chairman of the House Transportation Committee. When President Bush signed the final bill (acronymed SAFETEA-LU in honor of Young's wife, Lu), the Pine Bluff Connector got another seventy-two million dollars—one quarter of the amount earmarked for all other segments of the I-69 Corridor.

SAFETEA-LU became infamous for its more than six thousand earmarks, including a total of $450 million set aside for a pair of bridges in Alaska—the Gravina Island "Bridge to Nowhere" that became an issue for Sarah Palin, and the Knik Arm Bridge, which the bill officially renamed "Don Young's Way." These appropriations caused a public uproar, as did an earmark that Young inserted into the bill—*after* it was passed by Congress—that allotted ten million dollars for an interchange south of Fort Myers, Florida, at I-75 and Coconut Road. The Coconut Road earmark surprised local planners, and it was later revealed that the interchange would benefit a local real estate developer who had hosted a forty-thousand-dollar fund-raiser for Young. Watchdog groups filed ethics complaints and the Senate asked the Justice Department to look into the matter.

Nowhere outside of Alaska did Young raise more money than in Pine Bluff, Arkansas. Just a few months before the seventy-two-million-dollar earmark for the Pine Bluff Connector was added to SAFETEA-LU, Dickey and Governor Mike Huckabee had thrown Young a fund-raiser in Little Rock that netted the congressman more than sixty-five thousand dollars for his reelection campaign and political action committee. When confronted by a reporter from the *Arkansas Democrat-Gazette* about this coincidence, Young denied any relationship between the contributions and the I-530 money. "I've been to fund-raisers all over the country," he told the reporter gruffly. "No fund-raiser I've been to has ever influenced me on anything."

Dickey also insists there was never a quid pro quo. His friend Don Young simply had a human affinity for Arkansas. "The biggest pitch we made on this highway was that it was for a developing part of our nation," Dickey said. "And Don Young understood that. He'd say, 'This is exactly what Alaska is like!' I mean, he just more or less adopted the southern part of Arkansas. I raised some money, yeah. But our friendship was so solid and established on the basis of who we were trying to help, I don't think either one of us would think about the money part."

Money did have some effect. I pointed out to Dickey that "who he was trying to help" as a lobbyist was clearly determined by who paid him: He lobbied for the Pine Bluff Connector, but never on behalf of the main branch of I-69 or the Great River Bridge. He would have been happy to, he replied, if anyone had hired him to do so. "In Washington, they ask you, 'Who are you working for?' If I said I'm working for myself, volunteering—I can't see that working," he said. "There would be no constituency behind me." To lobby effectively, one has to speak for many dollars or many votes, he said. "You can't just say, 'I write a letter to the paper every now and then.'"

In any event, Dickey insisted that the construction of his Pine Bluff connector will, in a way, help the cause of I-69. The new southern terminus of I-530, near the small town of Monticello (population ninety-two hundred), would serve as an "anchor point," he said, that would create the sense that the main branch's construction was inevitable. What would a connector be, after all, without a connection? But proponents of I-69 don't entirely agree. They complain that Dickey's success in getting huge earmarks for an ancillary project forced the state highway department to siphon resources away from I-69 proper. Terry Sherwood, the director of the Southwest Arkansas Planning and Development District and the head of the state's delegation to the Mid-Continent Highway Coalition, was borderline morose when I met him in 2007. "I-69 is where the focus was, but it seems like it's no longer the priority," he said, his voice barely audible. "It's been frustrating for me. Someone else is calling the shots— a special interest—and they don't have the greater picture of you or the interest of the whole. It's me, me, me. That's rubbed me wrong from day one. And I'll never get over it."

Normally, the Arkansas State Highway Commission is all-powerful. Its five members are appointed by the governor to ten-year terms, and they dictate policy, as one local elected official put it, "like five little gods." Sherwood fears that Dickey's earmarks have embittered the state transportation department. "If I were AHTD, and I got trumped by someone who used to be in Congress that's got some wherewithal and is able to upstage me and determine where the priority was in this state and where the money was going to go, I probably would be relatively upset," he said, perhaps projecting a bit. "And I'd probably say the hell with it all."

In the summer of 2009, in the midst of the financial crisis, as Congress stalled on yet another transportation reauthorization bill, Arkansas State Highway Transportation Department director Dan Flowers told state legislators that I-69 was "going to be a long time coming." Since the early days of the I-69 effort, Flowers has led the steering committee of DOTs from the states along the route. He knew very well the status of individual segments and their cost. The bad news was that the route through Arkansas, approved by the Federal Highway Administration in 2006, would cost around $3.5 billion, and the full length of Interstate 69 could reach $30 billion. But the state was going to keep at it, Flowers assured them, despite the costs.

But meanwhile, the towns and counties of southeast Arkansas are hurting from a gradual decline in population, an exodus of educated young people (including Sherwood's two children), and an economy that has not diversified much beyond manufacturing and agriculture—all of which has some people in the region thinking they should set more realistic goals. "I was talking with a county judge over in the western part of the district not all that long ago about what we need to do to stimulate some growth," Sherwood told me. "And he said, 'To be honest with you, I've got people returning to my county that left for their career. They're retiring back to the county and they don't want to see any change.' They don't want to *enhance the traffic flow*. They don't want to deal with what they've been dealing with wherever they were located for their career. They're wanting to come back and enjoy the rural setting, the lifestyle of southwest Arkansas. So I think maybe we need to look and see what our niche is."

Don't get him wrong. Sherwood still thinks I-69 is a glorious idea, and he continues to collect money for the coalition so that Patton Boggs can continue to position the project as strongly as possible. "But right now we're waiting in the shadows," he said. "There's nothing I can do to stimulate the allocation of eighteen billion dollars or whatever it's going to be. With all the financial demands of the war in Iraq and everything, I think the cost is going to be insurmountable in terms of the lack of investment in our own infrastructure."

Mike Dumas, the mayor of El Dorado, Arkansas, worked for Sherwood for a time at the regional economic-development office. Like Sherwood, he is a quiet, serious, and plainspoken man. He has the presence of a stern but caring football coach, with a large build, glasses, and a mouth-width mustache. He agreed that I-69 now seems like a far-off fantasy and prescribed tough love. "The mayors in southeast Arkansas and our friends in county government, we've all taken the attitude that we can't look to the state and the feds anymore," he said. "We gotta do it ourselves. Little Rock's not coming down here to help us. Washington's not coming down here to help us. They've got their own problems."

El Dorado has a population of twenty thousand, making it the largest city in Arkansas south of Pine Bluff, and the largest anywhere in the state without four-lane access to an interstate. It's a major center for the oil and chemical industries. Every day on the two-lane roads surrounding El Dorado, trucks come and go full of hazardous crude oil, jet fuel, ammonium nitrate, and bromine. "A few years ago we worked very diligently and raised a lot of money for the governor's pocket and got a local guy appointed highway commissioner for a change," he told me. "In Arkansas, if you look around, you can go to the parts of the state that have real good highways and you'll know that they once had a highway commissioner." Dumas expects to have four-lane access to an interstate within a few years, he said, but not thanks to Arkansas. Neighboring Louisiana is widening U.S. 63 between the state border and I-20. "We'll get that before we get our four-lane highway to our state capital, which is eight to ten years off."

And when did he expect I-69? "It won't be in my lifetime," he said. "People here have heard about I-69 for what now? Fifteen years? They're like I am—nobody believes it. Nobody gets excited." The notion was thrilling at one time, Dumas said, but then it "got real politicked. It got bogged down." Trent Lott pulled the route into Mississippi, and then Jay Dickey got money for his Pine Bluff Connector, which Dumas considers a "highway to nowhere." "They're gonna extend I-530 down from Pine Bluff to Wilmar?" he scoffed. "I don't even think they have an active *store* anymore down in Wilmar. They've got a couple of churches and a post office." Dumas was so pessimistic that he actually predicted the Great River Bridge would never be built. The route of I-69 might be altered, he suspected, to include the new bridge at Greenville instead, and the road would eventually follow I-20 west, with only a short stretch through Arkansas, if any. He put the chances of I-69 being built along its current alignment near El Dorado at "fifty-fifty. Without a Great River Bridge, you don't have an I-69 in Arkansas."

Luckily, El Dorado has other things going for it. It's slowly shrinking, but not quite as much as some of the other towns that pop out of the telephone-pole pines of southern Arkansas. It's got good bones, and some life: a quaint courthouse square on a hill with renovated buildings, a historic theater, and open shops and restaurants. The afternoon I talked to Dumas, in the spring of 2007, I watched people under forty, under thirty even, come and go from these places, a few with crisp-collared shirts. Most cars looked recently washed, a sight unusual enough to write down. "There is a lot of money in this town," Dumas explained, owing to the enduring presence of the Murphy Oil Corporation, an international oil and gas company that has remained headquartered in El Dorado since its incorporation in 1950. "And the people are very community minded. They're tight. If they buy into a project, they'll really come out and support it." The wealthy elite of El Dorado, he said, had furnished the town with a better conference center, an arts center, a symphony, and a top-flight cardiology team that was hired away from a hospital in Springfield, Missouri. "The story goes, they're big pork up there. And these doctors were campaigning against pork, saying it will clog your arteries and kill you. The farmers were on them, so they moved to El Dorado. I think each doctor was assured a million dollars a year."

Generally, recruitment of talent to El Dorado hasn't been easy. But it might be much easier now. A few months before my visit, the city was handed a new tool. Murphy Oil, the hometown company, pledged fifty million dollars for a program it called the El Dorado Promise. If you graduate from high school in the El Dorado school system, Murphy Oil will help you pay for college. A student who attends the local public schools from kindergarten gets an amount equal to the highest in-state tuition for an Arkansas public university, and she can spend that at any accredited college or university. The deal was modeled after a similar program in Kalamazoo, Michigan, funded by a group of anonymous donors. Dumas considers it a lifesaver. "I assure you two days after that announcement, the attitude of this community turned one hundred and eighty degrees," he said.

The Murphy Oil executives took criticism from some of its employees for granting the benefits only to students in the public El Dorado schools. As in the Mississippi Delta, many white parents, including some who worked for Murphy Oil, sent their kids to private school, or moved out to the neighboring school district. "That's white flight out there," Dumas said. "It was a little-bitty school and everybody fled out there to get away from blacks over the last twenty years. You still get a terrible education, but you don't go to school with blacks." Now some are moving back. In the first year after the promise was announced, enrollment in the El Dorado school system jumped by 140 students. The size of the kindergarten class alone increased by 12 percent.

Murphy Oil's promise at first seems like a risky gambit. El Dorado, like the rest of the region, exports an overwhelming number of its brightest young people to bigger cities and more thriving markets. By sending more kids to college, Murphy Oil risks creating an even bigger brain drain. But as Dumas pointed out, the promise isn't necessarily meant to bring grateful graduates back to El Dorado. It's designed to attract their parents. It's a recruitment tool aimed at making El Dorado a more attractive place for young families, a demographic that strengthens a local economy. Dumas saw the promise working its magic as soon as it was announced. He met with his police chief, who had intended to take a job in Hot Springs. "One day after the El Dorado promise was announced, he was sitting in that chair right there," Dumas recalled with a smile. "He said, 'Mayor, but I'm not going anywhere.' He said, 'They'd have to pay me a hundred thousand dollars more, because I have two sons in school over here.'"

In an America where the big places are getting bigger and the small places are getting smaller, every dwindling town is looking for a game changer. They grasp for tourism, they allow gambling, or they beg for a highway. The Murphy Oil executives, in one bold stroke, had done as much good for El Dorado as people there had once dreamed I-69 might do. They gave the place momentum. "I have never felt this good about El Dorado as I have in the last three or four months," Dumas said. "And it's because we've got some things going for us. And my friends, the mayors of Magnolia and Camden, they're envious of what we have going. And that's the way I want it."

Towns across the border in Louisiana are jealous, too. If you follow Robert E. Lee Street southwest out of El Dorado, the road—one of those two-laners Dumas was griping about—cuts like a canyon through thick pines. Some of the roads off to the left and right are dirt, and you see a mobile home for every two stick-built houses. The yards are full of dormant cars and furniture. Oncoming log trucks sound like jet planes as they pass. Just over the state line, thirty-three miles southeast from El Dorado, you come to a town that oil money left behind—dwindling old Haynesville, with its cartoon Main Street storefronts, its fake-porch park, and its mural on which the I-69 shield was painted into the middle, as if the road will someday come.

Mickey Mayfield, the wry and ebullient former mayor of Haynesville, met me at his pipe-supply store a few blocks off Main Street, where a small group of customers in blue jeans and Carhartt jackets sat on stools around a counter in the showroom. "This seems to be a little political round table," Mayfield explained after ushering me into an empty office. "They come by and get free coffee and free Cokes and hang out, sit there by the fire and eat my peanuts. Some of it's not worth listening to. It'll turn into sexual innuendos and all kinds of garbage. This morning they're trying to get me to run for mayor again." Mayfield was dressed in a black Harley-Davidson T-shirt and blue jeans. He seemed younger than he was, in part because of his energy. He was a blend of good ol' boy and firebrand. "I'm sixty-three years of age, I work on my hot-rod cars, and I work in my little store," he told me. "I've got enough money that I can retire on. I got grandbabies and three wonderful sons. I've got a wife that loves me and still thinks I'm kinda handsome." He put his hands on his knees and leaned forward. "And I am getting *tired* of the can't-get-off-the-porch song."

Some of his fellow townspeople, Mayfield explained, are a bit backward in their thinking, and the talk surrounding Interstate 69 has made this all the more evident. "Somebody once said to me, 'Well, we don't want a truck stop here,'" he said, cocking his head. "I says, 'We don't? I'll bet you the guy that's got the little old tire store that sells twelve sets of tires a year will *love* to have a bunch of trucks runnin' up and down that interstate!' And next thing you know we're gonna have big ol' eighteen-wheelers pullin' on and off the highway, and then we're gonna have a Waffle House, and somebody'll put a motel up there. And if it's laid out right, it'll be the saving grace of Haynesville, the *only* thing that'll save Haynesville." Mayfield grew up here and has watched his town's businesses close one by one—the barbershop, the Dollar General, almost everything on Main Street—and he can't understand why someone would turn his nose up at commerce. "I mean, you could open a horse doo-doo factory in Haynesville and I'd be *so* proud."

It was this kind of passion, exhibited by Mayfield in the local public meetings about I-69, that caught the attention of John Caruthers, the president of the Mid-Continent Highway Coalition, who subsequently invited Mayfield to join the organization. Mayfield, who as it happened supplied Caruthers's oil-production company with pipes and other drilling equipment, jumped at the chance. But his dealings with naysayers over the years, he told me, has made him doubt whether anyone in Haynesville will be equipped to take advantage of a "shot in the arm" like I-69. "Maybe somebody can see the light, and maybe rural America will grow and prosper, but I'm becoming more skeptical," he said. "I just wish I-69 happened fifty years ago, when I was a young man. 'Cause I woulda taken it and done something with it. I would've *owned* the truck stop and the Waffle House and the wreckers and the garages."

Mayfield hasn't been as active in the last several years. As in Arkansas, the studies are done, and now everyone is just waiting for construction money. "Most of the people that are for it are hurting, really hurting. But if something don't change real quick, this is not gonna be my place of retirement. I've got a big old house over here, and I got about three acres of land, and two or three buildings full of junk. I could be happy over there," he said. "But what do you need for retirement? I want a movie theater. I want maybe somethin' besides a hamburger. You need health care. And we have none of that. You get that with young people that are innovative, that create money, that pay taxes to build those sort of things, and *then* your retirees will come."

Mayfield's grown children have left town, as grown children do, and as he gets older, he has less energy to drive long distances to see his kids and grandkids. Two of his children live down in the Shreveport-Bossier area, he mentioned, and I told him I was headed there next to meet with John Caruthers. "As a matter of fact, Mister Caruthers was raised in an old town of about two hundred people over here," Mayfield replied. "He came from a little backwoods community called Lisbon, Louisiana. He hit it big, but he has been the most civic-minded, selfless person I've ever known, and as straight as an arrow."

In 1982, Caruthers paid to have the house that his great-grandfather had built in Lisbon restored and moved it to a piece of land just south of Shreveport, where he now hosts large family gatherings with his kids and ten grandchildren. Shortly after my visit with Mayfield, Caruthers took me to see the old house. On our drive from downtown Shreveport, we stopped by to check out Provenance, the New Urbanist development (with arboricultural street names) that his son Witt had been involved with. It was a mile east of Interstate 49 on Southern Loop Road, and only a few houses were occupied, but many more were finished. His son had simply sold the land for the neighborhood—Anderson Oil and Gas was the main investor in the development—but Caruthers was warm with pride at how things were shaping up. We parked on the main drive between a village retail complex and a pond. "They put in this wonderful water feature. There's already a bank coming in on that corner. And you can see how much money they've invested on infrastructure, with these sidewalks and lampposts." A village market, a tea shop, and a pie store were soon to open, and they were hoping to lease space to a hair salon, fitness center, doctor's office, and dry cleaner. Once the retail complex was full, Provenance would have more businesses than Haynesville does.

It was just a mile south to Caruthers's ancestral house. A white picket fence along the road was interrupted by a metal gate. We drove up a gravel driveway, past the daffodils Caruthers had planted beneath pines, a tire swing, and a pond with a fountain and two small alligators out of sight. Caruthers took me inside the house and showed off the heart-pine floors and the cypress walls. A photograph of his great-grandfather, David Andrew Jonathan Caruthers, hung on one wall of the main room. David built this house himself, Caruthers told me. He was the town blacksmith in Lisbon and had a shop just across a dirt road from the house. There were no paved roads in Lisbon until 1960. "His father brought him over from northern Alabama in 1840," Caruthers said. "I'll tell you what pioneer living was. This was the bedroom of my great-grandparents and my great-grandmother had two old-maid sisters, and back then you had to build your kitchen out from the house. So what I made into a kitchen was the bedroom of these two spinsters. Then there were three girls and four boys that went upstairs to two rooms in the attic. So you really had eleven people living in here."

Caruthers wasn't brought up as a country boy. He grew up close to downtown. "When my parents bought in the late twenties, you bought there because you could get on the streetcar," he said. "When people began to get cars, no one rode the streetcars anymore after World War II. Everyone developed a two-car lifestyle." Standing in the old house, we were about half a mile as the crow flies from Interstate 49 and less than seven miles from the city's barge port, where I-69 is supposed to cross the Red River—now named the Senator Bennett Johnston Waterway after the man who won the money to improve it with locks and dams, the man who told John Caruthers on that private plane in 1991 that I-69 was "doable."

I asked Caruthers if he ever expected that I-69 would take so long to build. "No. I wouldn't have gotten involved if I had." Then he chuckled. "We're getting to be a *geriatric* organization." He was pushing eighty. I asked if he ever thought about giving up the reins of the Mid-Continent Highway Coalition. "I'm going to stay with it until we find some younger man or woman that will take over," he said. Then he reflected for a moment. "I would certainly relish that opportunity. But I've been so involved with the organization that I'm a little sentimental about just letting it go."

IV

Texas

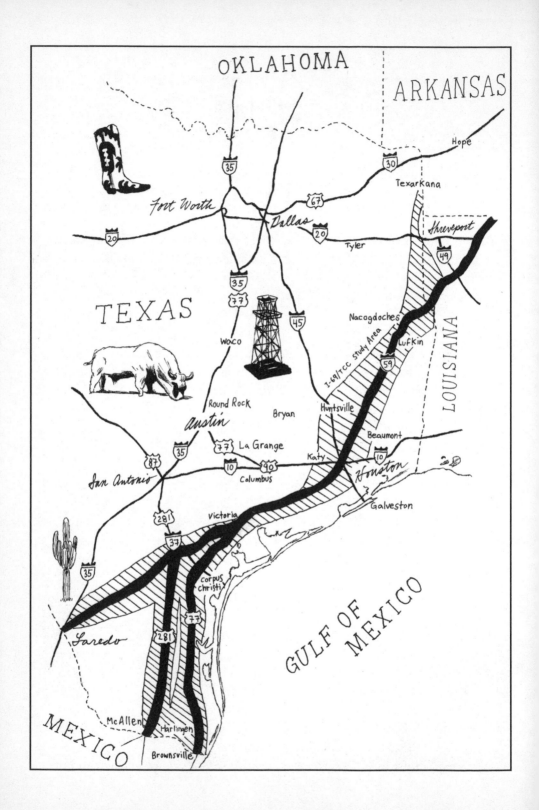

Boomstate

- - - - - - - - - -

The State—née the *Republic*—of Texas is a completely different story. This is true when it comes to Interstate 69, but also in general. The Lone Star State maintains a local identity as strong as you'll find, or perhaps want to find, anywhere in the United States. Texas, you may have heard, was once its own country. Its brief decade of independence—it separated from Mexico in 1836 and was annexed by the United States in 1845—still engenders enormous pride. And a few urban legends. One popular belief is that Texas, by the terms of its annexation, reserves the right to secede from the Union at any time. Governor Rick Perry, in the heat of the conservative Tea Party protests in April 2009, suggested this very possibility, but it is a myth. Another common legend is that the Texas flag is the only state banner that may be flown at the same height as the American flag. This, too, is false. But I think we get the point.

Everything is bigger in Texas. Even Texas itself. Over the last two decades, while the populations of the other I-69 states have remained relatively flat, Texas has boomed. From 1980 to 2008, the number of Texans swelled from fourteen to twenty-four million. During the nineties, the Houston metropolitan area alone grew by almost a million people (one third of the total population of Arkansas or Mississippi), and it took on another million between 2000 and 2008. In a state where inheriting an original Spanish land grant is as good as being a Mayflower descendant, this influx has led to some pedigree-related posturing. Those born and raised here have always worn it as a badge, but now they can wear it on their cars. In 2003, the state began offering a special "Native Texan" license plate. It costs an extra thirty dollars, and the proceeds go to preserve historic sites and promote the teaching of Texas history. Newcomers respond with popular bumper stickers that read, I WASN'T BORN IN TEXAS, BUT I GOT HERE AS FAST AS I COULD.

That Texans would carry out this conversation via the exhaust end of their cars makes a certain amount of sense. Texans spend a lot of time in their cars and like them big. I have seen, in the suburbs of Houston, crowded strip-mall parking lots where the unfortunate driver who takes the last spot in a row crowded with muscular pickup trucks and SUVs must shimmy out of her half-open door like Houdini. Many of the residents of Houston are in the business of producing oil, of course, and judging from their choice of vehicles and the looks of their newest neighborhoods, they're also committed to its consumption. The city is frequently cited by the New Urbanists and other smart-growth advocates as a nightmare of sprawl. Which is not to say that the subdivision planners here do not tip their hats to some of the amenities that New Urbanists champion. They build boulevards, lined not with storefronts and front porches but with privacy fences. There are sidewalks between these fences and the road, but they slalom gratuitously along the ground as if to signal that walking is a novel activity. There are town centers full of restaurants and shops, but these "lifestyle centers," as they are called, require a car to visit. You leave your neighborhood through its (often gated) entrance, take the traffic-aqueduct boulevard to the lifestyle center, pull into its entrance, and park. Yes, once there you can stroll from store to store like at an outdoor mall, but you can't stroll home without risking your life.

Roger Hord helps supervise the sprawl across the inland outskirts of Houston, where the suburbs have already swallowed the town of Katy, twenty-five miles from the city's center. Hord is the president of a non-profit called the West Houston Association, which tries to coordinate new master-planned development and encourage what it considers to be a base level of quality. We met at his headquarters in an office park just off I-10 near the Sam Houston Tollway (the city's outer loop, for now). Hord was a friendly and precise man with large wire-frame glasses and a certain respect for natural beauty. When I mentioned the contrasts between Houston and Austin, a city encouraging more transit and downtown residences, Hord spoke up for density in the capital city. He found the sprawl around Austin unseemly—"They're raping and pillaging those hills," he said. "But see, over here we don't have anything to rape and pillage." He pointed to a large map on the wall showing clusters of cul-de-sacs creeping out across empty ranch land. The meadows were sectioned off with dashed lines at one-mile intervals—a grid showing where major connector roads would be built as the low-density growth filled out. These roads would be paid for largely by developers, who would also have to fund new drainage systems and street-lights.

Beyond that, though, the developers could do pretty much whatever they wanted. Houston has no zoning laws, a condition that would make traditional urbanism easier to pull off if anyone wanted to build that way. But neither the developers nor the consumers crave New Urbanism's design or density, Hord said. The West Houston Association had projected what population growth would mean to the residential and commercial landscape through the year 2050, Hord told me, "and we don't believe that there are any public policies in the offing that will overcome the basic desires of a large portion of the home-buying population to want the kind of product that they have in the past. And what that means to us is that there will continue to be suburbanization." The association's land-use scenario predicted that Houston's sprawl will eventually consume all of Harris County, cover the northern half of neighboring Fort Bend County, and spill into now-rural Waller County. All of this growth requires transportation infrastructure, of course, which in Houston pretty much means roads.

Houston, like so many cities now dependent on cars, was once a trolley town. In the early twentieth century, the Galveston-Houston Electric Railway was the fastest interurban train in the country. When the automobile showed up, buses replaced those trolleys, and then cars replaced the buses. By 1956, the city was flirting with the idea of a monorail system to fight highway congestion. But the Eisenhower interstate system was born that same year, and the short length of demonstration track was abandoned after only seven months. Rail transit was forgotten by Houston—until this past decade. In March 2001, crews began construction of the city's first modern streetcar line, a seven-and-a-half-mile track along Main Street. The city broke ground without federal money, in defiance of Congressman Tom DeLay, who had maneuvered to withhold $65 million in funds for the project. "The Hammer," as he was known, considered streetcars a boondoggle. The city's voters disagreed. That November, they gave the Main Street rail line their retroactive blessing in a public referendum. And in 2003, before that first line opened, the voters doubled down, approving a $7.5 billion regional transit plan that called for twenty-two additional miles of light rail and forty-four new bus routes. Houstonians finally got a chance to board their downtown streetcar on New Year's Day 2004.

Given the local love of highways, Houstonians have been remarkably amenable to transit when given the chance. In 1978, when the city had just one loop freeway—it's now working on a third—the voters imposed a penny sales tax on themselves to support the creation of the Houston METRO Transit Authority. Back then, Roger Hord, a wet-behind-the-ears employee of the Greater Houston Partnership, was tasked with organizing the business community behind the transit referendum. "I cut my teeth going out on the stump giving speeches and supporting METRO," he told me. "That's how transportation got in my blood." Hord has left his mass-transit-booster beginnings behind, however. More recently, he worked to promote the widening of Interstate 10 out to Katy, a project considered crucial to support the explosive growth west of town. This, too, was a success, and today the stretch of I-10 sports new express toll lanes in its middle and, on the outside, multilane frontage roads that, in accordance with Texas custom, run the entire length of the interstate so that all adjacent property is accessible and developable. The I-10 Katy Freeway is now an imposing twenty-two lanes wide.

Hord relished his work on the expansion of I-10. He gloated a bit over how efficiently the project was completed. The city won special federal approval for the express toll lanes, and the projected revenues from them helped finance the construction. Everything came together—local control, political support, and money—and the thing was done within about ten years. This was more than Hord could say for another big road project that he worked on fifteen years ago. "I-10 was just total sweetness," he told me, "for as sour as I-69 was."

Hord's involvement with I-69 was brief compared to that of almost anyone else in the Mid-Continent Highway Coalition, but he left his mark. In the beginning, it was his lack of interest that made waves. When the coalition formed in the early nineties, Hord was leading the Greater Houston Partnership's transportation efforts. It was expected that Houston, by far the biggest city on the corridor (three times the population of Indianapolis or Memphis), would carry its weight in promoting I-69. But Hord and others demurred. It seemed to them that I-69 "didn't have anything to do with money for Houston," he explained. The Houston business community wanted badly to improve Corridor 20—U.S. Highway 59 down to Laredo and up to Texarkana—but they couldn't wrap their heads around how they would benefit from joining a cumbersome multistate coalition. If they could get U.S. 59 upgraded to an interstate, it would connect to I-20 west of Shreveport and to I-30 near Texarkana. "Where it went north of there, we didn't care," Hord told me.

But enthusiasm for I-69 had taken hold farther up U.S. 59, in the piney woods of east Texas, where the economy bears a stronger resemblance to that of northwest Louisiana and southern Arkansas. John Caruthers had found a compatriot in Louis Bronaugh, the mayor of Lufkin and an optician by trade, and the two became fast friends. I met Bronaugh in 2007, just after he'd ended an eighteen-year run as mayor. Like Bill Revell in Dyersburg, he retains enormous local popularity, and the townspeople we encountered around Lufkin still called him "Mayor." Bronaugh is a shorter man, with a full white beard cut round, a bald head, and glasses. He speaks with a soft and raspy tenor, and he was eager to show me some of the things he had worked to build. For instance, the Louis Bronaugh Regional Mobility Complex (also known as Jennings Station), where locals catch buses to the nearby towns of Diboll, Crockett, Livingston, and Nacogdoches. The bus system was Bronaugh's brainchild, and he was spending his postmayoral life hunting, fishing, refereeing youth boxing, and serving as the Brazos Transit District's vice chairman. "My secret as the mayor of the city of Lufkin was that I always tried to work for quality of life," he said.

Lufkin sits exactly midway between Shreveport and Houston, 120 miles from each, in a relatively pristine area with woods and lakes and plenty of water, a resource that the metropolitan behemoths of Dallas and Houston have their eye on. "The problem with the big cities is they start ruining the stuff that little cities need," Bronaugh complained. In fact, he said, he was somewhat sympathetic to the protesters he'd heard about in southern Indiana who were fighting to keep their region unspoiled. "I've often thought about blowing up a bridge between Lufkin and Houston," he joked, "to keep all those guys from coming over and screwing up our little town. But my philosophy, as a mayor in an underdeveloped area, is that whatever Houston gets, Lufkin will benefit from."

At the first meeting of the Mid-Continent Highway Coalition, Bronaugh was one of only four Texans, and Lufkin was the southernmost city represented. The absence of Houston was palpable, and Bronaugh spent the next several months trying to gain that city's cooperation and support. He made trips to Houston to meet with Hord and Harris County judge Jon Lindsay. The week before the coalition made its inaugural trip to Washington in February 1993, Bronaugh griped to the *Houston Chronicle* about the partnership's lackadaisical reaction, which he could not explain. "There's been a lot of follow-up from this end but not from that end," he told the paper.

But shortly thereafter, NAFTA was signed and a coalition sprang up to promote I-35 as the nation's "NAFTA highway." The Greater Houston Partnership—chaired by Ken Lay of Enron at the time—realized that I-35 would present strong competition for federal funds. Maybe the best way to promote the upgrade of U.S. 59 was to join the Mid-Continent Highway Coalition after all. They decided to enlist in the campaign to build I-69. "But," Hord said, "we also determined that if we were gonna get federal money, we needed to ratchet up the lobbying effort."

In 1994, Bronaugh got a call from Lindsay, who told him that Harris County and the City of Houston were prepared to support the coalition and were willing to put together three hundred thousand dollars to hire a lobbyist. "I said, 'Judge, I don't know how to spend three hundred thousand dollars in Washington,'" Bronaugh recalled. "And Lindsay said, 'That's all right. I'm also at liberty to offer you the Greater Houston Partnership as the administrator of that three hundred thousand.' In other words: 'We don't trust you with that money.'"

Hord and the partnership took charge of the Texas I-69 effort just in time to field advances from leaders in the Rio Grande valley, who were chagrined to discover that their towns had been left out of plans for the new NAFTA highway. By then the cities of Harlingen, Brownsville, and McAllen were already experiencing steep growth in truck traffic and trade activity, precipitated when Mexico signed the General Agreement of Tariffs and Trade, a precursor to NAFTA, in 1987. The cluster of cities at the southern tip of Texas had almost a million people, an expanding and dynamic economy, but no interstate highway. The closest interstate connections were over a hundred miles away—Interstate 37 up the Gulf Coast in Corpus Christi or Interstate 35 up the river in Laredo. So when the bankers and economic-development officials learned—from news accounts and overheard conversations on airplanes—that Laredo was the intended terminus of a newly planned international highway, they felt snubbed.

The selection of Laredo was inadvertent. When the coalition formed, the ISTEA-born Corridor 18 had been designated only as far south as

Houston, where it dovetailed with Texas's effort to upgrade U.S. 59, Corridor 20. But to those in the valley, it was a slap in the face. It confirmed their longstanding feeling—like that in southern Indiana, western Kentucky, western Tennessee, and the Delta region of Mississippi and Arkansas—that they were the state's unclaimed luggage. This insecurity had roots in Texas history: During the state's fling with independence, the area between the Nueces River and the Rio Grande was a dry, disputed no-man's-land. When President James K. Polk tried to claim it as part of the annexation of Texas, it sparked the Mexican War. But the valley has come a long way. Railroads and irrigation arrived at the turn of the last century, and as Alan Johnson, the chairman of the Texas State Bank in Harlingen, told me, the older people who grew up in the valley "have seen it go from brushland to farmland to subdivisions."

Mike Allen, a former priest who was the longtime president of the McAllen Economic Development Corporation, is certain that the growth will continue. "Mark my words, what we have from Brownsville to Laredo is the beginning of a new stretch of development similar to Los Angeles in 1963," he told me. U.S. Highway 83, which runs along the border, had already been replaced with a six-lane expressway between McAllen and Brownsville, "and that's not gonna be enough. Everybody's down on Mexico right now, but it's gonna come back."

Over the last ten years, the population in the valley has grown by more than 20 percent—80 percent of the current population is Hispanic—and some are projecting that it could double over the next twenty years. Bill Summers, the president of the Rio Grande Valley Partnership, the region's chamber of commerce, told me that in 1987, when he took over the post, the valley got only about twenty million dollars a year in highway money from the state. Its roads were in bad shape back then. U.S. 83 was just three lanes, and when two cars tried to pass at the same time in the middle "suicide lane," there would too often be head-on collisions. The state highway department came down in 1991, Summers recalled, "and they told us, 'If you guys start working together as a region, we'll give you more money.'" There has been a long-standing rivalry among the valley towns—Summers called it the "Friday-night mentality," a reference to high school football—but they collaborated on a regional transportation plan, and the state increased its budget for valley roadways. "We're like a big family. We'll beat the shit out of each other, but if somebody lays a hand on one of us, we all go after them."

When word got around that the valley had been left out of I-69, the Friday-night mentality was once again set aside in favor of a hive mentality. Johnson, Allen, and Summers contacted Hord and asked for a meeting. Because Houston is about three hundred miles from the valley, the men arranged to meet at Joe Cotten's BBQ in Robstown, outside of Corpus Christi. "We got there and realized they didn't have a meeting room," Johnson remembered. "So we went next door to the Farm Credit Bank. And in that boardroom we really took the Houston Partnership to task. They looked at us little country boys like, 'You guys don't have a clue what you're talking about, and why are you bothering us guys from Houston?'" The valley gang had brought ammunition. They presented traffic counts and border-crossing data showing that the eight bridges in the lower valley carried more trade than did Laredo's two. The Houstonians agreed to consider their case and discuss it with the coalition.

The next stop for the valley leaders was Laredo, Johnson said, "because we were fixing to have a showdown with them." Johnson, Allen, and Summers flew up to Laredo on a private plane provided by the International Bank of Commerce and met with a few of the city's luminaries in the bank's third-floor conference room. They ate lunch and exchanged pleasantries and then got down to business. "We came up here to talk to you and challenge you on this I-69 thing," Johnson told the Laredoans, "because the valley got left out again and we don't like it. And we're gonna stand pretty firm on this thing. Now here's the deal: You can either fight with us or you can fight against us, but we're gonna win. Because we think our numbers will show that you don't need this highway as bad as we do."

Jorge Verduzco, an executive vice president at the International Bank of Commerce, agreed that as long as it wasn't at the expense of Laredo, the valley should fight for an additional leg of I-69. "We in Laredo will do nothing to interfere," he told the group. Verduzco was sympathetic to the valley's crusade for a highway. ("When you talk transportation, transportation is power, money, influence, and anything else you can think of," he told me.) The border crossings downriver and the ports on the Gulf were under considerable strain, he understood, and an interstate connection was warranted. "Trade, ultimately, does not stop in Laredo, nor in McAllen, nor in Brownsville. We are pass-throughs. The more efficient we can become, the more efficient Texas becomes, the more competitive we become. We're talking, obviously, twenty-five years from now. But somebody's gotta start."

In late 1994, shortly after the summit in Laredo, Hord called the valley leaders to say that Houston too was on board with their inclusion—and, by the way, the partnership was planning to put together a few hundred thousand dollars to help the Mid-Continent Highway Coalition hire a lobbyist, and the new members would be expected to pay their share. "So then the challenge became, we gotta go change federal law," Johnson told me. But first, Hord and Bronaugh went to Memphis. In January 1995, a small cohort from the Greater Houston Partnership showed up at the coalition's annual Peabody Hotel meeting with their pile of money and some firm advice: It was time to work the back rooms in Washington. The coalition took the partnership's money and their guidance, and a few months later they hired Carolina Mederos of Patton Boggs, who had been handpicked by the partnership.

The sudden presence of Texans and money sent a jolt through the nascent coalition. The new members were considerably more assertive and savvy. Mike Allen, for instance, had left behind naïve idealism when he quit the priesthood. "How can you tell somebody about Jesus," he said to me, "if they don't have anything to eat?" Allen was a fighter now, with a penchant for hardball tactics. Like Lyn Arnold in Tunica, Mississippi, or David Cox in Washington, Indiana, he worked hard to lure new jobs. But when prospective employers came through McAllen, he wasn't left guessing who they were. "That doesn't happen to us," he told me. "Because we've got informants in all the hotels. Anybody comes into town and *breathes*, we know about it. Anybody buying land, we know about it. We're very, very seldom surprised."

As part of this tougher ethos, Allen had hired a lobbyist to represent McAllen: Randy DeLay. Like his friend Jay Dickey in Arkansas, DeLay liked to arrange visits by the chairman of the House Transportation and Infrastructure Committee, Bud Shuster of Pennsylvania. In 1995, DeLay brought Shuster to McAllen to tour the border region, and organized a fund-raiser at the home of a local construction company president in McAllen. "They invited some of us from Harlingen to come," Johnson recalled. "So we all went with our checkbooks and had a wonderful time and met the chairman and chatted with him." The schmoozing paid off. When Congress passed the National Highway System Designation Act later that year, Shuster and Texas senator Kay Bailey Hutchison ensured that I-69's Corridor 18 was extended from Houston to the valley.

Still, the legislation didn't say *where* in the valley the highway would go. There were two parallel U.S. highways down from the Corpus Christi area—U.S. 281 ran straight into McAllen and U.S. 77 led directly into Harlingen. Either would be a suitable corridor for I-69. And so if McAllen was going to have a lobbyist, Johnson decided, it behooved Harlingen to find one, too. "McAllen wanted Harlingen and Brownsville to hire Randy DeLay," Johnson told me. "But Harlingen said no. That's a conflict of interest because we'll eventually start battling for who's gonna get this spur of the highway." The Friday-night mentality had returned.

Soon Johnson stumbled onto another option. At the Shuster fundraiser in McAllen, he met the chairman's former chief of staff, Ann Eppard, and the two got along. Shortly thereafter, Johnson visited Washington, and Eppard helped arrange another meeting with Shuster. "As we were leaving the chairman's office that afternoon with Ann, she said, 'By the way, I just opened my own practice. I'm doing lobbying now on transportation issues,'" Johnson said. "I thought, this is made in *heaven*." He hired Eppard to lobby for Harlingen. "When McAllen found out, they were fit to be tied! They were focused on Randy DeLay being Tom DeLay's brother, and here we snuck in the back door and got who we thought was the perfect person."

Eppard got right down to business and won Harlingen money for a new interchange on Highway 83. "Ann always said, 'You hire me to be the person in the room at two A.M. the day the bill is being finally drafted and going to the deal. I'm gonna get that done.' And she did." In 1997, the House Ethics Committee launched an investigation into Eppard's relationship with Shuster after Ralph Nader's Congressional Accountability Project accused the two of an influence-peddling scheme. In April 1998, a grand jury in Boston indicted Eppard on felony charges of fraud and accepting unlawful gratuities in connection with the city's Big Dig project. In 1999, she pleaded guilty to a misdemeanor charge and was fined five thousand dollars. None of this troubled Johnson. Eppard represented the city of Harlingen until her death in 2005. (She also lobbied on behalf of Pine Bluff Sand and Gravel from 2000 to 2003, when hometown hero Jay Dickey opened his firm.)

On the subject of influence peddling, Mike Allen is refreshingly frank and unapologetic. Lobbyists raise money for influential members of Congress all the time—that's just the way it works. "Look, they all pay bribes, okay? Every damn consultant or lobbyist that you have," he said. "Now, in Mexico, they give a *mordida*. Over here in the United States, it's the same damn thing, except we legitimize it by calling it political contributions. The Mexicans are much more up-front about it, in saying exactly what it is. The lobbyist will never give you a report. He's never gonna tell you exactly who he talked to, and he doesn't tell you how he got it done. But I don't care *how* he got it done. All I want to do is get it done."

Randy DeLay would appear to agree. He declined to be interviewed for this book, but in August 2004 he was called before the Brownsville Navigation District board, another client, to answer for what the board believed were excessive charges. The district had hired DeLay in the hopes of getting $150 million to deepen its port, but his taxpayer-funded fees had climbed to $25,000 a month. The meeting was televised. DeLay answered questions about what a lobbyist does ("The short definition is, they're problem solvers") and defended receipts he had turned in for travel expenses and golf outings. He courted influential congressmen, he explained, in an attempt to educate them. "You've got a chairman of a committee that very much impacts this port. He's from Alaska," DeLay said, referring to Don Young. "He does not have a clue what Mexico is from Adam. Or our issues on our border. And it's like turning on a light in a dark room when you're bringing that person, that decision maker who's in control of the largest committee in the house, to this site and let them see firsthand what your problems are. It just turns those lights on."

Political donations also tend to illuminate these same dark rooms of the mind. "My wife and I contribute thousands—local, state, federal—which we believe helps us to get access," DeLay told the board. "It's not what people may jump to conclusions and think of as buying influence. It's not that at all. But as each one of you know, you have to have money to win elections, and you only have so much time per day, and you tend to devote priorities to those that—and so we usually coordinate site visits and other things along with fund-raisers. We're helping with the campaign process. We're helping for good government . . . If we're investing money to educate them, it's important for us to see that they stay in office."

DeLay was already hard at work on McAllen's behalf in January 1996, when the Greater Houston Partnership surprised the Mid-Continent Highway Coalition by bringing DeLay—in person—to its annual meeting in Memphis and insisting that he be added to the coalition's lobbying roster. In conversations with me, several long-standing members of the coalition expressed misgivings about DeLay's hiring, which remained the subject of rumor and speculation. Jerome Hafter of Greenville, Mississippi, recalled hearing of "a threat that the whole thing would be shut down if we didn't use Tom DeLay's brother. I think people from Texas were saying, 'We've gotten word you better do this.'" Randy Rohlfer, an accountant in Evansville whose activism dated back to the early Southwest Indiana Regional Highway days, told me in 2007, a few months before his death from cancer, that there had been an "intimation that Randy DeLay was a gotta-hire. There was never open discussion about it. And I don't think anybody who really knows is gonna tell you."

The coalition's executive committee did talk it through, of course. Caruthers and Bronaugh, who greatly respected each other's mettle, both worried aloud that hiring the majority whip's brother would present a conflict of interest, or at least the appearance of one. But in the end it was decided that, as long as it was legal, they would do it. And it was done.

DeLay was hired at an annual rate of $126,000. That same year, the Congressional Accountability Project, on the same day it made its complaint about Eppard, filed a request for investigation against Tom DeLay that specifically objected to Randy's work on behalf of Interstate 69. But the case against DeLay was circumstantial, and the House Ethics Committee dismissed the complaint in 1997. Still, the coalition was anxious. "Randy DeLay got his ass in a crack because he was using the weight of his brother as Speaker of the House to achieve certain things," Bronaugh said. "And so we fired him, because of the trouble he was creating. I never knew what Randy DeLay did. Other than play Speaker's little brother."

It can be hard enough to tell what lobbyists are accomplishing, given their often mysterious ways. But the Texas delegation had a particularly hard time sorting through the deeds of their various lobbyists. Randy DeLay took credit for many of the I-69-related accomplishments that Carolina Mederos at Patton Boggs claims were her own: the establishment of the special post-interstate programs funding national corridors and border infrastructure; the rule that allowed pieces of the new interstate to be designated I-69 as soon as they were connected to an existing interstate; the FUTURE I-69 signs along U.S. 77, 281, and 59 in Texas. Perhaps, as with a firing squad, it's best not to know who's responsible for wielding the decisive influence.

On at least one occasion, legislative language was advanced without the help of any of the hired lobbyists. Alan Johnson likes to tell the story of how he alleviated infighting in the valley by writing a route description that split the highway three ways—to Laredo, McAllen, and Harlingen. When Congress was working through the TEA-21 reauthorization in 1998, Johnson spent a lot of time in Kay Bailey Hutchison's office. "We went in there one afternoon and the bill was getting ready to be laid out," he told me. "And she said, 'I don't have time to talk about this right now. I'll make a copy of the page. You take it to your hotel room tonight and you figure it out. And you bring it back to us.'" Johnson chortled. "I thought, *okay*." Johnson and a colleague from Harlingen went back to the Madison Hotel, where they were staying. "And we went down to the bar, ordered up a scotch, sat down, and said, 'How do we wanna write this thing?'" Without Eppard, without Mederos, without DeLay, "he and I sat there in the bar and wrote two or three paragraphs," Johnson said. "And that's *exactly* the way it appeared in the bill. I mean, when it came out that way, it was just like, 'Wow. They bought it.' Word for word."

With the passage of TEA-21, the Texas delegation grew disenchanted with Mederos's performance. More to the point, they were tired of paying the lion's share of her fee. Summers complained that "for many years, Texas put in most of the money for the whole deal. And then finally we decided every state has gotta chip in. At that time the valley was very poor, and our share was forty-eight thousand dollars," he said. "Texas was paying two hundred thousand, and all the other states were paying twenty thousand."

"In retrospect we spent more money on lobbying than we should have," Hord told me. "The point was to get money to get I-69 started, get it institutionalized as best we could. That's why we joined I-69." That particular objective was achieved, Hord admitted, but there "wasn't much coming out of the gristmill in terms of money for the project." Yes, Mederos had helped to create new streams of revenue for which I-69 would qualify, but "everybody and his dog had a high-priority corridor. I think our first appropriation was like five or six million for Interstate 69. It didn't take someone quick with a pencil and calculator to figure out this would never get done."

After 2000, when Texas governor George W. Bush was elected president, the state delegation decided to assert itself: Bill Summers called Caruthers on his cell phone, found him on vacation, and told him there were other lobbyists whom the Texans would like to consider the next time the contract for Carolina Mederos came up for renewal. That didn't go over well. "John D. [Caruthers] got so pissed off at me. We've been on the outs ever since," Summers told me. "My personal opinion, and you can quote me on it: I think we would have gotten more done sooner if we'd had different lobbyists in Washington and different leadership in the Mid-Continent Coalition." I asked him whether there was a process in place to change the leadership. "You can do it," he replied. "There has to be a couple of *funerals*."

Bronaugh was less harsh. "We could not prevail upon John D. to fire Patton Boggs," he recalled with regret. "One little thing that I found over the years working in Austin, or in Washington, is that firing lobbyists is one of the hardest damn things you'll ever have to do."

The Texas delegation decided that if their concerns were not being addressed, they were no longer obligated to shoulder most of the cost of paying the lobbyist. Roger Hord resigned from the Greater Houston Partnership and went to work for the West Houston Association around this time, but not before breaking the news to the coalition that Texas was withdrawing its two-hundred-thousand-dollar-a-year support. In one motion the Mid-Continent Highway Coalition lost more than half of its funding and has lived hand-to-mouth ever since, frequently falling behind in its payments to Patton Boggs.

Texas remained a nominal part of the coalition—and Bronaugh remained the head of its delegation—but after the fight over lobbyists and money, the fabric of the organization was frayed forever. Other, more philosophical differences started to show. Texas believed it needed the interstate more than the other states because it was already growing and its infrastructure couldn't keep up; Texas had little patience for trying to win money so that the poorer, declining states could have a better chance at survival. "I mean, you know, it's a joke," Allen complained. "These things have to be business driven. Economic development? Okay. But we're saying, we've *got* it, and we've got to have the interstate *now*."

"TxDOT's philosophy has always been that they don't do build-it-and-they'll-come-type stuff," Johnson said. "You gotta show a need for it." An interstate to the valley is necessary, Johnson said, even if the rest of I-69 is not. The Texans were asserting their independence again. Hord, at first, didn't care where—or if—an upgraded U.S. 59 might go north of Texarkana; now the valley leaders didn't even care where it went north of Corpus Christi. "We always had a fallback position in Harlingen," Johnson said. "If we can't get I-69 to the valley, we want I-37 extended south from Corpus. We can't wait for I-69 to come from the north." Bill Summers agrees. A few years ago he told the Texas Transportation Commission that if the state built an interstate down to the valley, they could call it whatever they wanted.

In 2002, the Texas delegation, which calls itself the Alliance for I-69 Texas, hired its own lobbyist, Larry Meyers & Associates. Meyers encouraged a new strategy: The alliance would concentrate on getting money from the state and federal government for relatively small, quick improvements that would gradually transform U.S. 77 and U.S. 281 into interstate-standard highways. The results of this approach are already visible, if a little odd. If you were to drive south to the valley from Corpus Christi today, you would take bypasses around dusty towns like El Campo and Raymondville (unless you decided to try the old, slow "business" route) and you would speed on new multimillion-dollar overpasses stretching across lonely country roads not wide enough for their own yellow stripe of paint. These struggling ranch communities aren't plagued with traffic congestion. If anything, they suffer from whatever is the *opposite* of traffic congestion. To an unsympathetic eye—one accustomed, say, to the roads of the densely developed northeast, weathered like old stone walls—the brand-new infrastructure, with its landscaping and young trees, might seem like overkill, or a waste. But a real interstate can't stop for little old country roads. If the valley is to have its bold blue line from Houston, Raymondville must have it, too.

"People think one of these days they're gonna go out there and they're gonna bring all of the equipment and they're gonna start building I-69," Bill Summers told me. But in Texas, it's a more gradual process. "See, down here in the valley, we're already building. These overpasses that you saw when you came down, the new ones—that's I-69."

Freeway Isn't Free

At the coalition meeting in Washington in January 1996, the same morning the group hired Randy DeLay, another touchy subject was on the agenda: toll roads. Mederos had informed the highway boosters that the Eisenhower-born Interstate Construction Program had officially ended and wasn't coming back. And while much of the group's energy was still being spent haggling over the route—where I-69 would cross the Mississippi, how it would get to the valley, et cetera—the problem of how to pay for construction (then estimated at a modest seven billion dollars) was one they knew they had to face.

When the conversation about toll roads began—David Graham brought it up—Mederos timidly replied that the topic was "very controversial." The ensuing discussion confirmed this. A Mississippi member spoke up to say that the idea would never work in his state—they were looking to use the existing U.S. 61 corridor, and to replace a gas-tax-financed highway with a toll road would be double taxation. Roger Hord, on the other hand, piped up in favor of tolls as a way of financing I-69. Texas had a number of very successful urban toll roads, Hord argued, and it would behoove the coalition to keep its options open and at least allow flexibility state by state. Caruthers wasn't having it. "We are *not* pushing toll roads," he answered. The coalition's goal was to convince Congress to treat the project as an interstate and chip in 90 percent of the construction cost. "We should not be distracted by a discussion of toll roads," Caruthers said. The matter was dropped.

But it soon came up again. That November, four years after they had first assembled, the coalition held their annual organizational meeting on South Padre Island, off the coast near Brownsville, Texas. Everyone had a fine time. The setting was a diverting change of pace from downtown Memphis, and the Texas delegation, recently grown with the inclusion of the valley, was still playing well with the other states. Mike Allen and Bill Summers led members on a field trip to some of the factories on both sides of the border. In Mexico, they heard from the mayor of Reynosa, who hailed the *maquiladoras* in Tamaulipas and preached about how lower-wage manufacturing was boosting the economies of both countries. They ate in Reynosa, too. But their dinner there was not the spiciest nor the most foreign thing the coalition was asked to swallow that week.

Randy DeLay had invited Congressman Ron Packard, a Republican dentist from San Diego, to be a special guest luncheon speaker. Packard sat on both the Appropriations Committee and the Transportation and Infrastructure Committee, and had helped shape the 1991 transportation bill—ISTEA—that brought the interstate era to a close and established the high-priority corridors that would make up I-69. He was well acquainted with the direction of policy and funding, and he had some alarming insights to share with the coalition. Highway financing would be an even more difficult problem for states and local governments in the years ahead, Packard told them. Budgets would be tight and discretionary money was sure to shrink. He predicted that there would be greater emphasis on what he called "innovative financing."

For starters, this meant tolls. But not your grandfather's tolls, necessarily. In San Diego, Packard told them, they were about to open experimental high-occupancy toll lanes on a stretch of Interstate 15. HOT lanes were similar to HOV (high-occupancy vehicle) lanes in that carpoolers could drive in them for free. But under the new scheme, Packard explained, lone drivers (single-occupancy vehicles) could also buy access to these uncongested lanes. Initially one would buy a pass for a monthly fee. But eventually, once new technology was in place, use would be recorded with a transponder and the cost of access would be set dynamically so that it was higher at peak travel times. This "congestion pricing" would maintain an optimum flow of traffic while maximizing revenues. It would give people the option to buy their way out of traffic at market price. Transportation wonks call these managed lanes; critics call them "Lexus lanes."

The first managed-lane project, Packard told the coalition, was already up and running elsewhere in Southern California. State Road 91 in Orange County had been fitted with a four-lane toll road up its middle. The price for single drivers followed a set schedule based on the hour and day of the week. What's more, these lanes were built and operated not by the city, county, or state, but as a *for-profit* private business. The California Private Transportation Company had put up $130 million to build the new lanes, and in return it held a franchise to collect the tolls for the first thirty-five years. This kind of highway privatization "is the wave of the future," Packard told the group on South Padre Island, "and toll-financed projects will probably have to be at least a part of the funding mechanisms for I-69."

Apparently the coalition members who heard this wild prophecy didn't take it very seriously. The meeting minutes do not record any ensuing discussion of tolls or privatization, and most of the attendees I spoke with more than ten years later didn't remember much, if anything, about Packard's talk. Roger Hord was clearly listening—after leaving the I-69 coalition a few years later, he would advocate similar HOT lanes for I-10 in Houston—but the others must have regarded Packard's lunch lecture as crazy talk. Those high-tech toll lanes blooming in Southern California, the capital of congestion, were exotic specimens that bore little relevance to the rural freeways most of the members craved. The I-69 coalition was largely looking to stimulate traffic, not manage it. They wanted to win recognition as a national priority deserving of federal largesse, not to nickel-and-dime the very residents and companies they hoped to attract.

When Packard had finished speaking, Mederos took the floor to deliver a report on her own efforts in Washington. She hadn't been advocating tolls. Instead she was working to convince Congress and the Clinton administration to set aside tax money for new highway programs that could pay for I-69. This effort was a success—the corridors and borders programs that Mederos and DeLay worked into the 1998 transportation reauthorization directed more than $150 million to I-69—but it wasn't Eisenhower-era money. And it wasn't enough.

Angling for government appropriations was a Sisyphean struggle: Just as the coalition's lobbyists had won leverage with the Clinton administration, the election of George W. Bush brought in a new crop of bureaucrats with ideas and agendas of their own. Bush kept Clinton's secretary of commerce, Norman Mineta, as his secretary of transportation and appointed a new federal highway administrator, Mary Peters. In the House of Representatives, owing to chairmanship term limits, the Republicans appointed a new head of the House Transportation and Infrastructure Committee, Don Young. The delegation from Bush's home state of Texas, which by then was pulling away from the coalition, had new leverage in Washington, and they got an early start, briefing their former governor and his administration in the White House in March 2001. Mederos wasn't far behind. That spring and summer, she made the rounds trying to sell Peters and Young on the importance of Interstate 69.

Peters had come to Washington from the fast-growing city of Phoenix, where she had been director of the Arizona DOT. She is an avid motorcyclist—she rides a Harley—and a bit of a rebel when it comes to the orthodoxy of transportation policy. In May 2002, the full coalition met with Peters on its annual trip to Washington, and she assured the members that there was still a "federal interest" in I-69. But there was no money for it. "We are in a zero-sum game," she told them. The federal gas tax, which had been the main source of money for highways since 1956, was losing its effectiveness, she explained, because as cars were becoming more efficient, drivers were paying less per mile. Many would have suggested in their next breath that Congress should raise the gas tax—as mentioned, the 18.4-cent-per-gallon charge had remained unchanged since 1993, despite inflation and higher gas prices—but not Peters. She told the coalition that it was time to look hard at innovative financing to augment or even replace the gas tax.

Gas-tax-based road financing has become ingrained in our basic understanding of how highways are built, but it was not even fifty years old when Peters questioned its effectiveness in front of the coalition members. When Congress created the Interstate Highway Program in 1956, it set up the Highway Trust Fund through which gas taxes, diesel taxes, and excise taxes from the sales of vehicles and tires were pooled and redistributed to the states as transportation money. Before then, construction costs were drawn out of the Treasury's general fund, but the Eisenhower administration and Congress at the time thought it best to create a new, dedicated mechanism to pay for the immense new construction they had planned. Some argued for tolls; others, taxes. Some wanted to sell bonds; others wanted pay as you go. It was only after much debate and political compromise that they devised the tax-financed trust fund.

The debate over how best to pay for highways is older than the automobile. A variety of means have been tried since the colonial era, when able-bodied men were called upon to maintain local roads during lulls in farming. In the early 1800s, before steamboats and railroads, private turnpikes were common. More than ten thousand miles of for-profit toll roads were spread across the young country. Like many canals, these roads became obsolete, fell into disuse, and reverted to public control. When a new hunger for highways emerged in the early twentieth century, Carl Fisher formulated his scheme to have the auto industry build great continental highways. But that idea subsided once federal aid for highways began in 1916.

Franklin Roosevelt was the first president to plan seriously for a network of national highways—and had it been up to him, they would have been toll roads. As Tom Lewis narrates in his excellent history of the interstate program, *Divided Highways,* FDR summoned Thomas Mac-Donald, the head of the Bureau of Public Roads, to the Oval Office one day in 1937. Roosevelt showed him a map of the nation onto which he had sketched approximate routes for a set of six new transcontinental toll roads—three north-south and three east-west. He asked MacDonald to study the viability of building such a system.

In addition to being a fan of tolls, Roosevelt also championed an idea he called "excess land taking," in which the government would acquire more land than the actual right-of-way required and then, once the new road's presence increased the value of that extra land, capture that gain to pay for the road. "We all know that it is largely a matter of chance if a new highway is located through one man's land and misses another man's land a few miles away," he wrote in a letter to Congress. "Yet the man who, by good fortune, sells a narrow right-of-way for a new highway makes, in most cases, a handsome profit through the increase in value of all of the rest of his land."

Why, Roosevelt asked, should these "unearned increments" go to a mere handful of lucky citizens (the Grahams, let's call them)? Why shouldn't it be the public, which put up the cost of the highway, that keeps these proceeds as reimbursement? As Roosevelt imagined it, the government "buys a wide strip on each side of the highway itself, uses it for the rental of concessions, and sells it off over a period of years to home builders and others who wish to live near a main artery of travel." Some of Roosevelt's advisors also suggested the government could sell gasoline at stations along these new roads to raise even more money. The excess-taking concept was reminiscent of Lincoln's use of land grants along the transcontinental railroad as payment to the private companies who built the line. But many condemned Roosevelt's proposition—in which the government, and not private business, would control the extra land—as socialistic.

MacDonald, who wielded considerable power doling out general-fund monies for roads, hated the idea of tolls. In April 1939 his Bureau of Public Roads released a detailed study of Roosevelt's plan for the six major highways. It was titled, to the point, *Toll Roads and Free Roads*, and it was dismissive of the idea of excess taking and tolls. It cited "the general attitude of the courts that private property taken under the power of eminent domain may not exceed that needed for public use," and, on the question of tolls, it concluded that "a liberal estimate of revenue . . . is less than 40 percent of a conservative estimate of debt service, maintenance, and operating cost." Traffic projections were strong enough to justify building the roads, the bureau found, but they were not high enough to harvest sufficient toll money. The second part of the report was "A Master Plan for Free Highway Development."

There was evidence to suggest that tolls *could* work, at least in some places. Robert Moses had built toll roads and bridges in New York City, and, in 1940, just after the publication of *Toll Roads and Free Roads*, the Pennsylvania Turnpike opened. All of these performed beautifully— so much so that other states soon followed suit. In 1944, the Roosevelt administration released a more extensive report, *Interregional Highways*, which featured the contributions of Harland Bartholomew, another presidential plug for excess taking, and a diagram of the more extensive highway network that later became the interstate system. Through the late forties and early fifties, heavily populated states, unwilling to wait for Congress to fully fund the plan, started constructing toll roads in the interregional-highway corridors. New York state built its thruway, New Hampshire and Maine built state toll roads, and New Jersey built its turnpike. Ohio and Indiana built toll routes that met up with the western end of the Pennsylvania Turnpike. This modern toll route from the East Coast to Chicago was completed in 1955, just in time for Congress to tackle the financing of the interstate system.

Eisenhower, like Roosevelt, envisioned a network of toll roads. In his first year in office, his administration put together a report on possible stimulus spending called *The Potential Use of Toll Road Development in a Business Depression*. Two years later he ordered the preparation of a plan that would "get 50 billion dollars' worth of self-liquidating highways under construction." Exactly what "self-liquidating" meant was unclear, and fifty billion dollars was a lot of money. Where would it come from? Eisenhower appointed a committee, led by his trusted aide General

Lucius Clay, and asked them to come up with a scheme that would not add to the national debt. After consulting with bankers, the Clay committee recommended that a new national corporation be formed to sell bonds that would be paid off with gas taxes.

But there was no consensus. The American Automobile Association and the American Petroleum Institute were arguing, naturally, for the use of general-revenue funds. Several of the president's top advisors were making a strong case for tolls. In the eighteen months of congressional wrangling that followed, gas-tax financing won out but the Clay committee's idea of borrowing was set aside in favor of a pay-as-you-go approach. The federal government would spend only what gas-tax money it had collected—and the Highway Trust Fund was born.

Just as the building of the interstates changed the face of the country, the establishment of the Highway Trust Fund helped create a uniquely American attitude about highways. Though several existing turnpikes were grandfathered into the system, tolling was expressly forbidden on new interstates. Without tolls to pay, Americans grew to love "the open road." But the popular perception of the "freeway" has impaired the driver's appreciation for the direct and indirect costs of driving. It hastened the decline of ticketed rail and transit services and encouraged decentralized development across the landscape. It has led to congestion and has made it politically difficult to raise the gas tax—a move that would be an unwelcome reminder that driving costs money.

But freeways aren't free. And no system that pretends so is sustainable. That was the reality that Mary Peters was itching to confront when she first sat down with the I-69 Mid-Continent Highway Coalition. She was talking birds and bees, the seedy truth of where roads really come from and what they really cost. They're not brought by a federal stork; they have to be paid for. And the American system for doing so was nearly bankrupt. It was time to try new things. There was a pilot program—created by a relatively obscure provision in the 1998 reauthorization, TEA-21—that would allow three states to add tolls to existing interstates to offset the cost of maintenance. Peters wanted to explore more ways to make funding flexible and wean departments of transportation off their reliance on the gas tax.

The secretary's musings on potential reforms were the rumblings of a revolution in philosophy, one that would complicate the strategy for I-69. The Mid-Continent Highway Coalition had been swimming upstream in arguing, during the Clinton years, that despite the ostensible completion of the interstate system, it was in the nation's interests to build one last great highway. But now, ten years into their efforts, they were suddenly facing an administration eager to redefine—and reduce—the federal role in road building. It was already the job of each state to study, design, and construct its portion of I-69. But if what Peters was saying was true, the states might have to figure out their own way to pay for it, too.

Concrete Futures

Texas, being Texas, had already worked up some bold ideas about how to solve the problem of highway funding. In June 2002, a month after Peters met with the coalition, Governor Rick Perry and the Texas Department of Transportation circulated a document titled *Crossroads of the Americas: Trans-Texas Corridor Plan*. Texas, the report asserted, was not simply the "Crossroads of America" (which may or may not still be Indianapolis). It was—and had long been—the crossroads of *North America*. "This concept has never been more relevant," it continued, taking a page from the I-69 argument, "as trade between North and South America continues to grow." What's more, the population of Texas was projected to continue growing at a rate of thirty thousand new residents a month. The existing road system was nearing the end of its design life and would not be enough to accommodate the new traffic. Texas didn't need just one new highway. It needed several, and they needed to be big.

Quoting Sam Houston on the importance of transportation ("We must all lay our hands to it as a great and mighty work of national interest . . ."), the report invoked the sweep of history—the animal trails, the Indian paths, the Spanish Camino Real, the Chisholm Trail, the railroads—and went on to introduce the largest engineering project ever proposed for Texas. "The concept is simple," it said. The Trans-Texas Corridor would be a four-thousand-mile network of multimodal swaths up to twelve hundred feet wide, each potentially containing a six-lane passenger highway; a separate four-lane truck highway; six lines for high-speed passenger trains, commuter rail, and freight rail traveling both directions; and, finally, a two-hundred-foot-wide zone for underground and aboveground utilities like water, oil, natural gas, electricity, and fiber optics. An artist's rendering showed what this transportation smorgasbord would look like cutting majestically (and without congestion) through wide-open agricultural land. It did not look like a Harland Bartholomew "people-first" highway. It looked like an engineer's fantasy—and a farmer's nightmare. "Though other state transportation agencies also are looking to the future," the report boasted, "no other state has proposed such an ambitious and visionary project as the Corridor." This was safe to say.

The Trans-Texas Corridor would be to the interstates what the interstates were to the old U.S. highways—a quantum leap forward, a whole step larger, the thoroughfares of the *future*. The cost, too, was ahead of its time: The TTC (as it came to be known) would cost as much as $183.5 billion, and that was the state's estimate, which one might expect to be low. How would such a thing be built, if the state could hardly afford to maintain the roads it had? The answer was as avant-garde as the TTC itself. There would be tolls, but they wouldn't necessarily be collected by local agencies like the ones in Houston or Dallas–Fort Worth. Instead the state would have the option of entering into development agreements with private companies. As TxDOT and the governor imagined it, a developer would pay for the construction and/or maintenance of the corridor in exchange for the exclusive right to toll it for a period of time. A single private entity would be able to propose a new project, design it, finance it, build it, maintain it, and operate it. By taking on those responsibilities and risks at little or no cost to the state, the developer would have the opportunity to make a profit.

This type of arrangement has many names—privatization, a public-private partnership (or P3), a concession, a franchise—but all of them were unfamiliar to most Americans, at least when it came to transportation projects. Interstate-era federal law prohibited the use of trust-fund dollars on new toll roads, so examples of P3s were scarce and highly experimental. The privately built HOT lanes on State Road 91 in Orange County, California, which went into operation in 1995, were a ten-mile demonstration project in the median of an existing highway. Virginia had dipped its toe into the water as well, allowing two short privately operated toll roads—the twelve-mile Dulles Greenway, which opened a few months before the California HOT lanes, and the nine-mile Pocahontas Parkway, which was due to open in September 2002. To find the kind of massive P3 projects Texas was contemplating, one had to look to other continents. The highway networks in France, Spain, and Portugal were largely built by this long-term concession model, and there was a plethora of privatized toll roads, bridges, and airports in Mexico and South America.

Texans are not prone to taking public-policy cues from Europe or Mexico, but the Trans-Texas Corridor idea attracted some early local support. Its first official endorsement came from the Alliance for I-69 Texas, which had heard assurances from TxDOT that the new plans would include—and expedite—the I-69 project. The agency made it clear that its top priority was TTC-35, a parallel route to Interstate 35, which was badly congested through the key cities of San Antonio, Austin, and Dallas–Fort Worth. The second priority was I-69, and TxDOT suggested that no matter what private toll corridor emerged, the agency would continue making improvements to the existing roads until there was a free, interstate-style connection—an "I-69 regional" alongside the new TTC-69. The alliance kept pushing in Austin and Washington for incremental upgrades along the two U.S. highways already marked "Future I-69." But for a group whose members didn't necessarily care what number their interstate wore to the valley, or where it went north of Texarkana, what would be the harm in supporting yet another funding scheme, however extreme, put forth by the governor?

What the governor and TxDOT needed, more than approval, were new *laws*. The private-development agreements called for in the corridor plan were, technically speaking, illegal, but a small group of consultants had compiled a wish list of "statutory tools." The Texas legislature, which meets biennially during odd-numbered years, took up the matter in 2003, though it's not clear that it got a proper hearing. That year's session was a governmental circus.

In the 2002 elections, with the help of a political action committee organized by Tom DeLay, the Republicans had won control of the state house and senate for the first time since Reconstruction. Once in power, the Republicans moved to redraw the state's U.S. congressional districts to make them more GOP-friendly and boost the party's majority in Washington. During the regular session, fifty-three Democratic members of the Texas house fled to Oklahoma to prevent a quorum and stop the redistricting. Governor Perry called a special session and eleven Democratic senators fled to New Mexico. The Texas Rangers tried to bring the legislators back. A second special session was called, and then a third.

In the end a compromise map was drawn, but the political grudge match sullied a lot of reputations, including Tom DeLay's. Because candidates for the Texas legislature are restricted in accepting campaign contributions from corporate donors, a grand jury indicted DeLay on charges that he laundered illegal donations for state races through his Washington political action committee. The Republican takeover stuck, though, and the new majority brought with it new committee leadership, including a house transportation chairman, Mike Krusee, who was bullish on transportation reform and privatization. While his chamber fought over the congressional map, Krusee submitted a piece of legislation, House Bill 3588, that promised to forever change the road map.

HB 3588 provided all of the statutory tools outlined in the corridor plan, and then some. The Trans-Texas Corridor could include not just the roads, rails, and utilities, but also "ancillary facilities" like freight-transfer areas, warehouses, maintenance yards, gas stations, and restaurants. These roadside enterprises would be exempt from state and local property taxes, and land for them could be taken by eminent domain. The bill imposed new methods of financing that were not limited to the Trans-Texas Corridor. Multicounty areas could now form their own toll agencies ("regional mobility authorities") and enter into development agreements with private companies. Toll conversions—the imposition of tolls on existing free roads—would be permitted on state highways. And the public or private operators could charge whatever they wanted. Tolls, fares, and fees would not be subject to supervision or regulation by any governmental entity. *Crossroads of the Americas* had pitched privatization as a tool, not a mandate, but HB 3588 went further. It wasn't going to fool around with pilot programs and tests. "The department shall encourage the participation of private entities in the planning, design, construction, and operation of facilities," it read, "to the maximum extent practical and economical."

In spite of (or with the help of) the confusion that gripped the 2003 session, Krusee's transportation bill passed the house with only three nay votes, cruised unanimously through the senate, and Perry signed it into law that June. The passage of HB 3588 astounded even transportation wonks who had been advocating the very ideas it contained. Robert Poole, the founder, former president, and director of transportation research at the Reason Foundation, a libertarian think tank, told me in 2004 that he was floored by Texas's "brave strides." Poole's writings on privatization in the late eighties helped shape the California laws allowing the State Road 91 HOT lanes and other projects, but Texas's new enabling legislation was "by far the best, the broadest, most comprehensive, most flexible" he'd ever seen. "It's the first time any state has said, as a matter of policy, that *every* new addition to the limited-access highway system, whether it's adding lanes or building a new bridge or a new corridor, has to be evaluated to see if it can be done with tolls. Nobody's come anywhere *close* to that before." Poole, who referred to the interstate system as "that last bastion of socialism," was awed by the accomplishment. "I think they're really setting the pace for the rest of the country. This is a sea change."

The permissive new law also impressed transportation officials in other states, several of whom made pilgrimages to Texas. Krusee became a policy celebrity in high demand, meeting with Governor Schwarzenegger's advisors in California and traveling to the Midwest and Florida to hold forth on the future of transportation. I first met him in August 2004, when his victory was still fresh. The legislature was dormant that year, and he sat in his office in the Capitol wearing a short-sleeved golf shirt and suntan. Krusee is fiftyish, handsome, and blond, with the charm and slight impudence of someone who might have been a troublemaker as a child. He describes his younger self as precocious. On his wall hung a poster-size photograph of Bobby Kennedy, who Krusee says was his was his boyhood hero. "I was kind of a policy wonk at age ten," he said. He "gobbled up" *Time* and *Newsweek* before graduating to *Harper's* and the *Atlantic Monthly.* By age thirteen, he was spending afternoons in the library reading foreign-policy journals. Though Krusee is now unmistakably conservative—he signed Grover Norquist's no-tax pledge, for instance—back then "I wasn't old enough to start saying I was a Democrat or a Republican. But in '72, the Democrats just went nuts. They wanted to surrender in Vietnam and didn't care who went communist. And to me that was like, 'God, you don't remember the Treaty of Versailles?' It was like America in the 1920s." He pointed at Bobby. "And *he* wasn't like that. He tried to kill Castro! You know? He worked for Joe McCarthy. He was against welfare, in the form that it took. His politics weren't that different from Ronald Reagan's."

Krusee was a young star in the Texas Republican party. Months before the 2002 elections, he was made aware of Tom DeLay's efforts to orchestrate a new house majority, and the soon-to-be house speaker, Tom Craddick, told Krusee he could take over the House Transportation Committee if the plan succeeded. Krusee had never even been on the committee before becoming its chairman in 2003. But his district north of Austin had doubled in population since his election in 1992, and congestion was becoming an issue for his commuting constituents. Having been involved with Austin's Capital Area Metropolitan Planning Organization, Krusee understood that transportation was a key issue ripe for reform. "I knew in advance that we were going to take over, and I spent that summer of 2002 studying all the issues," he said. *Crossroads of the Americas* had been unveiled, and Krusee believed that in order to craft the kind of groundbreaking bill the governor wanted—and that he felt Texas needed—he needed to solicit advice from the very private sector whose participation he hoped to attract.

Krusee already had a well-connected advisor: a transportation and planning consultant named Mike Weaver, whose firm, Prime Strategies, works virtually every side of infrastructure development. In the early eighties, Weaver ran Houston's Metropolitan Planning Organization and helped set up the now-lucrative Harris County Toll Authority. Today he still advises various governmental entities on setting up toll programs, while also representing overseas contractors who are trying to win concessions and build toll roads. That summer, while DeLay worked his campaign-money magic, Weaver tutored Krusee, who, like most people, had to wrap his mind around the idea of paying directly for roads. "I came in not really understanding any of this," Krusee said. "And I had to basically start looking at transportation as another utility just like water, electricity, or cable TV. Not only do you have a meter, but you pay more for using during peak capacity. Same thing should be for roads. I'll be sitting at a conference table with mayors and county commissioners from a certain region, explaining this to them. And they say, 'We understand all that, Mike, but politically, our people won't accept it.' And I'll look around and I'll go, 'Well, I notice we're drinking bottled water here. Why? Water's free.' And then I'll go, 'How many people have cable TV?' Everyone raises their hand. 'Don't you understand the airwaves are free? They belong to the public.'"

Shortly after speaking with Krusee, I met Weaver, whose shy manner and modest workspace clashed with what I knew of his professional standing. His clients include multibillion-dollar construction corporations operating across the globe—in Canada, South America, Europe, Africa, and Asia—but he runs his firm out of a small converted house that is tucked between a head shop and a pool hall on South Lamar Avenue in Austin. Weaver made the same water and television analogies that Krusee had—though I could tell I was now hearing the original versions—and also pointed out that the sun is free and yet people go tanning. He compared road pricing to airline fares. "If I can plan my trip and I can fly whenever I want to go, I get a super discount," he said. "If I have to go but I can't stay on Saturday night, I pay another price. And if I find out I gotta go to Washington today, I pay a *lot*. And toll roads are the same way. If I'm in a hurry and I have to get downtown at seven thirty in the morning, I pay five bucks to be in a Lexus lane. If I can go at eight thirty and traffic's not that bad, then I won't."

On a shelf behind his desk, Weaver keeps at hand a dozen or so books on transportation and urban planning, including Caro's *The Power Broker*, Richard Florida's *The Rise of the Creative Class*, and one titled *Driving Forces: The Automobile, Its Enemies, and the Politics of Mobility*. In the summer of 2002, Weaver gave Krusee a copy of *Nothing Like It in the World*, Stephen Ambrose's tome on the building of the transcontinental railroad. Reading about the robber barons, Krusee says, helped convince him of the merit of working with the private sector to build infrastructure. He was also quite taken with the precedent of capturing the increase of land values to help fund construction—as FDR once imagined doing for roads with excess land taking.

"Basically they said, 'Look, when we build the railroad, we know that the property around it is going to increase tremendously in value,'" he said. "And I thought, you know, that really makes sense. Why shouldn't we take some of that?" This notion found its way into HB 3588 via the provision allowing the taking of land along the corridors for utility easements and "ancillary facilities" like truck stops, freight warehouses, and restaurants. If the private sector was going to build and operate the corridor, Krusee figured, it should have first crack at selling the amenities along it—which most definitely should be *sold*. "I have a problem with public rest stops," Krusee went on. "To me, we're just subsidizing truckers."

Krusee felt fortunate, he said, to be studying these issues under the radar, before anyone knew that the Republicans would be taking power. "The trucker unions didn't pay any attention to me," he said. "I never had to deal with any special interest." Some might put international corporations interested in private toll-road development under the umbrella of "special interests," but Krusee apparently does not. That summer, newly informed on the fundamentals of tolling and privatization, Krusee continued his education with a series of trips to visit toll projects in other parts of the country. Weaver went along and introduced him to some of the banking and construction interests with whom he had worked. Krusee listened hard. "I sat down with consultants and the private sector," he told me, "and I said, 'What works? What would really bring you in?' I basically formed a little kitchen cabinet. And we met almost every single weekend. I met with banks, with construction companies, with engineering companies—everybody who had an interest. Of course, their interest was to *build* a whole bunch more so they could make money off it. And that coincided with my interest, which was to take care of the capacity that we needed in Texas."

With his brain trust assembled, it was time for Krusee to start putting ideas on paper. After the elections, with the new balance of power clear, Weaver and Krusee began meeting with Governor Perry and his close friend Ric Williamson, whom Perry had appointed to the Texas Transportation Commission, the five-member body that makes policy for TxDOT. Perry and Williamson provided language about the Trans-Texas Corridor, which Weaver and Krusee collated with language written by their private-sector advisors, who had clear ideas about what perfect legislation might look like. They fielded suggestions from banks that financed toll projects—such as J.P. Morgan—from large domestic construction companies—including Kiewit, a client of Weaver's—and from international toll-road developers—specifically a Spanish firm named Cintra, a subsidiary of Ferrovial, the largest private infrastructure operator in the world. "We had a bunch of folks coming in who viewed a very favorable political climate in Texas," Weaver said. They knew that the governor, the new house speaker, and the new house transportation chairman were keen on P3s. "They were saying, 'This is the place. And if we're gonna do it, here's what we've learned.'" The new law itself would be a public-private partnership.

All of the concepts that Weaver and Krusee assembled had to be submitted and shepherded through markup, and for that task they brought in John Langmore, who had recently left his job as an executive at the construction-equipment manufacturer Caterpillar. A colleague of Weaver's had gone to middle school with Langmore and knew that he was looking for a career change. Langmore joined Krusee's staff as a legislative aide and took charge of HB 3588. "Everything that went in or out went through me," Langmore explained. "It was kind of a revolutionary bill in the transportation world. It's talked about all over the country. I didn't know that when I got down here. I just had to learn on the fly." One major challenge was negotiating between overlapping agendas—the governor was most interested in the Trans-Texas Corridor, local officials were itching for stronger regional control, and the private sector wanted friendly provisions about development agreements. "There were like eight or nine significant transportation bills in their own right when the session started. We started to feel that they were all gonna get picked apart," Langmore told me. "So what we decided to do—and it was a strategic move—was to roll them all together so everyone had to decide if they wanted this whole package. That's why it became so big. It was a three-hundred-plus-page bill."

Given the significance of the reforms contained in HB 3588, Langmore admits that there wasn't nearly as much discussion on the bill as one might think. "Not all the legislators are that into the details. They look to the committees. If it passes out of committee, they sort of take it at face value," he said. The hottest debate on the bill was over a relatively unrevolutionary increase in fines on drunk driving and other violations, and where the estimated $250 million of additional income would end up. "But all the rest of it—the Trans-Texas Corridor, even tolling—people didn't get it."

The governor and TxDOT didn't seem to be in any rush to educate the public about the new powers and projects that the legislature had approved—the department wouldn't hold the first public meetings on the Trans-Texas Corridor for another eight months. But it was eager to start making deals. On July 25, barely a month after Governor Perry signed HB 3588, TxDOT issued a request for proposals on the I-35 segment of the Trans-Texas Corridor. In August, the agency held a workshop for potential bidders at its headquarters in Austin. Phillip Russell, director of the Texas Turnpike Authority, told those assembled that the Transportation Commission and the governor "don't want any grass to grow under our feet . . . We will be moving very, very aggressively forward on this project." He hoped that TxDOT would be able to sign a contract for TTC-35 by the end of 2004. "And I would anticipate the I-69 corridor will probably be teed up in the next couple of years as well," he added.

The Alliance for I-69 Texas had publicly expressed support of HB 3588, just as it had for the Trans-Texas Corridor. But that summer the alliance's eyes were still on Washington, not Austin. The *Fort Bend Sun* ran a photo of Tom DeLay and Mary Peters standing over Secretary

Mineta as he wrote out a modest $6.5 million check for environmental studies in Texas. And in Brownsville, at a U.S. Senate field hearing on transportation, Rio Grande valley leaders lined up to complain that they weren't getting their fair share of tax dollars from the federal government—exactly the kind of futile supplication that Krusee and other privatization advocates hoped to make unnecessary.

In early 2004, TxDOT started to flex its new statutory muscles. The agency held public meetings on the Trans-Texas Corridor and started to strongly suggest tolling for a number of smaller projects around the state. There was resistance—more than TxDOT expected—but it pushed ahead. Paradigm shifts are always hard, they told themselves. Their new aggressive policies found a voice in Ric Williamson, who became the chairman of the Texas Transportation Commission that January. Williamson was a low-key but straight-talking man with a stubbly shaved head and hounddog eyes. If you disliked Williamson, you would say he was arrogant. If you liked him, you would probably *still* say he was arrogant, but you'd admire his strong belief that the citizens of Texas deserved to hear the truth. When the mayor of El Paso publicly complained that TxDOT was pressuring him to toll a long-awaited highway loop, Williamson answered directly: "It's either toll roads, slow roads, or no roads," he told the *El Paso Times.* When Houston rejected state plans to add tolls to its Tomball Parkway, Williamson said he could sympathize with the objections, but predicted that "in your lifetime most existing roads will have tolls."

In an earlier career as a Texas state legislator, Williamson had earned the nickname "Nitro" for what *The Dallas Morning News* once called his "energetic and sometimes volatile temperament." His evangelizing on transportation perpetuated that reputation, and in August 2004 Williamson was heralded as a reformer at the seventh annual Texas transportation summit in Irving. The conference, held at a hotel nestled in the tangle of freeways and suburbs between Dallas and Fort Worth, was packed with elected officials, economic-development types, and construction executives who attended seminars called "Aging Transportation Infrastructure: The Achilles' Heel of the Nation" and "The Use and Benefits of Toll Roads Throughout the Nation." Tom DeLay gave a keynote breakfast address, remarking that "the work of connecting our nation has been done," but "innovative, flexible financing tools are the only way we're going to meet all the needs we will have in the future." Over lunch, Williamson received the Johnson Transportation Excellence

Award. Congresswoman Eddie Bernice Johnson, for whom the honor is named, presented. "Ric Williamson is one person who, in a short period of time, has left an indelible positive mark on our transportation system," she said. "He has led us to a new level of thinking."

Williamson was humble, if a bit of a ham. He appreciated the accolades, he said, but they were more properly directed to Governor Perry. "I served twelve great years in the legislature doing something I wanted to do: serve people," he said. "And I left because he asked me to help, and because I was weary. I was weary of the easy way out. I was weary of the *whining*. And the waste of time and wasted energy and not solving the problem. So I was an easy target for my best friend." Williamson had known Perry for many years. In the late eighties, when the two were rookie state legislators, they shared an apartment in Austin and became close friends. "And I talk to him every night," Williamson said, his voice grown tender, "and I say, 'Are you okay? Is there a problem?' And he says, 'No. Somebody's got to pay for the roads. I could walk across this state and promise everybody that more money was on the way. But that doesn't get the road built.'"

I spoke to Williamson a few weeks after the summit in Dallas, and he described the predicament the governor was trying to fix. Texas was in a bind, he said, because it had never adequately imagined its future. "We were a rural state fifty years ago," when the interstate system was born, Williamson said. "We built our major highways right smack through the middle of our urban centers." It's not so much a rural state now. As Texas's cities and suburbs grew, frontage along urban interstates became crowded with valuable development. TxDOT scrambled to widen and stack highways as much as possible inside cities and to construct new loops on the outskirts. But the congestion only worsened, and it was now clear to Perry and Williamson that the only way to relieve it was to leapfrog the growth and build new mega-thoroughfares where land was still available: in the rural periphery of metropolitan areas.

I asked Williamson whether he and Perry foresaw a greater role for transit in the fight against congestion. He sighed. "As you know, public transit never really caught on too well in Texas," he said. He was well aware of the argument, made by the Sierra Club and others, that building more highways could never cure traffic problems, and that denser development and more robust public transportation was the only way to reduce the amount of required driving. But he, like the soothsayers at

Roger Hord's West Houston Association, didn't see that happening in Texas. "We don't have the population density for transit, because owning your own home is very important in Texas. Not owning your own *condo* or owning your own *flat*. Owning your own *home*. It's just one of the reasons people are here. Low taxes, low regulation, low services. Ours is a state of individual reward and punishment—across all ethnic lines, across all economic lines. People don't come to Texas to go on welfare. They come to Texas to work."

Williamson's description of the local mind-set was in complete harmony with the "ownership society" ideal that President Bush, Perry's gubernatorial predecessor, had been proposing that same year. "The more ownership there is in America," Bush said in 2004, "the more vitality there is in America and the more people have a vital stake in the future of this country." If it was good for the nation to have citizens take control and responsibility of their own homes, retirement savings, education, and health, maybe there was virtue in having *corporate* citizens take control and responsibility for the nation's transportation system.

When Governor Perry called for a new transportation plan, Williamson told me, "he said, 'I want a minimal amount of state tax money invested in this plan. I want the private sector to drive how fast we move and how aggressively we build. And the way we can do that is allow them to own a lot of it. Because they're not going to destroy their capital on purpose.'" The only transportation projects truly worth building, Williamson suggested, were the ones for which demand would furnish a profit. If transit advocates wanted streetcars and buses, Williamson said, they should come forward with a proposal to invest their own money to build them.

This business-minded philosophy was also bad news for roads to nowhere and other pork projects, Williamson insisted, but could be great news for justifiable endeavors like I-69 that had been pushed aside at the overcrowded federal trough. "There is no money to do any of these big transportation corridors that Congress, in its wisdom, says it's gonna build. The governor believes that some of these corridors *need* to be built—whether Congress eventually pays for it or individual states pay for it or, in the case of Texas, we turn to the private sector and say, 'Be our partners,'" Williamson explained. "Otherwise, the hollow promise of money to build I-69 will never be fulfilled. The governor knows that there is no pot of gold in Washington. There is no federal road fairy."

Not So Fast

Not to belabor the point, but Texas is a very, very big state. It's big enough to fit seven Indianas or thirty-five New Jerseys, with too many political microclimates to count. Census numbers may demonstrate a precipitous shift in population from rural to urban, but there's still a hell of a lot of country, which is occupied by 3.6 million rural residents who still experience Texas as a vast open land dotted with small towns and cattle. Out in their Texas, the transportation problems of growing metropolises such as Houston and Dallas seem academic. They drive on numbered two-lane highways labeled FM—"Farm to Market"—in the east and RM—"Ranch to Market"—in the west. They do not get stuck in traffic, and they do not pay tolls. At least not yet.

David and Linda Stall live in Fayette County, in a cattle community halfway between Houston and Austin. The Stalls are not ranchers—Linda works as an escrow officer at a law firm in the county seat of LaGrange, and David was the city manager of Columbus, a town off of I-10 twenty-five miles to the southeast—but they can look out any window of their farmhouse and see cows. They chose a rural Texas life after years in California, and have since made a point of immersing themselves in local history, tape-recording interviews with elderly neighbors and learning everything they could about the property on which they live. They look the part, too: The Stalls are big people, they drive a big truck, and they like to share meat-and-potato meals at small-town family restaurants. They weren't born in Texas, but they got there as soon as they could.

In the summer of 2002, David and Linda joined a few dozen of their neighbors at a chamber of commerce luncheon in LaGrange. The executive director of TxDOT had come to speak about the new Trans-Texas Corridor plan that the governor was proposing as a solution to their transportation problems. The residents of Fayette County were unaware that they *had* transportation problems, and when their visitor proudly handed out printed copies of the ninety-six-page *Crossroads of the Americas* report, with its artist's rendering of the mighty corridor cutting through the rural landscape, they were alarmed. "In the old days, if you got a road project in your community, you'd probably been hearing about it for ten years," Linda told me later. "You'd heard the whole drill for as long as you could remember. But this is coming from the governor's office, and there isn't a soul around here who understands why they need these giant toll roads. Mostly because they don't. This isn't something they asked for. This is someone's idea of revenue generation."

The Stalls had never before concerned themselves with the intricacies of transportation finance. But they were civic- and legal-minded people, and they knew a bad idea when they heard one. Like the Tokarskis a decade before them, the Stalls left that first mind-blowing highway meeting mad enough to holler. But *unlike* the Tokarskis ten years before, the Stalls had the Internet. "David's answer for everything was to build a website," Linda told me, "so that's what we did." David set up a home page, and Linda began compiling counterpoint arguments to each of the rationales offered by the state. David was a member of both the Lions and the Rotary clubs, and so he arranged for Linda to speak to the two groups (separately, as they are rivals) at a mom-and-pop restaurant called Schobel's, near the interstate exit in Columbus. She handed out copies of the executive summary of the *Crossroads of the Americas* report with their website address affixed to the cover.

Most people they spoke with assumed the plan was bull. Perry was running for reelection, trying to break out of George W. Bush's shadow, and surely the whole idea would dissolve after November, people said. "I talked to my state rep, and I talked to my farm bureau guy," Linda told me. "And they were like, 'Oh, pooh-pooh.' They thought it would need funding, and there wasn't any money, and so how could they do it? They didn't know about public-private partnerships, because that was all new. That power was in the state's legislative wish list, but none of us knew what we were reading, and neither did the legislature." The Stalls backed off. "Life moved on. My daughter was married, my granddaughter was born. We let it go," Linda said. "I will *never* do that again."

The next they heard of the corridor was in February 2004. Perry had been reelected, and House Bill 3588 had quietly passed through the legislature and across the governor's desk. The new law required TxDOT to

hold at least one corridor meeting in each affected county before it designated any routes. Naturally, the department wanted to get this unpleas-
antness out of the way as quickly as possible, and so in twenty-three days
it held 254 hearings, as many as 30 a day—a "blitzkrieg," the Stalls call
it. These meetings, despite the state-altering subject matter, were poorly
advertised and sparsely attended. The Stalls recounted how, at one rural
meeting, one citizen attended—and two reporters, who ended up interviewing each other. TxDOT held its meeting in LaGrange, a predomi-
nantly Catholic community, on Ash Wednesday. But the Stalls had spread
the word, and seventy-five people showed up. It was standing room only,
and the county judge demanded a second meeting, to which eight hundred people came. The unruly crowd bombarded the state officials with
angry questions. "How close does this corridor come to Crawford, Texas?"
one man in a cowboy hat, who evidently suspected a Bush-led conspiracy, yelled out. Another man took an unlit cigar out of his mouth to ask
whether there would be a vote on the plan. There would not.

The Stalls beefed up their website, CorridorWatch.org, and attracted
a few press interviews. Soon they were fielding calls from across the state
inviting them to come and speak. They traveled, over the next few years,
to more than five hundred meetings, some in towns they never knew
existed. One Saturday morning they arrived in a tiny hamlet near Hills-
boro and were sure there had been some mistake. "It was a ghost town,"
David said. "Most of it's boarded up." They drove around looking for the
small school where they were supposed to appear. "There was not a car on
the street. But we got to the school, and it looked like it was homecom-
ing! The whole *county* was there. They had handmade signs on everything.
It was really something."

Their audiences were enthusiastic and well-informed, too. People had
found their website, printed out pages of documents, and distributed
them to neighbors who didn't have Internet connections. Word spread at
cafés, churches, and stockyards. "Once you connect with one person in a
small community, they do the rest," David said. "We would e-mail them
a flyer, and they would print them. And when we got the hang of it, we
would use Kinko's, and we prepay it. We would just tell them, 'Can you
get to, you know, Kingsville? There's a Kinko's there. They'll have your
materials waiting for you.'"

The logistics required to run a statewide political operation would have
drowned most activists, but the Stalls were savvy and highly communi-

cative. I once rode in their truck with David, who was a police officer for twenty-two years, and the front seat was a tangle of cords and wires connected to a ham radio and three or four cell phones. David had set up one phone with a 202 area code because he found that people in Washington, D.C., were more likely to answer calls from inside the Beltway. He had a dashboard mount for his laptop, a mobile Internet card, and he wore a Bluetooth headset. Between this mobile command unit and their website, the Stalls were never out of touch, and their hyperconnectivity paid off. Thousands signed up to receive CorridorWatch's e-mail bulletins. In its first week of existence, the site enlisted members from eleven Texas counties. By June 2004, after just a hundred days online, its ranks included residents from fifty-five counties and elected officials from six.

The Stalls were just as methodical in working the political process. They started locally, convincing their LaGrange County Commissioners to draft a resolution denouncing the corridor plan. They got the State Farm Bureau, which had supported Perry's candidacy (the governor is, as he likes to point out, the son of tenant farmers), to do the same. And that summer, at the state Republican convention, the Stalls introduced a platform plank condemning the corridor. The party ratified it overwhelmingly, citing concerns about property rights and unnecessary spending, just a day before it nominated Perry for reelection. Buoyed by the populist embrace, the Stalls went around to state representatives and senators and solicited promises to roll back the more egregious portions of HB 3588. The legislators, who were running for reelection that year, were forced to take positions on the corridor plan. Many publicly came clean about not having read HB 3588 and insisted that they wouldn't have voted for it had they known what it contained.

By then, David and Linda had become experts on transportation policy and privatization. They read and reread HB 3588, perused and posted every relevant news article, and scrutinized the public comments being made by Ric Williamson and others. The more they learned, the more they found objectionable. "When we started initially, it was a NIMBY thing," Linda admitted. "We didn't want it coming through Fayette County anywhere near us. But as we read the plan more carefully, we realized this wasn't good for anyone." They saw that the reforms the legislature had passed would give inordinate economic and political power to corporations while moving the infrastructure-building process out of public reach. Unlike the Texas Railroad Commission, the Transportation

Commission was not an elected body, and there was no easy recourse to change the policies it set forth. "So now there's an appointed board making deals with private companies who get to operate a corridor in your backyard," she said. "That's two nightmares together: big business and government."

When I first met the Stalls in 2004, I had just interviewed Mike Krusee and Mike Weaver, and so I repeated the proponents' argument about bottled water and cable TV—how elsewhere in the economy, people willingly pay the cost of the conveniences they consume while private companies handle the transactions. But highways are not merely a convenience, the Stalls argued, and no matter how you finance it, the burden of paying for a road will rest ultimately on the average citizen, whether they be taxpayers or toll-payers. Any economic efficiency gained through privatization, they said, would be offset by the hunger for a profit margin. By letting a private company operate a toll road and set fares, the state will have succeeded only in privatizing taxation—while removing representation. "And you know what?" Linda said. "People in rural communities *don't* drink bottled water, and we *don't* get cable. So it's difficult for those guys to come down here and sell that banter. They get booed out of the room. People go, 'You're gonna take the nicest parts of the state and carve it up with this garbage!'"

David Stall likens HB 3588 to a pizza with everything on it. Krusee and the governor had sold it to legislators by hyping whatever aspect most appealed to them—local control, new highways, or high-speed rail. "But what we're finding out is when you put this together, not everyone likes anchovies and not everyone likes bell pepper," David said. What happens when the state starts using the corridor concept to allow privatized water infrastructure? What effect will the increased construction have on the environment? How much land would be taken from farmers and ranchers? As worries spread, a variety of groups with parochial interests began pecking away at the new transportation policies, and the Stalls saw an opportunity.

In November 2004, five months after Williamson accepted his award at the Texas transportation summit, the Stalls hosted their own conference. They rented out a small hotel ballroom just off I-35 in Austin and gathered the first toll-and-corridor summit. Some forty people from across the state and across the political spectrum attended: environmentalists from Houston, mass-transit gadflies, antitoll activists from Dallas and San Antonio and Austin, libertarians, and property-rights conservatives. There was even a Florida woman who happened to be passing through Texas: She had read about CorridorWatch online and sympathized with the cause. Political leaders in the growing Sunshine State had also flirted with toll hikes to build more highways. Her car sat in the parking lot covered in painted signs that said STOP TOLL ABUSE.

Linda Stall called the summit to order and told the story of how she and David had become involved: "I didn't know I was a grassroots activist until I read the Trans-Texas Corridor proposal and I read House Bill 3588." Who would have guessed, she said, that transportation would suddenly be the hot issue in Texas? But there they were, and even with agendas so disparate, they shared a legitimate and important concern about what was happening to their state, she said. Together, they could prevent a disaster. "We don't have any money," she said of CorridorWatch. "What we have is knowledge."

David rose from his seat to summarize what he saw as the many evils of HB 3588: the half million acres of land, by his calculations, that would be required for the corridor; the multidecade agreements allowed with private contractors; and the provision that gave those companies the ability to lease property along the corridor for "use as a facility and use for unrelated commercial, industrial, or agricultural purposes." He sprinkled his litany with some of Ric Williamson's more outrageous statements. " 'It's either toll roads, slow roads, or no roads'? That's the chairman of the state transportation commission. This is the guy that you look to, to make sure that your state highways are there," he said. " 'In your lifetime most existing roads will have tolls'? That's their vision for Texas?"

Over box lunches, Terry Keel, a Republican state representative from Austin, offered encouragements and ominous warnings. "I agreed to come speak today because I was so impressed, because this is a genuine grassroots movement that I have never seen the likes of before," Keel said. He hoped that House Bill 3588 would be reexamined and amended during the next session, in 2005, but "that's gonna be an uphill battle. Because there will be very powerful—*very* powerful—moneyed interests who are going to be fighting that every step of the way."

Sal Costello, a goateed freelance marketing consultant and the purveyor of AustinTollParty.com (now defunct), ranted about a local proposal to place tolls on a new, tax-funded expressway. He was leading an effort to recall the mayor of Austin and the state representatives who supported the plan—the protest equivalent of "a four-by-four with rusty nails at the end," he said, but he believed it was his only recourse. "These people can lease or sell our highways to *companies*," he said with incredulity. "Transportation is for *us*. These are *our* roads. And it's not right to take what is ours so that other companies can profit off of us." Costello had found what seemed to be a smoking gun online, a state document called "Toll Financing 101" that coached companies and public agencies on how best to implement turnpikes. A page titled "Limiting the Alternatives" advised toll operators that "free alternatives mean lower revenues"—clear evidence, Costello thought, that TxDOT was operating with complete disregard for the public welfare. His Googling had also turned up hefty contributions to Perry's campaigns from road builders and consultants— proof, he thought, that political payback was driving the road plans.

The presentations continued through the afternoon, each one introducing a new objection to the Trans-Texas Corridor. A Houston woman from the Sierra Club's antisprawl campaign lectured on the environmental and social evils caused by automobile-oriented development, which new roads would exacerbate. David Langford, an older rural conservative representing the Texas Wildlife Association, spoke somberly of the swaths of land that the new monster corridors would consume—including, potentially, land that had been in his family for seven generations— and then gave a pep talk on democracy. "Government is operating in this room right now," he said, "and it doesn't matter who the president of the United States is."

At the end of the summit, the delegates attempted to draft a joint resolution to release to the press. The group arranged long tables into a square. "This looks like the end of the Korean War," Langford joked.

"I hope it's more successful," Linda replied. But as the writing progressed, the synthesis of passions proved somewhat tricky. The Austin antitoll activists had to confess that although they were concerned about congestion, they weren't necessarily opposed to building more roads. The environmentalists *were* opposed to building more roads but didn't really mind the idea of tolls, since they thought that driving should be made more expensive. They were also for high-speed rail, the construction of which would surely require a sacrifice of land from the likes of Langford. The Stalls also weren't against toll roads per se but were wary of privatization and the Trans-Texas Corridor.

"We need to narrow the choke pattern of this shotgun," Langford said after the conversation had traveled in several circles. "I mean, what are we here to fix?" The answer was not a specific policy, they decided, but a law. The compromise statement, in the end, declared that House Bill 3588 "is bad for Texas." It listed a menu of reasons why, and ended with a pledge to "work together to further identify our specific concerns" and to "pursue all necessary revisions of such laws during the next session of the Texas legislature."

But would that be soon enough? Perry, Williamson, and TxDOT, well aware of the mounting political pressure, were moving fast to award their first privatization contract, a so-called Comprehensive Development Agreement for TTC-35. Three consortiums had submitted bids—one led by the American company Fluor, another by Skanska of Sweden, and a third led by Cintra, the Spanish firm with a reputation for aggressive proposals and big ambitions for American infrastructure. Few people in the United States had heard of Cintra before 2004, but that October the company made an ostentatious debut. The city of Chicago, eager for a way out of crushing debt, had decided to lease the Skyway, a 7.8-mile overland toll bridge between the Indiana Toll Road and the Dan Ryan Expressway downtown. Unlike the new roads being contemplated in Texas, the Skyway had proven traffic numbers. It was the favorite fast route into Chicago from the east, and city officials were hoping that a ninety-nine-year lease might fetch an upfront payment of hundreds of millions of dollars. Cintra, partnered with the Australian bank Macquarie, offered $1.8 billion, 50 percent more than the next highest bidder. Chicago politicians were giddy. The payment came out to more than four thousand dollars a foot. It was the best deal, they said, since the Dutch bought Manhattan.

Presumably they meant that they had swindled Cintra, not the other way around. But no one would really know for another century. Cintra had been in the tolling business for a long time, was patient, and didn't throw away money. That's why the company was able to put together the biggest deals. Once it had a road, it could do what politicians couldn't: raise tolls. On the Skyway, the fare had been a static two dollars since 1993. But Cintra would be able to charge up to five dollars by 2017, and without the risk of losing elections. The company would only risk losing customers, who would likely find congestion if they sought relief from tolls.

The Stalls had done their homework on Cintra and Macquarie, and they pointed to the companies' first North American lease, a toll-road bypass around Toronto called the 407, as a cautionary tale. Toronto 407 was the world's first all-electronic, open-access toll highway: Drivers with dashboard transponders paid through debit accounts (like E-ZPass), while those without transponders had their license plates photographed and were billed in the mail. Customers alleged erroneous charges, and when the companies jacked up the tolls, drivers complained of price gouging. In 2004, after the Liberal Party's Dalton McGuinty took over as premier, the provincial government of Ontario sued to rein in the concessionaires' toll increases, but an independent arbitrator and then the Ontario Superior Court both ruled that the government had no power over toll rates. The ninety-nine-year-lease contract, which the Conservative premier Mike Harris had awarded the Cintra-Macquarie consortium in 1999, was airtight.

This was bad news for unhappy drivers, and the Stalls feared that Texans would find themselves stuck with a similar case of seller's remorse. But it was good news for infrastructure investors. Jose Maria Lopez de Fuentes, the president of Cintra's operations in the U.S. and Canada, told me in 2007 that the company considers "a serious court system" a top requirement for investing in a country. "All we buy is a contract. This is all we have," Lopez de Fuentes said. "The winning bidder gives the government a number of billions. And all you get is a signature and a contract. That's all you have. You don't have highways. Highways? Who owns that? There's not even a building that you can close." Lopez de Fuentes showed me one of Cintra's contracts. It was as thick as a phone book. "Every word—it is very important," he said. "The government of today commits to behave in a manner for the next fifty years, seventy years. But the next government might not like the contract, or might have a different view."

In an effort to further bulletproof their investment, companies like Cintra often try to include non-compete clauses that prevent the government from building or improving any nearby free facilities in a way that might undercut the value of the company's toll road. The Stalls held up this practice as proof that partnering with the private sector could be hazardous to the public good. But to Lopez de Fuentes it was just good business. "The proposal we make is based on traffic and revenue forecasts. I have very clever guys telling me the number of people that are going to be willing to travel this portion of road. They take polls and they do a lot of research. There's a whole science around that."

The savvy Cintra was well positioned in Texas. In 2002, the consultant Mike Weaver brought in representatives from the company to advise Mike Krusee, the house transportation chairman, and his aide John Langmore on ideal language for House Bill 3588. The Spaniards were impressed with Langmore, evidently, because after the bill passed they hired him to help put together their bid on TTC-35. Langmore's seamless shift to consulting was never publicized—had it been, the Stalls and others would have made a stink about it—but it also didn't break any rule, nor was it abnormal. Dan Shelley, a Texan who had wandered between the private sector and the governor's office when it was occupied by George W. Bush, passed Langmore going the other way: In September 2004, Shelley left a consulting gig with Cintra to become a legislative aide for Perry. In 2005, he would return to Cintra as a lobbyist.

I asked Langmore about his Cintra job in the summer of 2004, and he did not apologize for his own personal privatization. "You *want* the expertise out there," he said. "I understood the concepts behind what the state was trying to accomplish. And obviously I knew the technical aspects of the bill. But a smart person reading it four or five times could get to the same point." Many who had read House Bill 3588 four or five times, I pointed out, were now furious about the Trans-Texas Corridor. Langmore had an interesting take on the public uproar. He told me the corridor would never happen. It was one small part of House Bill 3588, he said, and it was not what was attracting the private sector. He knew this for certain because he'd been talking it through with Cintra. "They're sitting there going, 'This little-bitty road makes sense. We'll build that one little stretch east of Dallas,'" he said. "'That's all we want. We don't want to touch trains. We aren't going to do development.'" It might make sense for the state to buy the entire length of right-of-way, he said, to connect these initial small pieces in thirty years or so. "But we don't need to build it today. It's not justified. The tolls won't pay for it, so the private sector isn't going to invest in it."

Langmore was particularly critical of the corridor drawing that TxDOT had circulated to the public—the one showing a quarter-mile-wide infrastructure orgy through the grasslands. Such a behemoth wasn't physically feasible, he said, because the engineering requirements for high-speed rail, for instance, were much higher than for highways. "Why the hell would you build a roadway to rail standards? Why put them in the same corridor? It makes no sense," he said. "And that's what

they're saying. Four football fields wide, fourteen hundred miles. That's what people are looking at, and freaking out." Perry and Williamson and TxDOT had overreached, he thought, by proposing a "pie-in-the-sky" corridor plan and by pressuring local governments to add tolls to tax-financed highways. "Now 'toll' is a four-letter word. The opponents saw right through this flawed plan, they didn't like it, and we gotta get past it," he said. "We blew it, for sure. And my big fear, on my policy-wonk side—I think tolling has a lot of merit. And I don't want to see the concept of tolling get drug under because we screwed up our local plan and got too aggressive."

Langmore is a Democrat, as it happens, and a devotee of the planner Andrés Duany and New Urbanism. He spoke excitedly about the potential use of innovative infrastructure financing to build commuter rail and bypass highways that would move trucks out of downtowns. "A lot of real progressives like the Sierra Club and others are into tolling," he said. "You allocate the true costs of use of roadways to the people using them. The gas tax today, you don't do that. People don't feel it. It doesn't factor into their decision on whether or not to drive." Commuters forced to pay the full cost of roads would be more inclined to ride trains, he said. That's what he hoped House Bill 3588 would accomplish, not the Trans-Texas Corridor. "Perry's gonna come and go," he told me. "If all of the sudden he's gone, I have a feeling this corridor idea will just evaporate."

For the time being, however, Cintra, with his help, was drawing up a plan that reflected Perry's dream. "These bids don't commit the companies to anything," he said. The state would merely be choosing a partner to create a master development plan for the corridor. "They're going to come back later and propose specific facilities. So at this point they're like, 'Just throw it in. Just call it twelve hundred feet wide everywhere. All we want to do is get chosen.'"

And chosen they were. At the December 16 meeting of the Texas Transportation Commission, TxDOT announced that it was awarding the TTC-35 contract to Cintra, which had partnered with the San Antonio construction firm Zachry on the bid. Turnpike director Phillip Russell, his voice quivering with excitement, outlined the winning plan. The consortium, Russell announced, had proposed $6 billion worth of construction over the next five years, including a completely new toll road connecting San Antonio, Austin, and Dallas. As a bonus, Russell revealed Cintra-Zachry proposed paying concession fees worth $1.2 bil-

lion, which the state could spend on whatever related public projects it wished.

None of these figures were binding—as Langmore knew, the contract actually only allocated $3.5 million to produce a master plan, from which the consortium could pick and choose projects to build later as it saw fit. But in the commission hearing room that day, it was spun as an extraordinary deal: A private company had offered to build the most expensive road project in Texas history without a dime of public funds or public debt, and would actually *pay* for the privilege. It was, for the career road men and politicians in the room, an emotional moment.

"You have made this, I think sincerely, the most historic day in transportation," Krusee told Governor Rick Perry and the commission, "not just for Texas, but for the United States since Eisenhower."

Federal-highway administrator Mary Peters was on hand for the occasion. "Texas is a national example for all states and a leader in unleashing the resources, innovation, and efficiency of the private sector to bring transportation improvements to the public faster and at less cost to American taxpayers," she said.

Governor Perry waxed poetic. "When our hair is gray, we will be able to tell our grandchildren that we were sitting in the Department of Transportation conference room when one of the most extraordinary plans was laid out for the people of the state of Texas," he said. He reminisced about having personally laid out the vision for the corridor three years before, but included himself when he said, "I have an idea that the people of the state of Texas don't realize just how big this is yet."

Ric Williamson, speaking to the press after the commission meeting, offered some ideological context to the day's events. When a reporter expressed concern that Cintra's proposal contained no short-term plans for a link to the interstate-starved Rio Grande valley, Williamson's answer was simple and blunt. The private companies had decided to start with the portions of the corridor that they believed would carry the most traffic, and therefore generate the most revenue, he said, and that same business rationale would drive the work of his public agency as well. It was time to stop whining for roads.

"I don't, at this great and happy moment, want to give offense, but let me be a little frank with you," he told the reporter. "I've been on the commission almost four years, and I tend to hear a lot of 'My fair share,' 'I'm last again,' and 'Why am I not important?' And that question is predicated upon the central-planning theory of government, which makes central plans for everybody to get a piece of the pie." He stared at her with a drooping, unblinking gaze. "But we're not central-planner people. We're market-driven Republicans."

Still, the leaders in the valley might have seen reason to celebrate the developments in Austin—TxDOT had succeeded in pushing forward its first corridor and had made it clear that TTC-69 was next in line. Jorge Verduzco, of Laredo, told me some time later that he was "absolutely in favor" of privatization, even for I-69. "No, it would not be an interstate as such. It would be a 'corridor,'" he said. "But we supported it, because it keeps I-69 alive."

But anger over the governor's new ideology was building, and to others in the valley and elsewhere it was less obvious whether tolling and privatization would be a blessing or a liability. The Stalls had made the rounds along the I-69 route, and their anti-corridor message had found footholds in towns such as El Campo, where the mayor and the economic development director made public statements against the corridor notion. They still supported plan A: seeking federal money to upgrade U.S. 59 and U.S. 77 to interstate standards.

Where the newfangled corridor might go was anyone's guess. The state's maps of the TTC-69 study area showed long, flat blobs stretching up and down the Gulf, as if the tidy U.S. highways—marked with those old FUTURE I-69 CORRIDOR signs—had been cut open and bled. In the Houston area, where U.S. 59 was already approaching interstate quality, the new study area cast a shadow bigger even than Houston's sprawl. In Lufkin, Louis Bronaugh complained to me that the TxDOT's new strategy had incited protest where there had been none before. "They showed maps as big as that wall," he said. "And people only look at the spot where their house is. Everyone who was touched by it was upset." Bronaugh was annoyed with Governor Perry, and he echoed Langmore's doubts that the grandiose corridor would ever be built. "It's not gonna happen," he predicted. "I can assure you that whoever is the next governor of the state of Texas will not accept that. And each time that the governors change, or the president changes, we start all over again."

Would the I-69 proponents get a regular old interstate, for which they had pined for so many years? Or might they have to live with a private corridor operated by some international corporation? The members of the Alliance for I-69 Texas were unsure, but the state's answer was clear.

At the Texas Transportation Commission meeting in November 2005, Ric Williamson reiterated his view that the federal government was "not going to send us any additional apportionment for I-69. It's not ever going to happen. Those politicians that promised that ought to admit it and quit promising people things they can't deliver. There's a way we can build I-69 using our approach, but it means tolling and it means freight rail; it means utility lines; it means water lines; it means doing things that some people don't want to do down there right now. That's how you get I-69."

That same month, Williamson's fellow commissioner Ted Houghton put it a different way. At a luncheon in the valley, Houghton told seventy-five local officials and business leaders that it was time to let go of the old free-highway idea. "I-69 is dead in the state of Texas," he said. "The road fairy has been shot."

V

A Line in the Dirt

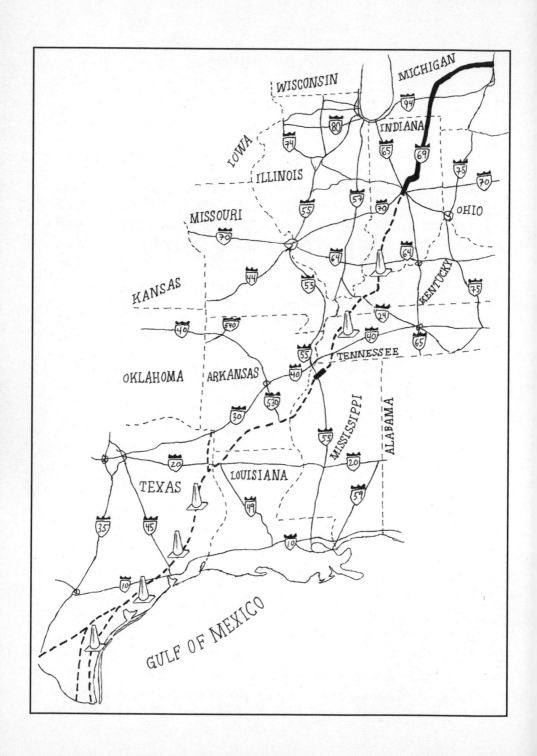

Major Moves

‑ ‑ ‑ ‑ ‑ ‑ ‑ ‑ ‑ ‑ ‑

The people of Indiana had been hearing tough talk about highway funding for years—not from self-assured government types, but from Thomas and Sandra Tokarski, the mother and father of the state's anti-I-69 movement. The couple never mocked an imaginary road fairy, but as we know, they did dress a fellow opponent as a pig and delivered a ham to the governor as a symbol of government waste. For entrenched opponents, the budgetary impossibility of I-69 was just one rationale for insisting that the state build the "common sense" route along existing highways—Interstate 70 and U.S. 41—if any new road at all. The Tokarskis had done the math and had been telling anyone who would listen that Indiana could not afford to build a new-terrain Interstate 69, at least not without neglecting roads elsewhere in the state.

To highway champions like David Graham and James Newland, the absence of money was also painfully obvious. Privately, they would grumble that the state's congressional representatives had been weak in winning earmarks, while publicly they pressed ahead, blustering through in the hopes of some eventual windfall.

Even after the environmental study process had officially ended and Governor Frank O'Bannon had announced the state's intention to build the new-terrain route—through the Tokarskis' backyard and the Graham family farm—the Tokarskis and their cohort continued to rehearse their stark logic. It gave Thomas and Sandra a kind of uneasy comfort to know that their worst fears were a financial absurdity. The country had been at war in Afghanistan for more than a year when O'Bannon declared his choice in January 2003, and two months later the United States invaded Iraq. War is expensive. So is nation building. It seemed likely to the Tokarskis that the next major highway built with American money would run not through the farms of the Midwest and South but through an occupied country half a world away.

The new-terrain opponents were pleasantly surprised in July 2003, when a new politician arrived on the state scene expressing similar skepticism about the I-69 project. Mitch Daniels, who had recently resigned as President Bush's White House budget director, had come back home again to Indiana to run for governor, and he was pitching himself as a man with an open mind and fresh eyes. Few were aware that Daniels had played a bit role in the early I-69 saga. He was friends with David Graham—they had worked together on Richard Lugar's 1976 Senate campaign—but he was also one of I-69's earliest doubters. As head of the Hudson Institute in the early nineties, Daniels first encountered the border-to-border NAFTA highway concept in David Reed's draft report on the future of southern Indiana, and he asked Reed to tone down his then-novel endorsement of the plan. But these obscure and inconclusive connections to Interstate 69 were unknown to the public. All they really knew was that Daniels had been in Washington during the climactic public hearings on I-69 and, before that, he had worked in the private sector as the CEO of the Indianapolis-based drug company Eli Lilly. If Daniels had preconceptions about the controversial highway, they were a mystery.

But a statewide candidate in Indiana cannot go long without being asked to take sides on the highway hobbyhorse. A mere week into his campaign, at a stop in Evansville, a member of the Tokarskis' Citizens for Appropriate Rural Roads asked Daniels if he would be open to reconsidering the route for Interstate 69. He said that he would. "Of course we need an I-69 and we need it in the fastest way possible," he said. But "the exact, final route selection, I think we need to look at very carefully, with the interest of all six million of us in mind." It may very well be that Governor O'Bannon's chosen path was the right answer, Daniels acknowledged. "But it's a very expensive answer and I think we need to understand whether there's going to be the money there to pay for it."

Noncommittal as Daniels was, his comments were a bright ray of hope for highway opponents. Here was a candidate willing to face the truth, even if that meant revisiting a controversy. If Daniels was indeed elected governor, he would have the power to unilaterally change the path of Interstate 69. And if he really did sit down and look hard at the facts, the Tokarskis and others believed, he would realize that the prudent thing to do—the only way to build anything soon—was to forgo the new-terrain route. E-mails of support for Daniels went out to members of CARR and John Smith's COUNT US! mailing list. Maybe they could still win this thing—on grounds of fiscal responsibility, at the hands of the man President Bush had nicknamed "the Blade" for his budget-cutting abilities.

Of course, there was now a second verse to the song about no money for transportation. It was already being sung in Texas and quietly hummed in Washington. President Bush never made comments about infrastructure financing or privatization of highways. Neither did Transportation Secretary Norman Mineta, the Clinton holdover who had declared a dozen years before that "America needs more of a transportation vision for the future than endless ribbons of asphalt, overpasses, and off-ramps." The avant-garde messaging was the province of Federal Highway Administrator Mary Peters. In 2002, it was Peters who broke the news to the members of the Mid-Continent Highway Coalition that the gas tax was doomed and that the administration would be exploring other options. By September 2003, it appears she had arrived at a solution. "I want to be clear about where the Bush administration stands, where U.S. DOT and Secretary Mineta stand, and where FHWA stands," she told the National Council on Public-Private Partnerships. "We are *for* public-private partnerships. We support them. We want to make them easier—much easier—to do."

If Daniels wasn't already thinking along these lines in 2003, he started to in the summer of 2004, once he had secured the Republican nomination for governor. His stance on I-69 settled into full support of the new-terrain route, and he was starting to tease out the "innovative funding" that might make it possible. "To build Indiana's infrastructure, we should look at any and all creative concepts like public-private partnerships," he wrote in an op-ed for *The Indianapolis Star*. "Toll roads could become one part of the solution." In the gubernatorial debate that October, Daniels went into full Ric Williamson mode: "Let's get honest about something. There is no money around to pay for [I-69]. The budget for highways in the years ahead is barely enough to maintain the roads we have now," he admonished. "This illusion that it's going to come like manna from heaven, from the federal government, is really not fair to float in front of people."

Governor O'Bannon died of a massive stroke in September 2003, and his lieutenant governor, Joe Kernan, was running against Daniels as a rookie incumbent. Like O'Bannon, Kernan supported the new-terrain I-69 route (though he rejected the idea of tolling to pay for it). To highway opponents, Kernan was the status quo, and they believed it was time for change. Sure, Daniels also favored new terrain, but, as John Smith put it in a lukewarm e-mail endorsement, he was "at least honest enough to acknowledge that there is no money to build I-69." Steven Higgs, the editor of the progressive *Bloomington Alternative* newspaper, echoed this sentiment and offered an appealing scenario: "Governor Daniels could shift his support from new terrain to common sense without violating his campaign position."

But the I-69 opponents did not understand the full ramifications of what Daniels was suggesting. And to be fair, how could they have? They had been fighting the same battles for a decade, and they didn't immediately realize that Daniels was proposing completely new rules of engagement. The notion of public-private partnerships and the awesome amount of money such arrangements could provide were not part of the policy vocabulary of most Americans. The outcry in Texas and the research done by David and Linda Stall, though just a few clicks away on the Internet, had not crossed the Tokarskis' radar.

That November, with the I-69 opponents' tepid blessings, Daniels won the election with 54 percent of the vote. His victory came just a few weeks after the city of Chicago announced its $1.8 billion deal for the Chicago Skyway—the deposit heard round the world—and Daniels wasted no time getting in line behind them. On New Year's Day 2005, even before he was sworn in as governor, Daniels named a fifty-seven-year-old retired aluminum executive as his new head of the Department of Transportation and declared that the agency would be run more like a business. He wanted to look into a possible lease of the Indiana Toll Road as a way to beef up the department's budget, he told *The Indianapolis Star.* "Other states have also had very large gaps, and have found creative ways to close them through asset sales," Daniels said. "This is happening all over the country and the world. It's something that we have been slow to imitate here in Indiana."

By this time, public-private partnerships for highways were becoming the new budget cure-all. That January, New Jersey governor Richard Codey announced a study on privatizing several of the state's highways including the New Jersey Turnpike, and New York governor George Pataki proposed legislation that would allow the lease of the Tappan Zee Bridge, the New York Thruway toll road, and New York City subway lines. In February, Congress took up the reauthorization of the transportation bill, and the Bush administration began pushing for policies that would encourage public-private partnerships on a national level.

In Indiana, I-69 opponents were finally waking up to the transportation-policy revolution. John Smith sent a worried e-mail to supporters over the Fourth of July holiday, imploring his fellow Hoosiers to educate themselves on the perils of privatization. "Do some Googles on the Trans Texas Highway," he told them. But his nemeses at INDOT were doing a lot more than Googling. That month, a fleet of Indiana transportation officials took a field trip to Texas, paid for by Peters's Federal Highway Administration. They flew down, over the proposed route of Interstate 69, to learn about how methods like public-private partnerships were being used to speed up projects.

Apparently, they picked up some good pointers. In September, Governor Daniels unveiled his own massive statewide highway plan, which he called Major Moves. Indiana would double its budget for new construction over the next ten years, fast-tracking projects including two new bridges over the Ohio River, several short expressways in the northern part of the state, and I-69. To pay for this, naturally, Indiana would turn to the private sector. The federal transportation reauthorization bill, which had passed a month before, made public-private partnerships easier and instituted new pilot programs that would allow limited tolling of new and rebuilt interstate highways. With this new authority, Daniels proposed building I-69 as a private turnpike. He also put the Indiana Toll Road up for lease. The Major Moves plan estimated that the deal might fetch in excess of two billion dollars.

Major Moves was not as jaw-dropping as the Trans-Texas Corridor, but it would still require new legislation to make its core elements legal. And while the law permitting the corridor passed quietly in Texas, Indiana's battle would happen in broad daylight. CARR, Smith's COUNT US!, and allied anti-new-terrain groups answered Major Moves with a report of their own, titled *Caution: Slippery Road Ahead!*, that laid out many of the things that could "go wrong," including the loss of public control of infrastructure, contracts laced with non-compete clauses, and the potential use of eminent domain for private profit. They covered all their bases, arguing that I-69 was doomed to failure as a toll road, and if it wasn't, then privatizing it would amount to piracy. Statehouse Democrats also criticized Major Moves as a risky overreach by Daniels, and a few baited the public with jingoism. Scott Pelath, a state representative from Michigan City, told a local newspaper: "I have grave reservations about the possibility of handing our state's roads over to the Germans, Russians or Chinese." (No mention of the Spanish.)

Daniels was already experienced in pushing through unpopular reform. He had made the instituting of daylight savings time a symbolic first priority, and had put just enough pressure on Republican state legislators to pass the change through the general assembly that April. With his transportation agenda, the governor was leaving little to chance. He had retained Goldman Sachs, the investment bank that handled the Skyway lease, and had hired Nossaman, Guthner, Knox & Elliott, a law firm in California that specialized in privatization, to draft a Major Moves bill. Daniels's biggest lure with politicians and the public was money, and the deal he was offering was about to get sweeter. In late January 2005, the governor announced the high bid for the Indiana Toll Road: $3.85 billion for a seventy-five-year lease. The offer was from Cintra and Macquarie, the consortium that now ran the Skyway and Toronto's 407. The governor was elated. "After closing, we will deposit this astonishing sum, equaling more than a decade of new construction funding at the current level, into a new trust fund, to be invested as fast as legally and humanly possible in the biggest building program in state history," Daniels said. "At last, we can stop dreaming and start digging."

The governor and his transportation department soon released a list of projects they intended to build with the billions gained from the toll-road lease. They set aside $700 million for I-69—enough, they said, to build about a third of the project. Opponents, it appeared, had been robbed of the argument that the state couldn't afford a new-terrain highway. John Smith was dejected. "I feel like I am reaching the end of my usefulness," he wrote to me in an e-mail. "I think this is going to become strictly a lawyer's game now, as we have only the hope that gas prices will go so high or whatever economic threshold that will stop I-69 before the project gets too far along. I feel all but totally defeated."

He kept at it, though, encouraging his supporters to write letters to their newspapers and call their lawmakers. The Major Moves legislation had a tough road ahead of it. At several points that winter, it seemed unlikely to pass. The bill made it through the senate only after amendments were added including one forbidding tolling on the northernmost segment of the I-69 extension. An *Indianapolis Star* poll showed Daniels's approval rating had fallen from 55 percent to 37 percent. On the last day of February, the embattled governor spoke to supporters gathered at the statehouse for a Major Moves rally. Daniels did not mince words: "You're either for this bill or you're against our future," he said.

Two weeks later, on the final night of the legislative session, Daniels's Major Moves bill passed. It allowed the lease of the Indiana Toll Road and granted the authority to privatize and/or toll I-69, but any further deals would require the approval of the general assembly. On March 30, the governor was booed at the Indiana Pacers game. On April 12, he closed the deal to lease the Indiana Toll Road to Cintra and Macquarie. The contract would take effect a few months later. On June 29, exactly fifty years after President Eisenhower signed the Federal Highway Act creating the interstate highway system, which was initially expected to cost $25 billion, Indiana handed over its 157-mile toll road to a private consortium in exchange for $3.8 billion. The amount was so huge that it took several wire transfers to complete the payment.

Looking back, Daniels believes the lease bid was about as high as it could have been. "Let's just say our timing was really good and we hit the perfect sweet spot," he told me in December 2009. The Skyway and Indiana Toll Road deals came before the recession, and the sellers had a "first-mover advantage. There was lots of money assembled." At the time, he predicted to his staff that there would be bigger deals—perhaps for the Pennsylvania or New Jersey turnpikes—but the other states dragged their feet. "It's amazing that people passed opportunities this large. Really it's always about protecting either legislative patronage control or somebody's government union dues, and the public loses out."

Not that the voters always see it that way. In retrospect, Daniels said, his window of opportunity had been narrow. "If we had gone any slower than we did, it just wouldn't have happened at all, for political reasons," he said—the same political reasons that kept the tolls too low for too long. "Any governor for twenty-five years could've raised the tolls. None of them did. You know, politics. That's why you still had a fifteen-cent tollbooth at Chicago. After I got elected, I asked somebody, 'What does it cost us to collect the toll?' They come back and they tell me, 'We think it's thirty-four cents.' I said, 'Listen, put out a cigar box. Go to the honor system. Somebody will pay and we're ahead!'" With its bulletproof contract, Cintra wouldn't have to worry about politics. Leasing the road, Daniels wrote in an essay for *Reason*, constituted "the freeing of trapped value from an underperforming asset." To say that the same value could have been realized by government, he told me, was "to assume that every future governor would be braver than every past governor" when it came to raising tolls.

Daniels's critics argue that he wasn't so much brave as selfish, accepting a windfall loan, essentially, that would have to be slowly paid back by seventy-five years' worth of motorists. But the governor has a response to that, too. "People say, 'Oh, in ten years the money will be gone.' And I'd say, 'No it won't. You'll be driving on it!'" he told me. "That was one of our cardinal rules: We said every penny must be reinvested. We're trying to address the infrastructure shortfall here. And this is not a cookie jar. It was an extremely difficult thing to get people to accept. They'd have had it in public education before they were done. But we said, 'No. We need this money to build Indiana's future. It's all going to be in concrete and asphalt and *real* stuff.'"

While the Daniels administration was waiting for its wire transfers to come in, the Mid-Continent Highway Coalition celebrated the interstate system's golden anniversary a few days early, in Memphis. Carolina Mederos, the group's lobbyist from Patton Boggs, had arranged to have a few guest speakers come to the annual meeting to educate the group on privatization. The coalition needed a pick-me-up. The year before, the organization had come close to going broke. It had struggled financially ever since the Greater Houston Partnership had withdrawn its support, and its lobbying costs over the course of the prolonged transportation reauthorization had been higher than expected. The executive committee had contemplated letting Mederos go after her work on the bill was finished. Instead they fired the coalition's sole employee, James Newland. The eighty-six-year-old executive director left gracefully, encouraging his fellow members that they were "rounding third base and headed home." That was partially true: The route for I-69 was all but solidified. But the coalition was tired. Many lamented that there were no younger people stepping up to the plate (to continue Newland's metaphor). They had gotten decent money from the reauthorization bill—$360 million, including $72 million for Dickey's pet connector in Arkansas—but they needed billions more, and they'd already been begging for years.

The weary coalition didn't have to go back to the same dry well. In 2002, Mederos had introduced the group to Mary Peters, who had explained that appropriation hunting was a "zero-sum game" and that the Highway Trust Fund was on track to become insolvent. Peters had alluded then to some innovative funding methods, which four years later were maturing as effective policy. Mederos brought the coalition together at the Peabody to talk about a new way forward. "The interstate program is over," she told them. "It's never coming back. We have to look at other sources of funding." There were a few people she thought they should meet—some gentlemen from Spain and Australia.

This coalition meeting would feel different from any before. The usual group of business and political leaders were joined around the conference-room table by representatives from the state DOTs. Big guns from Washington flew in, too: Tyler Duvall, the assistant secretary for transportation policy, and Jim Ray, the chief counsel at the Federal Highway Administration. The turnout was heavily Southern. The bookend states of Texas and Indiana had figured this stuff out already, so their six total delegates—three of whom were Department of Transportation bureaucrats—were there not so much to listen as to stand behind the very special guests: Trent Vichie from Macquarie, Carlos Ugarte of Cintra, a representative from Morgan Stanley, and a small platoon from the American construction giant Parsons Brinckerhoff.

News of the clashes in Texas and Indiana had not filtered through to the coalition, so many members were hearing for the first time about the great strides in privatization. Mederos compared the session to an economics class. Duvall began by reiterating that there was no federal money for new roads. The Morgan Stanley banker walked them through several different types of financing models—the asset lease, the design-build contract, the design-build-operate contract, the concession-and-development agreement—and Vichie followed up with an explanation of why his bank had so much money. The Australian government, he said, had mandated private retirement saving, and the banks, now fat with deposits, were seeking safe investments. American infrastructure, he told them, was about as safe as one could get. Ugarte talked about Cintra's TTC-35 deal in Texas, its leases of the Chicago Skyway and the Indiana Toll Road, and the 550 miles of roads it operated in Chile.

There were no reporters present at the Memphis meeting, and in Newland's forced absence, no minutes were produced. But the following year, when I spoke with Jose Maria Lopez de Fuentes, the president of Cintra's operations in the U.S. and Canada, I asked him how he normally handled talking to Americans about highways. "The general conception here is that roads are free," he said. "Which is weird. I mean, it's like you have been living in the house that your grandparents built, and now, suddenly, the roof needs repair. And that's a difficult concept. It is difficult for North Americans. In other places in the world, they see constant maintenance, constant construction. And they see their network going better and better. Here you see your network going worse and worse every day. Because of two things: because of severe wear and bad maintenance. And because of severe growth." The American people, he said, were experiencing denial and anger, the early stages of grief.

In Memphis, Caruthers at least arrived at acceptance. "I was impressed with the Australian and the Spanish," Caruthers told me. "Of course, I tend to accept what they tell me." He had been awed by the minutiae of the lease contracts and the level of service demanded of the private operators, particularly a detail about Cintra having only thirty minutes to remove any roadkill from the Indiana Toll Road. Caruthers was beginning to see how this kind of deal might work in Louisiana. "They made a pretty convincing case."

The meeting was not intended to get Cintra and Macquarie to invest in I-69, Mederos said. If anything, the sale was in the other direction. "I was just trying to get folks who were doing it and using different models to come and explain to the political leadership along the corridor just how this worked and what it was," she said. "The coalition folks are willing to do anything. So I'm just trying to say, as all of this evolves, 'Be a part of it, and make sure we're players.'" Most took the message to heart. Bill Revell went back to Dyersburg and began extolling privatization to his local newspaper. Months later, Tennessee would pass privatization-enabling legislation without fanfare or uproar.

Still, how exactly the public-private partnership model would work for I-69 wasn't entirely clear. The long rural stretches, though a compelling case for economic development, were poor prospects for tolling. But perhaps they could cobble together a mix of methods—build private toll roads in the urban areas, then use the concession fees to subsidize tax-funded construction of freeways through the less toll-worthy countryside. "I envision the best thing going is to focus on Memphis as the horse to ride, and to go out as far as we can justify a fee for using the road," Caruthers told me after the meeting. "I see at least a hope for Memphis and Tennessee to carry Mississippi, Arkansas, and Louisiana." Sharing concession fees across state lines might take some doing, he knew, but as he understood it, the Bush administration would do all it could to permit this hybrid solution. "If Mary Peters has anything to do with it, they will. She's very much in favor of putting poor areas with juicy spots."

Grand Opening

— — — — — — — — — — — — —

Three months after the Peabody summit with Cintra and Macquarie, John Caruthers stood with a small group of his fellow coalition members under a rented wedding-style tent out in the cotton fields near Tunica. It was an unusually hot October afternoon, a Tuesday, and Caruthers had driven the seven hours from Shreveport. Bill Revell, who didn't know he was nearing the end of his mayoral term, had come from Dyersburg, three hours away. Jerome Hafter was up from Greenville, Ancil Cox was there from Cleveland, and the Reverend J. Y. Trice had come from Rosedale in a three-piece suit. They stood in the shade, on the grass beside a newly paved piece of road, with Ron Hudson from Clarksdale, Lyn Arnold and Ken Murphree from Tunica, and Mayor Gene Alday from Walls. It was one thirty, and in a little more than an hour, they would each be holding a piece of newly cut red-white-and-blue ribbon. This was the day—October 3, 2006—that they had waited fourteen years for. They would get to drive on a new piece of Interstate 69.

In the northern Mississippi Delta, a place where a poor area meets a juicy spot, they hadn't been thinking about toll roads. They had come up with their own sort of innovative financing—a kind of public-public partnership. In Mississippi, the Department of Transportation can't issue bonds but cities and counties can. In 2004, a deputy director at MDOT unearthed an obscure state law that allowed the department to fund projects with locally borrowed money and then repay the bonds over time with federal highway dollars. The casino-rich county of Tunica was glad to hear it. In January 2005, while Mitch Daniels was musing about selling the Indiana Toll Road, Tunica County borrowed $45 million and handed it over to the state to expedite the first new piece of I-69.

Though it was Tunica that fronted the money, DeSoto County got the road—a fifteen-mile stretch from Interstate 55 near Hernando to the new four-lane Highway 61 near Robinsonville. This initial segment will one day be part of the flat bottom of Memphis's new wide loop, but Tunica County saw it differently. The first new piece of the great north-south NAFTA highway travels east-west, and the spur brings the interstate system to the casinos' front door. The project was scheduled to take seven years, but with the help of that clever funding, Mississippi had built it in eighteen months. Work had just finished when the coalition members and other honored guests assembled to celebrate.

Along Highway 61, signs for the new interstate were veiled in black fabric. A state trooper blocked the entrance ramp and checked invitations. The new road looked strange—empty and bright except for a few tracks left by hastily removed construction vehicles. A mile in, at a wide-open spot between two fields, the ribbon stretched across the road, tied in bows to orange-and-white cones. A dais-on-wheels with folding chairs and a podium blocked the way, too, and news vans clustered. Guests parked their cars in neat rows on the vacant concrete. Inside the tent, people held gift bags full of commemorative souvenirs: a deck of plastic-coated playing cards with the I-69 highway sign on the back, courtesy of the Gold Strike Casino, which had printed the slogan ROAD TO GOLD on the packaging; a round paperweight fashioned from a sample of core pavement; an I-69 shield-shaped hand fan. Caterers handed out highway-sign frosted cookies and pushed around wheelbarrows full of ice and plastic water bottles labeled I-69 RIBBON CUTTING CEREMONY.

The coalition members poked through their gifts, shook hands, and mingled with local politicians and DOT types. Ancil Cox mentioned Charles Dean, how he wished his friend could have seen this day, and Ron Hudson grumbled about the recent Peabody meeting—"I was trying to digest this toll-road stuff," he said with a frown. "I don't know about that."

Senator Trent Lott was working his way through the crowd, and everyone suddenly stood an inch taller. Mayor Revell introduced himself to the senator, who played dumb. "How much of I-69 have y'all built up there in Tennessee?" he asked, smiling. People chuckled. Lott shook hands with Caruthers. "You got this built all the way through Louisiana yet?" The men took the teasing with grace—it was a happy day—but the former majority leader's smack talk made me notice that there were no Mid-Continent members present from his rival state of Arkansas. Caruthers told Lott the coalition had been hearing a lot about public-private partnerships. Lott cocked his head and smiled. "We kind of like bonds," he said.

An aide prompted Lott to take his place on the platform, and the coalition members—who had not been invited onstage—made their way out into the sun as well. Someone recognized the Reverend Trice and expressed surprise that he wasn't part of the program. "I thought they'd let me do something," he said. "'Cause I prayed for the Lord to bless us to get the money. And he did, didn't he?"

The invocation was handled instead by James Q. Dickerson III, a district engineer for MDOT, who thanked God for the vision of those who had made the highway possible. "Father, this day is such a great opportunity for all of us," he said. The road would be a blessing "not only for safety, but also development, for the future of our lives." A state representative led the crowd in the singing of the national anthem, and a law-enforcement honor guard marched in with Old Glory and the state flag of Mississippi, with its Confederate corner. The scene could have been from the fifties. The twelve or so men on the dais were uniformly white. Their hair was short—graying or gray—and they stood in rolled shirtsleeves and ties, their hands on their hearts, each waiting for his chance to exalt a new interstate.

Murphree, the master of ceremonies, introduced Senator Lott, noting that "without his support during his time as Senate majority leader, I-69 would probably not be in our state today." The senator spoke briefly on the nonpartisan, nonracial delight that was a new highway. He was thrilled to be a part of it. "I want to pledge to you today that this is not a ribbon cutting for the end of a project. This is a ribbon cutting for the beginning of a project." There was applause. "Let's keep building on it. Better roads, houses, more jobs, more opportunity, safer roads, a good place to live. That's what this project symbolizes." He had learned a long time ago, he said, that when constituents are standing up in the heat, he should "shut up and sit down." And he did.

The heat was indeed a nuisance. I-69 fans fluttered madly and remarks were kept brief. Most of the other speakers (three of whom were named Billy) thanked their members of Congress—for "delivering the bacon," as the executive director of MDOT put it. Bill Minor, one of Mississippi's three transportation commissioners, was thoughtful enough to mention the coalition. "I know some of them are here," he said. "This road started when they started looking at trying to get it done."

Congressman Roger Wicker echoed that sentiment and reminded everyone that the interstate highway system had just turned fifty years old. Eisenhower "later wrote in a book that this move would change the face of America," Wicker said. "And certainly it has done that."

Mary Peters was not present. Secretary Mineta had retired in September, after the interstate-anniversary hoopla, and President Bush appointed Peters to replace him in the cabinet. She was off somewhere trying to change the face of transportation funding, presumably. The new federal highway administrator, J. Richard Capka, attended the ceremony and emphasized that I-69 was important not just to northern Mississippi but to the nation. "When completed, it will connect our southern border with our northern border," he said. "It is visionary."

For all the talk of history and vision, no one on the stage fully understood what events had brought them there. Neither David Graham nor David Reed had made the trip from Indiana. John Caruthers was there, at least, but no one bothered to mention him by name. The man who had drawn I-69 with a Magic Marker in Shreveport in 1991 stood in the crowd on the undriven concrete and watched while the Mississippians filed down off the stage and lined up along the ribbon with pairs of scissors. They grabbed the ribbon with their left hands and on the count of three they cut with the shears in their right. Each now held a piece of history, and camera shutters snapped. The spectators—Caruthers and the coalition members included—queued up for their pieces, which were cut unceremoniously from the leftover ribbon.

Then we got into our cars. The dais was rolled aside and a great open stretch was before us. The Studebaker Club of Tunica led the procession. Its members drove their antique cars—of Indiana pedigree—eastward. The speed limit was sixty miles per hour, but everybody drove forty. Because they wanted to savor the moment, because they weren't driving to get anywhere, or perhaps because the whole scene had transported everyone back in time. For years the I-69 champions had been harping on the need for a "modern highway," and here it was, like a postcard from a half century ago. The lines were new and clean—trees, fence, grass, shoulder, roadway, center dashes—and for now the only roadside ornaments were light poles and signs. Fifteen miles of 1956. There were no billboards yet, no fast-food places, no litter, no traffic.

To the people living along this new stretch of I-69, the coming of our cars was another milestone in a gradual transformation of their circumstances. For eighteen months they had watched as crews cut through woods and leveled the earth. Their country roads, which had previously puttered along flat dirt, were routed up new mounds of earth and over bridges. When I reached I-55—it didn't take long—I circled back and meandered through the small hamlets and farms. I found the local end of an unfinished exit at Tulane Road. Tulane was two-lane. It had existed for years as discontinuous sections along a north-south line from Horn Lake down past Hernando, and now the DOT was working to tie two of those pieces into a knot at I-69. Just to the south of the new highway, a section of Tulane that had been a quarter-mile-long back lane sat waiting to become a major crossroad. The sketch of its connector and exit ramps was already defined. A sign at the end of a driveway caught my attention, and I drove down a gravel entrance through a spread that could only have existed out here in the country. This was Southern Winds Ranch, a horse farm. It was Southern Cricket Wholesale, too. There were stocked ponds where one could fish and pay by the pound.

I parked in a dirt turnaround and walked to the open door of what I took to be the main house. The front room was full of boxes of chirping baby crickets, and over the noise I heard a hello. It was Eric Beené, the mild-mannered thirtysomething proprietor of this schizophrenic establishment. He had grown up here. His mother and her mother both lived here, as did his two children. The residence, in fact, was up on a hill at the other corner of the ranch, which totaled four hundred acres. Tulane Road was the eastern border of his piece, the northern edge of which was now I-69. I asked Beené how he felt about the highway. "We used to be out in the private out here," he said. "I was just standing outside listening to all the cars. You can hear them." The hum of traffic was an odd thing for a cricket farmer to complain about, and Beené saw the irony. But the hum wasn't going to be the end of it, he said. "You read in the paper every week about how this is gonna be such a great place for subdivisions and hotels. They haven't talked to *us* about it yet. But they got it in mind."

During the initial meetings about the highway, "I tried to do a little opposition against it," Beené said. "But you know, when they have something set, there's nothing you can do about it." Resigned, he had started to think about how he might make some money off his well-positioned land. That, too, proved frustrating at first. "We had offers from billboard companies wanting to pay us like ten thousand dollars a year per billboard, and then the county said, 'We're not going to allow any billboards.' They don't want it to look junky out here, they're saying." Now he's planning a gas station on his corner, and he might sell some acreage to a hotel chain. "I imagine we'll get offers," he said. "They're talking thousands per square foot. So I'm just sitting tight. I don't really want a subdivision on the place, but I wouldn't mind my corner to be hotels and shopping malls, whatever they want."

Eventually they will widen Tulane Road. The peace and quiet will slip away. "I figure I don't have many years left here," Beené told me. "Property taxes will be so high, I'll have to leave anyway. So we'll get what we can out of it, and go buy another big ranch somewhere in south Mississippi or something." In the meantime, I-69 would serve him well. Beené had recently divorced and had taken a job at a casino to give himself something to do at night. He dealt blackjack and ran a craps table at the Sheraton. He guessed that I-69 would shave ten minutes off his trip once they opened the exit. "I think you can go around the barricade now and get on," he said. "You're not supposed to, but I plan to just drive up there."

I left Beené's cricket farm/stock pond/horse ranch thinking about the letter that the Tokarskis had gotten from an INDOT official years before: "Loss of serenity is a non-compensable item." I turned left out the driveway, drove to where the blacktop of Tulane Road ended, and gingerly piloted my rented car across the dirt path to the newly paved bridge. On the other side the blacktop ended after a few hundred feet, but an aisle through the woods had been cleared. I figured in five more years there would be a turn light here. But that day, things were still a little wild. Birds landed in tall branches, and the weeds were lousy with grasshoppers—a buzzing sound that would soon be replaced by that of a gas station's fluorescent lights.

I maneuvered my sedan around the cones that blocked the on-ramp and headed west toward the casinos. Off near the river, I knew, the old two-lane Highway 61 was dusted in cotton, and the gambling meccas were lighting up, a sight as strange and enticing as the grand hotels in Carl Fisher's no-longer-swamp of Miami Beach. To my left and right, soybean fields were turning yellow. The farmland was two months pregnant with high-priced development, not yet showing. How many houses and golf courses and gas stations and shopping malls would come? How soon?

It was a little past seven in the evening. The sun was setting like a big red poker chip. The road was almost empty, and I drove fast. My dashboard GPS, which was unaware of the new interstate, gave up on giving me directions. The screen just said DRIVING WEST. A noise like the popping of popcorn startled me. It was the sound of hundreds of mosquitoes hitting my windshield. They didn't know about the new highway either. Last night at this time, this was just a hard strip of ground in a wide-open field.

Low Fuel

Up in Indiana, Thomas and Sandra Tokarski were determined not to become the proverbial bugs on anyone's windshield. Their position was precarious, though: Governor Daniels's lease of the Indiana Toll Road had conjured seven hundred million dollars for I-69, and the state was projecting it would break ground in the summer of 2008. INDOT planned to begin construction at the southern end, near Evansville, perhaps because the natives were more kindly disposed toward the project there or perhaps to encourage a sense of inevitable completion by creating a discontinuous piece—what Jay Dickey called an "anchor point."

In any case, the Tokarskis didn't believe in inevitability, and they still had one big card left to play. On October 2, 2006, the day before the ribbon cutting in Mississippi, Thomas and Sandra stood with a handful of other highway opponents to announce they were filing a federal lawsuit to block construction of I-69 in Indiana. Their suit argued that the Department of Transportation had not fairly considered the less expensive, less destructive "common sense" route along existing highways. "INDOT acts like we don't matter," Thomas told reporters, standing in a short-sleeved plaid shirt before a banner that read SAVE IT! DON'T PAVE IT! "INDOT is drunk on its own power—its sham studies are more like embarrassing stink bombs which are based on a political agenda. And the Federal Highway Administration is a rubber stamp."

The defendants—the state and federal agencies that had approved the new-terrain route through Bloomington—had acted in an "arbitrary" and "capricious" manner, opponents claimed. These adjectives were not meant merely to sting; they were the words used in 1969 by Justice Thurgood Marshall in handing down the Supreme Court's decision in Citizens to Preserve Overton Park vs. Volpe. The Indiana plaintiffs—CARR, the Hoosier Environmental Council, the Sassafras Audubon Society, and six individual citizens—were standing on the shoulders of the "little old ladies in tennis shoes" whom Charlie Newman had escorted to victory in Memphis almost forty years before. They were hoping that the environmental laws pioneered by Lynton Caldwell, who had recently died in Bloomington, would save southern Indiana from I-69 just as they saved Overton Park from I-40.

Which is to say: They hoped it would send INDOT back to the drawing board and frustrate the department into submission. As Sandy Ewing, the lawyer who had worked against I-69 at the Environmental Law and Policy Center in Chicago in the late 1990s, told me, a lawsuit is never a silver bullet. The courts don't dictate routes—only the process of choosing them—and so "all the legal stuff is just a weapon to win time to win the public-opinion battle." John Moore, Ewing's former boss at the ELPC, who was representing the plaintiffs in their lawsuit, admitted this tactic to *The Indianapolis Star.* "If we win," he said, "it will slow down the process and allow the legislature to step in."

If anyone needed assurance that political winds could change over time, they got it a month later. In the November elections, the Democrats won control of the Indiana House, and the new majority leader, Patrick Bauer, promised the voters that the body would now serve as a check on Governor Daniels's ambitious agenda. Days later, Daniels pulled back his proposal to build I-69 as a private toll road. Instead he suggested a new toll highway—an outer beltway around Indianapolis that would connect growing exurbs in the six counties to the east and south of the capital. It had never been clear that a rural I-69 would attract the interest of private-sector concessionaires, but Daniels was confident that the Indiana Commerce Connector, as he called it, would. A lucrative public-private partnership for the new beltway, Daniels guessed, would provide the state enough money to complete a free I-69.

The Commerce Connector idea came out of nowhere. The governor's office released only vague maps, which, like those of the Trans-Texas Corridor, showed a frighteningly wide strip of study area. The route would be left up to whatever private company the state chose to build the road, which Daniels thought could be completed within ten years. But the proposal didn't sit well with residents. To the eye of the average citizen, the proposed Commerce Connector appeared to plow through a whole lot of farms and take out a handful of small towns. To the wary eye of smart-growth champions, the beltway looked like a sprawl magnet. Even William Hudnut III, Indy's expatriate former mayor, reappeared to criticize the plan, saying that it would "suction economic development opportunities out of Indianapolis." A colleague of Hudnut's at the Urban Land Institute backed him up. "Building an outer belt is so 1970s," he said. Indianapolis residents, who had grown relatively quiet about I-69, were now as unsettled as their neighbors in Bloomington. The Commerce Connector became a foil for champions of commuter rail and improved mass transit, who were suddenly given a forum to promote their vision of a less car-centric city.

The I-69 opponents could hardly keep up with Daniels's sudden lurches in policy and plans. They started to wonder, privately, if the string of surprises might indicate that contractors such as Cintra were calling the shots. They sensed that something big was going on, and though their legal challenge was under way, they felt increasingly demoralized. The Tokarskis had been in touch with their counterparts in Texas, and a film director named William Molina had sent them a copy of his documentary on the Trans-Texas Corridor, *Truth Be Tolled*. In early November, Thomas and Sandra brought the DVD to the Bloomington home of Clark and Vicky Sorensen, where a group of anti-new-terrain activists gathered to watch. I drove there with John Smith, whose black Nissan pickup truck wore bumper stickers saying FIX THE ROADS WE HAVE. STOP THE I-69 HIGHWAY; WAR ISN'T WORKING; and DITCH MITCH.

Smith and I stopped to pick up bottles of locally brewed beer, and when we arrived, the Tokarskis and the Sorensens were already eating chili and applesauce with Terry and Brenda Buster, a middle-aged couple whose auto-body shop in Martinsville would be taken by I-69. The Busters had come late but fiercely to the crusade, rabble-rousing at meetings and joining in the federal lawsuit. They contributed a sarcastic sense of humor, too. Near the beginning of the film, when a montage juxtaposed scenes of rural tranquillity and urban rush, the screen showed a quick shot of a Porta-Potty next to a concrete overpass abutment. "That's where Terry and I will be living," Brenda joked.

An aerial shot of a tangled, stacked intersection of highways caused Sandra to shake her head. "This is Mitch's dream!" she said.

And when scenes of a TxDOT hearing revealed that speakers in Texas were given three minutes instead of the two customary in Indiana, Bill Boyd, a longtime CARR member, turned to his wife, Jan. "I guess everything *is* bigger in Texas."

But as the movie played on, the joking subsided. The group, scattered on couches and chairs and the floor, grew serious. The Texans on the screen were railing against government arrogance, the perversion of the democratic process, and the rabid hunger for development and private profit. They were fighting in city-council chambers, transportation commission meetings, and public hearings. The Tokarskis, John Smith, the Boyds, and the Busters were witnessing a drama not unlike the one they had been living, and the familiarity was no comfort. When two married ranchers facing the loss of their land spoke of what that meant to them, I noticed Brenda Buster wiping away tears.

Molina's narrative highlighted the 2006 Texas gubernatorial election and the candidacy of Carole Keeton Strayhorn, the Republican state comptroller, who ran against Perry as a staunchly antitoll Independent. (So did country singer and humorist Kinky Friedman.) The race had not been resolved when Molina released the film, but the vote happened just a few days before the screening in Bloomington. When the credits rolled and the lights came up, Brenda asked immediately if the Texans had thrown the bums out. John Smith, who had been spending a lot of time on the Internet, shook his head. "No," Sandra confirmed. And it was quiet for a long few seconds. The party, if it can be called that, broke up soon after.

It was poignant to watch the highway fighters in Indiana watching the fight in Texas. The film produced sharp pangs of déjà vu among the group of I-69 veterans, but reliving their own struggle had also evoked, I could sense, a kind of regret. In Texas, the battle was still fresh and full of energy. But in Indiana, the debate felt more like a quagmire: The two sides had hardened, the body politic was covered in scar tissue, and the last conventional weapon, the federal lawsuit, had been deployed. The Texans were still going at it the way people do when their quiet lives have recently been turned upside down. The Hoosiers had been hanging upside down for sixteen years.

With Thomas and Sandra's blessing, I interviewed their children, Lara and Ben. Lara was old enough to sign the Tokarskis' first handwritten letter to Senator Richard Lugar in 1990—she graduated from high school that year—and she says she has always been proud of what her parents were doing to fight the interstate. "They're amazing to watch, but it's pretty overwhelming," she told me. Though Lara went to a lot of the CARR meetings while she was in college, she had since drawn back in frustration, and feels guilty about that. "It's been so hard to see them struggle with it. But they've never talked about quitting. The most drastic thing they've ever said is that they wish this would all go away." Even if that were possible, Lara has trouble imagining it. "It's been so much a part of my life for so long, and for Ben even more so. I don't even think he remembers a time before this."

In fact, he doesn't. "I've forgotten what the mood was like at home before the highway," Ben told me. He was ten when the surveyor's notice showed up in his parents' mailbox, and he ended up going with his parents to most of their CARR events because there was nothing better to do. The meetings were really boring, he said, when people weren't yelling. "After a while I started to get mad. I was like, 'Stop talking about this. It's driving me nuts!'" But his peers around Bloomington, he told me, helped him appreciate what his parents were doing. "All my friends think it's gonna be built. But they're like, 'You know, your parents are using the system how it's supposed to be used. They're questioning.' I just don't know if it'll work. Hopefully they win and live happily ever after. But I'm a pretty pessimistic person."

Both Tokarski kids told me in low, regretful tones that they privately believed the highway would be built. But there was some hope that it wouldn't happen soon. "If they don't win this thing," Lara said with a wince, "it's going to *kill* them."

The Tokarskis and friends were winning some skirmishes. Governor Daniels had already retreated from building I-69 as a private toll road, and in March 2007 he withdrew his improvised proposal for a new highway loop around Indianapolis, owing to ferocious public resistance. But even without a new road to privatize, Daniels had billions from his lease of the Indiana Toll Road, and seven hundred million dollars for I-69 was burning a hole in his pocket.

I saw the Tokarskis later that spring. We sat at their kitchen table drinking tea. Sandra pointed out to me that it had been almost five years since I'd first interviewed them, and we marveled at how much had happened: O'Bannon had chosen the route, then died; Daniels had gotten their hopes up, then turned; a Spanish company had appeared seemingly out of nowhere to lease the toll road and change the rules of road funding. The construction of the interstate they had thwarted for seventeen years was scheduled to begin a year later, starting with a modest two-mile stretch down near Evansville. The state believed that its seven hundred million dollars would be enough to pave sixty miles, which would bring the highway within thirty miles of the Tokarskis. But construction costs were rising, Thomas pointed out. Sandra predicted that the road would never make it up to Bloomington. "Daniels understands that there is no money to complete it. That's what's scandalous," she said. "Without some huge infusion of money, it won't get here. I get a clutching in my gut to think that people could lose their farms and homes to something that only goes twenty miles or whatever."

"He's pushing it for political reasons," Thomas said. "They're rushing this first two miles for Daniels's reelection next year. They want to say, 'We started it, now we can't stop.'"

A similar air of inexorability propelled the Tokarskis. I had come that day, in fact, to collect some of their papers from the early nineties. Sandra brought these to the table from their den. It was a neat stack four inches thick, and these were just the highlights. "It's sickening to look at all of it," she said, leafing through the top few pages. "We typed out all of these long—"

"And it didn't make a damn bit of difference," Thomas cracked. "This is the same route they came up with seventeen years ago. And all that we've done hasn't made a *damn* bit of difference."

"We wrote all these letters to Frank McCloskey!" Sandra said incredulously. "We fussed a lot more back then. We're too tired now."

There came a sudden small thud against a picture window not far from where we sat, and our heads turned. Sandra let out a pitying "Oh," and Thomas stood up without a word and walked quickly outside. He crouched and scooped something up with his hands, and brought it inside to Sandra, who had already retrieved a paper grocery bag and held it open. "We get a lot of baby birds hitting that window this time of year," she told me. Thomas gently placed the bird inside the bag, folded over the top, and set it in a corner near the front door.

"Is it dead?" I asked.

Thomas shrugged. "It might be stunned," he said. "You have to just put it somewhere dark and hope it wakes up."

"It won't last long if you leave it outside," Sandra said. "The other day I saw a fox with one of our chickens in its mouth. I yelled at him and scared him off, and that hen was fine. But another time, a few years ago, we came home from a highway meeting and found thirteen chickens dead."

I mentioned David and Linda Stall in Texas, how the view from their kitchen involved a lot of grazing cattle and a couple of donkeys. They perked up at the mention of the Stalls. Thomas asked whether they had jobs—he couldn't believe how much they were able to accomplish. I told them yes, the Stalls have jobs, but they're on the Internet constantly.

"We've never used the Internet well," Sandra said. "But you have to learn how to do all that stuff."

"I never liked computers," Thomas said. Their pile of papers on the table proved it. Many of the pages had been produced with a pen or a word processor. But their lack of technological savvy was not his main regret. "If I had to do it over, I would have gotten political sooner. All of our methodical analysis of the state's studies didn't *do* anything. We should have spent that energy on politics, like they do in Texas."

"We suffered from the delusion that telling the truth would make a difference," Sandra said. "But people don't read these studies. Not even the politicians."

"We've always been right, though," Thomas said. "We told INDOT they should put us on their payroll." Sandra chuckled. "If they had just decided to use existing highways," Thomas continued, "they would probably be finished with it by now."

And so would the Tokarskis.

It came time for me to leave. The Tokarskis were having dinner that night with their son and daughter. They had made a pie from scratch. Sandra put a big rubber band around the heavy stack of documents and handed it to me. The three of us were walking to the door when we came to the paper bag in the corner. Thomas paused, lifted the bag, opened it slowly, and peered inside. He let out a sigh, reached in, and brought out the body of a small blue bird.

"Oh, that's too bad," Sandra moaned. "It musta hit too hard." It was a male indigo bunting, she told me, one of her favorite types of bird. "When you see them in the light, they're just *iridescent.*"

New Blood

Had they been too cerebral? Should they have tried to influence more elections? Thomas and Sandra were willing to admit they could have been more sophisticated in their campaign against Interstate 69, but one thing they didn't regret was their civility. The Tokarskis had always played by the rules, which is why they had been taken aback in early June 2005 when protesters at an anti-I-69 rally in Indianapolis defaced the state capitol. Someone scrawled I-69 IS THE ENEMY in spray paint on the building's limestone wall, and the Tokarskis were not amused. "CARR does not need to resort to such tactics," they wrote in a public statement immediately afterward. The group's eight-hundred-some families, they said, had employed careful research and rational argument, along with "accepted" forms of protest—yard signs, letters, and a petition, which by then wore 140,000 signatures. "We encourage all citizens to become more involved in the I-69 issue," they wrote, but "the questions raised by I-69 cannot be answered by vandalism."

No one was ever sure who exactly committed the un-Hoosierlike act. The police had some ideas—they rounded up a group of twenty-four younger protesters that afternoon, handcuffed them in a nearby park, charged them with disorderly conduct, and held them overnight. An eighteen-year-old suspect was eventually charged with the spray painting, but a jury found him not guilty; they were unable to determine with certainty that the young man in question was the person they saw in the state's video evidence.

Though the perpetrators' identities were unknown, their inspiration was less of a mystery. An anarchist website, Infoshop.org, had promoted the demonstration as a key moment of what a group calling itself Roadblock Earth First! had deemed the "Roadless Summer." "We are calling for a summer of community organizing, civil disobedience, and direct action," the Roadblock group wrote on its own website, "to finally stop this bid to

pave over tens of thousands of acres of forests and farms, displace hundreds of families, and destroy communities throughout the Midwest, all to serve the interests of multinational corporations." I-69, the group believed, was a linchpin of globalization, "a vital foundation for the Free Trade Area of the Americas." The NAFTA superhighway, as they loyally referred to it, was connected to something called the Plan Puebla Panama, they said, a scheme to force "Mesoamerica" to industrialize. "Roads are the veins of capital," one essay declared. "They should become a primary target as we confront global capitalism and strive to create another world." The Roadblock Earth First! group, whoever they were, had spent the spring of 2005 traveling up and down the Midwest, sharing their ideas with like-minded groups in such cities as Madison, Minneapolis, Chicago, and Cincinnati. They hoped to recruit fellow travelers from across the country, and it seems they had some success—ten of the twenty-four people arrested in June had come to Indianapolis from other states.

The anarchists were also mindful of the more mainstream highway opponents already among them—they had e-mailed Sandra Tokarski that winter to ask if she would speak at one of their early meetings—but the old guard held the radicals at arm's length. The anarchist ethos was significantly different from their own. The Tokarskis and Smith were accustomed to holding forth at public meetings at local fire stations and from their booth at the county fair. The anarchists held secretive strategy meetings called "consultas" and often operated under assumed names. The veteran opponents wrote letters to editors about irresponsible government, circulated petitions, and prepared to file a thoroughly documented federal lawsuit. Roadblock Earth First! was talking in more militaristic terms about "direct action," a term used to describe less legal tactics like banner drops, vandalism, and sabotage. "We will defend our communities," the group wrote on its website. "Roadless Summer WILL stop the construction of I-69."

Sure, John Smith was known to entertain a conspiracy theory or two over beers in the privacy of his backyard. And, yes, Thomas Tokarski did get himself arrested climbing the fence of a nuclear power-plant site in 1978. But the appearance of the young rabble-rousers complicated their efforts, especially with all the other changes in the air. The spray painting of the state capitol happened just weeks after Daniels won legislative approval for the sale of the Indiana Toll Road, and the Tokarskis found themselves answering reporters' questions about both Spanish turnpike

operators and their own plans for civil disobedience. Thomas and Sandra had no such intentions, but others did: That July, protesters smashed a glass door and window at the Department of Transportation's I-69 project office in Bloomington and threw lightbulbs filled with roofing tar at the building in what an INDOT spokesperson interpreted as an attempt to start a slow fire. In August, a dozen protesters descended on the Evansville headquarters of Bernardin Lochmueller and stood holding banners, chanting, and beating drums outside. A participant later bragged on the Infoshop website that "minor scuffles occurred as office workers moved to bar the doors," and that later that evening, "a number of BLA executives received visits and protests at their homes."

The next year, 2006, was relatively quiet on the anarchist front. One can't be sure exactly why, but it's likely that events in Oregon had a chilling effect in Indiana. That January, eleven activists affiliated with more extreme groups—the Earth Liberation Front (ELF) and the Animal Liberation Front (ALF)—were indicted for seventeen direct-action attacks, including the arson of a ski resort in Vail, Colorado, in 1998. These acts, according to FBI director Robert Mueller, constituted nothing less than domestic terrorism. "Terrorism is terrorism, no matter what the motive," he said at a press conference after the indictments. "There's a clear difference between constitutionally protected advocacy—which is the right of all Americans—and violent criminal activity." Preventing and prosecuting domestic terrorists, officials said, were among the bureau's top priorities.

When ten of the accused environmentalists in Oregon admitted to their crimes the year after, U.S. district judge Ann Aiken had to decide whether to apply a "terrorism enhancement" to their cases, a move requested by prosecutors that would increase the maximum sentence to thirty years to life in prison. The defense argued that terrorism laws did not apply—the fires had not injured or killed anyone, and had not been intended to, they said—but Judge Aiken disagreed. In a few of the cases, she ruled, the severity of the crimes and their stated motivation put the anarchists into a category with Timothy McVeigh. "It was your intention to scare, frighten, and intimidate people and government," she said in sentencing Chelsea Gerlach to nine years. These were the first terrorism enhancements applied to environmentalists, and the rulings cast a shadow across the radical community. Anarchist websites equated the federal government's rhetoric to the anticommunist witch hunts of the 1950s—the Green Scare, they called it.

A few months later, though, radical highway resistance was back in bloom. Earth First! had deemed the I-69 struggle worthy of national focus and decided to hold its annual meeting, the Round River Rendezvous, at an undisclosed wooded location near Spencer, Indiana. There, in July 2007, anarchists camped out, shared skills and stories, and discussed tactics. Workshops included "Basic Blockades," "Scouting/Moving Through Woods," and "Advanced Climbing Techniques." Sexual health and hide tanning were covered as well. A special "action camp" for women and the transgendered offered training on edible and medicinal plant identification and "Confronting Oppression Within." A week before the gathering, I e-mailed the anonymous organizers to ask if I might be welcome to observe the "Rondy," as they called it for short. A young woman who I later discovered was an Evansville resident named Gina "Tiga" Wertz told me no. Anarchists "don't really like the fly-on-the-wall thing," she said.

The Tokarskis likewise did not attend the Rondy. But they did go to a meeting held by Roadblock Earth First! the week prior. On the last Tuesday evening in June, the Tokarskis, the Boyds, John Smith and his wife, France, and other longtime I-69 foes took seats in a lecture hall at the Monroe County Public Library and listened while their junior counterparts briefly summarized their view of the situation. I heard a recording of this meeting later. Anarchists don't really like the leader thing either, but a young man who introduced himself only as Hugh was clearly the de facto master of ceremonies. Hugh, I later found out, was Hugh Farrell, a twenty-one-year-old who had graduated from North Central High School in Indianapolis, in the school district neighboring my own. The northern suburbs of Indy are a pretty moderate place, politically, though you might not have guessed that from Farrell's worldview: I-69, he said at the library session, was "a scheme, basically, to be able to move commodities and move goods from NAFTA corridors in Mexico *directly* to this part of the United States and Canada."

Two other young men gave talks on related plots to the north and the south—what economists might call regional integration projects, but what the presenters believed was, to the south, a plot "to move sweatshop-type industry from northern Mexico into southern Mexico and Central America and have the ability to ship all those goods into the United States." To the north, "the CEOs of these multinational corporations" were pushing to dissolve unions and drive down the minimum wage, "and then expand the port of Halifax to take in more international goods coming mostly from China." These schemes—Atlantica (to the north) and the Plan Puebla Panama (to the south)—were connected by the NAFTA superhighway, they said. "So you just have this massive shipment of these free-trade goods going down I-69 from both ways."

The connection the anarchists were trying to make between I-69 and various international economic efforts was highly interpretive. As John Smith pointed out later in the meeting, existing highways already connected America to our neighboring countries. The construction, or not, of Interstate 69 would have no real bearing on globalization. Even to highway proponents, the NAFTA label was more a marketing device than a core mission. But if the Roadblock group's extrapolations were irrelevant, their values were not. In arguing against capitalism, against the globalized economy as we know it, the anarchists were advocating for self-determination, simplicity, localism, and the primacy of nature. And in Bloomington, among I-69 opponents, that was common ground.

"We talk about these projects, the Plan Puebla Panama and Atlantica," Farrell said, because "they are very physically hooked up." But also, "we are inspired by the local resistance around these projects. The more we look at these projects, the more we can see Indiana in them." Farrell asked for the lights to be dimmed so that he could show slides from an exemplary antihighway campaign in England. "Folks moved on-site to resist construction," he said. Members of Earth First! teamed up with local citizens' groups to fortify endangered communities. "An entire neighborhood was draped with nets so that people could be up in the air all the time and more eviction-proof," Farrell said. "They constructed a gigantic, seven-story-tall tower with greased poles so you couldn't climb it without the permission of the folks on top, and they put a sound system up there so that when the eviction came everyone was able to dance, and basically it became a gigantic party." The struggle lasted a year, Farrell reported, and eventually the road pushed through. But the expulsion of the camps was extremely costly, the protests drained the state's momentum, and later projects were canceled.

"This is not necessarily something we seek to replicate," Farrell said, although the plans for "advanced climbing" lessons at the Rendezvous suggested otherwise. "But it definitely shows us there's potential for continuing the struggle well past the point at which the DOT says it's a done deal." Knowing he was in the presence of the Tokarskis and other longtime foes, Farrell tipped his hat to their years of work. "We have to continue building on the firm foundation that's been built over the past fifteen years," he said. "But especially as we get to construction, we feel it's not in anyone's interests except those of the road builders to throw in the towel."

Farrell ordered the lights brought up, and a girl who introduced herself as Katie gave a rundown of recent activity along the I-69 route. The record of decision—final federal approval—for the first eleven miles north of Evansville was imminent, and INDOT was already buying land. Members of Roadblock had conducted a "listening tour" through the towns in the highway's path, she said, and they had heard stories of evictions and land deals closed with the help of police intimidation. Several families they talked to hadn't yet agreed to the state's buyout terms, and they were hoping to encourage collective refusals, to tie up the project with eminent-domain lawsuits. This was the kind of organizing that even the stalwart old-timers could support, and lively brainstorming ensued. But it wasn't long before the elephant in the room was outed.

"It's not a question of what do we want or not want. It's more about the tactics, and what works," Kevin Enright, the Monroe County surveyor, said. "There was the attack on the office that got headlines. And then the spray painting of the statehouse in Indianapolis that got headlines. And all of this seems, from my perspective, to undermine the work of people who've been working to build the resistance, grassroots, along the route." He understood that the young were frustrated by a process that seemed not to be working, "but for us that have been in it for the long haul, we need to keep things clean and respectable and upright."

Farrell responded, choosing his words carefully. "I guess I feel that, in a lot of ways, we are entering a phase where those questions are, in some ways, becoming less relevant," he said. The countermeasures over the last fifteen years had built a strong foundation, "and had those not been in place and that work not been done, this road might have been built a very long time ago." But now the state was moving toward construction, he said. "Once they're on the ground evicting families, clearing trees and whatnot, what remains?" The pending lawsuits would help slow the state down and cost them more money and expose the absurdity of the project. "But I'm also in favor of basically creating the community infrastructure to make sure *every* option necessary is put into place, or is available, to stop this road."

France, John Smith's wife, spoke next. "Kevin brought up the difference in ages. It's true in some ways," she said. "I'm not going to be climbing up trees or any of that. But I'm very happy to know that there are people who will. I think we need to be protesting this in every way possible. Because the alternate final thing is that the bulldozers are going to crush someone's home and it's going to be gone forever." She was happy to read about actions that were "most unexpected and not nice." "The government expects everyone to always be nice and they get real upset when people aren't nice all the time, and they get a little bit scared." But people along the route were scared, too, and they'd been waiting for too long already, "not knowing, 'Am I gonna get to live here until I die or am I not?'" She supported the anarchists, she said, even if they broke the law. "I don't have the guts to do this. I don't have time. I teach school. I can't go to jail. But there are people who can do that. And I appreciate that it's done."

Sandra followed. "It's a very fine line," she said. "We need to build support in rural communities. And some kinds of actions are not going to do that. They're going to alienate people." She agreed that INDOT and the governor were behaving reprehensibly. Clearly times were changing. Things were moving into another phase, "and I don't have the answers to *any* of this," she said. "But acts that are destructive and wanton, wanton destruction, that isn't going to move us forward."

The room had grown a little tense, but Bill Boyd broke the ice. "Thank you for bringing new energy into this, because some of us have run out of gas," he said. Sandra let out a belly laugh in apparent agreement. "Those of us in the *geriatric* generation here have been fighting this for some time," Boyd said. The codgers had a very low tolerance for unlawful activities, and he, like Sandra, worried about turning off the same rural folks they sought to organize. "But I do agree that further action is necessary. If the state is going to continue to lie to us as they have, perhaps—all options are on the table, I guess. We need to look at everything. But I think our two groups will run on parallel paths. And that may be necessary. May be a good thing, too."

The torch was not exactly passed at the library that evening. But the two generations had at least expressed a certain degree of mutual respect, and each promised to continue in its own way, the one more diplomatic and the other more raucous.

On a Monday afternoon in July, a week after the Rondy, small teams of anarchists showed up at four of the INDOT I-69 offices along the route. In Oakland City and Petersburg, they "evicted" the workers. Calling themselves Hayduke's Moving Company—after the eco-radicalist hero of Edward Abbey's novel *The Monkey Wrench Gang*—they carried boxes and office equipment out to the curb. At two sites in Bloomington, they dropped banners or wrote anti-69 slogans in chalk and shoe polish before marching through the streets. A bystander told a reporter from the *Indiana Daily Student* that some of the marchers were barefoot. "They almost looked like they came from a commune, just of-the-earth-type people," he said. No arrests were made.

In August, the anarchists showed up to a meeting at a local high school, where Steve Smith, an INDOT project manager, was to brief local officials on grants the state was awarding to help communities plan for I-69. It was relatively benign for an I-69 meeting—if the road was going to come, planning could theoretically help mitigate sprawl and other environmental ills—but that didn't spare it. On a recording aired by WFHB, the Bloomington community radio station, you can hear Farrell pipe up after Smith's brief introduction. "It's a bribe!" he yelled. "You're selling out the people who are losing their homes! This is a fifty-thousand-dollar bribe to shut people up! But you can't shut people up, and this is a waste of time, because this road project is gonna get *shut down!*"

Smith remained calm. "This sounds like it might be a message for somebody who has to do with the choice of building a highway, which is not why we're here," he said. "We have nothing to do—" And then a chair hit the floor. The next day, the press would report that the chair had been thrown—thanks to former IU basketball coach Bobby Knight, chair throwing looms large in Bloomington—but it was only knocked over as protesters who had positioned themselves throughout the crowd rose to their feet. "Shut it down!" they yelled. They banged on tables and chanted, "Earth first! Profits last!"

The police arrived and warned the anarchists that they could be thrown in jail for disorderly conduct. Why don't they arrest the planning consultants for trying to bribe public officials, a demonstrator wanted to know.

"That's not the matter at hand right now," one officer responded coolly. "The matter at hand is you guys being loud." The cops radioed headquarters to ask if they should arrest anyone, or just stand by and make sure no one got physical. Evidently their orders were to remain as onlookers. The demonstration—and the meeting—ended shortly thereafter. Again, no arrests were made.

As unsettling as the performance may have been for the bureaucrats present, such misbehavior would soon be common in the heartland, as outrage over the Democrats' health-care plan made for several dicey town halls in 2009. Farrell and the Earth First! gang were ahead of that curve and also keeping up a proud antihighway tradition: As previously mentioned, author Jane Jacobs herself was known to raise some hell. At a New York City Planning Commission meeting in 1961, she and fellow activists tried to take over the proceedings and were thrown out. In 1968, when Jacobs was arrested and charged with second-degree riot and criminal mischief, it was for a performance not unlike Farrell's. As Anthony Flint describes the event in his book *Wrestling with Moses,* Jacobs came to the microphone at a hearing on the Lower Manhattan Expressway and warned, "If the expressway is put through, there will be anarchy." She then walked up onto the stage, followed by some fifty compatriots. They threw the stenographer's tape into the air, onto the floor. "Listen to this! There is no record!" Jacobs cried. "We're through with this phony, fink hearing!" The Indiana anarchists' complaints were the same: Public meetings were shams, useful only as flashpoints for anger and action. A charade of listening was not enough for them. They wanted to be heard.

Oddly, though, they didn't want to be interviewed. I sent e-mails to the generic Yahoo! address listed on their website. I sent word through the Tokarskis and John Smith. I tried to invite myself to their Rendezvous. But when my requests were answered, they were refused. Maybe the Earth Firsters were concerned about talking over e-mail or the telephone, I thought, so I decided to try showing up in person. Their website advertised an informational get-together in Chicago at a progressive bookstore called the New World Resource Center. On the last day of August it was clear and warm, and I parked on the street and came inside. I was early, so I browsed the books in a rack near the counter—Norman Mailer on the Chicago Conventions, *The Communist Manifesto,* Studs Terkel's *Working*—before walking back to a meeting room behind the shop, where a young girl in glasses and a guy with a patchy blond beard were figuring out how to fix the picture on a laptop projector.

I was older than thirty and wasn't interested in going undercover. I introduced myself to the girl, who seemed as in charge as anyone, and told her I was a writer working on a book about I-69. I had been trying to get in touch, I said, and hoped I could sit in, listen, and maybe take some notes.

She looked straight ahead, not at me. "Um, let me talk to some other folks," she said, and walked into yet another room.

For the next twenty minutes—among the longest in my life—I made small talk about vegan food and radical child care with the half dozen people in the room. Mercifully, one woman had lived in Brooklyn, where I do, and we talked about vegan restaurants in New York. Right about the time I found myself asking whether sorbet was vegan, a young man with an unwashed faux-hawk hairdo walked in from the other room and stood in front of me. "Hey, dude. We've come to the decision that we're not gonna allow members of the media here," he said, "so it would be really cool if you left."

I asked him if I might have a chance to explain myself a little better, and he invited me to step outside, where we were met by a tall, serious-faced young man with dark curly hair and glasses—this, I later learned, was Hugh Farrell. I tried to explain that I wasn't writing a newspaper article, but a complete history of the road and the efforts to build it and stop it. I was from Indiana and I'd been talking to the I-69 opponents there for five years, I told them. I had traveled the whole route, and I'd come to Chicago to meet them because they were now part of the story.

"I think our general feeling is we'll contact the media when we want to be portrayed, like, third person," the guy who had asked me to leave said, "and otherwise we'll speak for ourselves."

That's why I had come, I said. I was already familiar with the group's arguments and had been following their actions. I could cobble together a picture from their literature and news accounts. But I had come to meet them in person because I wanted to understand better who they were as people.

Farrell thought for a moment and looked at the faux-hawked guy. "I'm now for taking this back to the group," he said. They leaned inside and invited a few of the others out onto the sidewalk, where they huddled at a safe distance from me, conferring.

Inside, the girl in glasses was preparing her presentation on how I-69 was connected to oppressive infrastructure projects in Central and South America and corporate schemes in Canada, I knew. As it happened, I had met just the night before with David Reed, the unknown intellectual father of I-69 and the originator of its NAFTA branding. On my way to Chicago I had taken a drive along the newly privatized Indiana Toll Road and the existing stretch of I-69 in Michigan, and Reed, who teaches at Alma College, met me at his favorite Indian restaurant in Lansing, fifty miles south of his home. He was a tall, hefty man with dark hair and a lot to say.

We talked about his work at the Hudson Institute and his former boss, Mitch Daniels. Interestingly, Reed was against the privatization of highways, which he called a "license to print money." "I'm a conservative economist," he said, "but I understand, I think reasonably well, that some services cannot be provided for profit." Leasing toll roads, he said, "results from the laziness of politicians. They recognize the need to raise tolls, but they don't want to put themselves at risk."

Knowing I would be hearing about international conspiracies the next day in Chicago, I asked Reed about I-69's NAFTA moniker. For most proponents, the continental nature of the route was merely a way to get Washington's attention, and Reed himself had written an essay for the first newsletter of the Mid-Continent Highway Coalition in which he called the Canada-to-Mexico link an "accident of geography, history, and timing." But over Indian food, and so near Detroit, he defended the free-trade associations that had become so toxic. "We cannot build a world-class car in Michigan and be price-competitive with it," he said. "My mother raised us on wages paid by the auto industry—but the auto industry in the fifties and sixties was a very different animal." Detroit now was suffering under the weight of its unions; "a NAFTA highway would allow comparative advantage to play out more effectively. You would do the relatively low-skill, labor-intensive kinda work perhaps in Mexico." What Detroit and Flint should be doing, he told me, well before the idea became conventional wisdom, was retooling for the jobs of the future: "Let's use the auto industry as the central point around which we recon-struct the way we manufacture things in this country."

We left the restaurant in a rainstorm, and Reed stood under his umbrella and told me, "My one great unrequited desire, which I hope will be requited before my exit from this great world, is to drive the completed I-69. If that ever happens, I will feel as if my career has been reasonably successful—made at least some difference, if that's all it amounts to."

On the sidewalk in Chicago the next evening, I stood awaiting my fate. When the anarchist huddle broke up, the half dozen activists filed past me and inside with their heads down. The last of them, the guy with the faux-hawk, walked over to me. "I'm sorry, dude," he said. They weren't comfortable with me staying, but they wanted to send me away with some of their literature. I flipped through one flyer on the way to my car. "With the construction of I-69 comes a new vision of development that tears through Mesoamerica, transforming it into a massive, interconnected, industrial production site," an article titled "I-69 and the Plan Puebla Panama: The Global Connection" read. "It is clear that these projects are part of a single massive scheme."

There was a certain irony to all of this. The anarchists were certain that Interstate 69 was the fruit of collusion, a deal worked out by shady corporate interests. But the man who had come up with the NAFTA highway idea in a brainstorm seventeen years before had driven an hour to meet me and explain why he thought the road was important. It was the young environmentalists who wanted to stop it that insisted on meeting behind closed doors. The group so eager to take direct action was unwilling to take direct questions.

That December, the U.S. district court granted a motion for summary judgment in favor of the agencies seeking to build I-69. The Tokarskis et al. lost their case, and with it the last good chance at peacefully preventing construction. The ruling was handed down by Judge David F. Hamilton, a nephew of former congressman Lee Hamilton, at whose behest the Hudson Institute had hired David Reed to study the future of southern Indiana. Hamilton's opinion covered a lot of ground, including an extensive discussion of the hibernation habits of the endangered Indiana bat. But in short it said what Sandy Ewing had feared such a decision might: that the National Environmental Policy Act "does not mandate a particular outcome or contain substantive environmental standards." INDOT had successfully jumped through the hoops of the environmental-study process—one made more stringent and time-consuming by the Tokarskis' vigilance—and now the state could do whatever it wanted to.

The Tokarskis had always worked within the system and had expected the system to work for them. They had hoped that the lack of transportation funding would make I-69 impossible. They thought the highway advocates might fade first. But money appeared. Their lawsuit failed. Families near Evansville were being evicted from their homes, and the state was preparing to break ground. The legitimate remedies were all but exhausted. Thomas and Sandra were exhausted. The state still couldn't afford to build much, the Tokarskis told their supporters. It was no time to give up the fight. But Governor Daniels wasn't giving up either. And the anarchists—they had only just begun.

Don't Mess with Texas

Major international corridors, it turns out, can be just as terrifying to reactionaries as to radicals. The Earth Firsters in Bloomington weren't the only ones taking the antihighway rhetoric to new levels. In 2006, a quiet year for the anarchists, word of asphalt imperialism started to spread online among ultraconservatives. That June, Jerome Corsi, the man best known as the coauthor of *Unfit for Command: Swift Boat Veterans Speak Out Against John Kerry,* took to the Internet to sound the alarm about a new threat being advanced by the very man he had helped to reelect: "Quietly but systematically the Bush administration is advancing the plan to build a huge NAFTA Super Highway, four football fields wide, through the heart of the U.S.," he wrote on the website for the conservative weekly *Human Events.* "Once complete, the new road will allow containers from the Far East to enter the United States through the Mexican port of Lazaro Cardenas, bypassing the Longshoremen's Union in the process. The Mexican trucks, without the involvement of the Teamsters Union, will drive on what will be the nation's most modern highway straight into the heart of America."

For a conservative to complain about the circumvention of unions, the larger scenario must be pretty bad. And it was! "The American public," Corsi wrote, "is largely asleep to this key piece of the coming 'North American Union' that government planners in the new trilateral region of [the] United States, Canada and Mexico are about to drive into reality." The alleged North American Union, Corsi believed, would be a "super-regional political authority that could override the sovereignty of the United States on immigration policy and trade issues." Our borders with Mexico and Canada would be reduced to mere speed bumps, Corsi said, and the dollar would be discarded in favor of a new Eurolike currency called the Amero. Supposedly, all of this was being advanced under the auspices of the Security and Prosperity Partnership, a seemingly harmless pact to promote security and trade between the NAFTA nations. The fact that most Americans had no clue about these developments was, for Corsi, further proof that things were happening way too fast. "Missing in the move toward creating a North American Union is the robust public debate that preceded the decision to form the European Union," he wrote. "All this may be for calculated political reasons on the part of the Bush administration."

There were notable differences between the intrigue to which Corsi was alerting conservatives and the "massive scheme" warned of by Earth Firsters in Indiana. While the anarchists suspected global corporations, Corsi saw the hand of world leaders and quasigovernmental organizations; and while the radicals focused on the integrating economy, the reactionaries feared unified government. The perceived scope of the NAFTA superhighway varied, too, depending on where you were and when. It was defined as I-69, or I-35, or the Trans-Texas Corridor (in part or in full), or some combination of the above. But whatever it was, the pivotal instrument of these supposed evils looked the same to both groups: massive new highways run by private foreign companies carrying imported goods by nonunion means into the American heartland.

There was plenty of room in this dark vision for everyone. As with the Tea Party protests that arose in 2009, the anti–NAFTA superhighway campaign in Texas became the chosen vehicle for a cacophony of constituencies. For David and Linda Stall, this presented a challenge. Trying to wrangle the inconsistent messages emerging from their toll-and-corridor summit in 2004 had been difficult enough. But things were about to get downright absurd. On March 2, 2007, the Stalls agreed to speak at a Don't Tag Texas rally at the state capitol building in Austin. The event was pulled together by Hank Gilbert, a cattle rancher and former Democratic candidate for agricultural commissioner from northwest Texas. Gilbert was a cofounder, with Teri Hall, an activist from San Antonio, of Texans Uniting for Reform and Freedom. TURF was an antitoll, anti–Trans-Texas Corridor, anti–North American Union group, and the rally, held on Texas Independence Day, reflected all of these passions and then some. The Tag in "Don't Tag Texas" referred not only to TxTag, the state's windshield tolling transponder, but also to the proposed National Animal Identification System, which the USDA wanted to implement to better trace diseased livestock. It seemed to many of those gathered in Austin that day that the government would not rest until it could track every car and every cow and perhaps—God forbid—every citizen.

The rally began with a march up Congress Avenue to the capitol. The Stalls skipped this part, and maybe that was for the best. The procession was a dreamlike mélange of rage and paranoia. There were pickup trucks and tractors, horses ridden and caged chickens carried, black-clad skateboarders and gray-haired farmers in overalls. A bespectacled, Birkenstock-wearing highway hater walked his bicycle and talked to a man in a cowboy hat who was motoring along slowly in a red front-end loader. Several people waved full-size Texas flags and a banner from the Texas Revolution: a white flag with a lone black star, the silhouette of a cannon, and the taunt COME AND TAKE IT. A handful of marchers wore T-shirts that read 9-11 WAS AN INSIDE JOB, and many carried printed signs—STOP THE TRANS-TEXAS CORRIDOR, MY LAND IS *NOT* YOUR LAND, RON PAUL FOR PRESIDENT, and DON'T TAG MY ANIMALS. Handmade posters read NO CHIPS IN CHICK-ENS and THE MARK OF THE BEAST: WE'RE PREPARED TO RESIST UNTO DEATH. One older woman carried a Ziploc bag of soil marked BIGGEST AMOUNT OF DIRT I'LL GIVE TO RICK PERRY'S TTC TOLLROAD.

Alex Jones, a syndicated radio host, "investigative journalist," and the purveyor of the conspiracy-theory-laden site Infowars.com, was the dominant voice in the march. He carried a bullhorn, which he employed liberally. "Down with the North American Union!" he yelled frequently, and "Remember the Alamo!" He shouted non sequiturs for much of the ten-block hike until he was hoarse. "Governor Perry is a whore! Rick Perry is a piece of trash! We're gonna defeat his North American Union, his Trans-Texas Corridor, and his National Animal Identification System! Texas will not pay taxes to a Spanish king!"

Like the Tokarskis, the Stalls were uneasy with their new strange bedfellows. At a CorridorWatch meeting in Victoria later that month, I watched Linda's smile turn into a grimace as I stood chatting to members of the John Birch Society and people convinced that Muslims were taking over America. After the Don't Tag Texas rally, David proudly described his appearance that day on the Lou Dobbs show, but while he was happy that the Trans-Texas Corridor was becoming a national issue, the outrageous suspicions that were becoming attached to the transportation issue made him uncomfortable. "Alex Jones is Jerome Corsi turned up four or five notches. And we distance ourselves from those folks at every opportunity, because they damage our credibility. We just stay with the highway aspect of it."

The Stalls were characteristically focused in their remarks that afternoon. When they took their turn at the microphone on the statehouse steps, they made no mention of the North American Union and only polite passing reference to animal tagging. Gilbert introduced them as "the people who have fought this fight longer than anyone, the people who put the Trans-Texas Corridor on the map," and they soaked in the applause of a thousand people. David spoke first. "Our elected officials in this building behind me told my wife and I that they would never give TxDOT the sweeping powers and authorities they asked for to do the Trans-Texas Corridor," he said. "We thought that they would tell us the truth, and it turned out to be a lie." When they had heard in early 2004 that the state was in fact pressing forward, Linda asked him, "'What can two people do?' And I'm standing here today so proud I'm about to explode," David said, "because *this* is what two people can do."

The day before the rally, the Texas Senate Transportation Committee had held a hearing on the Trans-Texas Corridor, David told the crowd, and several bills had already been filed to put a stop to the plan. When Linda spoke, in a sweet schoolteacher tone, she implored the people to take advantage of the momentum they had created and to keep pushing their legislators. "It takes courage and it takes strength to go up against a governor who has a plan," she said of sympathetic lawmakers. "We need to have their backs. It's really, really important. We can make change happen, but we can't ever, ever be idle. So let them hear from you, and let them sometimes hear *kind* words. Let them hear 'thank you' when they do what you want."

The Stalls had their eye on the ball; the political landscape was primed. Governor Perry had won reelection in 2006 against a Democratic challenger and two Independents with a mere plurality of 39 percent. The voters were furious, and lawmakers were getting the drift that the corridor was poison. Senator John Carona, the chairman of the state Senate Transportation Committee, had said at his hearing that many of his colleagues who had voted for House Bill 3588 "would like a do-over," and support was building for a half dozen bills that called for a moratorium on private toll contracts.

The Stalls, to the envy of the Tokarskis, operated a fearsome online organizational machine, and they wielded it to full effect. CorridorWatch had members in 199 out of 254 Texas counties, and as the moratorium bills wound their way through committees and onto the floor, the Stalls fired off e-mail bulletins to supporters. With David's wireless Internet card, they could send dispatches from rural parking lots or the café in the basement of the state capitol. At their command, their followers would flood the phone and fax lines at the statehouse. Their CorridorWatch mailing list allowed them to work with devastating precision. If they heard that an individual lawmaker needed a nudge, they could send an urgent message to that person's constituents and overwhelm his or her office with well-informed demands.

David and Linda spent much of that April and May in Austin, and they didn't just have front-row seats. They had backstage passes, too. They gave their opinion on various bills at committee hearings, and aides frequently scrambled to find them and pull them into pivotal conversations. One afternoon they were seated in the house gallery and their representative, Lois Kolkhorst, climbed the stairs to get their opinion on changes to her bill. "She actually left the floor and came up into the gallery with her bill in hand, and we went down and sat down, off away from everybody else, and went through the bill, provision by provision," Linda told me over the phone after an intense day of horse-trading.

David was on the line, too. "Lois didn't realize that *we* had written some of the sections that they put in," he said gleefully. "We were working with the transportation staff and had offered those as things we wanted to see in the bill." David and Linda had enormous power that session. Transportation had become the hot issue in Texas, and the Stalls, better than anyone, spoke for the angry electorate—without showing anger themselves. "In four years of not burning anybody and not advancing some wild-eyed agenda," David said, "we also have credibility where the legislators can take us into confidence and work with us." As they maneuvered through the statehouse, they said, not a single state representative or senator turned them away. Private interests had collaborated with Krusee and Langmore and Weaver to craft HB 3588 to their liking, and now the Stalls were guiding the bill that could put the brakes on privatization.

On May 2, 2007, the Texas legislature passed House Bill 1892, which included almost everything the Stalls had wanted: a two-year moratorium on all private toll deals, greater legislative oversight and a forty-year cap on the term of future toll agreements, and more local public control over toll roads in Houston and Dallas, for which TxDOT had been urging leases. Both houses passed the bill by wide margins. The house approved it 139 to 1, with Krusee standing alone against it.

But on May 18, Governor Perry vetoed it, saying that it would jeopardize billions of dollars of infrastructure investment and prevent Texas from dealing with its projected population. "As a state that grows by 1,200 people each and every day," he wrote, "we must consider every viable option that will allow Texas to build a strong transportation infrastructure."

Another moratorium bill was making its way through the legislature. Senate Bill 792 was being carried by Senator Robert Nichols, whose district covered the northern end of I-69. Rather than try to override the governor's veto, the lawmakers decided to tweak SB 792 so that it would be acceptable to the governor. The new bill was passed on May 26, and Perry promised his signature. On the twenty-eighth, Memorial Day, the last day of the session, the Stalls sat triumphantly with a handful of their supporters in the house gallery when the assembly they had so expertly influenced gaveled to a close. William Molina, the director of *Truth Be Tolled,* was there shooting footage for a second edition of his documentary, and he asked the Stalls to sit alone in their favorite seats while he filmed them. They nuzzled and kissed and laughed. It seemed like their wedding day. As they left the gallery, still smiling, they walked past a composite picture of the Texas House from 1985. They paused to enjoy an old photo of Ric Williamson with slicked-back hair and a Doc Holliday mustache. They walked out onto a balcony under the rotunda, and three floors below an a cappella group called the Austin Chord Rangers happened to be launching into "This Land Is Your Land." Linda sang along.

The Trans-Texas Corridor was on the ropes, but privatization wasn't dead. Williamson, who no longer had a mustache or enough hair to slick back, was quick to point out to the press that the compromise moratorium bill was full of holes. The bill did not affect agreements that had already been signed, and while it forbade new private tolling contracts for two years, it did not prevent planning. What's more, a dozen or so private projects on which the state had been close to a concession agreement were exempted from the ban—including the portion of I-69 from Corpus Christi to the valley.

Stall had mixed feelings about the exemption of I-69. He didn't want to see anything resembling the Trans-Texas Corridor built anywhere, but the way he saw it, the I-69 group had been hoodwinked by Perry and his big ideas. "Those people have been lobbying for years, for more than a decade, to get an interstate," he told me. "They've been underserved and they want their road. So when they have the Trans-Texas Corridor dangled in front of them, that's funding to get a road that they figure, at this point, they'll never otherwise see." During the moratorium debate, Harris County judge Ed Emmett withdrew Houston's support of the ostensibly pro-TTC Alliance for I-69 Texas, which had already pulled back from the Mid-Continent Highway Coalition, and many longtime supporters found themselves wishing that the corridor genie could be put back in the bottle. They wanted to return to simpler times, when I-69 meant only the improvement of existing roads, and the only arguments were over which U.S. highway to improve first.

They soon got their wish. In January 2008, the state embarked on the environmental process for TTC-69 by holding a series of meetings along the route. In the rural counties around Houston, which the vast corridor threatened to divide, enraged landowners and other opponents turned out by the hundreds. The North American Union conspiracy theories were still in circulation. In fact, the Republican presidential-primary hopefuls had been getting questions about the NAFTA superhighway out on the trail. *The New York Times* reported that the candidates were having a hard time answering those questions. Rudolph Giuliani disavowed all knowledge in New Hampshire, and Mitt Romney, in Iowa, told voters that he wasn't aware of any such plan. But if there was one, he said, "I'll stop it." Ron Paul, a Texan, was the only one talking about it, and he talked about it a lot. Many of the people at the TTC-69 hearings wore Ron Paul stickers and shirts.

Ric Williamson had died suddenly over the holidays, and the agency he once ran with such sass was humbled by both his absence and the legislative session the year before. Transportation commissioner Ted Houghton, who had famously declared I-69 dead, was now doing penance as the public face of its resurrection. He stood for the entirety of the meetings, which lasted for hours. He took the abuse the agency had coming, and reassured the people that TxDOT was listening now. They were going to do what the people asked, he said, and he wouldn't be surprised if I-69 went back to being its old self.

For good measure, Hank Gilbert, who attended most of the TTC-69 hearings, organized a second TURF rally in Austin. The public meetings were over and the legislature wasn't in session, so turnout was sparser. There were a few tractors and a couple of horses, but no Alex Jones and no Stalls. Gilbert and Teri Hall led the march, which ambled past the Austin

Convention Center before turning up Congress to the statehouse. Inside the convention center, coincidentally, the Congress for the New Urbanism was holding its annual meeting. During their four days of programming, they talked about streetcars and compact development and roads for people as well as cars. The president of the CNU, John Norquist, moderated a panel on "Correcting the Robert Moses Freeways," a conversation that considered the virtues of tearing down urban expressways and fashioning them into boulevards—as Harland Bartholomew would have wanted from the get-go. Robert Caro, the author of the seminal book on Moses, gave a talk as well, and the planner Andrés Duany took part in a discussion on marketing New Urbanism to conservatives. There was something perfect about the anti-corridor protesters unknowingly marching past a building full of people trying to plan for a posthighway world. There was great irony, too: The New Urbanism conference was hosted by, among others, John Langmore and Mike Krusee, the two men most responsible for passing the bill that permitted the Trans-Texas Corridor.

Langmore, who gave a presentation on gentrification that featured his own photographs of the historically Hispanic neighborhoods of East Austin, had turned Krusee on to New Urbanism years before, when they went on a field trip with Duany to the Kentlands development in Maryland. "Krusee was into it, the dense development as an alternative to sprawl," Langmore told me. "He lives in the ultimate suburban sprawl, and he hates it." After many talks on the subject, Langmore had convinced the conservative Krusee to embrace trains, and the two were active in bringing commuter rail to Austin. Krusee was now a board member of the Congress for the New Urbanism and was working on a project in San Antonio that would turn an old strip mall along I-35 into a corporate campus and town center.

"What's New Urbanist about building a six- or twelve-lane bypass around Austin?" Krusee asked me, when I brought up the seeming paradox of his two passions. "With that bypass in place, we can go back into the small towns along I-35 and change the highway's design, change it into a boulevard. We've been trying to figure out a way to heal the scar between Austin and East Austin. Eisenhower was against bringing the interstates through cities. Now we can go back and correct those mistakes." That is what he had hoped for the Trans-Texas Corridor, he told me. He never expected to build the monstrosity that TxDOT showed in its conceptual drawings. "The farmers got all upset about it. Nobody understood it," he said. "When Ric Williamson started talking about twelve-hundred-foot swaths going through, and high-speed rail, he just basically put everything in the kitchen sink and said, 'This is what we're doing.'"

But Williamson was gone, and TxDOT was chastened. On June 11, 2008, the department announced that it would build I-69 along existing roadways wherever possible. The twenty-eight thousand comments from the public environmental process, TxDOT executive director Amadeo Saenz said, had expressed an "overwhelming sentiment" that the agency should focus on improving the roads it already had. Ted Houghton made good on his word. "TxDOT's recommendation would effectively shrink our environmental study down to roads such as U.S. Highways 77 and 281 in south Texas . . . and U.S. Highway 59 along the coastal bend," he said. "We are dropping consideration of new corridors that would run west of Houston." Houghton and the other commissioners had cleaned up their act. They swore by a new set of principles: Only new lanes would be tolled, and there would never be a reduction in the number of free lanes in any corridor; existing footprints would be used wherever possible; and the department would rededicate itself to obeying the wishes of the local communities. Later that month, TxDOT awarded the development contract for the planning of the I-69 corridor to Zachry Construction of San Antonio. Cintra, the great conquistadors of privatization, lost the bid.

Maybe the moratorium hadn't been all that the Stalls had hoped. But clearly the spirit of the law had been taken to heart. The Stalls and their supporters had stopped the stampede of the Trans-Texas Corridor. The tools for privatization that remained in TxDOT's hands were smaller and saner, and they had assurances that the agency would henceforth do its planning with its ears open. In four years, David and Linda had accomplished what the Tokarskis had been trying to do for almost two decades—they had tamed their state department of transportation and forced I-69 off of new terrain.

Broken Ground

Everyone more or less behaved on Earth Day, 2008. The Indiana anarchists had put together a protest parade through the streets of Bloomington for that Saturday, April 19. They hadn't bothered getting a permit, and some worried that the morning march would spiral into vandalism. But despite being noisy and mildly disruptive to traffic, the demonstration remained a peaceful family affair. Thomas and Sandra did their part to keep things light. They showed up with full-body cow costumes, which they provided to two fellow CARR members along with signs that said COWS NOT CONCRETE and I-69 IS UDDERLY CRAZY. Thomas had dressed himself as a tree, a vine of artificial leaves draped over his head and shoulders. The crowd gathered and unpacked banners and bucket drums, and Sandra glanced around at the younger marchers, who held harsher signs about NAFTA and sweatshops and wore camouflage print, plaid, and every shade of brown and black and gray. Sandra furrowed her brow and said to me, "They never smile." I looked over at Hugh Farrell, who nodded at me in recognition. Soon the fifty or so activists who had gathered in People's Park made their way out onto Kirkwood Avenue and blocked the street as they headed toward the courthouse square. Sandra followed but kept to the sidewalk.

The anarchists wound through the downtown grid, stopping cars and a public hybrid bus. "They wreck trees. We wreck roads," they chanted. People dining out under awnings looked up and a few cheered. When the procession passed in front of One City Center, the previously vandalized building that housed the I-69 offices, four Bloomington police officers stood in front of the door, watching with their arms folded. A few police cars idled along behind the throng, too, but no one intervened.

Such police presence had become routine. Thomas had been detained earlier that spring for taking pictures of soon-to-be-destroyed houses in the I-69 right-of-way down near Evansville. He was put into the back of a police car without handcuffs and questioned, he told me. "I saw it as just harassment and intimidation." He had also heard reports of a recent meeting between INDOT, Bernardin Lochmueller, the FBI, and the state and local police. The law-enforcement agencies were coordinating their activities, he said, and strategizing about how to deal with threats from protesters. Several of the anarchists that day told me that they were being followed, and I believed them, mostly because Robert Springer, an FBI special agent with the Joint Terrorism Task Force, had called my cell phone the week before. Springer knew that I was working on a book about I-69, and somehow he was aware that I'd tried to attend the Roadblock Earth First! meeting in Chicago—a detail that seemed to indicate that the FBI had infiltrated the group, or at least was monitoring its e-mail.

The afternoon before the Earth Day march, I met Agent Springer for coffee near the FBI's Indianapolis field office. He was a clean-cut man of about forty, wearing not a dark suit or sunglasses but khakis and an oxford shirt. I agreed to keep the content of our conversation off the record, but that turned out to be no great loss: Springer revealed nothing and was more interested in asking me questions I couldn't answer about the anarchists' intentions. He had already spoken publicly about the bureau's focus on I-69, however. In November 2007, Springer gave a talk in Bloomington at IU's School of Environmental and Public Affairs. The session, titled "Terrorism, Civil Liberties and Mediation: A Delicate Balance," was advertised as an educational lecture, but it was clearly meant as a warning, too. Springer told the seventy-five or so in attendance that domestic and international terrorism were, together, the bureau's number one priority, and he framed antihighway actions in very serious terms. "We recognize there is potential for conflict regarding I-69," the Bloomington *Herald-Times* quoted Springer as saying. "The number of people opposed to the construction of the highway breeds the possibility of eco-terrorist acts. My job is to investigate any such acts that occur."

The definition of terrorism is a subjective thing, of course, and Springer refused to say whether any incidents related to I-69 had crossed that threshold. But he did offer a few examples of acts that might be considered terrorism, two of which—destroying property and targeting private homes for harassment—were things for which anonymous I-69 activists on anarchist websites had already claimed responsibility.

I didn't see Special Agent Springer in Bloomington on Earth Day, but it was easy to imagine that some number of his FBI colleagues were sprinkled among us. The anarchists certainly assumed as much, though the idea didn't seem to bother them. When the march ended in Dunn Meadow on the IU campus, Farrell asked for everyone's attention. "Thank you so much for parading with us today," he said. The contract for the first two miles of I-69 had been awarded that month, and four homes in the highway's path had already been demolished. Now was the time to act, he said. "We're within a month of setting up camps against I-69. That means we're going down to stop this road! Please join us, talk to us, get involved." That Tuesday, April 22, Farrell announced, would be a day for "decentralized direct action," which would be followed by an old-time jamboree that evening at a local pizza joint, Max's Place.

The day of direct action passed anticlimactically—whether a dud or a decoy, no one could say for sure. I spent that Tuesday afternoon in Washington, Indiana, in the company of David Graham. Had the anarchists known who Graham was, that it was he and not a group of multinational corporations who had planted the seeds of the road they were fighting, he might have seemed like a risky person to hang around on a day of supposed direct action. But we spent the day in peace. Graham had recently lost his wife, Stuart, to a heart attack, and he seemed a little lonely and nostalgic. We ate lunch at an Amish restaurant—there wasn't much food in the house—and then drove into town to see two old Graham Brothers automobiles he and Stuart had donated to the city.

The first was a farm wagon built at the Grahams' Evansville factory in 1927. It was being kept under a tarp at a municipal garage, and a man named Ernie uncovered it for us. Graham's face lit up. "Well, I'm just thrilled to death that you're keeping it up so well," Graham said. "I mean, look at this." The truck was in nice shape. Ernie had chased down a few parts, fixed it up a bit, and was hoping to drive it in a parade before too long. "The more it's used, the better off it is," Graham said. The city had mounted a plaque on the back gate to commemorate its donation by David and Stuart, and Graham seemed genuinely moved. "Thank you for taking such good care of it," he told Ernie. "I was afraid it'd be a pile of junk over in the corner."

We made our way across town to a fire station where an old Graham fire truck was on display, a 1924 model that had belonged to the town of Elnora. We went inside, and Graham took a slow walk around the bright red truck. He had bought it from Elnora some years back and had given it to the city of Washington shortly after he and Stuart moved from his father's house to the place on U.S. 50. It was unsafe trying to pull out of the driveway because the old truck couldn't get up to speed fast enough. "I used to drive this around town all the time," he said. He pulled a rope to ring the old bell on the dashboard, and reached up to a handle near the steering wheel and gave the siren a crank. The sound seemed like something out of an old cartoon. "That came off a World War I ambulance," Graham said. A young fireman who had joined us smiled at Graham and told him that the siren was a big hit with visitors. The truck hadn't been driven in a while, but one of the guys was trying to rebuild the water pump in his spare time. So maybe it would ride again soon. "You're doing a fine job," Graham told him, taking one last look at the truck before we left.

Seeing the old Graham vehicles brought to mind the mules that Ron Hudson in Clarksdale, Mississippi, had described to me and how the Omega plantation workers had fed and cared for them even after they'd become obsolete. The same could be said of these old Grahams but not of the B&O shops. We drove over to a shabbier part of town to see what was left of the bustling engine of growth and prosperity that Graham's grandfather Ziba had helped lure to Washington in the 1880s, and I almost drove right past it. "Slow down," Graham said. "This is where the old shops were. And I think if you look over there you can still see where the roundhouse was." On a flat weedy piece of ground along the railroad tracks to my left was the circular ghost of the steam-engine turntable. Sections of the concrete foundation remained visible, with traces of track radiating from the center. "Each little bay was where they worked on the steam engines," Graham said. "You'd pull in, onto the turntable. And over there was a shop for the railroad cars." A hundred years ago, locomotives running all day between Cincinnati and Saint Louis would stop at the roundhouse. Now its footprint looked barren and strange, like it might have been the site of a UFO landing.

Back at the house, Graham offered me a drink. We sat in his living room, where a painted portrait of his wife hung by the fireplace. He told me about Stuart's sudden death. The day of her funeral, he said, the governor came down from Indianapolis. Daniels was expected, but the style of his arrival took Stuart's mourners by surprise. "He pulled in on his motorcycle with his Harley-Davidson shirt on," Graham said, chuckling. "My sophisticated relatives from the East Coast couldn't believe it." Though it was Daniels's first visit to the home, the two had remained friends since working together on Richard Lugar's Senate campaign in

1976. After Lugar was elected, Daniels asked Graham for help getting into Georgetown Law School. "My good friend was the dean of admissions," Graham told me. "Daniels is so smart, he wouldn't have had any trouble. But I called up my friend."

Decades had passed, and now it was Daniels who was in a position to help Graham fulfill his dream. If it wasn't for Daniels and his bold lease of the Indiana Toll Road, Graham said, the I-69 effort would still be floundering. It became poignantly clear to me, having spent the afternoon checking in on the various relics of the local Graham-family legacy, that David was still waiting for his contributions to materialize. "The governor sat right there," he said, pointing to a dainty antique sofa, "and he told us that they were gonna break ground this summer on I-69. And I think they're gonna do it."

There were those who were working to prevent that ground breaking. I drove back to Bloomington that evening through the dusk and farms and small towns. When I arrived at Max's Place, the anarchist hootenanny was in full swing. A string band played on a small stage in the front window, people danced and drank beer, and the tables were crowded with a mix of opponents new and old. The Tokarskis didn't show, but their neighbor Brian Garvey was there. I found a seat between him and John Smith, who was eager to tell me that his attitude had evolved. He'd decided he had already won his own private battle with I-69. "Seventy-two is about the life expectancy, right?" he said. "I'll be seventy-two in seventeen years, and with construction costs and gas prices the way they are, I can't imagine they'll make it this far north before then."

This was a different tone than I was used to hearing from the veteran antagonists. With new-terrain construction mere months away, it appeared they had given up all hope of preventing it completely. Now they just wanted it to be as slow and painful as possible for INDOT and the governor. "I hope it's trouble and misery for those assholes every step of the way," Garvey said. He wasn't necessarily advocating anything violent or destructive, though. "Trouble can be a granny on the front porch saying, Go fuck yourselves."

It was the new, younger crowd that would provide the sweet, life-affirming optimism that evening. At a break in the music, a wholesome-looking Indianapolis native in her early twenties took the stage to make a little speech. "I can give you guys a lot of numbers and facts about why I-69 shouldn't be built," she said. "But I think one of the most important things, besides the habitats that will be ruined, are the homes which have already been demolished. And there are homes that could potentially be demolished where people like us are dancing, and meeting people, and singing, and sharing their stories. And growing. And growing *things*." She had closed her eyes, and now she opened them and looked around the room. "I think that's one very noble cause to fight for: the continuation of our own sense of self and our own humanity."

There were those, of course, who expected I-69 to boost humanity. The road would bring jobs, so the thinking went, and help provide opportunities for the people dancing and singing and meeting each other. That was the other side's noble cause. But was it true? The Tokarskis had always argued that the promise of interstate-borne revitalization was exaggerated and hollow, and in May they were seemingly vindicated when the University of Southern Indiana released the findings of a yearlong study on highways and economic development. The USI team had set out to decode why some towns historically prospered from highway construction while others withered—and to garner lessons to help the towns of Oakland City, Petersburg, and Washington shape their post-interstate future. After studying the evolution of analogous towns in Georgia, Maryland, and Texas, the USI economists Sudesh Mujumdar and Timothy Schibik offered a prognosis for southern Indiana that was mixed at best. I-69 might not be a panacea after all. In the short term, the study suggested, it might even be a curse.

Of the three towns Mujumdar and Schibik dealt with, Washington was the only one sure to thrive, the researchers projected, because it was far enough from any competing small city, and its exit (on land belonging to Graham Farms) was convenient to its center and would therefore be a prime location for an industrial park or other development. Petersburg, by contrast, would be more or less bypassed by I-69. Its best bet for survival, Mujumdar thought, was to pour resources into "some kind of Main Street program that would be unique enough to make people want to come." Now, before I-69, people are *forced* to come to Petersburg if they're traveling on U.S. 57. The highway runs straight through downtown, and the locals have lowered the speed limit on that main drag to twenty miles per hour in an apparent attempt to lull travelers into stopping. They'll have to find some new tricks, the study suggests, to reinvent themselves as a "destination town." Oakland City had some work to do, too. Because the town is a mere thirty miles from Evansville, I-69 could actually siphon off jobs to the bigger city, the report warned. On the bright side, Oakland City can look forward to becoming a bedroom community of Evansville—but only if it spends a lot of money to improve its schools and other city services. That wasn't likely in the near future. The USI study didn't mention it, but Governor Daniels had pushed through statewide limits on property taxes, forcing many small towns to cut their already anemic budgets. Oakland City had to slash its own by $130,000 over two years. Mayor Alfred Cooper wasn't thinking up ways to improve the schools; he was contemplating laying off police officers.

That spring of 2008 was certainly no time to be cutting police budgets in Gibson County, Indiana. Not long after the USI study made its waves, the anarchists arrived and occupied trees near the construction site. The right-of-way itself had been cleared, so the protesters set up their camp in a patch of woods near the north end of the two-mile corridor. They hung large banners from the trees and constructed two platforms in the branches some thirty-five feet up, where a pair of Bloomington residents, Harriet Ray and Grant Reynolds, sat and vowed to remain. The authorities, who learned about the encampment through an online press release, decided to play it cool. State police and conservation officers arrived in cars and helicopters, gave the scene a once-over, asked the perchers to come down, but left, as in previous cases, without making any arrests. The protesters were technically trespassing, but they weren't harming anything. So they let them sit.

That day Harriet Ray appeared by cell phone on the Bloomington community-radio program *The EcoReport*. Listeners could hear helicopters flying nearby. "It's been pretty sunny and pleasant," Ray said. She had been trying to identify the trees around her, which were mostly beech, maple, and oak. From where she sat, she could see a field of yellow flowers. There was a lot of poison ivy and a gorgeous creek. "I saw—I think it was a yellow-tailed woodpecker and we've seen all kinds of squirrels. There are birds chirping. It's just really, really beautiful in this little-bitty patch," she said. "But on either side it's surrounded by complete clearing and devastation. It's very dramatic and heartbreaking to think this is what's going to be happening down the entire course of our country."

The ground camp was an environmentalist's paradise. Over the next month, supporters arrived to move in and take shifts in the trees. Tents were erected, a rustic kitchen assembled, and "community hangout space" was set aside. The goal was for the initial camp to grow into a wider occupation, a "tree village" where even sympathetic landowners would feel comfortable. Some locals did come to visit, but the organizers' vision never quite came to fruition. About a month after it began, the tree sit ended in the wee hours of Friday, June 20, when state troopers and INDOT officials arrived with a cherry-picker truck. The two tree occupants, Emily Cross and Andrew Joyce, were removed and placed under arrest. Three activists who were on the ground at the time were allowed to leave, but they later returned to the site and were also arrested for trespassing. Another trio was pulled over at a police checkpoint on their way to the scene. The driver allegedly spit in the face of his arresting officer and was charged with felony battery. News reports pointed out that seven of the eight arrested had come from other states: Tennessee, Michigan, California, and New York.

The Department of Transportation wanted to make clear that it wasn't trying to squelch dissent. It fenced off a "protest zone" near the construction site, which it announced would be open daily from dawn to dusk. But the members of Roadblock Earth First! would not be tamed. They were incensed about the tree-sit evictions, which they claimed had been careless and had endangered the lives of the activists. The Roadblock website announced an emergency demonstration of solidarity for the next night in Bloomington. It was the first full day of summer, and, thanks to daylight savings time, the sky was still electric blue at nine P.M., when the crowd assembled once again at Peoples Park. As on Earth Day, there were banners and signs and bucket drums, but the similarities trailed off there. The Tokarskis and their cow costumes were replaced by young anarchists with bandannas over their faces. Someone was handing out baseball-bat-size torches, and others sent bottle rockets screaming into the air.

The scene took on a lynch-mob feel. Activists spilled out onto Kirkwood around nine thirty, and the next half hour was a tense blur. The paraders went wide, from curb to curb, and meandered among stopped cars. In the courthouse square, masked marchers overturned trash cans and dragged them into the street. Policemen righted the barrels and did their best to block cross traffic, but the anarchists were hostile nonetheless. "Fuck you, pigs! Burn in hell," people yelled, and a chant broke out: "You can't put our friends in jail! We will drive the final nail!" Torches were refueled on the go by a bandanna-faced man in camo shorts who sloshed the flammable liquid from a plastic jug. An angry young marcher took offense at the sight of an SUV full of Saturday-night revelers and punched its hood. He taunted the driver to get out of his car, and when he did, the two men had to be pulled apart. A twenty-two-year-old man was arrested for obstructing traffic after blocking an unmarked police car, but the march went on. The hollering and drumming and menacing crescendoed as the throng arrived back at Peoples Park, where Hugh Farrell climbed atop a picnic table and cried out, "The trees will win!" That was finale enough for the activists, small groups of whom wandered off in various directions into the short summer night.

It would be a busy week for the anarchists. On Monday, a crowd stormed the Bloomington offices of the Indiana Department of Natural Resources, an agency the activists believed was complicit in dismantling the ground occupation. The dissidents rushed through the front door, pushed papers off desks, and destroyed a potted plant. On Tuesday in Evansville, a dozen people calling themselves the River City Animal Defense League showed up at the office of Bernardin, Lochmueller & Associates and smashed a window while yelling through a bullhorn. And on Saturday, in the small town of Haubstadt, a crew descended on Gohmann Asphalt Company, the paving business that had been awarded the contract for the first two miles of new-terrain I-69. They stopped a semi leaving the company's driveway and deflated its tires. Four protesters attached themselves to the undercarriage of the trailer, and a fifth climbed between the cab and the trailer and used a bicycle lock to secure his neck to the truck.

The Gohmann lockdown lasted more than three hours and was as skillful as the tree-sit camp had been. The four protesters underneath the truck had affixed themselves to its frame using a maneuver called the sleeping dragon—they chained their hands together inside PVC piping that was wrapped in duct tape, making it dangerous and difficult for police to disconnect them. They decided not to try. A healthy crowd of police officers, local residents, media, and supportive protesters had gathered, and a local prosecutor negotiated by cell phone for the protesters to leave quietly. One twenty-one-year-old woman from central Indiana had already been taken into custody for allegedly flattening the tires on the truck, and the rest decided, according to an Earth First! journal account, that "the hours of lost business and the media spectacle were more important than symbolic arrests." The protesters walked away without being identified, the report said, "freeing up more bodies and legal funds to continue the fight."

The anarchists would need those funds sooner than they realized. In early July, Kathleen Cornetta, the young woman who had been arrested for deflating the tires, was sued by Gohmann for sixteen thousand dollars—the value of the business the company claimed the protesters impeded. Her codefendants were each listed as John and Jane Doe, and Cornetta was asked in court to provide the names of her fellow activists. She refused. On July 14, five protesters chained themselves across the driveway at Gohmann again, and the police arrested fifteen people. Their bail was set at a total of thirty thousand dollars, and the asphalt company promptly added the new arrestees to its civil lawsuit and increased the claim to twenty-seven thousand dollars. Gohmann then got a restraining order against the protesters—the fifteen defendants by name, plus all members of Earth First!, Roadblock Earth First!, the River City ADL and Root Force (two names under which groups had posted online action reports), and anybody arrested under the names of Jane or John Doe. The blanket order prevented anyone matching that description from coming within one hundred yards of any site in which Gohmann had a monetary interest. This would include, of course, the first two miles of Interstate 69 construction.

Ironically, the restraining order would not have prevented the anarchists from coming to the official ground-breaking ceremony, which took place on Wednesday, July 16, just two days after the second lockdown at the asphalt yard—and a month after Texas announced its I-69 segments would follow existing roads as much as possible. The event was planned in secret, and with the looming threat of an unpleasant scene, the organizers decided to hold the ground breaking not on the actual site of construction but safely indoors at the Evansville Convention Center, twenty miles to the south. I was among the lucky few journalists to be admitted that day to the center, which had been turned into a fortress. The authorities had surrounded the building and its adjacent streets with high fencing, and there were men on the roof with cameras and binoculars—and, according to rumor, rifles and tear gas. A K9-unit van, a black armored bomb-squad truck, and a mobile command center were parked near the entrance, while dozens of patrolmen covered the area on foot, bicycle, and motorcycle. At a checkpoint inside the front door, plainclothes police with earpieces and cops in riot helmets stood staring through the glass doors at the designated protest area across the street, which was eerily empty—except for Thomas and Sandra Tokarski and Bill and Jan Boyd.

I went over to say hello. "I thought we might see you." Sandra smiled. "We almost didn't come, but Bill said, 'I think we gotta be there.'" She wore a straw hat and held a sign that said, HOMEWRECKER HIGHWAY: 400 HOOSIER HOMES DEMOLISHED. She also wore tennis shoes, which made me think of the little old ladies in Memphis who had defeated their piece of highway. Sandra and I stood on either side of the police fencing. "They've got you all cooped up in there," she said. She teased me about my suit jacket and joked that I might not want to be seen consorting with them if I wanted to be allowed inside. She pointed up to the roof, where a man was pointing a camera in our direction. "Now you're branded," she said.

I walked inside and immediately ran into Bill Revell, the former mayor of Dyersburg, Tennessee, who was looking well, beaming at no one in particular, waiting to introduce himself and shake hands. I said hello and asked him whether anyone else from the Mid-Continent Highway Coalition would be coming. I had expected to see maybe John Caruthers, or Gerry Montgomery and Bill Paxton from down the river in Paducah. "I think I'm the only one from outside of Indiana," he said. "I thought more of us would be here, too." We followed the herd of guests into Exhibition Hall B, where orange construction barrels separated the crowd of eight hundred from a small stage in the front of the room. A dump truck and a Caterpillar excavator were parked to either side, and green placards resembling exit signs listed the towns and counties along the route: LINTON WELCOMES INTERSTATE 69, DAVIESS COUNTY WELCOMES I-69. I paced the room and read them all, but I didn't see a sign for Bloomington.

A few minutes before the program was to begin, David Graham emerged from a door near the stage with Governor Daniels and James Newland. Three of Graham's eight children had come for the big day—Ellen from Louisville, Darnall from Virginia, and Beau from South Bend. Beau is David B. Graham Jr., and he brought his son, David B. Graham III. Newland and Graham took seats on the dais, and a local drum crew, the Boom Squad, did a booty-shaking dance on a blue tarp up front. A high school show choir sang the national anthem, and Joe Dedman, an old friend of Graham's and the chairman of what had once been the Southwest Indiana Regional Highway Coalition, took the podium to thank what must have been a hundred people by name. But there were two very special people who deserved recognition, he said: Graham, "a gentleman who I believe is the backbone of the I-69 effort from the very beginning," and Newland, "who as the executive director of the Mid-Continent Highway Coalition worked hard on the state and national level." The two men stood, to great applause, and received awards from INDOT commissioner Karl Browning—framed I-69 highway shields signed by the governor.

Daniels, who was dressed like a workman in khakis, a blue shirt, and no tie, spoke last. "These are days when the toughest old men choke up," he said. "Days like this one are beautiful beginnings. But days like this are also an end. Today we end the eternal waiting, the unfulfilled hopes, the empty promises. Starting today, I-69 becomes real." The highway meant more than a simple connection between cities. It meant new hope for young people. And it meant the triumph of the Hoosier spirit. "Let the rest of America erode," Daniels said. "Let them deteriorate if they haven't the guts or the imagination to do what we did. In Indiana, we're building a new future."

The governor wanted to say a word to those who had disagreed with the project. "Those few who may come from out of state to tell us how to live, you came with violence and destruction in your heart. Hoosier hospitality will be suspended in your case," Daniels said. But they were a mere handful of people. There was a larger number of opponents for whom he had more regard. "We respect the sincerity of your viewpoints. You have brought good arguments. I believe you brought improvements to the design of this road," he said. "We thank you for your citizenship even though we came to a different conclusion in our own good faith, in the sincerity of our own hearts." The interstate was not a black-and-white issue, to be sure. "But in the end, public leadership is about choices. It is about decisions and not dithering. It is about actions and not words." The world was brutal and competitive, the governor said. It waits for no one. And it won't wait on Indiana. "We chose to make history, not surrender to it," he said. "Hoosiers have shown America how to grab hold of our destiny, to commit ourselves to a brighter future with more opportunity to everyone, including the spaces that have been left behind."

When Daniels was done, the Boom Squad erupted in a racket of drumbeats, and a ballroom wall up front was moved aside. From behind it, a front-end loader emerged. Behind the wheel was a vice president of Gohmann Asphalt, and in the front shovel was a load of dirt from the I-69 construction site—a big dollop of earth from a space that had been left behind. The Gohmann man pulled forward to the square of blue tarp near the stage and dumped the pile of soil down.

The governor and six other public officials lined up along the mound with golden-bladed shovels. On cue they dug in and held their scoopfuls for the cameras before throwing the dirt back over the pile. Other dignitaries stepped forward for a second round of make-believe digging, and the people to Daniels's right yielded their shovels to Graham and Newland. The men had wanted this moment for twenty years, though perhaps they had imagined it differently. Graham was eighty-one. Newland

was eighty-nine. But they went at it like kids in a sandbox and tossed their heaps of dirt with all of their modest might. The governor staked his shovel into the dirt and put his arms around Graham and Newland. He spoke privately to them for a moment in the flicker of camera flashes, and I noticed that Newland had kept hold of his shovel handle. When the governor walked away, and everyone had broken into small, chatty groups, and the cameras were pointed elsewhere, Graham and Newland took one more moment to make a last plunge with their spades.

On my way out I grabbed a few of the souvenirs on offer—a rubber-stopped test tube of soil from the construction site and a tiny oak sapling that a yellow tag explained was "a token of our efforts to protect the environment while building the infrastructure that will bring economic vitality to the Hoosier State." I stepped out into the sunshine to find the Tokarskis still there, talking to television reporters about the homes and forests and wetlands that would be destroyed. They repeated their assertion that the project would never be completed—there was just no more money for it—and said that they were appalled that the governor would allow construction to start on a road that would never get to Bloomington. Sandra saw me at the fence and asked how the ground breaking had gone. I told her that Daniels had mentioned all of the good arguments, and how they had made the project better. "Don't tell Thomas that!" she said. "The top will blow off his head." She noticed the tree start I was holding and read the attached card, which asked the bearer to plant and care for the oak as a symbol of "the symbiotic relationship between economic growth and environmental stewardship." Her face fell. "That is such a slap in the face," she said.

That afternoon I stopped by Graham's house in Washington. When I pulled into his driveway, his housekeeper was in the barn-size detached garage, freshening up Graham's motor home, a luxury Newmar model with a washer-dryer and a bedroom and living room that expanded at the push of a button. Graham had told me he would be leaving for New Mexico the next day with his daughter Darnall. He planned to spend the rest of the summer on the road, traveling around the country and visiting his children and brothers. Inside the house, Darnall and Beau were busy packing up to leave—Ellen had already left—and Graham was alone in the kitchen. I asked him what he had thought of the ceremony. It was tiring, he replied, and he needed a nap. Graham stared forward, exhausted or thoughtful. "It was nice of them to recognize Jim and me," he said. "Because we're just a couple of has-beens."

I could tell that he wasn't joking. "Isn't that ground breaking proof that you've been pretty effective?" I asked.

"Maybe in our day," he answered, "but we've got a war on now." Graham was concerned about the budget and the economy, and he worried that the government wouldn't be able to afford to build the entire highway. "I read in the paper this morning that the market went to hell again."

Beau and Darnall came into the kitchen just then and admired Graham's award, which sat on the table. Graham said he wasn't sure what to do with it.

"Maybe you ought to put it in the RV," Beau said, "and parade it around so everyone can see it." The two kids talked about how they might get a copy of a commemorative video that had been produced for the ground breaking, and which featured their father. Graham asked them why on earth they would want it.

"For preserving history!" Darnall said. "Like George Washington, when you're dead a hundred years, there'll still be a picture of you, Dad."

The governor had said these were days where the toughest old men choke up, and apparently he was right. The day was a beginning, the governor said, but also an end to the waiting and the empty promises. But for Graham it was the end of a mission that, he once told me, had kept him young. Later that week, after I'd left Indiana, I got an e-mail from Graham's friend Joe Dedman, who told me he was worried about Graham. "I hope that reaching this milestone in the highway process does not cause him to feel he has less purpose," Dedman wrote. "Losing his wife last year was tough, and now the highway is finally under construction. I hope traveling and his grandchildren will keep him active and going for a long time."

It might be far-fetched to suppose that David Graham was envious of the Tokarskis that day. But Thomas and Sandra certainly weren't finished. They, too, were concerned about the economy, albeit for different reasons, and they were anxious for the day when declining home prices and rising gas prices and global warming would bring the country to its senses. "They want to strangle us with more highways, but the roads we have are crumbling. We need to look at fixing Amtrak and providing more rail," Thomas told me that summer. "The world is changing. And I don't know where it's going. I think if we can hold I-69 off for a few more years, it'll be totally dismissed as an old-fashioned way of doing things." He let out a nervous chuckle. "I just don't know if I can wait that long."

The Road Ahead

Days after the indoor dirt-digging in Evansville, Roadblock Earth First! held a potluck picnic at a park in Oakland City. It was intended as outreach for the affected landowners near the construction site, but non-anarchist turnout was limited, and the event evolved into a mix of strategy and group therapy. The ground breaking had been a gut-check moment for the I-69 activists, an unpleasant reminder of the limitations of their activism. It meant something that state officials had held the ceremony indoors—Mayor Jonathan Weinzapfel even complained to David Graham at the convention center that morning that the anarchists "got what they wanted"—but the movement was feeling the squeeze of oppression (to use the word they preferred). Their militant idealism had been criminalized. They had been arrested, restrained, and sued, and it seemed like it was time to regroup and rethink.

Gina "Tiga" Wertz wore a long paisley dress and no shoes. She had brought her mother along, and the two laid out a spread of mostly vegan food over two picnic tables while a few of the protesters who had been arrested in recent weeks swung on playground swings nearby. I arrived with Thomas Tokarski and four cantaloupes we had bought from a farm stand in Washington on the drive down. There were about thirty people there if you counted the uninvited guests: Fifty yards away from us, in the parking lot of the park, a state-police car sat, its occupants watching us from the front seat.

We had some food and chitchat, and then the group sat down in a circle under a grove of fully leafed trees and Wertz facilitated a postmortem on the months prior. The anarchists complained that law-enforcement officers—in particular a state-police detective named Brad Chandler—had been following them around, staking out their homes and hangouts. Fear was spreading among the activist community. Thomas Tokarski felt for them but saw a lesson in all of it, too. He told them that the police had also detained him, for taking pictures of houses in the path of construction—but what did the Roadblock members expect after their recent antics? "It doesn't help your image when there are people marching in the streets of Bloomington at night with hoods over their heads carrying torches. I can't tell you how many people told me it looked like the Ku Klux Klan." Many of the anarchists agreed that their public-relations efforts needed some work, but Thomas wasn't finished. "Years ago I protested the construction of the Marble Hill nuclear power plant," he said. "When we did that, we had lawyers lined up. We *wanted* to go to court. That was the whole point. We wanted to go on trial and put the plant on trial. A lot of times, what I see here is there's not any cohesive goal." At the library a year before, the anarchists had resisted the idea that their methodology might be counterproductive. But things weren't quite so hypothetical and exciting anymore. Thomas's age and experience were a comfort to them now, and the group took his advice to heart. They talked about how they might shift their energies from troublemaking to community organizing. Maybe it was time to get political, like the Stalls had in Texas. Maybe it was time to flood the newspapers with letters to the editors.

Direct actions by Earth First! waned steeply after that week of the ground breaking and the soul-searching picnic. Then they came to a screeching halt nine months later, in April 2009, when Wertz and Hugh Farrell were arrested and charged with two counts each of intimidation, two counts each of conversion (the unauthorized use of another's property), and one count each of corrupt business influence, or racketeering, a class C felony often used against the Mafia. Their arrest warrants, filed by their police nemesis Brad Chandler, invoked the pranklike office "evictions," the disrupted planning meeting in Bloomington, and the postings to the Roadblock website that threatened those responsible for the highway with visits to their homes. The description of each charge ended with the same boilerplate refrain, that their alleged crimes were "against the peace and dignity of the State of Indiana."

In a long letter from the Pike County jail, Wertz told supporters how the police had offered to cut her a deal if she told them everything she knew about her fellow activists, and that she had refused. "They're trying to demonize me and Hugh," she wrote, "not just to scare those willing to physically stop construction with nonviolent civil disobedience, but to also scare those brave and hardworking souls that for twenty years have spoken loudly and proudly for their communities and against I-69." Wertz alluded to a posting by an anonymous writer on an anarchist website that accused Farrell of being a snitch; she wanted her friends to know that this was no more than a shameless attempt to divide their community. "I stand by him with the utmost solidarity and love." Wertz and Farrell soon made bail, but they no longer felt free to protest the highway. The racketeering charges against them were dropped in March of 2010—under Indiana law, criminal conspiracy cannot stem from misdemeanor charges—but for a year, the threat of felony prosecution hung heavy over their compatriots. If the rap had stuck, no one whom prosecutors could prove was a member of Roadblock Earth First! would have been safe. As of May 2010, no trial date had been set for Farrell or Wertz, and preliminary hearings have been repeatedly delayed. The remnants of the anarchist energy in Bloomington are now channeled into their legal defense. FREE TIGA AND HUGH T-shirts are for sale, and a benefit album is planned.

In the absence of tree sits and vandalism, Thomas and Sandra once again have the anti-I-69 pulpit to themselves, and since the ground breaking they've grown louder in their insistence that the state of Indiana cannot afford I-69. According to the Tokarskis' calculations, the road from Evansville to Indianapolis will cost about a billion dollars more than the state claims. Lately their lonely jeremiads about infrastructure funding have been well corroborated. In September 2008, two months after the ground-breaking ceremony in Evansville, the U.S. Department of Transportation announced that the Highway Trust Fund was "essentially broke." With high oil prices and the economic downturn, people were driving less and buying more fuel-efficient cars, and gas-tax revenues could no longer cover the costs of construction and maintenance of roads. Congress rushed to fill the hole with general-fund money, but they punted on the bigger problem: the transportation bill that was due for reauthorization that fall. Everyone understood that the legislation couldn't just be a matter of negotiating earmarks. A truly responsible bill would have to answer—finally—what to do about the dying stream of transportation funds.

The outgoing transportation secretary for the Bush administration, Mary Peters, had been trying for years to warn her colleagues that the trust fund was headed for bankruptcy, and she used the occasion of its insolvency to once again declare the gas tax "an antiquated mechanism." She urged Congress and the individual states to consider tolling and privatization. But there was another idea that was slowly gaining traction with lawmakers and transportation wonks: a mileage tax, under which motorists would pay for every mile they drove, rather than for every gallon of gasoline they burned. The state of Oregon piloted the concept in 2006, and the results had been encouraging. Many observers are dubious about the effects on privacy—having the government track a motorist's mileage and possibly even location is a hard sell among libertarians and many others, and there is no consensus on how to outfit vehicles or manage such a system—but the mileage tax has won supporters from across the political spectrum. So much so that Ray LaHood, the new secretary of transportation under President Obama, felt comfortable telling the Associated Press in February 2009 that "we should look at the vehicular miles program." But Obama's press secretary followed with a harsh statement to the contrary. The economy was in full recession then, and it was no time to be musing publicly about creating a mileage tax or raising the gas tax, however fair or necessary either might be.

Rather, it was time for spending. A week before LaHood went out on his limb about the mileage tax, Congress (or at least the Democratic majority of it) passed a $787 billion stimulus package, $45 billion of which was aimed at transportation-infrastructure investment. To anyone even halfway listening, Obama had made clear his preference for rail and transit over new highways, but the mission of the stimulus was to spend money as quickly as possible, and a vast majority of shovel-ready projects were asphalt-related. The Obama administration has dropped hints that this Jekyll-and-Hyde disparity between the rush to build and the hunger for reform is temporary. A fraction of the stimulus money—$1.5 billion—was set aside for "merit-based" grants, which were awarded largely to freight-rail and transit projects. The president himself slipped in $8 billion for high-speed intercity passenger rail—a down payment, Vice President Joe Biden later said, on "the economy that's going to drive us in the twenty-first century in a way that the highway system drove us in the mid-twentieth century."

The mid-twentieth-century economy, of course, was alive and well in Indiana. Sort of. In May 2010, Governor Daniels announced that he intended to finish the road all the way from Evansville to Bloomington by 2014. The poor economy, he said, had led to lower construction costs, and the state wanted to build while it was still cheap to do so. But the Tokarskis accused Daniels of trying to rush the job and do it on the cheap. In the summer of 2009, INDOT had announced a variety of cost-saving measures, including building the road to lower engineering standards—thinner pavement and narrower shoulders and medians—and delaying the construction of two planned interchanges, one near Petersburg and another near Elnora, in northern Daviess County.

Eliminating those two exits, the Tokarskis were quick to point out, would undercut the economic benefit that supporters claimed was the main purpose of the highway. On the other hand, making interchanges scarcer will greatly benefit the ones that are built. The exit that sits between the two to be delayed, for instance, will be the only access point for forty-five miles. If factories or truck stops or housing developments are to arise, they'll likely concentrate near the on- and off-ramps at U.S. 50 in Washington—where Graham Farms owns several hundred acres. Even luckier for the Grahams, the state has decided to alter the alignment of U.S. 50 in a way that will give the Grahams land on all four corners, not just three.

What eventually emerges at the Washington interchange will be up to the eight family members that constitute the board of Graham Farms—two of David's children and two each of his three brothers'. In June 2009 I spoke with Graham's nephew Tom, who since the retirement of his cousin Robert Graham III was the last Graham still involved with the family business—his generation, the sixth in Daviess County, ran the farm more or less remotely from adopted cities across the country. Tom was sixty. His kids had moved away and he lamented the fact that the younger Grahams had never worked the farm save for a few summer stints in their youth. Tom was the last of a breed, and he felt ambivalent about the pending plans to turn a sizable chunk of Graham Farms into subdivisions or retail strips. "We've always said we'd put the land to the highest and best use," he told me. "So far, that's still agriculture. But with I-69, it'll be something else."

The city and county had received a community-planning grant—the kind that Hugh Farrell called a bribe during his disruptive tirade at the Bloomington meeting in 2007—and they used it to hire Bernardin, Lochmueller & Associates, Graham's old friends. BLA had completed the multiple environmental studies justifying I-69; they were now working on the design of the highway; and here they would have a chance to see through the highway's transformative effect on land use. When I spoke with Tom, who sits on the city planning commission, as his uncle David once did, BLA had just finished a master plan for the town that anticipated industrial development on the north side of the exit and new residential communities on Graham Farms land to the south.

The Washington interchange is not slated for completion until the year 2015, and David Graham won't be around to see what develops. In the summer of 2009 he moved to Florida. The icy Indiana winters were giving him bronchitis and pneumonia, he told me, so he bought a brand-new house in the Villages, a vast master-planned "active adult" retirement community northwest of Orlando. When I saw Graham that spring before he left Washington, he was giddy to be getting out. "I have a modest house, and I'm gonna put furniture in it and have a good time, ride around in my golf car—they don't call them golf *carts*," he said. "There's two town squares, where they have music and dancing every night— every night! And then there are little villages with a fine grocery store and a bank. It's golf-car-friendly all over." The Villages is no Miami Beach, but Graham will still be close to Carl Fisher's legacy—his new house sits just a few miles from a stretch of the old Dixie Highway.

It seemed strange that the man who wanted to build a highway through Indiana so that people would stay was leaving—to a place where everyone drove golf carts. I didn't make this observation aloud. Instead we got to talking about how nice it is to live in a place where you don't need a car for everything. Graham, to my surprise, expressed a wish that this might become the case in southern Indiana. He brought up the old interurban trains that used to crisscross the state and said he hoped they would come back. "It makes so much sense. Of course, we had the B&O Railroad, with beautiful passenger cars. You could get on the train here and go to New York or Denver or Dallas," he said. Graham told me that when he was in college in the 1940s, he used to take the B&O back and forth to Georgetown. "I used to go down here and get on a train, go to Cincinnati and have dates and go out and have a good time, then get on the later train and go on to Washington."

In 1990, just as he started working on the Evansville-to-Indianapolis highway, Graham contributed to a local campaign to renovate the old B&O depot in town. The station, where the funeral train for interstate father Dwight D. Eisenhower stopped in 1969, became the new office for the Daviess County Chamber of Commerce. Graham Farms once had its own freight stop north of town—it still appears as Graham, Indiana, on detailed maps—but that hasn't been active for years, Graham told me. "I don't think the freight train goes through here very often anymore. But

I don't want to lose that. There's some people in town that think it's too noisy. But they're not thinking *ahead*. One of these days, we're going to have trains go through here that have passengers on them."

Graham couldn't stop talking about trains. He had seen a map in *USA Today*, he told me, of Obama's high-speed-rail plan. "It showed a route going from Cincinnati to Indianapolis and then Indianapolis to Saint Louis," he said. "I mean, that bypasses here! And I don't think our chamber of commerce is working on that very hard." They're probably focused on I-69, I suggested. "Well, you gotta do both," Graham said. His new home of Florida will see the American train renaissance before Indiana does. At a town hall in Tampa in January 2010, President Obama announced the recipients of the $8 billion in stimulus money for high-speed rail. The Tampa-to-Orlando line was a big winner, with $1.25 billion.

Graham's old friend Mitch Daniels isn't quite as keen on rail. "It's a lovely vision," the governor told me when I asked him about a line through Indiana that showed up on the Obama administration's map, "but if it comes up on my watch, I want to know what will a taxpayer who never rides that train pay for every backside that sits on it? What's the subsidy? I'd love to see that high-speed rail works in practice. But I would want to know—before committing Indiana to something expensive—why this isn't another Amtrak."

Of course, construction of new-terrain I-69 was being subsidized, essentially, by an advance on future tolls from drivers on a different road. And, as Mary Peters or Mike Krusee (or Governor Daniels, speaking in a different context) might point out, users haven't exactly been paying the full cost of using the nation's highways. But Daniels was being consistent: He had proposed tolling I-69 to cover its costs with direct user fees. And, when pressed, he did have a few kind things to say about transit. "I'm an enthusiast about mass transit in the right place. What is the right place? Well, it will always involve a subsidy. But where there's enough population density and ridership, that subsidy is clearly justified by the societal and environmental benefits. But, you got to be very hardheaded about knowing that you're going to get that positive return."

Perhaps the Memphis area might be such a place? When I stopped in to see Jim McDougal, the planning director for DeSoto County, Mississippi, in April 2009, he was late to welcome me into his office. He apologized—he'd been on the phone, he said, with the Federal Railroad Administration. The national plan for high-speed rail showed no corridor through Memphis, and McDougal thought that was a terrible mistake. During the hour we were together, McDougal talked more about smart growth and public transportation than he did about interstates. Like former Mississippi development director Leland Speed, Walls mayor Gene Alday, and others, McDougal saw the fast growth of northern Mississippi as a chance to do something special. In SAFETEA-LU, the earmark-laden reauthorization bill of 2005, Congress allocated seventy million dollars to study transit along the I-69 corridor near Memphis and Hernando, and McDougal pitched possibilities at a public meeting in January. "Bus rapid transit is very realistic to fit our needs in twenty, thirty, or fifty years," he said. "It would be very advantageous and very efficient for commuters. Who wouldn't want that option?"

But for some in Memphis, McDougal's vision of a transit wonderland along I-69 was ringing hollow. As construction of the I-269 loop around the city progresses, some Memphians are worried that the new road might drain taxpayers and vitality from the city's urban neighborhoods. Consultant Tom Jones, writing on his blog, Smart City Memphis, in January 2010, complained that I-269 would foster "greater economic segregation" in the already divided metropolitan area. "Someone from North Mississippi said in an article in the *Commercial Appeal* that the task now is to apply smart growth principles to I-269," Jones wrote. "We're not sure when we've heard such a contradiction of terms." In my conversations with Jones and his fellow urbanists, they seemed to understand that the plans for the new loop were too far along to stop. But if they must live with it, Jones wrote, "we must change policies so that the interstate does in fact mitigate its negative impact. For example, we've said previously that I-269 and Tennessee 385 should be toll roads. They would produce more than $100 million a year that could be invested in strategies to strengthen our core city."

There is talk of tolling near the I-69 corridor in Texas, of course, but those revenues wouldn't be poured into urban transit projects. They would go toward building more highway. The consortium, led by Zachry American Infrastructure, that holds the contract to develop I-69 has proposed two new toll expressways—one near the border at Brownsville and another from the Gulf shore to I-37 at Corpus Christi—the proceeds from which they plan to use to upgrade U.S. 77 to a toll-free I-69. In 2009, Zachry hired a highly qualified consultant to help with this strategy: former transportation secretary Mary Peters, who had suggested to the

Mid-Continent Highway Coalition in 2006 that tolls from the higher-traffic "juicy spots" along I-69 (as John Caruthers put it) might help carry the cost of construction in the poorer, more rural stretches. When I talked to Peters this spring, she told me that Zachry was looking at other ways to use "cross-collateralization" in Texas. "We're looking at power generation in the corridor," she said, "and probably some intermodal freight centers."

Peters said that Zachry had invested a lot of time in "grassroots organizing" up and down the route. Committees made up of local officials and business owners had been advising the company, and the pursuit of I-69 in Texas had become "significantly less controversial" since TxDOT decided to follow existing roads as much as possible. "That's a whole lot more palatable than taking football-field-wide swaths of land and calling it some future Trans-Texas Corridor," she said. "And I think TxDOT suddenly realizes now that that was probably a good idea but not well executed, and they would do it differently if they were doing it again today."

Indeed, the backtracking in Austin was at full speed. In October 2009, Governor Perry was entering into a fierce reelection primary against Senator Kay Bailey Hutchison, and the Trans-Texas Corridor fiasco was a major liability. His campaign worked hard to convince voters that the plan was dead, and so did his transportation department. At a press conference in the newly rededicated Ric Williamson Hearing Room at TxDOT headquarters, the agency announced the end of the environmental study for TTC-35. Five years before, Williamson, Perry, Mike Krusee, and Mary Peters had gathered in that very room with executives of the Spanish firm Cintra to tout a historic six-billion-dollar commitment to a vast new private toll road. Now they were happily declaring that it would never be constructed. The agency had sent notice to the Federal Highway Administration that it was recommending the "no-build" option. The contract with Cintra was to be terminated, and the department was committing itself to starting over, involving the public more, and building, only as needed, pieces that were locally popular.

This was a most unheard-of conclusion to an environmental study. But the event was not without its familiar touches. Ted Houghton, the brash transportation commissioner who had upset the valley by prematurely declaring I-69 dead, gave a little tough talk for old times' sake. "We ask people that come before us to state their name," he said. "I am Ted Houghton, the most arrogant commissioner of the most arrogant state agency in the history of the state of Texas." He admitted that TxDOT had done a poor job of explaining the Trans-Texas Corridor to the people of Texas. "We're not very good marketers here," he said. "And I've got scars to prove it." He picked at some scabs a bit, describing what he said were the four groups of opponents that the plan had brought together: "You had the North American Union conspiracy theorists who thought we were putting together Canada, the United States, and Mexico. And then you had the antitoll crowd. And then you had the anti-immigrant crowd. And the one I have affection for and really listen to are the landowners. By the blue line on that map, we tainted that property. And we really didn't understand that until we got out in those regions and listened to those landowners."

Houghton didn't mention the Stalls by name, but David and Linda were overjoyed by the news. I met them that night at Schobel's restaurant in Columbus, where Linda had first spoken out against the corridor at meetings with the Lions and Rotary clubs. It had been tricky, they said, to channel the energies of the other more extreme opponents without getting caught up in their messages. "It was a delicate dance," David told me. "Linda went to Dallas to talk to people with the John Birch Society. And we'd tell them the same consistent story. And then they would all come up to us afterward and say, 'Well, you know what's *really* behind this?' You know, hey, if that works for you, run with it."

Linda said she was looking forward to having time to play with her grandchildren. "We're having our life again. You know, the first time I spoke to the Lions Club, I didn't really realize we were talking about the odyssey, a seven-year journey." David is taking a little rest now, too, but he's already dreaming of his next project. He wants to take the high-tech fundamentals he perfected with CorridorWatch and apply them to a new Internet-based political-organizing tool that will let people indicate the issues they care about and their zip code, and then inform them when relevant things happen in the state and national legislatures. He already owns the domain: CapitolCorps.org. "It'll be a dynamic thing," he said, "where we feed you the information you're interested in, and don't bury you with stuff you don't care about. When something happens that can be impacted, we tell you what you can do where your call means something. It's about engaging people."

The defeat of the Trans-Texas Corridor plan might portend trouble for other ambitious designs. Former Harris County judge Robert Eckles, who at one time headed up the Alliance for I-69 Texas, is now the chairman of the Texas High Speed Rail and Transportation Corporation, which is working to advance a fast-train "Texas Triangle" or "Texas T-Bone" connecting Houston, Dallas, San Antonio, and Austin. But the impact of a true bullet train on the rural land through which it passes would be even more onerous than that of a highway, and Houghton, among others, expects that the rural coalition that formed against the Trans-Texas Corridor will have a field day with high-speed rail. "It's gotta be straight, and they're gonna go fast, and they're gonna need a hundred to two hundred feet of right-of-way," Houghton told me. "So where are you gonna put it? Guess what: You're gonna disenfranchise the landowners. Here you go again. 'Not in my backyard,' all that kind of stuff." The Farm Bureau in Texas, he said, had long ago fought the interstate system and even the farm-to-market roads. "So any progress is tough."

Transportation progressives may face a debilitating irony: The very techniques they have perfected for slowing down highway projects might be brought into play against more eco-sensitive endeavors like transit and high-speed rail. The bastardization of Lynton Caldwell's Environmental Impact Statement would be complete if NEPA turns out to be as useful in stopping environmentally friendly projects as it is impotent in stopping highways and dams. And then there is the cost. John Langmore, the New Urbanist who found himself shepherding the legislation that allowed the Trans-Texas Corridor to flower, has become active in promoting commuter rail in Austin. But national train initiatives, he says, will run into the same funding problems that I-69 has. "To talk about a multibillion-dollar project, and all the good it's gonna do, and all the reasons that it's needed," he told me in the fall of 2009, "well, that's virtually meaningless if you are not coupling it with a realistic assessment of how you pay for it."

Mary Peters believes that when Congress finally takes up the transportation reauthorization bill, it will probably have to pass a modest gas-tax increase. But that will only be a temporary measure, she believes. Eventually—in ten to twenty years—the nation will transition to a mileage tax. "We've got to get the public acclimated to it," she told me. "And if we can attract private investment to do at least fifteen percent of our projects, that would be fantastic. But it is really time to start over, and say, 'What is in the federal interest to do?' and to focus what federal money there is on where you're truly furthering those interests. If you do that, I-69 comes out strong."

Whether Interstate 69 is deemed to be in the federal interest to build, it's clearly stimulating business interest in the rural South, where tolling and privatization fear to tread. Last summer, Lyn Arnold in Tunica, Mississippi, finally found a taker for her megasite. Word leaked out in June 2009 that Greentech Automotive, a Chinese manufacturer of hybrid vehicles, is planning to build a billion-dollar plant just south of that first open stretch of I-69. The helicopter pilots who used to fly anonymous suitors over the flat Delta country might suffer from a loss of business, but the car-assembly operation should more than make up for that—the facility is expected to create as many as forty-five hundred jobs once it ramps up to full production. Another international company, a German pipe manufacturer, announced in January 2010 that it, too, would build a factory along I-69 in Tunica County. Some five hundred workers will be employed there.

In Union City, Tennessee, just south of the Kentucky state line, a multimillionaire gift-shop mogul named Robert Kirkland is creating a few jobs himself. In a bold effort to put his small town on the map, Kirkland has put one hundred million dollars toward the Discovery Park of America, a massive roadside attraction that will sit near the town's I-69 interchange. Kirkland is a heavy, bald, bespectacled man, jovial and revered, who dislikes income taxes, death taxes, and capital-gains taxes. When I met him last year, he told me that he'd started thinking about how "if I died right now, old Uncle Sam is going to get a *hunk*." His lawyers told him that in lieu of paying taxes, he could give his money away, and Kirkland went straight to work brainstorming ideas for an educational museum and tourist oasis. Most of the ideas stuck, apparently: Discovery Park of America will feature exhibits on regional history, natural history, the military, science and technology, space, and transportation. Road-weary visitors and wide-eyed locals will have access to botanical gardens, an art gallery, dinosaur bones, antique cars, Indian artifacts, and a pioneer village with a working farm. While I interviewed Kirkland, crews were out digging the foundation of the main building. He showed me drawings of the wave-shaped glass structure, which would feature a clear-bottomed observation deck where visitors could stand and look down on Interstate 69. That bird's-eye view of the NAFTA highway may never materialize—Kirkland has since parted ways with his original architect, and the plans are being reimagined—but with so much private funding, Discovery Park probably will. A grand opening is projected for 2012, right around the time that Union City's piece of Interstate 69 opens for traffic.

Just thirty-five miles south of there, in Dyersburg, Bill Revell had gone back into business. When I spoke to him in August 2009, he had opened a used-car lot; with the economy in a slump, he said, a lot of people were too broke to buy new. "And they know me," he said. "I've got a good name, thank God." He was doing well. Revell still had his I-69 office, too, and he was still hustling for I-69. "I just sent out letters to all the state departments of transportation along the route asking for contributions to the Mid-Continent Highway Coalition." The membership had grown lackadaisical about fund-raising, he told me, and they were fifty thousand dollars behind in payments to their lobbyist, Carolina Mederos at Patton Boggs. The grand old Peabody crew had waned considerably. Jim Newland had been let go, of course. People had gotten older, and tired. And John D. Caruthers had stepped down as president.

"I decided just before I turned eighty that we should get a younger man to run the organization," Caruthers told me in 2009. His replacement was Bossier City mayor Lo Walker, who is technically younger but not exactly young. Caruthers was in Colorado for two weeks on a ski trip when we spoke by phone. He sounded relaxed. "I'm trying to outlive my heirs," he joked. "I'm taking every vitamin known to man." Caruthers was still waiting for a federal record of decision for the stretch of I-69 through northwest Louisiana. The studies had to be revised, he told me, when a Louisiana State University experimental pecan farm near the port of Shreveport raised hell because the highway was going to take out several old trees. No one had set up camp in the trees—there aren't too many anarchists in that part of the world—but the concrete yielded nevertheless.

The big news in Shreveport these past few years has been the discovery of a massive reserve of natural gas trapped in a layer of shale about two miles underground. The play, called the Haynesville shale, is thought to hold as much as two hundred trillion cubic feet of natural gas—the equivalent of thirty-three billion barrels of oil, enough to fuel America's crude habit for two decades. Extracting that gas is expensive and beyond the capabilities of the Caruthers family business, and its discovery has driven the price of leases through the roof. In 2007, a year before the Haynesville find was made public, Caruthers Producing paid three hundred dollars an acre for a three-year lease nearby. Now landowners are getting more than ten thousand dollars an acre. "It's had an effect on everybody that has land south of town," Caruthers said. It's carrying the Shreveport region through the recession. "It's almost a reproduction of Depression times. Most fields of any importance around here were found in the late twenties and early thirties. The city was almost surrounded by meaningful discoveries that kept the economy thriving, as bad as it was for most folks in the rest of the country."

But natural-gas plays, like highways, are a hit-or-miss blessing. One town that's been left out of the Haynesville gas boom, oddly enough, is Haynesville, home of the butterfly festival, the Golden Tornado football team, and the town mural celebrating these and the long-awaited Interstate 69. The Haynesville shale got its name a long time ago, before it was worth much. There has been little gas found under Claiborne Parish. Overnight millionaires were made within fifty miles, but Haynesville had none. The Golden Tornado did win the state high school football trophy in 2009, though. The already fourteen-time state champions played the big game at the Superdome in New Orleans just a few months before the resident Saints won the Super Bowl. The "Welcome to Haynesville" mural might need an update, when its creator, Keith Killgore can find the time. Killgore recently painted a new picture of a 1923 Model T Ford and two old barns onto the side of the abandoned Garrett Mercantile (which had opened in 1923), and he tells me he has several more murals planned. There are certainly enough blank walls to keep him busy awhile.

"In small towns you have a lot of dilapidated old buildings. When there's no demand for them they start going down, and we have our share of that here," Killgore told me when we spoke in March 2010. His civic-beautification work began out of frustration. His pharmacy sits on the corner diagonal from where the old Planters Bank burned down, and Killgore got tired of looking at the rubble. He got a crew together and transformed the empty lot into the park with the fake porch, and then he painted the empty Main Street storefronts and the "Welcome to Haynesville" wall. "The mural thing was, in my mind, to get something off of negative and onto positive. If somebody can come through our town and look and see a lit-up mural at night, that's a lot more attractive than seeing a dark place with an old burnt-down building beside the road." He wanted the artwork to reflect all of the special things that made Haynesville worth visiting. And that included the faraway, long-awaited Interstate 69.

"I-69 is the shining star out there that we hope we get to. It's the single biggest thing that we look forward to as far as this town ever growing in size." Small towns across the country had been hit hard, Killgore said, "as far as big corporate stores coming in and mom-and-pops on Main Street going out of business." But he was excited about the highway's two interchanges near Haynesville because "we're hoping that they create some businesses along the interstate that will help our little town."

Killgore was being sincere, but his observations presented a paradox: Many small towns like Haynesville, born by resources or rivers or railroads, have been done in by the economics and ethos of Interstate America—and yet some believe an interstate can make them whole. But what exactly are proponents of the highway trying to save? A name, a zip code? If I-69 comes, and if anything comes of it, development will happen along that new road. New restaurants and new hotels and new houses and new stores will pop up in the fields near the new exits, and, if experience is any guide, the "business routes" through town will become anything but.

And what if I-69 is never built? What if it remains an awkward, half-finished monument to the people who've tried to build it and the people who've tried to stop it? Some will say the lack of wherewithal and resolve is a sign of a once-great nation faltering. And others will say it's progress, a welcome signal that our highway binge is done and we're ready to rebuild the rails and sidewalks that we've ignored for too long.

One thing is certain: Whatever places are revived or destroyed or left alone, life will adapt, and people will forget. Killgore tells me that folks in Haynesville don't talk about I-69 as much as they used to. "It's kinda quieted down," he said, "but it's still in the back of everybody's mind." Killgore's in his mid-fifties now, and he's sure he'll be an old man before the highway comes through. He's lived in Haynesville since he was two, and he likes it just fine the way it is. "All the basic things are here, the necessity things, and that's about it. But we're just like we were twenty years ago. When I first came back from pharmacy school, people said, 'You're a nut for coming back here. This town's gonna be dried up and blowed away.' And I said, 'Well, I may be a nut, but I'm gonna try it.' And I did. I've been working in this drugstore for thirty years. And I'm gonna retire right here on this corner. And hopefully someone will take over what I'm leaving here."

Acknowledgments

I am enormously grateful to the many people in the path of this road who ended up in the path of this book. Their collective concern about the future of their communities was both inspiring and contagious. My reporting took eight years, during which the people along the route of I-69—particularly David Graham, Thomas and Sandra Tokarski, and David and Linda Stall—gave generously of their time and energy. This book would not exist were it not for their dedicated participation.

Many of the documents that were essential to my reconstruction of this history could have come only from its participants, and I am indebted to all those who provided primary source material, especially Bill Revell, James Newland, and Jorge Verduzco, who trusted me with the private records of the Mid-Continent Highway Coalition, and the Tokarskis and Alexander Ewing, who provided me with the copious files produced in their effort to thwart that coalition. Independent researcher Carolyn Klepser was amazingly helpful in verifying details about Fisher-era Miami Beach and Robert Graham's Bal Harbour, as was the staff at the Historical Museum of Southern Florida. Wendy Wertz in Bloomington (no relation to Tiga) guided me through Lynton Caldwell's work and philosophy, and I can't wait to read the biography of Caldwell she's writing.

My research leaned considerably on decades' worth of reporting by journalists at local newspapers including *The Indianapolis Star,* the Bloomington *Herald-Times,* the *Bloomington Alternative,* the *Evansville Courier & Press,* the Memphis *Commercial Appeal,* the *Memphis Flyer,* the *Delta Democrat Times, The Clarksdale Press Register,* the *Arkansas Democrat-Gazette,* the *Shreveport Times, The Lufkin Daily News,* the *Houston Chronicle,* the *Austin American-Statesman,* the *Corpus Christi Caller-Times,* and *The Brownsville Herald,* among many others. Their accounts preserved not only events but also the full array of evolving attitudes about I-69, and it was this body of work that opened my ears to the important conversations around this road and laid the foundation for my own research.

It may seem strange to acknowledge a behemoth Internet company here, but it is no exaggeration to say that the free services offered by Google were absolutely crucial to this work. A constant stream of Google News Alerts into my e-mail inbox ensured that my research was comprehensive and nagged me when other work and life conspired to distract me; as I was writing, Google Street View helped me reconstruct the towns and minor highways I had traveled; and Google Wave streamlined the complicated fact-checking process. No website can replace personal conversations and observation, but the tools available online are a blessing to even the most ink-stained journalist, and those who provide those tools deserve credit for doing so.

My knowledge of Memphis—not to mention my enjoyment of it and my waistline—would have been much thinner without the maternal care and friendship of Suhair Lauck at the Little Tea Shop. I spent many hours there with Suhair, her husband, Jimmy, Paula Casey, and others, discussing Memphis politics and history. They introduced me to a number of important and compelling characters, all while feeding me cornbread sticks and turnip greens.

My editor and friend Brant Rumble demonstrated remarkable faith in this book, heroic tolerance for my pace in completing it, and great skill in making it better. During freshman orientation at DePauw University, Brant was my randomly assigned upperclassman mentor. He eased my transition into college, and I have been lucky to have him shepherding me into publication. My eternal thanks to him and to everyone at Scribner who helped bring this book into the world, including Susan Moldow, Nan Graham, Roz Lippel, Anna deVries, Meredith Wahl-Jones, and Tyler LeBleu. I also owe much gratitude to my agent, David McCormick, who trusted my passion for this subject, and to Daniel Menaker, who coaxed the proposal out of me after I e-mailed him from a parking lot in Mississippi.

Several people worked very hard to make the book you are holding beautiful. John Ritter, whose work I have greatly admired since my time as an illustration editor at *The New Yorker*, created the cover of my dreams at the direction of Rex Bonomelli. Andy Friedman, a dear friend and a brilliant artist, drew the beautiful and informative country-music maps. Gus Powell, an enormously gifted photographer and great friend, made my author photo a work of art.

A number of insightful reader chums gave me critical feedback on early and late drafts. My special thanks to Joshua Hersh, Tara Gallagher, Ben McGrath, Anne Stringfield, Willing Davidson, Melanie Redman, Brian Bennett, and Sophie Fels.

I am fortunate to have found a fact checker fascinated by the Interstate 69 story. My fellow Hoosier Barry Harbaugh waded through the piles of source material with conscience and care and put in extra hours making sure this account was honest and complete. Dylan Byers, a *New Yorker* intern who became a friend, contributed research and transcription and jolts of enthusiasm.

Paul Reyes and Mark Smirnoff at the *Oxford American* magazine were the first editors to recognize the significance and appeal of the I-69 story. In 2005 they published my article on the Great River Bridge, an act of faith that propelled me forward with confidence. Before and after that, they offered me a forum for my reporting on Mississippi Delta blues tourism and post-Katrina planning, and in doing so encouraged and sharpened the eccentric curiosity that informed this book.

I had the unspeakable fortune to work for eleven years at *The New Yorker*, and it would be impossible for me to overstate the value of that experience. I learned most of what I know about literary journalism from the people who worked there, and I am especially grateful to Christine Curry, who took a chance on hiring a kid from Indiana in a cheap suit; David Remnick, who gave a twenty-four-year-old the chance to publish in the best magazine in the world; John Bennett, who kept telling me I needed to get out and write; Pam McCarthy, who granted me a three-month reporting leave from the interesting work that made me want to stay; and Stanley Ledbetter, a dear friend and a giant who opened many doors for me. A number of writers whom I greatly admire—at *The New Yorker* and elsewhere—were kind enough to give me much-needed advice, encouragement, and sympathy, including Katherine Boo, Ian Frazier, Mark Singer, Ken Auletta, James Howard Kunstler, Susan Orlean, Philip Gourevitch, Alec Wilkinson, Seymour Hersh, Lawrence Wright, James Stewart, Rebecca Skloot, and Robert Caro.

The rest of what I know about writing I learned from a succession of teachers who told me I could write and taught me how to do it better, including Richard Roth, Barbara Bean, Tom Chiarella, Susan Gooch, Ma Booth, and Jim Meyers.

I want to thank profusely and categorically my family and friends, who for years listened with genuine interest or generous patience as this complicated story unfolded.

My parents, Dennis and Laura Dellinger, and my four brothers, Jeff, Steve, Kenny, and Terry, never faltered in their support of my professional endeavors, however quixotic. They stood behind me when I moved to New York City with no job, and again a decade later when I quit my job at *The New Yorker* to pursue this book. The "brain drain" of college-graduate children from the Midwest to more cosmopolitan cities is a theme that runs throughout this book. Perhaps writing this has been, in some small part, a way of atoning for my own expatriation. It has certainly been a very welcome excuse for frequent visits to family in Indiana and Texas.

Creating this book required a lot of travel, and I owe a great deal to everyone who provided me roofs and beds and food and company during my reporting and writing, including my father and his wife, Lyn; my brother Steve, his wife Theresa, and my nephew Jake; Wally Wallace (with fond memories of Judy), his sons Jed and Daniel, and the staff of the National Ornamental Metal Museum; Keith Porteous and the Dockery clan (with fond memories of Big Keith); Jon and Jeni Howe and family; Chad Darbyshire and family; Rebecca Skloot and David Prete; Doug Britt; Brian Keane; Jay Erickson; Nancy Rullo (with fond memories of Tony); Andy Weaver and Nicole Martins; Bayard and Lisa Snowden; and Richard and Lisa Howorth. As soon as I live somewhere with a guest room, you all are welcome to it.

To my traveling companions Dylan Byers, Sarah Stern, Yancey Allison, Jason Spellings, and Brian Gallagher: You made the road more fun and reassured me that I wasn't just imagining the allure of the people and places along I-69.

Notes

This is a work of nonfiction. I have not changed or fabricated any names, events, or other details. In limited cases, the style and punctuation (not the words) of quoted printed material have been corrected for consistency and clarity.

My research for *Interstate 69* included hundreds of hours of recorded interviews, thousands of documents and news clippings, and my own observations from 2002 to 2010. Whenever possible, descriptions of events have been based on audio and video recordings or deduced from the written record or the accounts of multiple people who were present.

My sources are too numerous to list in their entirety, but in the notes below I offer directions to some of the more valuable publicly available resources for researchers and readers who may want to learn more.

For further notes, including an extended bibliography, a full list of interviews I conducted, links to government studies and maps, and downloadable primary-source materials, please visit www.mattdellinger.com/i69.

I. A LINE ON THE MAP
Overture

3   The facades of Haynesville, Louisiana, like those of many small towns, may be observed using Google Street View at maps.google.com.

7   *More than $2.5 billion in federal and state money has been devoted to the project, much of it for pre-construction planning*   This figure does not include any federal funds devoted to upgrading U.S. highways not yet designated as Future I-69 at the time of investment. Carolina Mederos (Patton Boggs lobbyist for the Mid-Continent Highway Coalition), recorded interview with the author, March 2010.

7   *the full cost is estimated to be $27 billion*   Mederos, 2010.

9   *Lou Dobbs took regular umbrage at these highway plans*   The instance quoted is one of many: Lou Dobbs, commentary on *Lou Dobbs Tonight*, CNN, February 20, 2008, http://transcripts.cnn.com/TRANSCRIPTS/0802/20/ldt.01.html (accessed on March 20, 2010).

9   *President Obama has championed high-speed rail and mass transit over new highways. "The days where we're just building sprawl forever, those days are over," he told a Florida audience in 2009*   Ben Fried, "Obama: The Days of 'Building Sprawl Forever' Are Over," DC.Streetsblog.org, February 10, 2009, http://dc.streetsblog .org/2009/02/10/obama-the-days-of-building-sprawl-forever-are-over/(accessed on March 20, 2010).

315

A Big Breakfast

11 The history of David Graham's family came from Graham's own recollections and memorabilia, but this book was a rich trove of details: Michael E. Keller, *The Graham Legacy: Graham-Paige to 1932* (Paducah, KY: Turner Publishing, 1998).

14 *The post-interstate period in southwestern Indiana has seen a slow deterioration of the area's agricultural and manufacturing economy* David Reed, with contributions by David J. Weinsehrott et al., *The Future of Southern Rural Indiana: Paradigms and Prospects for Rural Development* (Indianapolis: Hudson Institute, 1991).

14 *To move forward, the report said, "would assume that the highway is the highest priority for each of the counties along the route"* Donohue & Associates et al., *Major Conclusions of the Southwest Indiana Regional Highway Feasibility Study* (Prepared for the Indiana Department of Transportation, 1990).

The Long Drive

18 *When the first Pan-American Congress for Highways convened in Buenos Aires in 1925, the Graham Brothers truck company sent a delegate to the meeting, where he joined a few dozen other Americans* This and other information on the Pan American Highway was taken from the First Pan American Congress of Highways, General Minutes and Appendixes (Buenos Aires, 1925). Accessed in 2007 at the Pan American Union's Columbus Memorial Library in Washington, D.C.

22 *At a meeting in August 1990* David Graham provided me with the minutes of this meeting of the "Evansville-Indianapolis Road Sub-Committee" of the Metropolitan Evansville Chamber of Commerce. The membership of this committee overlapped heavily with that of the Southwest Indiana Regional Highway Committee, and I considered this meeting to be a SWIRHC event.

23 *In the summer of 1991, on the way home with Stuart, Graham did a little soliciting himself* David Graham provided me with copies of two memoranda in which he reported to SWIRHC on his meetings with people along the proposed route of I-69. One was dated August 19, 1991, and the other was dated February 21, 1992.

24 *Michael Keller, a funeral director and amateur Graham-Paige historian, quotes David* Keller, *The Graham Legacy*.

A Plane Ride

25 *Some years back, John D. Caruthers sent a warm and rambling reminiscence* Caruthers's essay was excerpted in an article by the editor of the newspaper: Judy Pace Christie, "Share Your Neighborhood Memories with Us," *Shreveport Times*, May 27, 2001.

27 *By 1834, Shreve had opened up the river* and other references to the clearing of the Red River by Captain Henry Miller Shreve: Federal Writers' Project, Writers' Program, *Louisiana: A Guide to the State* (Washington, D.C.: U.S. History Publishers, 1945).

27 *the Caddo set aside an unspecified 640-acre piece of land for an interpreter, Larkin Edwards, who was friendly with the tribe and who had married one of the Caddo chief's daughters* Jacques D. Bagur, *A History of Navigation on Cypress Bayou and the Lakes* (Denton: University of North Texas Press, 2001), 47.

28 *As John McPhee writes* John McPhee, "The Control of Nature: Atchafalaya." *The New*

Yorker (February 23, 1987), 39, http://www.newyorker.com/archive/1987/02/23/
1987_02_23_039_TNY_CARDS_000347146 (accessed on March 10, 2010).

31 *by February 1992, Senator Johnston was talking up I-69* Bill Cooksey, "Johnston Says
I-69 Plans Could Be Revitalized," *Shreveport Times,* February 15, 1992.

The Hotel Lobby

33 *"The Mississippi Delta begins in the lobby of the Peabody Hotel," David Cohn, from
Greenville, Mississippi, wrote in 1935* David Lewis Cohn, *God Shakes Creation*
(New York: Harper & Brothers, 1935).

34 *Those assembled were pillars of their local communities* The details of this and other
meetings of the Mid-Continent Highway Coalition come largely from minutes of
those meetings kept by James Newland and provided to me by Mayor Bill Revell.

35 *Their report,* Interregional Highways, *offered maps of ideal routes, traffic and population
analysis, design recommendations, and, most important, a compelling vision of a highly
connected and mobile America* This seminal document is mentioned frequently
throughout the book. *Interregional Highways: Message from the President of the United
States Transmitting a Report of the National Interregional Highway Committee, Outlining and Recommending a National System of Interregional Highways,* 78th Cong., 2nd
sess., House Document 379 (Washington, D.C.: U.S. Government Printing Office,
1944).

35 *The Clay Committee proposed financing the interstate construction through bonds, an
idea supported by Connecticut senator Prescott Bush* Many facts about the history
of the interstate system, particularly the roles of the elder Bush and Gore in the
debate over the Federal-Aid Highway Act of 1956, came from the writings of
Richard F. Weingroff, a historian at the Federal Highway Administration. Many of
his writings are compiled at http://www.fhwa.dot.gov/infrastructure/publicroads
.cfm (accessed on March 10, 2010). Another crucial resource for information
regarding the history of the interstate highway system: Tom Lewis, *Divided Highways: Building the Interstate Highways, Transforming American Life* (New York:
Penguin, 1999).

36 *California congressman Norman Mineta, the chairman of the House Surface Transportation Subcommittee, stood before a conference of the American Road and Transportation
Builders Association and told them* Richard F. Weingroff, "Creating a Landmark: The
Intermodal Surface Transportation Efficiency Act of 1991," http://www.fhwa.dot
.gov/infrastructure/rw01.cfm (accessed on April 10, 2010).

36 *The final bill, signed a week before Christmas, was called the Intermodal Surface Transportation Efficiency Act, or ISTEA* U.S. Congress, House, *Intermodal Surface Transportation Efficiency Act of 1991,* HR 2950, 102nd Cong., 1st sess. The various versions
of the bill may be accessed on the Library of Congress's information page, http://
thomas.loc.gov/.

The Washington Lobby

40 *The first newsletter of the I-69 Mid-Continent Highway Coalition was mailed out
from the group's downtown Indianapolis headquarters in 1993* This newsletter, and
many other Mid-Continent Highway Coalition papers, were provided to me by
Bill Revell.

41 *In 1995, the firms released their report, which concluded that the project did indeed make*

sense Wilbur Smith Associates and HNTB Corporation, *Corridor 18 Feasibility Study: Final Report,* Submitted to the Arkansas State Highway & Transportation Department, November 1995.

43 *Louis Bronaugh, the mayor of Lufkin and the leader of the Texas contingent to the Mid-Continent Highway Coalition, complained* James Robinson, "I-69 Plan Would Connect Canada and Mexico," *Houston Chronicle,* February 14, 1993.

45 *The coalition's entire annual budget had started out at $140,000, but it would have to increase* Taken from meeting minutes of the Mid-Continent Highway Coalition provided to me by Bill Revell.

45 *In the end, the bill did not address where exactly the highway would cross the river* U.S. Congress, House, *National Highway System Designation Act of 1995,* HR 2274, 104th Cong., 1st sess. The various versions of the bill may be accessed on the Library of Congress's information page, http://thomas.loc.gov/.

46 *the House Ethics committee would make that clear in 1997 when it dismissed a complaint filed against Tom DeLay* Christi Harlan, "Ethics Panel Dismisses Complaints Against DeLay," *Austin American-Statesman,* November 8, 1997.

48 *In 1998, a year late, Congress passed the Transportation Equity Act for the 21st Century, or TEA-21. The law did wonders for I-69* U.S. Congress, House, *Transportation Equity Act for the 21st Century,* HR 2400, 105th Cong., 2nd sess. The various versions of the bill may be accessed on the Library of Congress's information page, http://thomas .loc.gov/.

II. INDIANA

The Crossroads of America

53 *"It was an ordinary bus trip"* Jack Kerouac, *On the Road* (New York: Penguin, 1976), 14.

53 *"I became impatient, stuck to the huge toll road that strings the northern border of Indiana"* John Steinbeck, *Travels with Charley: In Search of America* (New York: Penguin, 1986), 114.

55 *Dreiser put a premium on authenticity, insisting they take "the scenic route" west* and other quotes taken from: Theodore Dreiser, *A Hoosier Holiday* (Bloomington: Indiana University Press, 1997).

58 Description of the Indiana interurban trains came from facts obtained at the Indiana State Museum and from a well-researched book full of wonderful photographs and maps: George K. Bradley, *Indiana Railroad: The Magic Interurban* (Chicago: Central Electric Railfans' Association, 1991).

When This Was All Field

74 Quotes from letters and literature written by and to Thomas and Sandra Tokarski and my account of their battle against I-69 came from papers provided by Alexander Ewing, formerly of the Environmental Law and Policy Center in Chicago, and by the Tokarskis themselves.

How Things Have Changed

84 *"The NEPA process has overshadowed the NEPA purpose"* Lynton K. Caldwell, "Achieving the NEPA Intent: New Directions in Science, Politics, and Law," in

Environmental Analysis: The NEPA Experience, Stephen G. Hildebrand and Johnnie
B. Cannon, eds. (Boca Raton, FL: CRC Press, 1993), 12–21.

84 *"There is a NEPA process larger than impact statement procedure"* Lynton K.
Caldwell, *The National Environmental Policy Act: An Agenda for the Future* (Bloomington: Indiana University Press, 1998), xvii. Both Caldwell essays above are cur-
rently accessible through Google Books, and both are well worth reading in their
entirety.

87 *This strange synergy was on dramatic display that August at three public hearings following the release of the revamped-draft EIS* The quotes from the Bloomington meeting
were taken from VHS videotapes of the public hearing provided to me by the Indiana Department of Transportation in 2003.

93 *Mitch Rice, who served as master of ceremonies, brought out a guitar and sang a song he
wrote* "I-69 Revisited," from the album *Save It—Don't Pave It,* compiled by Citizens for Appropriate Rural Roads, November 2004.

New Developments, Old Dreams

98 *George Washington, the first president and the man after whom David Graham's town
was named, was into real estate* Joel Achenbach, *The Grand Idea: George Washington's
Potomac and the Race to the West* (New York: Simon & Schuster, 2005).

98 *"Nature then has declared in favor of the Potomac," Jefferson wrote to Washington in
1784* Peter L. Bernstein, *Wedding of the Waters: The Erie Canal and the Making of a
Great Nation* (New York: W. W. Norton, 2005), 382.

99 *A clever entrepreneur, a gifted pitchman, and a travel-hungry Hoosier, Fisher made his
initial fortune* Most of my account of Carl Fisher's real estate and road ventures
was gathered from a biography compiled by a relative: Jerry M. Fisher, *The Pacesetter:
The Untold Story of Carl G. Fisher* (Fort Bragg, CA: Lost Coast Press, 1998).

99 *"The automobile industry should be willing to finance a road across the country," Fisher told
his friend James Allison* This and the scene of Fisher drawing out Miami Beach in
the sand come from a biography of Fisher by his ex-wife: Jane Fisher, *Fabulous Hoosier* (New York: Robert M. McBride, 1947).

102 *"In fact, my father bought one of the houses that Carl Fisher had built himself down
there"* The fact that Robert Graham's house in Miami Beach, in which David grew
up, was built by Carl Fisher, was difficult to confirm, but I did so with the help of
the staff at the Historical Museum of Southern Florida and independent researcher
Carolyn Klepser, who dug up old work permits for the dwelling.

III. DOWN SOUTH

The Scenic Route

109 *the Tennessee Valley Authority also built a dam on the Cumberland River* William and
Cora Kappele, *Scenic Driving Kentucky* (Helena, MT: Falcon Publishing, 2000).

109 *Governor Edward T. Breathitt . . . spoke triumphantly to a conference of highway builders
in March 1964* Edward T. Breathitt, *The Public Papers of Edward Breathitt, 1963–
1967* (Lexington: The University Press of Kentucky, 1984), 167.

111 *The state transportation secretary at the time, Bill Nighbert, told the Henderson* Gleaner
that the work might need to be spread out over twenty years Chuck Stinnett, "'Future
I-69' Signs Set to Grace Parkways," Henderson *Gleaner,* May 16, 2006, http://www

.courierpress.com/news/2006/may/16/future-i-69-signs-set-to-grace-parkways/ (accessed on April 10, 2010).

Best-Laid Plans

126 *His longtime colleague Eldridge Lovelace, in a biography of his friend and former boss* Eldridge Lovelace, *Harland Bartholomew: His Contributions to American Urban Planning* (Urbana: University of Illinois Office of Printing Services, 1993), http://stlouis.missouri.org/heritage/bartholomew/ (accessed on March 10, 2010).

126 *In 1924, Memphis had hired Bartholomew to do a comprehensive city plan, and the volume that he produced was chock-full of society-first prescriptions* Harland Bartholomew, *A Comprehensive City Plan, Memphis Tennessee* (City Plan Commission, 1924), 53, 93, plate 47.

127 *As Jeffrey Brown at the UCLA Institute of Transportation Studies pointed out in a 2002 paper* Jeffrey Brown, "A Tale of Two Visions: Harland Bartholomew, Robert Moses, and the Development of the American Freeway," *Journal of Planning History,* vol. 4, no. 1, 2005.

130 *The Court's decision, handed down on March 2, 1971, was unanimous* Citizens to Preserve Overton Park v. Volpe, 401 U.S. 402 (1971), http://laws.findlaw.com/us/401/402.html (accessed on April 10, 2010).

131 *in January 1973, Volpe refused to approve the Overton Park route* Citizens to Preserve Overton Park v. S. Brinegar, 494 F.2d 1212 (1974), http://openjurist.org/494/f2d/1212/citizens-to-preserve-overton-park-inc-v-s-brinegar-w (accessed on April 10, 2010).

131 *In May 1973, the industry newspaper* Transportation Topics *ran a full-page article* Jesse H. Merrell, "Environmentalists Spilling Blood," *Transportation Topics,* May 21, 1973, 28.

135 *The article, 'A Good Place to Live,' by Philip Langdon, began* Philip Langdon, "A Good Place to Live," *Atlantic Monthly,* March 1988, http://www.theatlantic.com/past/docs/issues/96sep/kunstler/langdon.htm (accessed on April 10, 2010).

Highway 61 Remade

139 *When Speed took over the Development Authority, he went around passing out copies of Seaside planners Duany and Plater-Zyberk's book* Andrés Duany, Elizabeth Plater-Zyberk, and Jeff Speck, *Suburban Nation* (New York: North Point Press, 2001).

143 *The 1980 Census found that 53 percent of residents [in Tunica] were living below the poverty level* Jason DeParle, "Tunica Journal; The Shacks Disappear, but the Poverty Lives On," *New York Times,* March 10, 1991.

143 *as of 2007, one third of county residents still lived in poverty* This and other demographic information for Tunica and other towns came from City-Data.com, http://www.city-data.com/county/Tunica_County-MS.html (accessed on March 10, 2010).

143 *"The past is never dead. It's not even past," William Faulkner, a Mississippi local, once wrote* William Faulkner, *Requiem for a Nun* (New York: Random House, 1951).

147 *In Tunica, the public Rosa Fort High School is 98 percent black, while the private Tunica Institute of Learning is 97 percent white* This and the details of the racial makeup of secondary schools in Clarksdale were gathered from High-schools.com, http://high-schools.com/schools/17610/rosa-fort-high-school.html (accessed March 10, 2010).

149 *The cabins were featured in* Time *magazine's "50 Authentic American Experiences" package in 2009* Reed Tucker, "50 Authentic American Experiences," *Time,* July 13, 2009.

The Great River Bridge
153 *As John Barry describes in his definitive history* John M. Barry, *Rising Tide: The Great Mississippi Flood of 1927 and How It Changed America* (New York: Touchstone, 1998).
153 *Mark Twain visited Napoleon on several occasions* Mark Twain, *Life on the Mississippi* (New York: Signet Classics, 1961).

The Long Wait
169 *The language of the Federal-Aid Highway Act of 1944, he reminded me, called for the connection of the country's principal cities and industrial hubs by routes as "direct as practical"* Federal Highway Administration, "Dwight D. Eisenhower National System of Interstate and Defense Highways," http://www.fhwa.dot.gov/programadmin/interstate.cfm (accessed on April 10, 2010).
170 *His biggest client—from whom he received $729,000 over five years* Facts and figures about Dickey's lobbying clientele, as well as other lobbying records cited throughout this book, were retrieved from the website Opensecrets.org, http://www.opensecrets.org/lobby/firmsum.php?year=2003&lname=Jd+Consulting&id= (accessed on April 10, 2010).
171 *TEA-21 added an extra little piece to I-69, an interstate-quality spur from the main route up to Pine Bluff* U.S. Congress, House, *Transportation Equity Act for the 21st Century,* HR 2400, 105th Cong., 2nd sess., http://thomas.loc.gov/.
172 *"That was nowhere on our radar screen, or anyone's radar screen," an AHTD spokesman told a local paper* Michael DeVault, "Road to Nowhere: Proposed Interstate Throttles Arkansas/Louisiana Project," *Ouachita Citizen,* February 14, 2008, http://www.ouachitacitizen.com/archives.php?id=1811 (accessed on April 10, 2010).
172 *Watchdog groups filed ethics complaints, and the Senate asked the Justice Department to look into the matter* Paul Kiel, "Coburn Pushes for Investigation of Young's Secret Earmark Edit," Talking Points Memo, December 18, 2007, http://tpmmuckraker.talkingpointsmemo.com/archives/004937.php (accessed on April 10, 2010).
173 *When confronted by a reporter from the* Arkansas Democrat-Gazette *about this coincidence, Young denied any relationship between the contributions and the I-530 money* "How Did Millions for I-530 Get in Bill?" *Arkansas Democrat-Gazette,* May 17, 2004.
177 *In the first year after the promise was announced, enrollment in the El Dorado school system jumped by 140 students. The size of the kindergarten class alone increased by 12 percent* "One Year Later Ark Scholarship Program Boosts Economy," *Community College Week,* February 11, 2008.

IV. TEXAS

Boomstate
185 *From 1980 to 2008, the number of Texans swelled from fourteen to twenty-four million* U.S. Census Bureau, Population Division (accessed through Google.com on April 10, 2010).
185 *During the nineties, the Houston metropolitan area alone grew by almost a million people*

Texas A&M University Real Estate Center, http://recenter.tamu.edu/data/popm00/pcbsa26420.html (accessed April 10, 2010).

187 *the short length of demonstration track was abandoned after only seven months*   J. R. Gonzales, "When Monorail Came to Houston," *Houston Chronicle's* Bayou City History blog, October 22, 2008, http://blogs.chron.com/bayoucityhistory/2008/10/when_monorail_came_to_houston.html.

194 *In April 1998, a grand jury in Boston indicted Eppard on felony charges*   David Stout, "Lawmaker's Aide Indicted on Fraud Charges," *New York Times,* April 10, 1998, http://www.nytimes.com/1998/04/10/us/lawmaker-s-aide-indicted-on-fraud-charges.html (accessed March 10, 2010).

194 *In 1999, she pleaded guilty to a misdemeanor charge, and was fined five thousand dollars*   David Stout, "Lobbyists Plead Guilty, Ending Inquiry into a Lawmaker," *New York Times,* November 2, 1999, http://www.nytimes.com/1999/11/02/us/lobbyists-plead-guilty-ending-inquiry-into-a-lawmaker.html (accessed on March 10, 2010).

195 *DeLay answered questions about what a lobbyist does*   VHS videotape of this August 2004 meeting was offered by the Brownsville Navigation District in response to an open records request by the author.

199 *Meyers encouraged a new strategy*   A copy of Larry Meyers & Associates' proposal to represent the coalition, and other papers related to the Alliance for I-69 Texas were provided to me by Jorge Verduzco of Laredo, Texas.

Freeway Isn't Free

200 *At the coalition meeting in Washington in January 1996*   The accounts of this and other meetings of the Mid-Continent Highway Coalition were gathered from minutes kept by James Newland and provided to me by Bill Revell.

204 *Franklin Roosevelt was the first president to plan seriously for a network of national highways*   and other historical references throughout this chapter came from Lewis, *Divided Highways*

205 *In April 1939 his Bureau of Public Roads released a detailed study of Roosevelt's plan for the six major highways*   U.S. Government Printing Office, *Toll Roads and Free Roads: Message from the President of the United States Transmitting a Letter from the Secretary of Agriculture, Concurred in by the Secretary of War, Enclosing a Report of the Bureau of Public Roads, United States Department of Agriculture, on the Feasibility of a System of Transcontinental Toll Roads and a Master Plan for Free Highway Development* (Washington, D.C.: U.S. Government Printing Office, 1939).

205 *Through the late forties and early fifties, heavily populated states, unwilling to wait for Congress to fully fund the plan, started constructing toll roads in the interregional-highway corridors*   Weingroff, "Federal-Aid Highway Act of 1956: Creating the Interstate System," http://www.fhwa.dot.gov/infrastructure/rw96e.cfm (accessed on March 10, 2010).

Concrete Futures

208 *Governor Rick Perry and the Texas Department of Transportation circulated a document*   Texas Department of Transportation, *Crossroads of the Americas: Trans-Texas Corridor Plan,* June 1, 2002. This document is available through a number of websites, including CorridorWatch.org and the City of Brownsville: http://www.cob.us/files/50/trans_texas_corridor_2004.pdf (accessed April 10, 2010).

209 *This type of arrangement has many names—privatization, a public-private partnership (or P3), a concession, a franchise* An excellent, if biased, resource for learning about road privatization in the United States and around the world is the pro-toll online newsletter run by Peter Samuel, www.Tollroadsnews.com.

210 *a grand jury indicted [Tom] DeLay on charges that he laundered illegal donations for state races through his Washington political action committee* Among the many news reports on the indictment was Philip Shenon and Carl Hulse, "DeLay Is Indicted in Texas Case and Forfeits G.O.P. House Post," *New York Times,* September 29, 2005.

211 *HB 3588 provided all of the statutory tools outlined in the corridor plan, and then some* Texas State Legislature, House, *An Act Relating to the construction, acquisition, financing, maintenance, management, operation, ownership, and control of transportation facilities and the progress, improvement, policing, and safety of transportation in the state; imposing criminal penalties,* HB 3588, http://www.legis.state.tx.us/tlodocs/78R/billtext/html/HB03588F.htm (accessed April 10, 2010).

216 *In August, the agency held a workshop for potential bidders at its headquarters in Austin* The transcript of the August 20, 2003, Texas Department of Transportation Preproposal Workshop, once posted on the TxDOT website, has been removed, but a copy survives on Corridorwatch.org, http://www.corridorwatch.org/ttc/cw-ttc35-wkshp20030820.htm (accessed April 20, 2010).

217 *Williamson said he could sympathize with objections, but predicted that "in your lifetime most existing roads will have tolls"* Rad Sallee, "Planners Put Brakes on Converting Segment of Texas 249 into Toll Road," *Houston Chronicle,* October 12, 2004.

V. A LINE IN THE DIRT

Major Moves

238 *when a new politician arrived on the state scene expressing similar skepticism about the I-69 project* The article that first gave anti-highway activists hope about Mitch Daniels was "Daniels Willing to Reopen Debate on I-69 Extension Plan," Associated Press, July 13, 2003.

238 *"it's a very expensive answer and I think we need to understand whether there's going to be the money there to pay for it"* "Daniels Still Open on Route for I-69," *Evansville Courier & Press,* July 23, 2003.

239 *"We are for public-private partnerships. We support them. We want to make them easier—much easier—to do"* Mary Peters's September 24, 2003, speech can be found on the website of the National Council for Public-Private Partnerships, http://www.ncppp.org/resources/papers/peters_speech.pdf (accessed April 10, 2010).

241 *The federal transportation reauthorization bill, which had passed a month before, made public-private partnerships easier* U.S. Congress, House, *Safe, Accountable, Flexible, Efficient Transportation Equity Act: A Legacy for Users (SAFETEA-LU),* 2005, HR 3, 109th Cong., 1st sess., http://thomas.loc.gov/.

244 *the Mid-Continent Highway Coalition celebrated the interstate system's golden anniversary a few days early, in Memphis* The accounts of this meeting cited in the text and the list of meeting participants were supported by an e-mail from Carolina Mederos to the executive committee of the Mid-Continent Highway Coalition on May 30, 2006.

Grand Opening

247　*a deputy director at MDOT unearthed an obscure state law that allowed the department to fund projects with locally borrowed money* That deputy director was Brenda Znachko, and the news of her discovery was reported by Lynn Lofton, "New Bonding Program Puts Projects on Faster Track," *Mississippi Business Journal,* August 29, 2005.

Low Fuel

255　*"Building an outer belt is so 1970s," he said* Hudnut's quote about the Indiana Commerce Connector proposal comes from "Selling Our Toll Roads: Good or Retrograde Idea?" *Government Finance Review,* June 1, 2007.

255　*a film director named William Molina had sent them a copy of his documentary on the Trans-Texas Corridor* Trailers of the film and other information may be found at http://truthbetolled.com/ (accessed on April 15, 2010).

New Blood

260　*Someone scrawled I-69 IS THE ENEMY in spray paint on the building's limestone wall* Photos of the vandalized walls and a list of those arrested came from the website of Indianapolis Channel 6 News, June 5, 2005, http://www.theindychannel .com/news/4570146/detail.html# (accessed April 15, 2010).

260　*An anarchist website, Infoshop.org, had promoted the demonstration as a key moment of what a group calling itself Roadblock Earth First! had deemed the "Roadless Summer"* Many of the anarchists' postings were from the Infoshop website, where the dispatches I cited were still online as of April 15, 2010. A full search here: http://news .infoshop.org/search.php?query=i-69&type=all&mode=search.

262　*eleven activists affiliated with more extreme groups—the Earth Liberation Front (ELF) and the Animal Liberation Front (ALF)—were indicted* The details of this indictment and the quotes surrounding it came from a Federal Bureau of Investigation press release, "ECO-TERROR INDICTMENTS 'Operation Backfire' Nets 11," January 20, 2006, http://www.fbi.gov/page2/jan06/elf012006.htm (accessed April 15, 2010).

262　*Judge Aiken disagreed. In a few of the cases, she ruled, the severity of the crimes and their stated motivation put the anarchists into a category with Timothy McVeigh* William Yardley, "Radical Environmentalist Gets 9-Year Term," *New York Times,* May 26, 2007, http://www.nytimes.com/2007/05/26/us/26sentence.html (accessed April 15, 2010).

263　*longtime I-69 foes took seats in a lecture hall at the Monroe County Public Library and listened while their junior counterparts briefly summarized their view of the situation* The recording on which I based my account of this meeting was provided by Lauren Taylor, a reporter with WFHB community radio in Bloomington. This audio is posted on my website, mattdellinger.com/i69.

267　*In August, the anarchists showed up to a meeting at a local high school* This audio is also posted on my website, mattdellinger.com/i69.

Don't Mess with Texas

272　*"Quietly but systematically the Bush administration is advancing the plan to build a huge NAFTA Super Highway, four football fields wide, through the heart of the U.S."* Jerome

R. Corsi, "Bush Administration Quietly Plans NAFTA Super Highway," *Human Events,* June 12, 2006, http://www.humanevents.com/article.php?id=15497 (accessed April 15, 2010).

278 *the Republican presidential-primary hopefuls had been getting questions about the NAFTA superhighway out on the trail* Michael Luo, "Overheard; Road or Rumor, They're Against It," *New York Times,* July 31, 2007.

278 *There were a few tractors and a couple of horses, but no Alex Joneses and no Stalls* A video of this second Don't Tag Texas rally may be seen at http://www.youtube.com/watch?v=_ObxG1BOcdQ (accessed April 15, 2010).

Broken Ground

282 *He had also heard reports of a recent meeting between INDOT, Bernardin Lochmueller, the FBI, and the state and local police* Bryan Corbin, "Daylong Protests, Warn I-69 Opponents," *Evansville Courier & Press,* April 22, 2008, http://www.courierpress.com/news/2008/apr/22/daylong-protests-warn-i-69opponents/ (accessed on April 20, 2010).

282 *"We recognize there is potential for conflict regarding I-69," the Bloomington* Herald-Times *quoted Springer as saying* Dann Denny, "FBI Agent Challenged by I-69 Opponents," Bloomington *Herald-Times,* November 8, 2007.

286 *the University of Southern Indiana released the findings of a yearlong study on highways and economic development* Sudesh Mujumdar and Tim Schibik, *I-69 and the Economic Development of Oakland City, Petersburg and Washington: Some Insights from Other Highway Projects* (Evansville: University of Southern Indiana, 2008), https://www.usi.edu/newsinfo/images/articles/communitydevelopmentstudy.pdf (accessed April 15, 2010).

287 *That day Harriet Ray appeared by cell phone on the Bloomington community-radio program* The EcoReport WFHB, *The EcoReport,* May 22, 2008, http://www.wfhb.org/ecoreport-may-22-2008 (accessed on April 15, 2010).

The Road Ahead

296 *Their arrest warrants, filed by their police nemesis Brad Chandler, invoked the prank-like office "evictions"* The arrest warrants for Wertz and Farrell were downloaded from the "Free Tiga and Hugh" website, http://mostlyeverything.net/resources.html (accessed April 15, 2010). They are also available at mattdellinger.com/i69.

298 *In the summer of 2009, INDOT had announced a variety of cost-saving measures* Bill Ruthhart, "I-69 project: Can State Finish What It Started?" *Indianapolis Star,* August 17, 2009.

Selected Bibliography

Achenbach, Joel. *The Grand Idea: George Washington's Potomac and the Race to the West*. New York: Simon & Schuster, 2005.

Ambrose, Stephen E. *Nothing Like It in the World: The Men Who Built the Transcontinental Railroad, 1863–1869*. New York: Simon & Schuster, 2000.

Bagur, Jacques D. *A History of Navigation on Cypress Bayou and the Lakes*. Denton: University of North Texas Press, 2001.

Barry, John M. *Rising Tide: The Great Mississippi Flood of 1927 and How It Changed America*. New York: Touchstone, 1998.

Bernstein, Peter L. *Wedding of the Waters: The Erie Canal and the Making of a Great Nation*. New York: W. W. Norton, 2005.

Bradley, George K. *Indiana Railroad: The Magic Interurban*. Chicago: Central Electric Railfans' Association, 1991.

Breathitt, Edward T. *The Public Papers of Edward Breathitt, 1963–1967*. Lexington: The University Press of Kentucky, 1984.

Brown, Jeffrey. "A Tale of Two Visions: Harland Bartholomew, Robert Moses, and the Development of the American Freeway." *Journal of Planning History*, vol. 4, no. 1, 2005.

Caldwell, Lynton K. "Achieving the NEPA Intent: New Directions in Science, Politics, and Law." In *Environmental Analysis: the NEPA Experience*, edited by Stephen G. Hildebrand and Johnnie B. Cannon. Boca Raton, FL: CRC Press, 1993.

———. *The National Environmental Policy Act: An Agenda for the Future*. Bloomington: Indiana University Press, 1998.

Caro, Robert A. *The Power Broker*. New York: Vintage Books, 1975.

Connelly, Seán. *I-69 Does Not Stop*. Bloomington, IN: Unknown Arts Press, 2003.

Corsi, Jerome R. *The Late Great USA: The Coming Merger with Mexico and Canada*. Los Angeles: WND Books, 2007.

Donohue & Associates, Cambridge Systematics, Congdon Engineering Associates. *Major Conclusions of the Southwest Indiana Regional Highway Feasibility Study*. Prepared for the Indiana Department of Transportation in cooperation with the U.S. Department of Transportation and the Federal Highway Administration, 1990.

Dreiser, Theodore. *A Hoosier Holiday*. Bloomington: Indiana University Press, 1997.

Duany, Andrés, Elizabeth Plater-Zyberk, and Jeff Speck. *Suburban Nation*. New York: North Point Press, 2001.

Federal Writers' Project, Writers' Program. *Louisiana: A Guide to the State*. Washington, D.C.: U.S. History Publishers, 1945.

First Pan American Congress of Highways. *General Minutes and Appendixes*. Buenos Aires, 1925.

Fisher, Jane. *Fabulous Hoosier: A Story of American Achievement*. New York: Robert M. McBride, 1947.

Fisher, Jerry M. *The Pacesetter: The Untold Story of Carl G. Fisher*. Fort Bragg, CA: Lost Coast Press, 1998.

Flint, Anthony. *Wrestling with Moses: How Jane Jacobs Took on New York's Master Builder and Transformed the American City*. New York: Random House, 2009.

Foster, Mark S. *Castles in the Sand: The Life and Times of Carl Graham Fisher*. Gainesville: University Press of Florida, 2000.

Goddard, Stephen B. *Getting There: The Epic Struggle Between Road and Rail in the American Century*. Chicago: The University of Chicago Press, 1996.

Jacobs, Jane. *The Death and Life of Great American Cities*. New York: Vintage Books, 1992.

Kappele, William, and Cora Kappele. *Scenic Driving Kentucky*. Helena, MT: Falcon Publishing, 2000.

Keller, Michael E. *The Graham Legacy: Graham-Paige to 1932*. Paducah, KY: Turner Publishing, 1998.

Lewis, Tom. *Divided Highways: Building the Interstate Highways, Transforming American Life*. New York: Penguin Books, 1999.

Lovelace, Eldridge. *Harland Bartholomew: His Contributions to American Urban Planning*. Urbana: University of Illinois Office of Printing Services, 1993. http://stlouis .missouri.org/heritage/bartholomew/ (accessed on March 10, 2010).

McPhee, John. "The Control of Nature: Atchafalaya." *The New Yorker*, February 23, 1987.

Mujumdar, Sudesh, and Tim Schibik. *I-69 and the Economic Development of Oakland City, Petersburg and Washington: Some Insights from other Highway Projects*. Evansville: University of Southern Indiana, 2008. https://www.usi.edu/newsinfo/images /articles/communitydevelopmentstudy.pdf (accessed on April 15, 2010).

Mumford, Lewis. *The Highway and the City*. New York: Harcourt Brace Jovanovich, 1963.

Reed, David. *The Future of Southern Rural Indiana: Paradigms and Prospects for Rural Development*. With contributions by David J. Weinsehrott, Karl O'Lessker, John Thomas, and Judith A. Carley. Indianapolis: Hudson Institute, 1991.

Texas Department of Transportation. *Crossroads of the Americas: Trans Texas Corridor Plan*. June 1, 2002.

Texas State Legislature. House. *An Act Relating to the construction, acquisition, financing, maintenance, management, operation, ownership, and control of transportation facilities and the progress, improvement, policing, and safety of transportation in the state; imposing criminal penalties*. HB 3588. http://www.legis.state.tx.us/tlodocs/78R/billtext/ html/HB03588F.htm.

Twain, Mark. *Life on the Mississippi*. New York: Signet Classics, 1961.

U.S. Congress. House. *Department of Transportation and Related Agencies Appropriations Act, 1993*. HR 5518. 102nd Cong., 2nd sess. http://thomas.loc.gov/.

U.S. Congress. House. *Food Security Act of 1985*. HR 2100. 99th Cong., 1st sess. http:// thomas.loc.gov/.

U.S. Congress. House. *Intermodal Surface Transportation Efficiency Act of 1991*. HR 2950. 102nd Cong., 1st sess. http://thomas.loc.gov/.

U.S. Congress. House. *Interregional Highways: Message from the President of the United States Transmitting a Report of the National Interregional Highway Committee, Outlining and Recommending a National System of Interregional Highways*. 78th Cong., 2nd sess., House Document 379.

U.S. Congress. House. *National Highway System Designation Act of 1995*. HR 2274. 104th Cong., 1st sess. http://thomas.loc.gov/.

U.S. Congress. House. *Safe, Accountable, Flexible, Efficient Transportation Equity Act: A Legacy for Users*. HR 3. 109th Cong., 1st sess. http://thomas.loc.gov/.

U.S. Congress. House. *Transportation Equity Act for the 21st Century*. HR 2400. 105th Cong., 2nd sess. http://thomas.loc.gov/.

U.S. Congress. Senate. *National Highway System Designation Act of 1995*. S 440. 104th Cong., 1st sess. http://thomas.loc.gov/.

U.S. Government Printing Office. *Toll Roads and Free Roads: Message from the President of the United States Transmitting a Letter from the Secretary of Agriculture, Concurred in by the Secretary of War, Enclosing a Report of the Bureau of Public Roads, United States Department of Agriculture, on the Feasibility of a System of Transcontinental Toll Roads and a Master Plan for Free Highway Development*. 1939.

Wilbur Smith Associates and HNTB Corporation. *Corridor 18 Feasibility Study: Final Report*. Submitted to the Arkansas State Highway & Transportation Department, November 1995.

Index